수능 VOCA EDGE RED

3판 1쇄 발행 2020년 1월 15일

지은이   정오은
발행인   조상현
마케팅   조정빈

펴낸곳   더디퍼런스
등록번호 제2018-000177호
주소   경기도 고양시 덕양구 큰골길 33-170
문의   02-712-7927
팩스   02-6974-1237
이메일   thedibooks@naver.com
홈페이지 www.thedifference.co.kr

ISBN   979-11-6125-240-7 53740

수VOCA EDGE

정오은 지음

고등학생을 위한 일상 생활 속
스토리텔링 단어 학습법

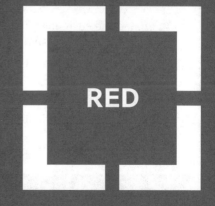

RED

더디퍼런스

Introduction

Every student knows acquiring English vocabulary is a basic necessity for learning the English language. However, not many are aware that simply memorizing vocabulary words is not enough. In order to master a language, students need to spend more time learning how to use these words and what they really mean. Yet, students still spend countless hours memorizing rather than learning.

Even worse is the fact that most vocabulary books are extremely difficult and boring. Fortunately, there is a way for everyone to change their perspective on learning vocabulary. Now you can develop your vocabulary in an enjoyable way. The VOCA EDGE series will help you simultaneously enlarge your vocabulary and improve your English.

This series uses an integrated approach to learning English.
Listening, reading, writing and comprehension are all covered in this series.

One of the key features of this series is that it revolves around the daily lives of several characters and the challenges they face in growing up. By reading each episode, students will learn the natural and functional use of English vocabulary.

Each level of this series comes with one textbook and one audio component. Each book is organized into 12 chapters, each of which consists of 2-4 related units. Each book also deals with a variety of unique and interesting topics, and the series is graded to an appropriate length and depth to suit the needs of students with varying levels of English proficiency.

After studying each unit, students will be challenged to review the words and expressions they learned through a series of related questions and activities. Students can listen to the entire script in MP3 format or use the attached CD. We invite you to let this series help you take the next step in your journey towards becoming a more proficient speaker of English. We are confident that the VOCA EDGE series can help you make a dramatic improvement in your English ability.

Structure

- **Reading Passages**

  The Reading passages cover a wide variety of topics ranging from teen life to social issues. Each sentence in the reading passages contains target vocabulary students have to learn. Each of the characters has their own personality and the real life topics will help students understand the context more easily. In addition, it will motivate students to learn vocabulary used in the passages with confidence.

- **Words**

  Students are encouraged to read the definitions in English, which provides them with greater exposure to English vocabulary. They are also encouraged to read the sentences and derivations of the target vocabulary that students need to learn.

- **Check Again!**

  These sections provide students with a chance to practice words and idiomatic expressions learned in each unit using a variety of approaches.

- **Check More!**

  In the section, students are encouraged to apply their understanding of the words learned in each unit to the K-SAT test.

- **Voca Plus**

  The Voca Plus section is added at the end of each chapter. This section provides students with basic information about how some English words are composed including their derivations. In addition, culture tips related to each chapter are included.

Contents

Bomi

A high school first grade student. An inquisitive teenage girl.

Hoony

Bomi's younger brother

Seri

Bomi's younger sister

Sara
Bomi's best friend

Mom
Bomi, Hoony, and Seri's mother

Dad
Bomi, Hoony, and Seri's father

We're teens. I had my cell phone taken away. Goodbye, Brownie Life is full of contradi

campus tour. If I were a judge,... How can we survive in a jungle? I became a Santa C

oney-wise. oony goes to an herbal clinic. We became a rescue team. Grandma goes

u want to meet? Are mom and dad compatible? I can't understand this painting. Ther

ve illusions about boys. I can't understand politicians. Wearing an electronic tag is hor

e economics camp. construction a thriving business? How amazing our life has becon

pace. I attended the Arbor Day ceremony. We can make the earth a better place. A

VOCA
EDGE
RED

ife is full of contradictions. Goodbye, Sara. I learned about the earth. I went to a natu

became a Santa Claus. Sara attends a community party. Mom's got a new hobby. Are th

Grandma goes to a laughter clinic. The Volcanoes are back. We have great brothers. Wh

painting. There was telepathy between us! Sara goes to Turkey. Home decorating is n

electronic tag is horrible. The war should be stopped. Mom, are you going to cut my allc

our life has become! I should have been more careful. Forgery should be stopped. Hoo

better place. A super hurricane hit the village. We're teens. I had my cell phone taken

went to a natural science museum. I had a campus tour. If I were a judge,... How can w

hobby. Are they my bosses? Hoony is money-wise. Hoony goes to an herbal clinic. We

great brothers. What historical figures do you want to meet? Are mom and dad compat

decorating is not easy. Hoony thinks girls have illusions about boys. I can't understand po

cut my allowance? Hoony is back from an economics camp. construction a thriving b

topped. Hoony wants to explore outer space. I attended the Arbor Day ceremony. We

phone taken away. Goodbye, Brownie Life is full of contradictions. Goodbye, Sara. I lear

How can we survive in a jungle? I became a Santa Claus. Sara attends a community

Goodbye, Sara. I learned about the earth. I went to a natural science museum. I had c

a attends a community party. Mom's got a new hobby. Are they my bosses? Hoony is

ighter clinic. The Volcanoes are back. We have great brothers. What historical figures do

lepathy between us! Sara goes to Turkey. Home decorating is not easy. Hoony thinks girls

war should be stopped. Mom, are you going to cut my allowance? Hoony is back from

ild have been more careful. Forgery should be stopped. Hoony wants to explore oute

ricane hit the village. We're teens. I had my cell phone taken away. Goodbye, Brownie

e museum. I had a campus tour. If I were a judge,... How can we survive in a jungle?

osses? Hoony is money-wise. Hoony goes to an herbal clinic. We became a rescue team

cal figures do you want to meet? Are mom and dad compatible? I can't understand thi

Hoony thinks girls have illusions about boys. I can't understand politicians. Wearing ar

Hoony is back from an economics camp. construction a thriving business? How amazing

to explore outer space. I attended the Arbor Day ceremony. We can make the earth o

odbye, Brownie Life is full of contradictions. Goodbye, Sara. I learned about the earth.

n a jungle? I became a Santa Claus. Sara attends a community party. Mom's got a new

Chapter 1. Teen Life

a rescue team. Grandma goes to a laughter clinic. The Volcanoes are back. We ha

Unit 1. We're teens.

n't understand this painting. There was telepathy between us! Sara goes to Turkey. Ho

Unit 2. I had my cell phone taken away.

Wearing an electronic tag is horrible. The war should be stopped. Mom, are you going

Unit 3. Goodbye, Brownie.

ow amazing our life has become! I should have been more careful. Forgery should be

e the earth a better place. A super hurricane hit the village. We're teens. I had my ce

the earth. I went to a natural science museum. I had a campus tour. If I were a judge,..

got a new hobby. Are they my bosses? Hoony is money-wise. Hoony goes to an herba

Chapter 1
Teen Life

Unit 1. We're teens.

freeze while waiting for favorite stars

imitate the hairstyles of favorite stars

pretend to **concentrate on** one's studies

squeeze pimples

Episode

Dear Mom,

How can you define teenagers? • Mom, what were you like when you were an adolescent? • Were you obedient? • Were you rebellious? • What do you think typical teens are like? • I'm talking about ordinary teens like me. • Teens are energetic. • We don't mind freezing while waiting outside for our favorite stars.

We like to imitate the hairstyles of our favorite stars. • We want our privacy. • We don't like to have our privacy interrupted. • We have our own individual phones. • We like decorating our phones with stickers. • Mom, I know you chat on the phone. • We prefer to text on the phone. • We post images of celebrities on our blogs. • We even put anonymous messages on the Internet. • Sometimes harsh comments can cause problems, though. • Now, more teens are eager to have their own blog.

Some blogs provide practical tips. • They even help us keep up with fashions that are in vogue. • Some tips are about effective study habits. • Tips like how to pretend to concentrate on our studies while sending text messages. • Do you know what we like to do when we feel stressed? • We're reluctant to spend time on schoolwork and prefer to hang out with friends. • We like to have big feasts of dukbokki and kimbab. • We often stand in front of the mirror squeezing pimples on our faces. • Mom, when you were a teenager, were you like me?

엄마에게,
십대를 어떻게 정의할 수 있나요? 엄마, 엄마는 청소년이었을 때 어땠어요? 순종적이었나요? 반항적이었나요? 전형적인 십대는 어떻다고 생각하세요? 저와 같은 일반적인 십대에 대해 이야기하는 거예요. 십대는 활기가 넘치죠. 우리는 좋아하는 스타를 밖에서 기다리는 동안 몸이 어는 것도 상관하지 않아요.
우리는 좋아하는 스타의 헤어스타일을 모방하는 것을 좋아해요. 우리는 우리만의 사생활을 원해요. 우리는 사생활이 방해받는 것을 좋아하지 않아요. 우리는 개인 전화를 가지고 있어요. 우리는 스티커로 전화를 장식하는 것을 좋아해요. 엄마, 엄마는 전화로 수다 떠시죠. 우리는 전화로 문자 보내는 것을 더 좋아해요. 우리는 유명인의 이미지를 블로그에 올려요. 우리는 인터넷에 익명의 글을 올리기도 해요. 때로는 무자비한 비판이 문제가 되기도 하지만요. 요즘은 더 많은 십대들이 자신만의 블로그를 가지고 싶어해요.
어떤 블로그는 실질적인 조언을 제공해요. 그런 블로그는 우리가 유행하는 패션을 따라갈 수 있도록 도움을 주기도 해요. 어떤 조언은 효과적인 공부 습관에 관한 것이에요. 문자 메시지를 보내면서 공부에 집중하는 척하는 방법과 같은 조언이죠. 우리가 스트레스를 받을 때 무엇을 하고 싶어하는지 아세요? 우리는 학교 공부를 하는 데 시간을 보내지 않고 친구들과 돌아다니는 것을 더 좋아해요. 떡볶이와 김밥 먹는 걸 좋아해요. 우리는 얼굴에 난 여드름을 짜면서 종종 거울 앞에 서 있죠. 엄마, 엄마가 십대였을 때 엄마도 저와 비슷했나요?

define
[difáin]
v. 정의를 내리다

to explain the meaning of a word (short definition or synonym)
• definition n. 정의

How can you define teenagers?
십대를 어떻게 정의할 수 있나요?

adolescent
[ӕdəlésənt]
n. 청소년
a. 청소년의

a teenager, a person aged between thirteen and nineteen
• adolescence n. 청소년기

Mom, what were you like when you were an adolescent?
엄마, 엄마는 청소년이었을 때 어땠어요?

obedient
[oubí:diənt]
a. 순종적인

obeying instructions or orders, well-behaved
• obey v. 순종하다   • obedience n. 순종

Were you obedient?
순종적이었나요?

rebellious
[ribéljəs]
a. 반항적인

defiant or disobedient of orders
• rebel v. 반항하다 n. 반항아   • rebellion n. 반항

Were you rebellious?
반항적이었나요?

typical
[típikəl]
a. 전형적인

normal, ordinary, usual, average
• type n. 전형

What do you think typical teens are like?
전형적인 십대는 어떻다고 생각하세요?

ordinary
[ɔ́:rdənèri]
a. 일반적인

normal, common, not special

I'm talking about ordinary teens like me.
저와 같은 일반적인 십대에 대해 이야기하는 거예요.

energetic
[ènərdʒétik]
a. 활기가 넘치는

having a lot of energy, being very active
• energy n. 기운, 에너지

Teens are energetic. 십대는 활기가 넘치죠.

freeze
[frí:z]
v. 얼다, 얼리다

to become ice or become covered in ice
- freezing a. 어는 • frozen a. 냉동된

We don't mind freezing while waiting outside for our favorite stars.
우리는 좋아하는 스타를 밖에서 기다리는 동안 몸이 어는 것도 상관하지 않아요.

imitate
[ímitèit]
v. 모방하다

to follow the style of someone or something else
- imitation n. 모방

We like to imitate the hairstyles of our favorite stars.
우리는 좋아하는 스타의 헤어스타일을 모방하는 것을 좋아해요.

privacy
[práivəsi]
n. 사생활

the state of spending time alone
- private a. 사적인

We want our privacy. 우리는 우리만의 사생활을 원해요.

interrupt
[ìntərʌ́pt]
v. 방해하다

to temporarily stop a person from doing something
- interruption n. 방해

We don't like to have our privacy interrupted.
우리는 사생활이 방해받는 것을 좋아하지 않아요.

individual
[ìndəvídʒuəl]
a. 개인적인
n. 개인

personal, belonging to one person
- individually ad. 개별적으로

We have our own individual phones.
우리는 개인 전화를 가지고 있어요.

decorate
[dékərèit]
v. 장식하다

to make something more attractive by adding things to it
- decoration n. 장식 • decorative a. 장식의

We like decorating our phones with stickers.
우리는 스티커로 전화를 장식하는 것을 좋아해요.

chat
[tʃǽt]
v. 수다를 떨다
n. 잡담

to talk to each other in an informal and friendly way

Mom, I know you chat on the phone.
엄마, 엄마는 전화로 수다 떠시죠.

prefer
[prifə́:r]

v. 선호하다, 더 좋아
하다

to like one thing more than another
- preference n. 선호

We prefer to text on the phone.
우리는 전화로 문자 보내는 것을 더 좋아해요.

celebrity
[səlébrəti]

n. 유명인사

a famous person

We post images of celebrities on our blogs.
우리는 유명인의 이미지를 블로그에 올려요.

anonymous
[ənǽniməs]

a. 익명의

without giving one's name, unidentified
- anonymity n. 익명, 작자 불명

We even put anonymous messages on the Internet.
우리는 인터넷에 익명의 글을 올리기도 해요.

harsh
[hɑ́:rʃ]

a. 무자비한, 심한

unkind, cruel

Sometimes harsh comments can cause problems, though.
때로는 무자비한 비판이 문제가 되기도 하지만요.

eager
[íːgər]

a. 열망하는

having a desire to do something
- eagerness n. 열망, 갈망 • be eager to+ V ~하는 것을 좋아하다

Now, more teens are eager to have their own blog.
요즘은 더 많은 십대들이 자신만의 블로그를 가지고 싶어해요.

provide
[prəváid]

v. 제공하다, 주다

to give something to a person
- provider n. 공급자

Some blogs provide practical tips.
어떤 블로그는 실질적인 조언을 제공해요.

vogue
[vóug]

n. 유행, 유행하는 것
a. 유행의

a thing that is popular for a short time
- in vogue 유행하는

They even help us keep up with fashions that are in vogue.
그것들은 우리가 유행하는 패션을 따라갈 수 있도록 도움을 주기도 해요.

effective
[iféktiv]
a. 효과적인

productive, producing a good result
- effect n. 효과 • effectively ad. 효과적으로

Some tips are about effective study habits.
어떤 조언은 효과적인 공부 습관에 관한 것이에요.

concentrate
[kánsəntrèit]
v. 집중하다

to focus on something
- concentration n. 집중 • concentrate on ~에 집중하다

Tips like how to pretend to concentrate on our studies while sending text messages.
문자 메시지를 보내면서 공부에 집중하는 척하는 방법과 같은 조언이죠.

stressed
[strést]
a. 스트레스가 쌓인

anxious and tense
- stress v. 강조하다, 괴롭히다 n. 스트레스

Do you know what we like to do when we feel stressed?
우리가 스트레스를 받을 때 무엇을 하고 싶어하는지 아세요?

reluctant
[rilʌ́ktənt]
a. 망설이는

unwilling to do something
- reluctance n. 망설임 • be reluctant to+ V ~하는 것을 망설이다

We're reluctant to spend time on schoolwork and prefer to hang out with friends.
우리는 학교 공부를 하는 데 시간을 보내지 않고 친구들과 돌아다니는 것을 더 좋아해요.

feast
[fíːst]
n. 진수성찬, 잔치

a large and special meal

We like to have big feasts of dukbokki and kimbab.
우리는 떡볶이와 김밥 먹는 걸 좋아해요.

squeeze
[skwíːz]
v. 쥐어짜다

to press something firmly from several sides

We often stand in front of the mirror squeezing pimples on our faces.
우리는 얼굴에 난 여드름을 짜면서 종종 거울 앞에 서 있죠.

Check Again!

A Translate each word into Korean.

1. adolescent ....   2. obedient ....

3. rebellious ....   4. ordinary ....

5. freeze ....   6. interrupt ....

7. anonymous ....   8. harsh ....

9. privacy ....   10. define ....

B Translate each word into English.

1. 전형적인 ....   2. 활기가 넘치는 ....

3. 선호하다 ....   4. 수다를 떨다 ....

5. 효과적인 ....   6. 망설이는 ....

7. 진수성찬, 잔치 ....   8. 쥐어짜다 ....

9. 모방하다 ....   10. 장식하다 ....

C Fill in the blank with the appropriate word. Refer to the Korean.

1. Teens are e   to have their own cellular phone.

   십대들은 자신들만의 휴대 전화를 가지고 싶어한다.

2. When you feel s   , what do you do?

   스트레스를 받을 때 어떻게 하십니까?

3. It's not always easy to keep up with fashions that are in v

   유행하는 패션을 따라가는 것이 늘 쉬운 일은 아니죠.

4. It's time to c   on our studies. The final tests are around the corner.

   지금은 공부에 집중해야 할 때이다. 기말 고사가 코앞이다.

5. I'm r   to waste time hanging out with friends today.

   오늘 친구들과 어울려 놀면서 시간낭비하고 싶지 않다.

Check More!

다음 밑줄 친 부분에 알맞은 어휘를 고르시오. 아래의 영영 풀이를 참조하시오.

If we want to describe our society in terms of age, we may come up with four age groups – childhood, adolescence, **(A)** maturity / mutuality, and old age. We take it for granted that people of different ages behave differently. For example, we feel that a man in his thirties should act his age and not behave like an **(B)** adolescent / adolescence or an old man. Equally, we expect that, as they go through life, people of the same age will in some ways **(C)** underscore / understand each other better than people of different ages. This is all part of the way we are expected to behave in our social life, but it is not something that we can apply in formal **(D)** institutions / constitutions governed by hard-and-fast rules.

(A) the state of being fully grown or developed:

....

(B) a teenager; youthful: ....

(C) to perceive the meaning of; be thoroughly familiar with:

....

(D) an organization founded and united for a specific purpose:

....

Chapter 1
Teen Life

Unit 2. I had my cell phone taken away.

persist listening to music

force someone to give something

Episode

When do you feel frustrated? • Is it when you get poor grades on your report card? • How about when you feel isolated from friends? • I've had successive bad luck. • It reminds me of a proverb that it never rains but it pours. • In the morning, I had a big argument with my mom. • She compelled me to put my pajamas back in the closet. • I refused to do it. • I covered my ears and persisted listening to my music. • Mom was furious with me. • She said I misbehaved. • I slammed the door hard and left home. • I got on the bus and inside the bus it was stuffy because of the poor ventilation. • Later I regretted my behavior. • I felt uneasy.

During class, my cell phone vibrated. • My teacher forced me to give it to him. • Then the teacher announced to the whole class that he would keep it for one month. • I couldn't use my transportation pass. • It was attached to the cell phone, so I had to walk home temporarily. • I was supposed to see my friends, but we had to cancel our plans because I couldn't contact them. • Now, I realize how indispensable my cell phone is. • At home, my mom told me to apologize to my teacher. • I guess I'd better listen to my mom's advice.

당신은 언제 좌절감을 느끼나요? 성적표에 점수가 좋지 않을 때인가요? 친구들로부터 따돌림을 당할 때인가요? 저는 불행이 연속적으로 닥친 적이 있어요. '비가 오면 억수로 퍼붓는다' 라는 속담이 생각나요. 아침에 저는 우리 엄마와 심한 말다툼을 했어요. 엄마는 저에게 잠옷을 장롱에 다시 집어넣으라고 강요하셨어요. 저는 싫다고 했어요. 저는 귀를 막고 음악을 계속 들었어요. 엄마는 저에게 화가 많이 나셨어요. 엄마는 제가 못되게 굴었다고 말씀하셨어요. 저는 문을 세게 닫고 집을 나왔어요. 저는 버스를 탔고 버스 안에는 환기가 잘 안되어서 공기가 탁했어요. 나중에 저는 제 행동을 후회했어요. 마음이 불편했어요.

수업 중에 제 휴대 전화가 진동으로 울렸어요. 선생님이 저에게 휴대 전화를 달라고 강요하셨어요. 그리고 나서 선생님은 반 전체 학생들에게 선생님이 제 휴대 전화를 한 달 동안 가지고 계실 거라고 말씀하셨어요. 저는 교통카드를 쓸 수가 없었어요. 교통카드가 제 휴대 전화에 달려 있어서 저는 한동안 집까지 걸어다녀야 했어요. 저는 친구들을 만나기로 되어 있었는데 연락을 할 수가 없어서 우리는 계획을 취소해야 했어요. 이제는 제 휴대 전화가 얼마나 필수적인지 알게 되었어요. 집에서 우리 엄마는 저에게 선생님께 사과하라고 말씀하셨어요. 우리 엄마의 충고를 듣는 게 좋을 것 같아요.

frustrated
[frástreitid]

a. 좌절감을 느낀, 실망한

disappointed, discouraged
- frustrate v. 좌절(실망)시키다 • frustration n. 좌절, 실망

When do you feel frustrated?
당신은 언제 좌절감을 느끼나요?

report card
[ripɔ́:rt kà:rd]

성적표

a document that records one's grades

Is it when you get poor grades on your report card?
성적표에 점수가 좋지 않을 때인가요?

isolated
[áisəlèitid]

a. 고립된

being separated from other people
- isolate v. 고립(격리)시키다 • isolation n. 고립

How about when you feel isolated from friends?
친구들로부터 따돌림을 당할 때인가요?

successive
[səksésiv]

a. 연속하는

happening one after another

I've had successive bad luck.
저는 불행이 연속적으로 닥친 적이 있어요.

proverb
[právə:rb]

n. 속담

a well-known sentence that often gives advice

It reminds me of a proverb that it never rains but it pours.
'비가 오면 억수로 퍼붓는다' 라는 속담이 생각나요.

pour
[pɔ́:r]

v. 억수같이 퍼붓다

to flow quickly, to empty a large amount of liquid

It reminds me of a proverb that it never rains but it pours.
'비가 오면 억수로 퍼붓는다' 라는 속담이 생각나요.

argument
[á:rgjəmənt]

n. 말다툼

a disagreement with another person
- argue v. 말다툼하다

In the morning, I had a big argument with my mom.
아침에 저는 우리 엄마와 심한 말다툼을 했어요.

compel
[kəmpél]
v. 강요하다

to force or make someone do something

She compelled me to put my pajamas back in the closet.
그녀는 저에게 잠옷을 장롱에 다시 집어넣으라고 강요하셨어요.

refuse
[rifjúːz]
v. 거절하다

to say no, to choose not to do something
• refusal n. 거절

I refused to do it. 저는 싫다고 했어요.

persist
[pəːrsíst]
v. 지속하다

to continue to do something
• persistence n. 지속성, 끈기   • persistent a. 지속적인

I covered my ears and persisted listening to my music.
저는 귀를 막고 음악을 계속 들었어요.

furious
[fjúəriəs]
a. 격노한

extremely angry
• fury n. 격노

Mom was furious with me.
엄마는 저에게 화가 많이 나셨어요.

misbehave
[mìsbihéiv]
v. 못되게 굴다, 버릇
없이 행동하다

to behave badly
• misbehavior n. 버릇없음

She said I misbehaved.
그녀는 제가 못되게 굴었다고 말씀하셨어요.

slam
[slǽm]
v. (문 등을) 세게 닫다

to shut something e.g. the door noisily

I slammed the door hard and left home.
저는 문을 세게 닫고 집을 나왔어요.

ventilation
[vèntəléiʃən]
n. 환기

a state of allowing fresh air to get inside
• ventilate v. 환기시키다

I got on the bus and inside the bus it was stuffy because of the poor ventilation.
저는 버스를 탔고 버스 안에는 환기가 잘 안되어서 공기가 탁했어요.

regret
[rigrét]
v. 후회하다
n. 후회

to feel sorry about something someone has done
• regretful a. 후회하는 • regrettable a. 유감스러운
Later I regretted my behavior.
나중에 저는 제 행동을 후회했어요.

uneasy
[ʌníːzi]
a. 불편한

uncomfortable
I felt uneasy.
저는 마음이 불편했어요.

vibrate
[váibreit]
v. 진동하다

to shake or fluctuate
• vibration n. 진동
During class, my cell phone vibrated.
수업 중에 세 휴내 선화가 신농으로 울렸어요.

force
[fɔ́ːrs]
v. 강요하다

to compel or make someone do something
My teacher forced me to give it to him.
선생님이 저에게 그것을 달라고 강요하셨어요.

announce
[ənáuns]
v. 알리다

to tell several or many people about something
• announcement n. 공표
Then the teacher announced to the whole class that he would keep it for one month.
그리고 나서 선생님은 반 전체 학생들에게 선생님이 제 휴대 전화를 한 달 동안 가지고 계실 거라고 말씀하셨어요.

transportation
[trænspərtéiʃən]
n. 교통

any type of vehicle used to travel from one place to another
I couldn't use my transportation pass.
저는 교통카드를 쓸 수가 없었어요.

attach
[ətǽtʃ]
v. 달다, 첨부하다

to connect or stick one thing onto another
• attachment n. 부착
It was attached to the cell phone, so I had to walk home temporarily.
그것은 제 휴대 전화에 달려 있어서 저는 한동안 집까지 걸어다녀야 했어요.

temporarily
[tèmpərérəli]
ad. 일시적으로

for a short time, not permanently

It was attached to the cell phone, so I had to walk home temporarily.

그것은 제 휴대 전화에 달려 있어서 저는 한동안 집까지 걸어다녀야 했어요.

suppose
[səpóuz]
v. ~하기로 하다, 추정하다

to intend to do something

• be supposed to + V ~하기로 되어 있다

I was supposed to see my friends, but we had to cancel our plans because I couldn't contact them.

저는 친구들을 만나기로 되어 있었는데 연락을 할 수가 없어서 우리는 계획을 취소해야 했어요.

cancel
[kǽnsəl]
v. 취소하다

not to do something that someone planned to do

• cancellation n. 취소

I was supposed to see my friends, but we had to cancel our plans because I couldn't contact them.

저는 친구들을 만나기로 되어 있었는데 연락을 할 수가 없어서 우리는 계획을 취소해야 했어요.

contact
[kántækt]
v. 연락하다
n. 연락

to speak or write to someone

I was supposed to see my friends, but we had to cancel our plans because I couldn't contact them.

저는 친구들을 만나기로 되어 있었는데 연락을 할 수가 없어서 우리는 계획을 취소해야 했어요.

indispensable
[indispénsəbl]
a. 필수적인, 없어서는 안 될

essential, absolutely necessary

Now, I realize how indispensable my cell phone is.

이제는 제 휴대 전화가 얼마나 필수적인지 알게 되었어요.

apologize
[əpálədʒàiz]
v. 사과하다

to say sorry

• apology n. 사과

At home, my mom told me to apologize to my teacher.

집에서 우리 엄마는 저에게 선생님께 사과하라고 말씀하셨어요.

advice
[ædváis]
n. 충고

a helpful suggestion

• advise v. 충고하다

I guess I'd better listen to my mom's advice.

우리 엄마의 충고를 듣는 게 좋을 것 같아요.

Check Again!

A Translate each word into Korean.

1. frustrated ....   2. successive ....

3. pour ....   4. slam ....

5. compel ....   6. misbehave ....

7. regret ....   8. vibrate ....

9. force ....   10. announce ....

B Translate each word into English.

1. 교통 ....   2. 일시적으로 ....

3. 취소하다 ....   4. 연락하다 ....

5. 필수적인 ....   6. 사과하다 ....

7. 충고 ....   8. 거절하다 ....

9. 격노한 ....   10. 고립된 ....

C Fill in the blank with the appropriate word. Refer to the Korean.

1. I was s   to visit my grandparents.

   저는 조부모님을 방문하기로 되어 있었어요.

2. I had a big a   with my boss today.

   오늘 나는 상사와 크게 말다툼을 하였다.

3. Three files were a   to his e-mail.

   파일 3개가 그의 이메일에 첨부되어 있었디.

4. What were your grades on your r   card for each subject?

   각 과목에 대한 너의 성적표 상의 점수가 얼마였니?

5. She p   with her studies in spite of financial problems.

   그녀는 재정상의 문제에도 불구하고 그녀의 학업을 지속했다.

Check More!

(A), (B), (C) 각 밑줄 친 부분에 알맞은 어휘를 짝지은 것으로 가장 적절한 것을 고르시오.

Have you ever hurt another person? If so, get in touch with the person you wronged and ask for forgiveness in all sincerity. You must **(A)** applaud / apologize for what you did. Promise yourself now to carry it out immediately. Even after many years, it's still possible to find people. If the person has died or really can't be found, you can make a contribution in some way to help others who have suffered from similar acts. If your **(B)** determination / frustration is firm, clear, and sincere, then you will be able to put that emotion and **(C)** memory / regret aside and find peace of mind.

(A)	(B)	(C)
① applaud	frustration	memory
② apologize	frustration	regret
③ applaud	determination	memory
④ applaud	frustration	regret
⑤ apologize	determination	memory

Chapter 1
Teen Life

Unit 3. Goodbye, Brownie.

be **identical**

balance on a board

express one's **condolences**

Episode

Dear Brownie,

Goodbye, Brownie. I'm sure you're in heaven. • Brownie, you were such a good companion to Sara and me. • I remember how gracious you were. • We dyed your hair purple. • You were athletic. • You could balance on a board. • You liked tuna when you were pregnant. • Last month your three puppies were born. • They are so adorable. • Do you know the puppies are identical?

They resemble you. • Your puppies are a blessing to us. • They are all pure-bred like you. • We were shocked at the news that you had terminal cancer. • Sara told me that you were taken to the intensive care unit. • I heard the heartbreaking news. • This morning we all mourned. • Sara said there would be a funeral. • I read an elegy. • Sara wept all day. • She was in despair. • I sympathized with her feelings.

I tried to comfort Sara. • It was unbearable for her. • Other friends expressed their condolences. • We unanimously agreed to bury you. • We put a grave stone above you with these words - Goodbye, Brownie. • You will stay immortal in our memories.

....

브라우니에게,

잘 가, 브라우니. 나는 네가 천국에 있을 거라고 생각해. 브라우니, 너는 사라와 나에게 정말 좋은 친구였어. 나는 네가 얼마나 상냥했는지 기억해. 우리는 너의 털을 보라색으로 염색했어. 너는 운동 신경이 있었어. 판자 위에서 균형을 잡을 수 있었어. 너는 임신했을 때 참치를 좋아했어. 지난달에 너의 강아지 세 마리가 태어났어. 그들은 정말 귀여워. 그 강아지들이 똑같이 생긴 거 알고 있니?

강아지들이 너를 닮았어. 너의 강아지들은 우리에게 축복이야. 그들은 너처럼 모두 순종이야. 우리는 네가 말기 암에 걸렸다는 소식을 듣고 충격을 받았어. 사라는 네가 중환자실로 보내졌다고 나에게 말했어. 나는 마음 아픈 소식을 들었어. 오늘 아침에 우리 모두는 슬퍼했어. 사라는 장례식이 있을 거라고 말했어. 나는 애가를 읽었어. 사라는 하루 종일 울었어. 사라는 절망에 빠져 있었어. 나는 사라의 감정에 공감했어.

나는 사라를 위로하려고 했어. 그건 그녀에게는 견딜 수 없는 일이었어. 다른 친구들도 슬픔을 표현했어. 우리는 만장일치로 너를 묻어주기로 동의했어. 우리는 '잘 가, 브라우니'라는 말을 너의 묘비에 새겨 놓았어. 너는 우리 기억 속에 영원히 남아 있을 거야.

heaven
[hévən]
n. 천국

the place where God and angels live and where Christians believe they go after they die
- heavenly a. 천국 같은, 하늘의

Goodbye, Brownie. I'm sure you're in heaven.
잘 가, 브라우니. 나는 네가 천국에 있을 거라고 생각해.

companion
[kəmpǽnjən]
n. 친구

a person whom someone spends time with
- companionship n. 교제 - company n. 동료

Brownie, you were such a good companion to Sara and me.
브라우니, 너는 사라와 나에게 정말 좋은 친구였어.

gracious
[gréiʃəs]
a. 상냥한

well-mannered, polite
- grace n. 고상함, 은혜

I remember how gracious you were.
나는 네가 얼마나 상냥했는지 기억해.

dye
[dái]
v. 염색하다

to change one's hair color

We dyed your hair purple.
우리는 너의 털을 보라색으로 염색했어.

athletic
[æθlétik]
a. 운동 신경이 있는

strong and healthy, full of life and energy
- athlete n. 운동선수

You were athletic.
너는 운동 신경이 있었어.

balance
[bǽləns]
v. 균형을 잡다
n. 균형

to be steady and not fall off

You could balance on a board.
너는 판자 위에서 균형을 잡을 수 있었어.

pregnant
[prégnənt]
a. 임신한

having a baby inside one's body
- pregnancy n. 임신

You liked tuna when you were pregnant.
너는 임신했을 때 참치를 좋아했어.

bear
[bέər]

v. 낳다

to give birth to a child
- birth n. 출생 - be born 태어나다

Last month your three puppies were born.
지난달에 너의 강아지 세 마리가 태어났어.

adorable
[ədɔ́:rəbəl]

a. 귀여운

cute, attractive
- adore v. 아주 좋아하다

They are so adorable. 그들은 정말 귀여워.

identical
[aidéntikəl]

a. 똑같은, 동일한

looking exactly alike, the same
- identify v. 구별하다, 확인하다 - identity n. 동일함, 신원

Do you know the puppies are identical?
그 강아지들이 똑같이 생긴 거 알고 있니?

resemble
[rizémbəl]

v. 닮다

to look similar to another person or thing
- resemblance n. 유사

They resemble you. 그들은 너를 닮았어.

blessing
[blésiŋ]

n. 축복

a good thing, a happy circumstance
- bless v. 축복하다

Your puppies are a blessing to us.
너의 강아지들은 우리에게 축복이야.

pure-bred
[pjúər-bréd]

a. (동물이) 순종인

from the same bloodline or type, not mixed

They are all pure-bred like you.
그들은 너처럼 모두 순종이야.

cancer
[kǽnsər]

n. 암

a serious disease
- cancerous a. 암에 걸린

We were shocked at the news that you had terminal cancer.
우리는 네가 말기 암에 걸렸다는 소식을 듣고 충격을 받았어.

intensive care unit
[inténsiv kɛ́ər jùːnit]
중환자실(집중 치료실)

a special hospital unit to treat patients in a critical situation

Sara told me that you were taken to the intensive care unit.
사라는 네가 중환자실로 보내졌다고 나에게 말했어.

heartbreaking
[háːrtbrèikiŋ]
a. 마음이 아픈

causing great pain

I heard the heartbreaking news.
나는 마음 아픈 소식을 들었어.

mourn
[mɔ́ːrn]
v. 슬퍼하다

to be sad because someone has died

• mourning n. 슬픔   • mournful a. 슬픔에 잠긴

This morning we all mourned.
오늘 아침에 우리 모두는 슬퍼했어.

funeral
[fjúːnərəl]
n. 장례식

a ceremony after someone has died

Sara said there would be a funeral.
사라는 장례식이 있을 거라고 말했어.

elegy
[élədʒi]
n. 애가

a sad poem

I read an elegy. 나는 애가를 읽었어.

weep
[wíːp]
v. 울다

to cry

Sara wept all day. 사라는 하루 종일 울었어.

despair
[dispɛ́ər]
n. 절망
v. 절망감을 느끼다

depression, hopelessness

• in despair 절망에 빠진

She was in despair.
그녀는 절망에 빠져 있었어.

sympathize
[símpəθàiz]
v. 공감하다, 동정하다

to understand someone's feeling
- sympathy n. 공감, 동정 · sympathetic a. 공감하는, 동정하는

I sympathized with her feeling.
나는 그녀의 감정에 공감했어.

comfort
[kʌ́mfərt]
v. 위로하다
n. 위로

to make someone feel less worried or unhappy
- comfortable a. 편안한

I tried to comfort Sara.
나는 사라를 위로하려고 했어.

unbearable
[ʌ̀nbɛ́ərəbəl]
a. 견딜 수 없는

unable to accept, intolerable
- bear v. 견디다 · bearable a. 견딜 수 있는

It was unbearable for her.
그건 그녀에게는 견딜 수 없는 일이었어.

condolence
[kəndóuləns]
n. 애도

giving sympathy
- condole v. 위안하다, 문상하다

Other friends expressed their condolences.
다른 친구들도 슬픔을 표현했어.

unanimously
[juːnǽnəməsli]
ad. 만장일치로

in a way everybody agrees, with one accord
- unanimity n. 만장일치 · unanimous a. 만장일치의

We unanimously agreed to bury you.
우리는 만장일치로 너를 묻어주기로 동의했어.

grave
[gréiv]
n. 무덤

a place someone is buried in the ground after they die

We put a grave stone above you with these words - Goodbye, Brownie.
우리는 '잘 가, 브라우니' 라는 말을 너의 묘비에 새겨 놓았어.

immortal
[imɔ́ːrtl]
a. 불멸의

lasting forever and never dying, opposite of mortal
- immortality n. 영원함, 불멸

You will stay immortal in our memories.
너는 우리 기억 속에 영원히 남아 있을 거야.

Check Again!

A Translate each word into Korean.

1. companion ....   2. gracious ....

3. dye ....   4. athletic ....

5. pregnant ....   6. adorable ....

7. identical ....   8. sympathize ....

9. unbearable ....   10. condolence ....

B Translate each word into English.

1. 천국 ....   2. 암 ....

3. 슬퍼하다 ....   4. 불멸의 ....

5. 장례식 ....   6. 애가 ....

7. 균형을 잡다 ....   8. 위로하다 ....

9. 절망 ....   10. 무덤 ....

C Fill in the blank with the appropriate word. Refer to the Korean.

1. I heard the h   news.

   나는 마음 아픈 소식을 들었어.

2. Children are a b   to those who desire them.

   간절히 원하는 자들에게 자녀는 축복이다.

3. My pet is p   like yours.

   나의 애완동물은 네 것처럼 순종이야.

4. He was elected as a student representative u   .

   그는 만장일치로 학생 대표로 선출되었다.

5. His grandfather was taken to the i   care unit.

   그의 할아버지는 중환자실로 보내졌다.

Check More!

다음 밑줄 친 부분에 알맞은 어휘를 고르시오. 아래의 영영 풀이를 참조하시오.

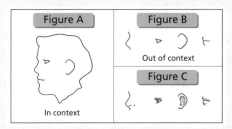

Object identification rarely occurs in isolation. Face perception seems to work the same way. Notice that when seen as part of a face presented in Figure A, any bump or line will be sufficient to **(A)** depict / define a feature. However, the result may be different when the features are separated from the context as shown in Figure B. The features in Figure B are basically **(B)** identical / individual with those in Figure A, but, out of context, they are less identifiable. As in Figure C, we actually require a more detailed presentation than in Figure B, to identify facial features **(C)** unambiguously / unanimously when presented in isolation. Thus, our understanding of context **(D)** compensates / concentrates for lack of detail in the feature identification process.

(A) to portray; to outline; to illustrate: ....

(B) exactly the same: ....

(C) clearly: ....

(D) to make equal return for; to make up for:

....

+ 접두사 in- / im- / un-

접두사 in- / im- / un-은 단어 앞에 붙어 부정의 뜻을 만들어 주는 역할을 한다.
in-은 발음상의 편의를 위해 b, m, p 앞에 올 때 im-으로 변형된다.
un-은 동사에 붙어서 반대의 뜻을 나타내기도 한다.

in-

accurate 정확한
in + accurate = inaccurate 부정확한, 틀린
ex) It was an inaccurate quote of what I really said.
　　그것은 내가 실제로 했던 말을 정확하게 인용한 것이 아니었어요.

- **ability** 능력　　　　　**inability** 무능력
- **definite** 명확히 한정된　**indefinite** 한계가 없는
- **gratitude** 감사　　　　**ingratitude** 배은망덕
- **tolerable** 참을 수 있는　**intolerable** 참을 수 없는
- **credible** 신뢰할 수 있는　**incredible** 믿을 수 없는
- **hospitable** 손님 접대를 잘하는　**inhospitable** 손님을 냉대하는
- **voluntary** 의도적인　　　**involuntary** 무의식 중의

im-

mortal 죽어야 할 운명의
im + mortal = immortal 불사의, 불멸의
ex) A human girl and an immortal vampire fall in love.
　　인간인 소녀와 불사의 흡혈귀가 사랑에 빠져요.

- **moral** 도덕적인　　　**immoral** 부도덕한
- **mobile** 이동할 수 있는　**immobile** 움직일 수 없는
- **practical** 실용적인　　**impractical** 비실용적인
- **balance** 균형　　　　**imbalance** 불균형
- **measurable** 잴 수 있는　**immeasurable** 헤아릴 수 없는
- **partial** 편파적인　　　**impartial** 공명정대한
- **purity** 청결　　　　　**impurity** 불결

un-

acceptable 받아들일 수 있는
un + acceptable = unacceptable 받아들일 수 없는
ex) Texting messages in class is simply unacceptable.
수업 시간에 문자 메시지를 보내는 것은 절대로 용인할 수 없습니다.

- **authorized** 권한을 부여 받은   **unauthorized** 권한이 없는
- **worthy** 가치 있는   **unworthy** 가치 없는
- **orthodox** 정통파의   **unorthodox** 정통이 아닌
- **willingly** 자진해서   **unwillingly** 마지못해
- **favorably** 유리하게   **unfavorably** 불리하게
- **employment** 고용   **unemployment** 실직
- **tangle** 얽히게 하다   **untangle** 얽힌 것을 풀다

Funeral 장례식

⁺coffin 관 / ⁺casket (고급스러운) 관

⁺hearse 영구차

⁺pallbearer 운구하는 사람, 관 곁에 따르는 사람

⁺funeral home 장례식장

⁺hold a wake 초상집에서의 밤샘을 치르다

⁺express one s condolences to ~에게 조의를 표하다

⁺give a eulogy 고인에 대한 송덕문을 낭독하다

VOCA
EDGE
RED

We're teens. I had my cell phone taken away. Goodbye, Brownie Life is full of contrad
campus tour. If I were a judge,... How can we survive in a jungle? I became a Santa (
oney-wise. Hoony goes to an herbal clinic. We became a rescue team. Grandma goe
u want to meet? Are mom and dad compatible? I can't understand this painting. The
ve illusions about boys. I can't understand politicians. Wearing an electronic tag is ho
economics camp. construction a thriving business? How amazing our life has becon
space. I attended the Arbor Day ceremony. We can make the earth a better place. A
Life is full of contradictions. Goodbye, Sara. I learned about the earth. I went to a natu
became a Santa Claus. Sara attends a community party. Mom's got a new hobby. Are
Grandma goes to a laughter clinic. The Volcanoes are back. We have great brothers. W
painting. There was telepathy between us! Sara goes to Turkey. Home decorating is r
electronic tag is horrible. The war should be stopped. Mom, are you going to cut my all
our life has become! I should have been more careful. Forgery should be stopped. Hoc
better place. A super hurricane hit the village. We're teens. I had my cell phone taken
went to a natural science museum. I had a campus tour. If I were a judge,... How can v
hobby. Are they my bosses? Hoony is money-wise. Hoony goes to an herbal clinic. We
great brothers. What historical figures do you want to meet? Are mom and dad compa
decorating is not easy. Hoony thinks girls have illusions about boys. I can't understand p
cut my allowance? Hoony is back from an economics camp. construction a thriving
stopped. Hoony wants to explore outer space. I attended the Arbor Day ceremony. W
phone taken away. Goodbye, Brownie Life is full of contradictions. Goodbye, Sara. I lec
How can we survive in a jungle? I became a Santa Claus. Sara attends a community p

Goodbye, Sara. I learned about the earth. I went to a natural science museum. I had a
attends a community party. Mom's got a new hobby. Are they my bosses? Hoony is
ughter clinic. The Volcanoes are back. We have great brothers. What historical figures do
epathy between us! Sara goes to Turkey. Home decorating is not easy. Hoony thinks girl
war should be stopped. Mom, are you going to cut my allowance? Hoony is back from
uld have been more careful. Forgery should be stopped. Hoony wants to explore outer
ricane hit the village. We're teens. I had my cell phone taken away. Goodbye, Brownie
e museum. I had a campus tour. If I were a judge,... How can we survive in a jungle?
osses? Hoony is money-wise. Hoony goes to an herbal clinic. We became a rescue team
cal figures do you want to meet? Are mom and dad compatible? I can't understand this
Hoony thinks girls have illusions about boys. I can't understand politicians. Wearing an
Hoony is back from an economics camp. construction a thriving business? How amazing
o explore outer space. I attended the Arbor Day ceremony. We can make the earth a
odbye, Brownie Life is full of contradictions. Goodbye, Sara. I learned about the earth.
n a jungle? I became a Santa Claus. Sara attends a community party. Mom's got a new

Chapter 2. My home and Neighborhood

a rescue team. Grandma goes to a laughter clinic. The Volcanoes are back. We ha

Unit 4. Life is full of contradictions.

't understand this painting. There was telepathy between us! Sara goes to Turkey. Ho

Unit 5. Goodbye, Sara.

earing an electronic tag is horrible. The war should be stopped. Mom, are you going

Unit 6. I learned about the earth.

ow amazing our life has become! I should have been more careful. Forgery should be
e the earth a better place. A super hurricane hit the village. We're teens. I had my cel
the earth. I went to a natural science museum. I had a campus tour. If I were a judge,...
got a new hobby. Are they my bosses? Hoony is money-wise. Hoony goes to an herba

Chapter 2
My home and Neighborhood

Unit 4. Life is full of contradictions.

fight for **dominance**

compliment someone

Episode

Dear Daddy,

Daddy, do you agree that life is **contradictory**? • Are you sure adults are **mature**? • At times I **assume** kids are mature. • Adults seem to miss their **childhood**. • Like kids, at times they fight for **dominance**. • Sometimes kids and adults need to **reverse** roles. • You say your dictionary doesn't **contain** words such as fight.

You always say men are **generous**. • Did I **misunderstand** you? • Did you change your **attitude**? • Last night my brother and I thought you and mommy put on an act. • Both of you were **absorbed** in acting, but we could feel the cold **atmosphere**. • We were aware that the **situation** was serious. • Daddy, you looked troubled and **concerned**. • You needed **professional** help. • You seemed to be **desperately** looking for help. • **Ironically**, that help came from me.

Hoony asked me, "Are they going to **divorce**?" • I'm **convinced** that you can stop this from happening. • Daddy, why don't you **apologize** first? • Just **admit** to mom that she is right. • Your generous act will **impress** her. • Just **compromise** with her. • Prove to her that you're not **stubborn**. • **Compliment** her and tell her that she is the best wife and mother. • Am I a good **counselor** for you?

....

아빠에게,

아빠, 아빠는 인생이 모순적이라는 데 동의하세요? 어른들이 성숙하다고 확신하세요? 가끔은 저는 아이들이 성숙한 것 같아요. 어른들은 어린 시절을 그리워하는 것처럼 보여요. 아이들처럼 가끔 어른들은 주도권을 차지하려고 싸우곤 해요. 때때로 아이들과 어른들은 역할을 바꿀 필요가 있어요. 아빠는 아빠 사전에는 싸움이라는 단어는 없다고 말씀하시죠.

아빠는 항상 남자들은 관대하다고 말씀하시죠. 제가 아빠를 오해한 건가요? 생각을 바꾸신 건가요? 어젯밤에 동생과 나는 아빠와 엄마가 연기를 한다고 생각했어요. 두 분 모두 연기하는 데 열중하셨지만, 우리는 차가운 분위기를 느낄 수 있었어요. 우리는 상황이 심각하다는 걸 알았어요. 아빠, 아빠는 괴롭고 걱정스러워 보였어요. 아빠는 전문적인 도움이 필요했어요. 아빠는 필사적으로 도움을 찾고 있는 것 같았어요. 아이러니하게도 그 도움은 저에게서 나왔어요.

후니는 저에게 "두 분이 이혼하실까?"라고 물었어요. 저는 아빠가 이런 일을 막을 수 있다고 확신해요. 아빠, 아빠가 먼저 사과하시는 게 어때요? 그냥 엄마가 옳다고 인정하세요. 아빠의 자상한 행동이 엄마를 감동시킬 거예요. 그냥 엄마와 화해하세요. 아빠가 완고하지 않다는 걸 엄마에게 증명해 보이세요. 엄마를 칭찬하고 엄마가 최고의 아내이자 엄마라고 말하세요. 제가 아빠에게 훌륭한 상담자이죠?

contradictory

[kɑ̀ntrədíktəri]

a. 모순적인

opposite to what someone expects or believes

• contradict v. 모순되다   • contradiction n. 모순

Daddy, do you agree that life is contradictory?

아빠, 아빠는 인생이 모순적이라는 데 동의하세요?

mature

[mətjúər]

a. 성숙한

acting responsibly, fully grown, ripe

• maturity n. 성숙

Are you sure adults are mature?

어른들이 성숙하다고 확신하세요?

assume

[əsjúːm]

v. 생각하다

to think or believe something is true

• assumption n. 가정

At times I assume kids are mature.

가끔은 저는 아이들이 성숙한 것 같아요.

childhood

[tʃáildhùd]

n. 어린 시절

the time period when someone is a child

Adults seem to miss their childhood.

어른들은 어린 시절을 그리워하는 것처럼 보여요.

dominance

[dάmənəns]

n. 우위, 주도권

influence over other people

• dominate v. 우세하다, 지배하다   • dominant a. 우세한, 지배하는

Like kids, at times they fight for dominance.

아이들처럼 가끔 어른들은 주도권을 차지하려고 싸우곤 해요.

reverse

[rivə́ːrs]

v. 거꾸로 하다, 뒤집다

to change positions with someone else

• reversal n. 역전, 반전

Sometimes kids and adults need to reverse roles.

때때로 아이들과 어른들은 역할을 바꿀 필요가 있어요.

contain

[kəntéin]

v. 포함하다

to hold something inside

• container n. 용기

You say your dictionary doesn't contain words such as figh

아빠 사전에는 싸움이라는 단어는 없다고 말씀하시죠.

generous
[dʒénərəs]
a. 관대한

giving a lot, considerate
- generosity n. 관대

You always say men are generous.
항상 남자들은 관대하다고 말씀하시죠.

misunderstand
[mìsʌndərstǽnd]
v. 오해하다

to make a mistake, not to understand
- misunderstanding n. 오해

Did I misunderstand you?
제가 오해한 건가요?

attitude
[ǽtitʃùːd]
n. 사고방식, 태도

a person's thoughts and feelings towards something

Did you change your attitude?
생각을 바꾸신 건가요?

act
[ǽkt]
n. 연기

someone's behavior that does not express real feelings
- put on an act 연기하다

Last night my brother and I thought you and mommy put on an act.
어젯밤에 동생과 나는 아빠와 엄마가 연기를 한다고 생각했어요.

absorbed
[əbsɔ́ːrbd]
a. 열중한

very interested in something or someone
- absorption n. 열중 • be absorbed in ～에 열중하다, 몰두하다

Both of you were absorbed in acting, but we could feel the cold atmosphere.
두 분 모두 연기하는 데 열중하셨지만, 우리는 차가운 분위기를 느낄 수 있었어요.

atmosphere
[ǽtməsfìər]
n. 분위기

how a place or situation feels

Both of you were absorbed in acting, but we could feel the cold atmosphere.
두 분 모두 연기하는 데 열중하셨지만, 우리는 차가운 분위기를 느낄 수 있었어요.

situation
[sìtʃuéiʃən]
n. 상황

what is happening to someone at a specific time or period

We were aware that the situation was serious.
우리는 상황이 심각하다는 걸 알았어요.

concerned
[kənsə́:rnd]
a. 걱정하는

worried or troubled about something
- concern v. 걱정하다 n. 걱정, 염려

Daddy, you looked troubled and concerned.
아빠, 아빠는 괴롭고 걱정스러워 보였어요.

professional
[prəféʃənəl]
a. 전문적인
n. 전문가

relating to a job which requires special training
- professionalism n. 전문성

You needed professional help.
전문적인 도움이 필요했어요.

desperately
[déspəritli]
ad. 필사적으로

badly, seriously
- desperation n. 자포자기 - desperate a. 필사적인

You seemed to be desperately looking for help.
필사적으로 도움을 찾고 있는 것 같았어요.

ironically
[airánikəli]
ad. 아이러니하게도,
반어적으로

unexpectedly, sarcastically
- irony n. 풍자

Ironically, that help came from me.
아이러니하게도 그 도움은 저에게서 나왔어요.

divorce
[divɔ́:rs]
v. 이혼하다
n. 이혼

to end a marriage
- divorced a. 이혼한

Hoony asked me, "Are they going to divorce?"
후니는 저에게 "두 분이 이혼하실까?"라고 물었어요.

convinced
[kənvínst]
a. 확신을 가진

sure and certain, believing in something
- convince v. 확신시키다, 설득하다 - conviction n. 확신

I'm convinced that you can stop this from happening.
저는 아빠가 이런 일을 막을 수 있다고 확신해요.

apologize
[əpálədʒàiz]
v. 사과하다

to say sorry
- apology n. 사과

Daddy, why don't you apologize first?
아빠, 아빠가 먼저 사과하시는 게 어때요?

admit
[ædmít]
v. 인정하다

to tell the truth, to agree that something is true
- admission n. 승인

Just admit to mom that she is right.
그냥 엄마가 옳다고 인정하세요.

impress
[imprés]
v. 감동시키다

to make someone feel admired
- impression n. 감동, 인상 - impressive a. 인상적인

Your generous act will impress her.
자상한 행동이 그녀를 감동시킬 거예요.

compromise
[kámprəmàiz]
v. 화해하다   n. 화해

to reach an agreement with someone

Just compromise with her.
그냥 그녀와 화해하세요.

stubborn
[stʌ́bərn]
a. 완고한

unwilling to change one's mind
- stubbornness n. 완고 - stubbornly ad. 완고하게

Prove to her that you're not stubborn.
완고하지 않다는 걸 그녀에게 증명해 보이세요.

compliment
[kámpləmənt]
v. 칭찬하다
n. 칭찬

to say something nice to someone, to praise
- complimentary a. 칭찬의, 무료의

Compliment her and tell her that she is the best wife and mother.
그녀를 칭찬하고 그녀가 최고의 아내이자 엄마라고 말하세요.

counselor
[káunsələr]
n. 상담자

a person who gives advice
- counsel v. 상담하다 n. 상담 - counseling n. 카운셀링, 상담

Am I a good counselor for you?
제가 훌륭한 상담자이죠?

Check Again!

A Translate each word into Korean.

1. contradictory ....   2. mature ....

3. assume ....   4. stubborn ....

5. reverse ....   6. contain ....

7. generous ....   8. misunderstand ....

9. dominance ....   10. apologize ....

B Translate each word into English.

1. 열중한 ....   2. 분위기 ....

3. 상황 ....   4. 사고방식 ....

5. 전문적인 ....   6. 필사적으로 ....

7. 이혼하다 ....   8. 감동시키다 ....

9. 상담자 ....   10. 화해하다 ....

C Fill in the blank with the appropriate word. Refer to the Korean.

1. Sara looked uneasy and c   when she heard the news.

   사라는 그 소식을 들었을 때, 불편하고 걱정스러워 보였다.

2. They c   the mayor on his service to the community.

   그들은 시장이 지역사회에 봉사한 것을 칭찬하였다.

3. I'm c   that you can take care of this challenging job.

   나는 네가 이 까다로운 일을 처리할 수 있다고 확신한다.

4. Just a   to us that you are the person who broke into the building.

   당신이 그 건물에 침입했던 사람이란 것을 우리에게 그냥 인정하세요.

5. He has been a   in reading the mystery novel all afternoon.

   그는 오후 내내 그 추리소설을 읽는 데 열중하고 있다.

Check More!

(A), (B), (C) 각 밑줄 친 부분에 알맞은 어휘를 짝지은 것으로 가장 적절한 것을 고르시오.

(A) Ironically / Cynically, even our most highly educated guesses often go disastrously wrong. Albert Einstein remarked, "There is no chance that nuclear energy will ever be obtainable." Why is predicting the future so difficult? Would it be smart not to try to guess what's coming next? Not predicting the future would be like driving a car without looking through the windshield. We **(B)** desirably / desperately need people who can foretell the future. They help us narrow the infinity of possible futures down to one or, at least, a few. We look at the present and see the present; they see the seeds of the future. They are our advance scouts, going secretly over the border to bring back **(C)** priceless / valueless information to help the world to come.

*windshield: 자동차 앞유리

	(A)	(B)	(C)
①	Cynically	desperately	priceless
②	Ironically	desirably	valueless
③	Cynically	desirably	priceless
④	Cynically	desperately	valueless
⑤	Ironically	desperately	priceless

Chapter 2
My home and Neighborhood

Unit 5. Goodbye, Sara.

quarantine something from someone

begin to **ascend**

embrace something

Episode

Today is a sad and happy day. ● Sara's family **emigrated** to the U.S. and I got an email from her.

Dear Bomi,

Bomi, it is so **complicated** to leave for another country. ● Yesterday my pet, Choko, was **vaccinated**. ● Choko had an **immunization** shot. ● This morning my family went to the **international** airport. ● It's much bigger than the **domestic** airport.

First, we checked our **baggage**. ● Then, we went through the next **procedure**. ● An officer tried to **quarantine** Choko from me. ● Please don't **separate** us. ● I **pleaded** with him. ● But my pleas were in **vain**. ● He carried Choko to a **freight** cabin. ● I wondered when we would **reunite**. ● I asked if I could go with Choko, but he said it was a **restricted** area. ● I went through **security**. ● What's that metal **detector** for? ● I saw that it **inspected** everything. ● I **boarded** the plane.

The captain announced that we must **fasten** our seat belts. ● The plane began to **ascend**. ● On the ground, houses started to **shrink**. ● Can you imagine flying at an **altitude** of 42,000 feet? ● Suddenly, the plane started shaking and I felt **threatened**. ● Finally, the plane landed and I **embraced** Choko. ● After the 18 hour flight, I experienced **jet lag** and I was **extremely** tired. ● It was a really hard day.

오늘은 슬프고 기쁜 날이다. 사라의 가족은 미국으로 이민을 갔고 나는 그녀에게서 이메일을 받았다.

보미에게,
보미, 다른 나라로 떠나는 것은 정말 복잡해. 어제 내 애완견인 초코가 예방접종을 받았어. 초코는 면역 예방 주사를 맞았어. 오늘 아침에 우리 가족은 국제 공항으로 갔어. 국제 공항은 국내 공항보다 훨씬 커.

먼저, 우리는 짐을 부쳤어. 그리고 나서 우리는 다음 절차를 밟았어. 공항 직원은 나에게서 초코를 떼어놓으려고 했어. 우리를 떼어놓지 마세요. 나는 그에게 간청했어. 그렇지만 나의 간청은 허사였어. 그는 초코를 화물칸으로 데리고 갔어. 나는 우리가 언제다시 만날지 궁금했어. 나는 초코와 함께 갈 수 있는지 물어보았지만, 그는 그곳이 제한 구역이라고 말했어. 나는 보안 검색대를 지났어. 저 금속 탐지기는 무엇을 위한 거지? 나는 그 기계가 모든 물건을 검사하는 걸 보았어. 나는 비행기에 올랐어.

기장은 우리가 안전벨트를 매야 한다고 방송했어. 비행기가 올라가기 시작했어. 땅에 있는 집들이 작아지기 시작했어. 42,000피트의 고도에서 날아가는 걸 상상할 수 있니? 갑자기 비행기가 흔들리기 시작했고 나는 무서웠어. 마침내 비행기는 착륙했고 나는 초코를 껴안아 주었어. 18시간의 비행 후에 나는 시차로 인한 피로를 느꼈고 매우 지쳐 있었어. 정말 힘든 날이었어.

emigrate
[émagrèit]

v. 이민가다

to leave one's home country to live in another country
- emigration n. 이주

Sara's family emigrated to the U.S. and I got an email from her.
사라의 가족은 미국으로 이민을 갔고 나는 그녀에게서 이메일을 받았다.

complicated
[kámpləkèitid]

a. 복잡한

difficult and complex, opposite of simple
- complicate v. 복잡하게 하다   • complication n. 복잡

Bomi, it is so complicated to leave for another country.
보미, 다른 나라로 떠나는 것은 정말 복잡해.

vaccinate
[væksənèit]

v. 예방접종을 하다

to give medicine to prevent disease
- vaccination n. 예방접종

Yesterday my pet, Choko, was vaccinated.
어제 내 애완견인 초코가 예방접종을 받았어.

immunization
[ìmjunizéiʃən]

n. 예방 주사

medicine that prevents a disease from affecting someone
- immunize v. 면역시키다   • immune a. 면역의

Choko had an immunization shot.
초코는 면역 예방 주사를 맞았어.

international
[ìntərnǽʃənəl]

a. 국제적인

involving many countries

This morning my family went to the international airport.
오늘 아침에 우리 가족은 국제 공항으로 갔어.

domestic
[douméstik]

a. 국내의

involving only one's own country
- domesticate v. 길들이다

It's much bigger than the domestic airport.
그것은 국내 공항보다 훨씬 커.

baggage
[bǽgidʒ]
n. 짐

travelling bags, luggage

First, we checked our baggage.

먼저, 우리는 짐을 부쳤어.

procedure
[prəsíːdʒər]
n. 절차

a process, a way of doing something

Then, we went through the next procedure.

그리고 나서 우리는 다음 절차를 밟았어.

quarantine
[kwɔ́ːrəntìːn]
v. 격리시키다, 검역하다
n. 격리, 검역

to separate or remove one thing from another

An officer tried to quarantine Choko from me.

공항 직원은 나에게서 초코를 떼어놓으려고 했어.

separate
[sépərèit]
v. 떼어놓다, 분리하다

to pull two things apart so they are not joined

• separation n. 분리

Please don't separate us.

우리를 떼어놓지 마세요.

plead
[plíːd]
v. 간청하다

to beg, to ask with strong feelings

• plea n. 탄원 • plead with ~에게 간청하다

I pleaded with him. 나는 그에게 간청했어.

vain
[véin]
n. 허사

failure in achieving what was intended

• in vain 허사인, 쓸모없는

But my pleas were in vain.

그렇지만 나의 간청은 허사였어.

freight
[fréit]
n. 화물

goods that are transported separately from personal items

He carried Choko to a freight cabin.

그는 초코를 화물칸으로 데리고 갔어.

reunite

[rìːjuːnáit]

v. 재회하다

to see someone again after having been separated

• reunification n. 재회, 통일

I wondered when we would reunite.

나는 우리가 언제 다시 만날지 궁금했어.

restricted

[ristríktid]

a. 제한된

allowed to only people with special permission; limited

• restrict v. 제한하다 • restriction n. 제한

I asked if I could go with Choko, but he said it was a restricted area.

나는 초코와 함께 갈 수 있는지 물어보았지만, 그는 그곳이 제한 구역이라고 말했어.

security

[sikjúəriti]

n. 보안

all the measures taken to protect a place

• secure v. 확보하다 a. 안전한

I went through security. 나는 보안 검색대를 지났어.

detector

[ditéktər]

n. 탐지기

a machine used to look for items in people's luggage

• detect v. 탐지하다 • detection n. 탐지

What's that metal detector for?

저 금속 탐지기는 무엇을 위한 거지?

inspect

[inspékt]

v. 검사하다

to carefully look at something to check if it is okay

• inspection n. 검사

I saw that it inspected everything.

나는 그 기계가 모든 물건을 검사하는 걸 보았어.

board

[bɔ́ːrd]

v. 탑승하다

to get into the plane

I boarded the plane.

나는 비행기에 올랐어.

fasten

[fǽsn]

v. 묶다

to close something

The captain announced that we must fasten our seat belts

기장은 우리가 안전벨트를 매야 한다고 방송했어.

ascend
[əsénd]
v. 올라가다

to move upwards
- ascension n. 상승

The plane began to ascend.
비행기가 올라가기 시작했어.

shrink
[ʃríŋk]
v. 작아지다

to become smaller in size

On the ground, houses started to shrink.
땅에 있는 집들이 작아지기 시작했어.

altitude
[ǽltətjùːd]
n. 고도

the height above sea level

Can you imagine flying at an altitude of 42,000 feet?
42,000피트의 고도에서 날아가는 걸 상상할 수 있니?

threatened
[θrétnd]
a. 무서운

worried, feared or bullied
- threaten v. 협박하다 - threat n. 협박

Suddenly, the plane started shaking and I felt threatened.
갑자기 비행기가 흔들리기 시작했고 나는 무서웠어.

embrace
[embréis]
v. 껴안다

to hug

Finally, the plane landed and I embraced Choko.
마침내 비행기는 착륙했고 나는 초코를 껴안아 주었어.

jet lag
[dʒét-lǽg]
시차로 인한 피로

a feeling of tiredness after a long flight

After the 18 hour flight, I experienced jet lag and I was extremely tired.
18시간의 비행 후에 나는 시차로 인한 피로를 느꼈고 매우 지쳐 있었어.

extremely
[ikstríːmli]
ad. 매우

more than expected, very much (superlative)
- extreme n. 극단 a. 극심한

After the 18 hour flight, I experienced jet lag and I was extremely tired.
18시간의 비행 후에 나는 시차로 인한 피로를 느꼈고 매우 지쳐 있었어.

Check Again!

A Translate each word into Korean.

1. plead ....
2. vaccinate ....
3. immunization ....
4. inspect ....
5. quarantine ....
6. separate ....
7. jet lag ....
8. ascend ....
9. embrace ....
10. freight ....

B Translate each word into English.

1. 복잡한 ....
2. 재회하다 ....
3. 제한된 ....
4. 국내의 ....
5. 짐 ....
6. 절차 ....
7. 묶다 ....
8. 작아지다 ....
9. 매우 ....
10. 허사 ....

C Fill in the blank with the appropriate word. Refer to the Korean.

1. The plane made a dive to a lower a   .

   그 비행기가 고도를 낮추어 급강하했다.

2. The animals only bite if they feel t   .

   그 동물들은 위협을 느꼈을 때만 문다.

3. She p   with the kidnapper to return her son safely.

   그녀는 아들을 무사히 돌려보내달라고 납치범에게 애원하였다.

4. What is the new way to q   the infected animals?

   그 감염된 동물들을 격리시키는 그 새로운 방법이 뭐니?

5. His family e   to the U.S. except his two sisters.

   그의 가족은 누나 둘을 제외하고는 미국으로 이민 갔다.

Check More!

다음 밑줄 친 부분에 알맞은 어휘를 골라 빈칸에 쓰시오. 아래의 영영 풀이를 참조하시오.

Painting restorers are highly trained in their techniques, but they would have to be the **(A)** original / oriental painter to know exactly what to do with the work at hand. Technical aspects of the work, such as dirt removal, are not **(B)** complicated / competitive. They are quite straightforward. What is important is to bring a painting back to an artist's original intent. In order to do so, they have to decide if they should add something to the painting or leave it as it is. They admit it is **(C)** extraordinary / extremely difficult to determine what should and should not be retouched. "Our goal is to respect the artist's intent, but at the same time to make it a visually **(D)** coherent / cooperative work of art," says Michael Duffy of the Museum of Modern Art in New York.

(A) not copied, imitated, or translated; genuine:

....

(B) not simple, complex: ....

(C) more than expected, very much: ....

(D) logically connected; consistent: ....

Chapter 2
My home and Neighborhood

Unit 6. I learned about the earth.

consist of 5 oceans and 6 continents

see polar bears **inhabiting** the ice

go to **Antarctica** and see emperor penguins

Episode

Dear Sara,

Sara, I'm looking at the globe. • I enclosed a map in your envelope. •
Today I had a geography class. • I learned that the earth consists of 5
oceans and 6 continents. • Sara, can you find your continent? • It's
just a few inches away from Korea, right? • How did people discover
that earth is oval, not square?

Can you see the equator line in the center? • It's lucky that we are not
living in a tropical area. • I remember how much we hate hot and
humid weather. • Imagine living in weather that is 40 degrees Celsius.
• It's equivalent to 104 degrees Fahrenheit. • Isn't it lucky that we live
in mild climates? • Luckily, we live in a temperate zone. • We both
live in the northern hemisphere. • In the southern hemisphere, it
must be summer now. • See the horizontal lines? • I mean the
parallel lines.

If you move your finger north, you can find the Arctic ocean. •
Someday we'll go on a cruise tour together to see the glaciers. • We
can see vast glaciers there. • We will see polar bears inhabiting the
ice. • Or we can go to Antarctica and see emperor penguins. • Do you
know what is related to the time difference? • You can see vertical
lines. • They are called longitude lines. • Sara, I wonder what the
population of your city is. • What kind of plants do people cultivate
there?

....

사라에게,
사라, 나는 지구본을 바라보고 있어. 나는 지도를 너에게 보낼 편지에 함께 넣었어. 오늘 나는 지리학 수업을 들었어. 나는 지구
가 5개의 대양과 6개의 대륙으로 이루어져 있다는 걸 배웠어. 사라, 네가 사는 대륙을 찾을 수 있니? 그건 한국에서 몇 인치밖에
떨어져 있지 않아, 그렇지? 사람들은 지구가 정사각형이 아니라 타원형이라는 걸 어떻게 발견했을까?
중앙에 있는 적도선이 보이니? 우리가 열대 지방에 살지 않는 건 행운이야. 우리가 덥고 습한 날씨를 얼마나 싫어하는지 나는 기
억해. 섭씨 40도의 날씨에서 산다고 상상해봐. 화씨로는 104도가 되는 거야. 우리가 온화한 기후에서 사는 건 운이 좋은 거 아니
니? 다행히도 우리는 온대 지역에 살고 있어. 우리는 둘 다 북반구에 살아. 남반구는 지금 여름일 거야. 가로로 된 선이 보이니?
평행한 선 말이야.
손가락을 북쪽으로 움직이면, 북극해를 볼 수 있을 거야. 언젠가 우리는 빙하를 보러 함께 배를 타고 여행하게 될 거야. 그곳에서
거대한 빙하를 볼 수 있어. 우리는 얼음에서 사는 북극곰을 볼 거야. 아니면 우리는 남극에 가서 황제 펭귄을 볼 수 있어. 너는 무
엇이 시차와 관련이 있는지 아니? 수직으로 된 선이 보일 거야. 그 선들은 경선이라고 불려. 사라, 네가 사는 도시의 인구가 얼마
나 되는지 궁금해. 거기에서는 사람들이 어떤 식물을 경작하니?

globe
[glóub]
n. 지구본

a model of the earth
- global a. 세계적인

Sara, I'm looking at the globe.
사라, 나는 지구본을 바라보고 있어.

enclose
[enklóuz]
v. 동봉하다

to put something inside an envelope

I enclosed a map in your envelope.
나는 지도를 너에게 보낼 편지에 함께 넣었어.

geography
[dʒiːágrəfi]
n. 지리학

the study of the countries of the world
- geographical a. 지리학적인

Today I had a geography class.
오늘 나는 지리학 수업을 들었어.

consist
[kənsíst]
v. 이루어져 있다

to be made of separate things
- consist of ~로 이루어져 있다

I learned that the earth consists of 5 oceans and 6 continents.
나는 지구가 5개의 대양과 6개의 대륙으로 이루어져 있다는 걸 배웠어.

continent
[kántənənt]
n. 대륙

a large area of land that consists of several countries
- continental a. 대륙의

Sara, can you find your continent?
사라, 네가 사는 대륙을 찾을 수 있니?

inch
[íntʃ]
n. 인치

a unit for measuring distances

It's just a few inches away from Korea, right?
그건 한국에서 몇 인치밖에 떨어져 있지 않아, 그렇지?

oval
[óuvəl]
a. 타원형의

shaped like a circle but slightly flat and longer

How did people discover that earth is oval, not square?
사람들은 지구가 정사각형이 아니라 타원형이라는 걸 어떻게 발견했을까?

equator
[ikwéitər]
n. 적도

a line around the center of the earth

Can you see the equator line in the center?
중앙에 있는 적도선이 보이니?

tropical
[trápikəl]
a. 열대의

referring to the hottest part of the earth
• tropics n. 열대 지방

It's lucky that we are not living in a tropical area.
우리가 열대 지방에 살지 않는 건 행운이야.

humid
[hjú:mid]
a. 후덥지근한, 습한

referring to weather that is hot and very damp
• humidity n. 습기

I remember how much we hate hot and humid weather.
우리가 덥고 습한 날씨를 얼마나 싫어하는지 나는 기억해.

Celsius
[sélsiəs]
n. 섭씨

a unit for measuring temperature

Imagine living in weather that is 40 degrees Celsius.
섭씨 40도의 날씨에서 산다고 상상해봐.

equivalent
[ikwívələnt]
a. 동등한
n. 동등물

the same, alike, being equal
• equivalence n. 동등함 • equivalent to ~에 상당하는

It's equivalent to 104 degrees Fahrenheit.
화씨로는 104도가 되는 거야.

mild
[máild]
a. 온화한

relating to weather that is not very hot or very cold

Isn't it lucky that we live in mild climates?
우리가 온화한 기후에서 사는 건 운이 좋은 거 아니니?

temperate
[témpərit]
a. 온대의, 성품 등이
온화한

neither extremely hot nor too cold, mild

Luckily, we live in a temperate zone.
다행히도 우리는 온대 지역에 살고 있어.

zone
[zóun]
n. 지역, 지대

an area that has particular features

Luckily, we live in a temperate zone.
다행히도 우리는 온대 지역에 살고 있어.

hemisphere
[hémisfìər]
n. 반구

one half of the earth

We both live in the northern hemisphere.
우리는 둘 다 북반구에 살아.

southern
[sʌ́ðərn]
a. 남쪽의

in the south side, opposite of northern

In the southern hemisphere, it must be summer now.
남반구는 지금 여름일 거야.

horizontal
[hɔ́:rəzántl]
a. 수평의, 가로의

sideways, opposite of vertical

• horizon n. 지평선   • horizontally ad. 수평으로

See the horizontal lines? 가로로 된 선이 보이니?

parallel
[pǽrəlèl]
a. 평행한

being the same distance along the whole length

I mean the parallel lines.
평행한 선 말이야.

Arctic
[á:rktik]
n. 북극
a. 북극의

the very cold area around the North Pole

If you move your finger north, you can find the Arctic ocean.
손가락을 북쪽으로 움직이면, 북극해를 볼 수 있을 거야.

glacier
[gléiʃər]
n. 빙하

a large mass of ice on land

• glacial a. 빙하의

Someday we'll go on a cruise tour together to see the glaciers.
언젠가 우리는 빙하를 보러 함께 배를 타고 여행하게 될 거야.

vast
[vǽst]
a. 거대한

big, huge, very large and wide

• vastly ad. 광대하게

We can see vast glaciers there. 그곳에서 거대한 빙하를 볼 수 있어.

inhabit
[inhǽbit]

v. 살다

to live in a place

• inhabitant n. 거주자 • inhabitation n. 거주

We will see polar bears inhabiting the ice.

우리는 얼음에서 사는 북극곰을 볼 거야.

Antarctica
[æntá:rktikə]

n. 남극

the very large cold area around the South Pole

Or we can go to Antarctica and see emperor penguins.

아니면 우리는 남극에 가서 황제 펭귄을 볼 수 있어.

related
[riléitid]

a. 관련이 있는

connected, associated

• relate v. 관련시키다 • relation n. 관계

Do you know what is related to the time difference?

너는 무엇이 시차와 관련이 있는지 아니?

vertical
[və́:rtikəl]

a. 수직의, 세로의

going upwards, going from top to bottom

• vertically ad. 수직으로

You can see vertical lines.

수직으로 된 선이 보일 거야.

longitude
[lándʒətjù:d]

n. 경도

imaginary lines around the earth that show the position of things

They are called longitude lines.

그 선들은 경선이라고 불려.

population
[pàpjəléiʃən]

n. 인구

all the people or things that live in a place

• populate v. 거주시키다 • populated a. 거주하는

Sara, I wonder what the population of your city is.

사라, 네가 사는 도시의 인구가 얼마나 되는지 궁금해.

cultivate
[kʌ́ltəvèit]

v. 경작하다

to grow or develop

• cultivation n. 경작

What kind of plants do people cultivate there?

거기에서는 사람들이 어떤 식물을 경작하니?

Check Again!

A Translate each word into Korean.

1. globe ....
2. enclose ....
3. oval ....
4. continent ....
5. hemisphere ....
6. glacier ....
7. equator ....
8. Antarctica ....
9. tropical ....
10. humid ....

B Translate each word into English.

1. 북극 ....
2. 지리학 ....
3. 평행한 ....
4. 거대한 ....
5. 거주하다 ....
6. 온대의 ....
7. 수직의 ....
8. 인구 ....
9. 경작하다 ....
10. 수평의 ....

C Fill in the blank with the appropriate word. Refer to the Korean.

1. 1,000 won was roughly e   to one U.S. dollar.

   천 원은 대략 미화 1달러에 해당했다.

2. People who live in m   climates suffer more when it gets col

   온화한 기후에 사는 사람들이 추워지면 더 고생한다.

3. Do you know what everything on the earth c   of?

   지구상의 모든 것이 무엇으로 이루어졌는지 아세요?

4. Some people argue that the season of birth is r   to childhood intelligence.

   어떤 사람들은 태어난 계절이 어린이 지능과 관련이 있다고 주장한다.

5. The most famous line of l   is the prime meridian, which passes through Greenwich, England.

   가장 유명한 경선은 본초 자오선으로 영국의 그리니치를 통과한다.

Check More!

(A), (B), (C) 각 밑줄 친 부분에 알맞은 어휘를 짝지은 것으로 가장 적절한 것을 고르시오.

It was very hot and **(A)** humid / humiliated. One summer night a man stood on a low hill overlooking a wide **(B)** expense / expanse of forest and field. By the full moon hanging low in the west, he knew that it was near the hour of dawn. A light mist lay along the earth, partly veiling the lower features of the landscape, but above it, the taller trees showed in well-defined masses against a clear sky. Two or three farmhouses were visible through the mist, but in none of them, naturally, was a light. Nowhere, indeed, was any sign or suggestion of life except the barking of a distant dog, which served to **(C)** accentuate / escalate the solitary scene.

(A)	(B)	(C)
① humid	expense	accentuate
② humiliated	expanse	escalate
③ humid	expanse	accentuate
④ humiliated	expense	escalate
⑤ humid	expanse	escalate

+ 접두사 re- / en- / mis-

re-는 'again,' 'back'이라는 뜻의 접두사로, '무언가를 반복하거나 되돌려놓다'
라는 뜻의 단어를 만든다. en-은 'make'라는 뜻의 접두사로, '어떤 상태가 되게
하다'라는 뜻의 단어를 만든다. mis-는 'wrong'이라는 뜻의 접두사로, '잘못되거
나 나쁘다'라는 뜻의 단어를 만든다.

re-

assign 임명하다
re + assign = reassign 재임명하다
ex) I've been reassigned to another department.
나는 다른 부서로 재임명되었어요.

- **act** 행하다 **react** 반응하다
- **bound** 튀어오르다 **rebound** 다시 튀어오르다
- **fresh** 새로워지다 **refresh** 원기를 회복하다
- **formation** 형성 **reformation** 개조
- **habilitate** 훈련시키다 **rehabilitate** 사회 복귀시키다
- **imburse** 지불하다 **reimburse** 상환하다
- **consider** 고려하다 **reconsider** 재고하다

en-

large 큰
en + large = enlarge 크게 하다
ex) How big should we enlarge these photos?
이 사진들을 얼마나 크게 확대시킬까요?

- **courage** 용기 **encourage** 용기를 북돋우다
- **compass** 한계, 범위 **encompass** 둘러싸다, 포위하다
- **title** 직위, 권리 **entitle** 칭호를 주다, 권리를 주다
- **tail** 꼬리, 끝 **entail** 수반하다
- **trap** 덫 **entrap** 덫에 걸리게 하다, 함정에 빠뜨리다
- **vision** 상상력, 미래상 **envision** 상상하다, 계획하다
- **twine** 끈 실 **entwine** 얽히게 하다

mis-

understand 이해하다

mis + **understand** = **misunderstand** 오해하다

ex) Men and women often misunderstand each other's actions.

남자와 여자는 서로의 행동을 종종 오해한다.

• **treat** 대하다	**mistreat** 학대하다
• **lead** 인도하다	**mislead** 잘못 인도하다
• **hap** 운	**mishap** 불운
• **fortune** 행운	**misfortune** 불운, 불행
• **demeanor** 처신, 행실	**misdemeanor** 비행
• **conception** 개념, 생각	**misconception** 오해, 잘못된 생각
• **shapen** ~모양의	**misshapen** 보기 흉한, 기형의

Climate 기후

+ tempcrate zone 온대

+ subtropical zone 아열대

+ tropical zone 열대

+ subpolar zone 냉대

+ polar zone 한대

+ oceanic climate 해양성 기후

+ continental climate 대륙성 기후

VOCA EDGE

RED

we're teens. I had my cell phone taken away. Goodbye, Brownie Life is full of contrad
campus tour. If I were a judge,... How can we survive in a jungle? I became a Santa
money-wise. Hoony goes to an herbal clinic. We became a rescue team. Grandma goe
you want to meet? Are mom and dad compatible? I can't understand this painting. The
have illusions about boys. I can't understand politicians. Wearing an electronic tag is ho
an economics camp. construction a thriving business? How amazing our life has beco
space. I attended the Arbor Day ceremony. We can make the earth a better place. A
Life is full of contradictions. Goodbye, Sara. I learned about the earth. I went to a natu
became a Santa Claus. Sara attends a community party. Mom's got a new hobby. Are
Grandma goes to a laughter clinic. The Volcanoes are back. We have great brothers. W
painting. There was telepathy between us! Sara goes to Turkey. Home decorating is
electronic tag is horrible. The war should be stopped. Mom, are you going to cut my all
our life has become! I should have been more careful. Forgery should be stopped. Hoo
better place. A super hurricane hit the village. We're teens. I had my cell phone taken
went to a natural science museum. I had a campus tour. If I were a judge,... How can w
hobby. Are they my bosses? Hoony is money-wise. Hoony goes to an herbal clinic. We
great brothers. What historical figures do you want to meet? Are mom and dad compa
decorating is not easy. Hoony thinks girls have illusions about boys. I can't understand p
cut my allowance? Hoony is back from an economics camp. construction a thriving
stopped. Hoony wants to explore outer space. I attended the Arbor Day ceremony. W
phone taken away. Goodbye, Brownie Life is full of contradictions. Goodbye, Sara. I lea
How can we survive in a jungle? I became a Santa Claus. Sara attends a community p

Goodbye, Sara. I learned about the earth. I went to a natural science museum. I had a

attends a community party. Mom's got a new hobby. Are they my bosses? Hoony i

ghter clinic. The Volcanoes are back. We have great brothers. What historical figures do

lepathy between us! Sara goes to Turkey. Home decorating is not easy. Hoony thinks girl

war should be stopped. Mom, are you going to cut my allowance? Hoony is back from

Jld have been more careful. Forgery should be stopped. Hoony wants to explore oute

ricane hit the village. We're teens. I had my cell phone taken away. Goodbye, Brownie

e museum. I had a campus tour. If I were a judge,... How can we survive in a jungle?

osses? Hoony is money-wise. Hoony goes to an herbal clinic. We became a rescue team

cal figures do you want to meet? Are mom and dad compatible? I can't understand thi

Hoony thinks girls have illusions about boys. I can't understand politicians. Wearing ar

Hoony is back from an economics camp. construction a thriving business? How amazing

o explore outer space. I attended the Arbor Day ceremony. We can make the earth

odbye, Brownie Life is full of contradictions. Goodbye, Sara. I learned about the earth.

n a jungle? I became a Santa Claus. Sara attends a community party. Mom's got a nev

Chapter 3. Learning

a rescue team. Grandma goes to a laughter clinic. The Volcanoes are back. We ha

Unit 7. I went to a natural science museum.

't understand this painting. There was telepathy between us! Sara goes to Turkey. Ho

Unit 8. I had a campus tour.

earing an electronic tag is horrible. The war should be stopped. Mom, are you going

Unit 9. If I were a judge,...

ow amazing our life has become! I should have been more careful. Forgery should be

e the earth a better place. A super hurricane hit the village. We're teens. I had my ce

the earth. I went to a natural science museum. I had a campus tour. If I were a judge,..

got a new hobby. Are they my bosses? Hoony is money-wise. Hoony goes to an herba

Chapter 3
Learning

Unit 7. I went to a natural science museum.

live **together with** dinosaurs

speculate and **observe** things

make **hypotheses** and **theories**

Episode

Dear Sara,

Our class went to a natural science museum. • One of the most interesting things was that it was powered by renewable energy. • We were surprised to learn that the huge buildings were heated by solar energy. • We went upstairs and looked at the exhibits on display. • They included remains from our ancestors. • We also saw fossils. • Our teacher explained that some organisms became fossilized. • They can show us how life originated. • There were even dinosaur bones. • They were enormous. • Sara, isn't it a relief that we don't live together with dinosaurs? • We saw dinosaur skulls, too. • The displays showed how humans evolved. • Anthropologists believe that humans evolved from apes. • Sara, can you imagine our great, great ancestors were apes?

We moved over to the astronomy section. • The displays there explained how our universe originated from a dot. • The dot exploded. • Then it expanded. • Wow, our universe is full of mystery. • How can scientists analyze such a vast universe? • It must have given them chronic headaches. • Maybe they took painkillers to help them think. • I thought for a few moments about the ancient Greek philosophers. • How were they able to explain natural phenomena? • Our teacher said they speculated a lot. • They observed things and made hypotheses. • They also made many theories. • Whew, what a complicated process!

....

사라에게,
우리 반은 자연 과학 박물관에 갔어. 가장 흥미 있는 것 중 하나는 재생 에너지를 연료로 쓴다는 사실이었어. 우리는 커다란 건물이 태양 에너지로 난방이 되고 있다는 것을 배우고 놀랐어. 우리는 위층으로 가서 진열된 전시품들을 보았어. 우리 조상들의 유해도 포함하고 있었어. 우리는 화석도 보았어. 우리 선생님은 어떤 생물이 화석이 되었다고 설명해 주셨어. 그 화석들은 생명체가 어떻게 생겨났는지 우리에게 보여줄 수 있어. 공룡 뼈도 있었어. 그것들은 거대했어. 사라, 우리가 공룡과 함께 살지 않는 것이 안심이 되지 않니? 우리는 공룡 해골도 보았어. 전시품들은 인간이 어떻게 진화했는지 보여주었어. 인류학자들은 인간이 유인원에서 진화되었다고 믿고 있어. 사라, 우리의 아주 먼 조상이 유인원이었다는 걸 상상할 수 있니?

우리는 천문학 구역으로 옮겨갔어. 그곳에 있던 전시품은 우주가 어떻게 하나의 점에서 시작되었는지 설명해주고 있었어. 그 점이 폭발했어. 그리고 나서 팽창했어. 와, 우리의 우주는 신비로 가득 차 있어. 과학자들은 그렇게 광대한 우주를 어떻게 분석할 수 있는 걸까? 그것은 틀림없이 과학자들에게 만성 두통을 불러일으켰을 거야. 아마도 그들은 생각하기 위해서 진통제를 복용했을 거야. 나는 잠시 동안 고대 그리스 철학자들에 대해 생각해 보았어. 그들은 어떻게 자연 현상을 설명할 수 있었을까? 우리 선생님은 그들이 많은 사색을 했다고 말씀하셨어. 그들은 사물을 관찰했고 가설을 만들었어. 그들은 많은 이론을 만들기도 했어. 휴, 정말 복잡한 과정이야!

renewable
[rinjú:wəbəl]

a. 재생 가능한

constantly replenishing
• renew v. 새롭게 하다 • renewable energy 재생 에너지

One of the most interesting things was that it was powered by renewable energy.

가장 흥미 있는 것 중 하나는 재생 에너지를 연료로 쓴다는 사실이었어.

heat
[hí:t]

v. 난방을 하다,
  가열하다

to raise the temperature inside the buildings

We were surprised to learn that the huge buildings were heated by solar energy.

우리는 커다란 건물이 태양 에너지로 난방이 되고 있다는 것을 배우고 놀랐어.

solar
[sóulər]

a. 태양의

relating to the sun
• solar energy 태양 에너지

We were surprised to learn that the huge buildings were heated by solar energy.

우리는 커다란 건물이 태양 에너지로 난방이 되고 있다는 것을 배우고 놀랐어.

exhibit
[igzíbit]

n. 전시품
v. 전시하다

a thing that is displayed for people to look at
• exhibition n. 전시

We went upstairs and looked at the exhibits on display.

우리는 위층으로 가서 진열된 전시품들을 보았어.

remains
[riméinz]

n. 유해

the parts of a living thing's body that remain after it dies
• remain v. 잔존하다 • remainder n. 나머지

They included remains from our ancestors.

우리 조상들의 유해도 포함하고 있었어.

fossil
[fásl]

n. 화석

the hardened body of an old animal or plant
• fossilize v. 화석으로 만들다 • fossilized a. 화석이 된

We also saw fossils. 우리는 화석도 보았어.

organism
[ɔ́:rgənìzəm]

n. 생물

any plant or animal, anything that is alive

Our teacher explained that some organisms became fossilized.

우리 선생님은 어떤 생물이 화석이 되었다고 설명해 주셨어.

originate
[ərídʒənèit]

v. 생기다, 유래하다

to come into existence, to start, to begin
- origin n. 기원   - origination n. 시작, 발생

They can show us how life originated.

그것들은 생명체가 어떻게 생겨났는지 우리에게 보여줄 수 있어.

bone
[bóun]

n. 뼈

the hard parts inside one's body that make one's skeleton
- bony a. 뼈만 남은, 앙상한

There were even dinosaur bones.

공룡 뼈도 있었어.

enormous
[inɔ́ːrməs]

a. 거대한

very large, huge
- enormously ad. 막대하게

They were enormous. 그것들은 거대했어.

relief
[rilíːf]

n. 안심

a feeling of gladness that something bad did not happen
- relieve v. 경감시키다   - relieved a. 누그러진

Sara, isn't it a relief that we don't live together with dinosaurs?

사라, 우리가 공룡과 함께 살지 않는 것이 안심이 되지 않니?

skull
[skʌ́l]

n. 해골

the bones of a head

We saw dinosaur skulls, too.

우리는 공룡 해골도 보았어.

evolve
[ivάlv]

v. 진화하다

to change gradually over a long time into a better form
- evolution n. 진화, 발전   - evolutionary a. 진화의

The displays showed how humans evolved.

전시품들은 인간이 어떻게 진화했는지 보여주었어.

anthropologist
[æ̀nθrəpάlədʒist]

n. 인류학자

a scientist who studies people, society, and culture
- anthropology n. 인류학

Anthropologists believe that humans evolved from apes.

인류학자들은 인간이 유인원에서 진화되었다고 믿고 있어.

ape
[éip]
n. 유인원

an animal that is similar to a monkey or a gorilla

Sara, can you imagine our great, great ancestors were apes?

사라, 우리의 아주 먼 조상이 유인원이었다는 걸 상상할 수 있니?

section
[sékʃən]
n. 구역, 부분

division, one of the parts of something

We moved over to the astronomy section.

우리는 천문학 구역으로 옮겨갔어.

universe
[júːnəvə̀ːrs]
n. 우주

the earth, stars, and planets

• universal a. 전 세계적인, 보편적인

The displays there explained how our universe originated from a dot.

그곳에 있던 전시품은 우주가 어떻게 하나의 점에서 시작되었는지 설명해주고 있었어.

explode
[iksplóud]
v. 폭발하다

to loudly burst and break apart

• explosion n. 폭발 • explosive a. 폭발의

The dot exploded. 그 점이 폭발했어.

expand
[ikspǽnd]
v. 팽창하다

to become larger

• expansion n. 팽창 • expanded a. 팽창된

Then it expanded. 그리고 나서 팽창했어.

mystery
[místəri]
n. 신비

something that is strange and can't be explained

• mysterious a. 신비한

Wow, our universe is full of mystery.

와, 우리의 우주는 신비로 가득 차 있어.

analyze
[ǽnəlàiz]
v. 분석하다

to think about something in order to understand it

• analysis n. 분석

How can scientists analyze such a vast universe?

과학자들은 그렇게 광대한 우주를 어떻게 분석할 수 있는 걸까?

chronic
[kránik]
a. 만성의

very painful and lasting a long time

It must have given them chronic headaches.

그것은 틀림없이 그들에게 만성 두통을 불러일으켰을 거야.

painkiller
[péinkìlər]
n. 진통제

medicine that makes pain go away

Maybe they took painkillers to help them think.
아마도 그들은 생각하기 위해서 진통제를 복용했을 거야.

philosopher
[filásəfər]
n. 철학자

a person who studies and creates ideas about many things

• philosophy n. 철학 • philosophical a. 철학의

I thought for a few moments about the ancient Greek philosophers.
나는 잠시 동안 고대 그리스 철학자들에 대해 생각해 보았어.

phenomenon
[finámənàn]
n. 현상

an event, a thing that happens

• phenomena plural. phenomenon의 복수형

How were they able to explain natural phenomena?
그들은 어떻게 자연 현상을 설명할 수 있었을까?

speculate
[spékjəlèit]
v. 사색하다,
   깊이 생각하다

to think about something, to wonder

• speculation n. 심사숙고

Our teacher said they speculated a lot.
우리 선생님은 그들이 많은 사색을 했다고 말씀하셨어.

observe
[əbzə́:rv]
v. 관찰하다

to examine something, to discern

• observation n. 관찰 • observant a. 관찰하는

They observed things and made hypotheses.
그들은 사물을 관찰했고 가설을 만들었어.

hypothesis
[haipáθəsis]
n. 가설

an idea that attempts to explain how something happens

• hypotheses plural. hypothesis의 복수형

• hypothesize v. 가설을 세우다 • hypothetical a. 가설의

They observed things and made hypotheses.
그들은 사물을 관찰했고 가설을 만들었어.

theory
[θíəri]
n. 이론

an idea that is intended to explain something

• theorize v. 이론을 세우다 • theoretical a. 이론의

They also made many theories.
그들은 많은 이론을 만들기도 했어.

Check Again!

A Translate each word into Korean.

1. enormous ....
2. chronic ....
3. speculate ....
4. universe ....
5. philosopher ....
6. phenomenon ....
7. originate ....
8. analyze ....
9. renewable ....
10. section ....

B Translate each word into English.

1. 생물 ....
2. 화석 ....
3. 관찰하다 ....
4. 가설 ....
5. 이론 ....
6. 진화하다 ....
7. 인류학자 ....
8. 신비 ....
9. 폭발하다 ....
10. 팽창하다 ....

C Fill in the blank with the appropriate word. Refer to the Korean.

1. Nobody can explain how the story o_____ .

   그 이야기가 어떻게 유래되었는지 아무도 설명할 수가 없다.

2. What a r_____ ! The test has been postponed.

   정말 다행이야. 시험이 연기되었어.

3. People seemed interested in the e_____ on display.

   사람들이 전시물에 관심이 있는 것 같았다.

4. A researcher found fossilized r_____ of a dinosaur.

   한 연구자가 공룡의 화석 유해를 발견했다.

5. Most ancient cultures described natural p_____ as acts of God or several gods.

   대부분의 고대 문화권은 자연 현상들을 유일신 또는 여러 신들의 행위로 묘사했다.

Check More!

다음 밑줄 친 부분에 알맞은 어휘를 고르시오. 아래의 영영 풀이를 참조하시오.

I think it is rather unfair to decide our children's career paths based on the results of an **(A)** altitude / aptitude test taken when they are 11 or 12 years old. You may not believe in the **(B)** hypothesis / hypertension that areas which children are considered good at in sixth grade may be the same ones in which they excel by the end of their senior year. Secondary school should be a time for **(C)** expanding / exploding horizons - not limiting them. The only thing students should be required to do is to study a broad **(D)** language / range of subjects throughout middle and high school. By the end of high school, they would have a much better idea of what they would like to study at university. The time for specialized study is in university and graduate school, not earlier.

(A) an ability to learn something quickly and well:

....

(B) an idea created to explain how something happens:

....

(C) to make bigger: ....

(D) a series of things in a line: ....

Chapter 3
Learning

Unit 8. I had a campus tour.

assemble in the auditorium

look up and **serenade** someone

Episode

Dear Diary,

My uncle is a **college** student. • He gained admission to a **prestigious** college. • It has the best **reputation** in Korea. • After the entrance ceremony, there was an **orientation** for freshmen. • Students and guests **assembled** in the auditorium. • It was big enough to **accommodate** about 5,000 people. • The principal **praised** the students. • He said how **competent** they were.

Then he introduced the **faculty** members. • After that, he explained the **guidelines** of campus life. • Then the school **advisor** came on stage. • She said being a college student is a big **responsibility**. • She explained how they **assess** students and she talked about how important **term papers** are. • Whew, three years of cramming and studying? • How do students **tolerate** it? • Don't they **deserve** time off to play? • After the ceremony, we went to the **dormitory** where my uncle will stay. • It didn't look very **luxurious**. • There was a **laundromat** on the first floor. • Students can do **laundry** there. • There were signs on the doors of some rooms that said "Do not make **disturbances**." • Although the school was **co-ed**, the girls' dormitory was separate. • It reminded me of the **play**, Romeo and Juliet. • Romeo looked up at Juliet's window and **serenaded** her. • My uncle seemed to be **disappointed** that the dormitories were separate. • There are **supervisors** in the girls' dormitory. • They **rotate** their shifts every night. • Don't be disappointed, uncle. • You can climb a ladder to the girls' dormitory if you find a perfect **match**.

....

다이어리에게,

우리 삼촌은 대학생이야. 그는 일류 대학에 입학 허가를 받았어. 그 학교는 한국에서 가장 명성 있는 학교야. 입학식 후에 신입생을 위한 오리엔테이션이 있었어. 학생들과 손님들은 강당에 모였어. 그곳은 약 5,000명 정도를 수용할 만큼 컸어. 학장님은 학생들을 칭찬하셨어. 그는 학생들이 얼마나 유능한지 말했어.

그리고 나서 그는 교직원들을 소개했어. 그 후에 그는 학교 생활의 지침을 설명했어. 그리고 나서 학교 신입생 지도 교수님이 무대로 올라오셨어. 그녀는 대학생이 되는 것은 커다란 책임이 따른다고 말씀하셨어. 그녀는 교수님들이 학생들을 어떻게 평가하는지 설명해 주셨고 학기말 리포트가 얼마나 중요한지에 대해 말씀하셨어. 휴, 3년 동안 틀어박혀서 공부를 해야 한다고? 학생들은 그걸 어떻게 견디지? 그들은 나가서 놀 시간을 가질 만하지 않니? 식이 끝난 후에 우리는 삼촌이 살게 될 기숙사로 갔어. 기숙사는 그렇게 호화로워 보이지는 않았어. 1층에는 빨래방이 있었어. 학생들은 그곳에서 세탁을 할 수 있어. 몇 개의 방 문에는 "방해하지 마세요"라는 표시가 붙어 있었어. 그 학교는 남녀공학이었지만, 여학생 기숙사는 분리되어 있었어. 그건 나에게 로미오와 줄리엣이라는 연극을 상기시켰어. 로미오는 줄리엣의 창문을 올려다보면서 그녀에게 세레나데를 불러주었어. 우리 삼촌은 기숙사가 분리되었다는 것에 대해 실망하는 것처럼 보였어. 여학생 기숙사에는 감독관이 있어. 그들은 매일 밤 근무를 교대해. 실망하지 마세요, 삼촌. 이상적인 상대를 발견하면 여학생 기숙사에 사다리를 놓고 올라갈 수 있잖아요.

college
[kálidʒ]
n. 대학교

a place where students study to get a qualification like a university

My uncle is a college student.

우리 삼촌은 대학생이야.

prestigious
[prestídʒiəs]
a. 일류의, 명문의

well-known, important and admired

• prestige n. 명성, 평판

He gained admission to a prestigious college.

그는 일류 대학에 입학 허가를 받았어.

reputation
[rèpjətéiʃən]
n. 명성, 평판

people's opinion about how good something is

• reputable a. 평판이 좋은

It has the best reputation in Korea.

그것은 한국에서 가장 명성 있어.

orientation
[ɔ̀:rientéiʃən]
n. 오리엔테이션

an event where students receive helpful information about the college

• orientate v. 환경에 순응하다, 적응시키다

After the entrance ceremony, there was an orientation for freshmen.

입학식 후에 신입생을 위한 오리엔테이션이 있었어.

assemble
[əsémbəl]
v. 모이다

to come together

• assembly n. 집회

Students and guests assembled in the auditorium.

학생들과 손님들은 강당에 모였어.

accommodate
[əkámədèit]
v. 수용하다

to provide for, to supply with food, housing, etc.

• accommodation n. 수용

It was big enough to accommodate about 5,000 people.

그곳은 약 5,000명 정도를 수용할 만큼 컸어.

praise
[préiz]
v. 칭찬하다
n. 칭찬

to compliment and say nice things about something

• praiseworthy a. 칭찬할 만한

The principal praised the students.

학장님은 학생들을 칭찬하셨어.

competent
[kάmpətənt]

a. 유능한

having ability, talents, and skills
- competence n. 능력

He said how competent they were.
그는 그들이 얼마나 유능한지 말했어.

faculty
[fǽkəlti]

n. 교직원

the staff of a college or university

Then he introduced the faculty members.
그리고 나서 그는 교직원들을 소개했어.

guideline
[gάidlàin]

n. 지침

a set of rules and instructions that tell someone how to behave

After that, he explained the guidelines of campus life.
그 후에 그는 학교 생활의 지침을 설명했어.

advisor
[ædváizər]

n. 신입생 지도 교수

a person who gives advice, a counselor
- advise v. 충고하다 - advice n. 충고

Then the school advisor came on stage.
그리고 나서 학교 신입생 지도 교수님이 무대로 올라오셨어.

responsibility
[rispὰnsəbíləti]

n. 책임

a duty that someone has because of their job or position
- responsible a. 책임이 있는

She said being a college student is a big responsibility.
그녀는 대학생이 되는 것은 커다란 책임이 따른다고 말씀하셨어.

assess
[əsés]

v. 평가하다

to test, to evaluate
- assessment n. 평가, 감정

She explained how they assess students and she talked about how important term papers are.
그녀는 그들이 학생들을 어떻게 평가하는지 설명해 주셨고 학기말 리포트가 얼마나 중요한지에 대해 말씀하셨어.

term paper
[tə́:rm péipər]

학기말 리포트

a long document that students must write and which they will receive a grade for

She explained how they assess students and she talked about how important term papers are.
그녀는 그들이 학생들을 어떻게 평가하는지 설명해 주셨고 학기말 리포트가 얼마나 중요한지에 대해 말씀하셨어.

tolerate
[tálərèit]
v. 견디다

to cope or deal with a situation
- tolerance n. 관용 • toleration n. 묵인
- tolerant a. 관대한 • tolerable a. 참을 수 있는

How do students tolerate it? 학생들은 그걸 어떻게 견디지?

deserve
[dizə́:rv]
v. ~할 만하다,
~할 자격이 있다

to receive something because of what someone has done;
to have a legitimate claim to have or receive something
- deserving a. ~할 가치 있는

Don't they deserve time off to play?
그들은 나가서 놀 시간을 가질 만하지 않니?

dormitory
[dɔ́:rmətɔ̀:ri]
n. 기숙사

a place where students live on campus

After the ceremony, we went to the dormitory where my uncle will stay.
식이 끝난 후에 우리는 삼촌이 살게 될 기숙사로 갔어.

luxurious
[lʌgʒúəriəs]
a. 호화스러운

comfortable and expensive
- luxury n. 사치

It didn't look very luxurious.
그것은 그렇게 호화로워 보이지는 않았어.

laundromat
[lɔ́:ndrəmæt]
n. 빨래방

a room with machines where someone can wash their clothes

There was a laundromat on the first floor.
1층에는 빨래방이 있었어.

laundry
[lá:ndri]
n. 세탁물, 빨래

dirty clothes that need to be washed
- do laundry 세탁하다

Students can do laundry there.
학생들은 그곳에서 세탁을 할 수 있어.

disturbance
[distə́:rbəns]
n. 방해, 소란

disturbing something, bother, acts that annoy or irritate people
- disturb v. 방해하다 • disturbing a. 방해가 되는

There were signs on the doors of some rooms that said "Do not make disturbances."
몇 개의 방 문에는 "방해하지 마세요"라는 표시가 붙어 있었어.

co-ed
[kóuéd]
a. 남녀공학의
n. 남녀공학

allowing boys and girls to learn together

Although the school was co-ed, the girls' dormitory was separate.

그 학교는 남녀공학이었지만, 여학생 기숙사는 분리되어 있었어.

play
[pléi]
n. 연극, 희곡

an acting performance

It reminded me of the play, Romeo and Juliet.

그건 나에게 로미오와 줄리엣이라는 연극을 상기시켰어.

serenade
[sèrənéid]
v. 세레나데를 부르다

to sing a song to a person

Romeo looked up at Juliet's window and serenaded her.

로미오는 줄리엣의 창문을 올려다보면서 그녀에게 세레나데를 불러주었어.

disappointed
[dìsəpɔ́intid]
a. 실망한

a little sad and upset

• disappoint v. 실망시키다 • disappointment n. 실망

My uncle seemed to be disappointed that the dormitories were separate.

우리 삼촌은 기숙사가 분리되었다는 것에 대해 실망하는 것처럼 보였어.

supervisor
[súːpərvàizər]
n. 감독관

a person who ensures other people behave correctly

• supervision n. 감독

There are supervisors in the girls' dormitory.

여학생 기숙사에는 감독관이 있어.

rotate
[róuteit]
v. 교대하다

to take turns doing a job

• rotation n. 교대

They rotate their shifts every night.

그들은 매일 밤 근무를 교대해.

match
[mætʃ]
n. 어울리는 짝

a partner, someone you are compatible with

You can climb a ladder to the girls' dormitory if you find a perfect match.

이상적인 상대를 발견하면 여학생 기숙사에 사다리를 놓고 올라갈 수 있잖아요.

Check Again!

A Translate each word into Korean.

1. prestigious ....
2. reputation ....
3. praise ....
4. rotate ....
5. competent ....
6. accommodate ....
7. faculty ....
8. guideline ....
9. responsibility ....
10. deserve ....

B Translate each word into English.

1. 감독관 ....
2. 견디다 ....
3. 평가하다 ....
4. 기숙사 ....
5. 호화로운 ....
6. 연극 ....
7. 방해 ....
8. 남녀공학의 ....
9. 실망한 ....
10. 학기말 리포트 ....

C Fill in the blank with the appropriate word. Refer to the Korean.

1. Choosing right t_____ paper topics is very important.
   올바른 학기말 리포트 주제를 선정하는 것이 아주 중요하다.

2. I'm honored to get admission to such a p_____ college.
   이런 명문대에 입학하게 되어 영광입니다.

3. This will help to teach you how to do l_____ efficiently.
   이것이 세탁을 능률적으로 하는 법을 가르치는 것을 도와줄 것이다.

4. Students may not make d_____ in the parking lot.
   학생들은 주차장에서 소란을 피워서는 안 된다.

5. A huge crowd a_____ in the City Square to see the new President.
   신임 대통령을 보기 위해 거대한 군중이 시 광장에 모였다.

Check More!

다음 밑줄 친 부분에 알맞은 어휘를 골라 빈칸에 쓰시오. 아래의 영영 풀이를 참조하시오.

Our nursing college is one of the most **(A)** prestigious / pretentious schools in our nation. One day a professor gave us a quiz. I had easily answered all the questions until I read the last one: "What is the name of the woman who cleans the school?" I knew she was tall, short-haired, and in her fifties, but how would I know her name? I **(B)** handed in / gave away my paper, leaving the question blank. Collecting the papers, the professor said the last question would count. Then she added, "In your careers, you will meet many people. All are **(C)** substantial / significant. They **(D)** deserve / derive your attention and care, even if all you do is smile and say hello." I've never forgotten that lesson. I also learned that her name was Dorothy.

(A) well-known: ....

(B) to submit: ....

(C) important; vital; meaningful: ....

(D) to be entitled to; to have a right to: ....

Chapter 3. Learning **81**

Chapter 3
Learning

Unit 9. If I were a judge,···

enrich one's mind

order not to **violate** one's freedom of speec

Episode

Dear Mom,

I read an article about my favorite band, the Volcanoes. • It really aroused anger in me. • It says they won't be on TV for some time and this stirs me. • Some officials made a decision to censor the band. • They said there are some problems with the contents of some songs. • They said their songs are uneducational. • They claim the songs will ruin students. • They seem to think that the Volcanoes are criminals. • What an outdated idea! • What criteria did they use to decide this? • I'm in a rage.

Undoubtedly, they don't know what art is. • Mom, you said it's an absurd decision. • Their songs enrich my mind. • You said we live in a democracy. • In a democracy, people have a right to free speech. • But what's happening here? • Mom, you checked my text messages. • You can't deny it. • Hoony is my witness. • Mom, are you going to betray your own beliefs? • I want you to be objective. • Are you trying to confine me? • When you check my messages, you violate my freedom of speech. • Even prisoners have a right to say what they want. • If I were a judge, I would order you not to do this. • You're not allowed to touch my phone. • Any objections, mom?

....

엄마에게,

저는 제가 좋아하는 밴드인 볼케이노에 대한 기사를 읽었어요. 그것은 정말로 저를 화나게 했어요. 그들이 한동안 텔레비전에 나오지 않을 거라고 쓰여 있고 그것이 저의 감정을 자극해요. 몇몇 관계자들은 그 밴드를 검열하기로 결정했어요. 그들은 노래 몇 개의 내용에 문제가 있다고 말했어요. 그들은 그 밴드의 노래가 비교육적이라고 말했어요. 그들은 그 노래들이 학생들을 망칠 거라고 주장해요. 그들은 볼케이노가 범죄자라고 생각하는 것 같아요. 정말 시대에 뒤떨어진 생각이에요! 이걸 결정하는 데 그들은 어떤 기준을 사용했나요? 저는 화가 치밀어요.

의심할 여지 없이 그들은 예술이 무엇인지 몰라요. 엄마, 엄마는 그것이 불합리한 결정이라고 말씀하셨죠. 그들의 노래는 제 마음을 풍성하게 해요. 엄마는 우리가 민주주의 사회에서 산다고 말했어요. 민주주의 사회에서 사람들은 언론의 자유에 대한 권리가 있어요. 그런데 여기에선 무슨 일이 일어나는 거죠? 엄마, 엄마는 제 문자 메시지를 확인하셨어요. 엄마는 그걸 부인할 수 없어요. 후니가 증인이에요. 엄마, 엄마는 자신의 믿음을 배신하실 건가요? 저는 엄마가 객관적이면 좋겠어요. 엄마는 저를 가두려고 하시는 건가요? 엄마가 제 문자 메시지를 확인할 때, 엄마는 저의 언론의 자유를 침해하는 거예요. 죄수들조차도 자신이 원하는 것을 말할 권리가 있어요. 제가 판사라면, 엄마에게 그런 행동을 하지 말라고 명령할 거예요. 엄마는 제 전화를 만질 수 없어요. 이의 있으세요, 엄마?

article
[ɑ́ːrtikl]
n. 기사

a piece of writing in a newspaper or magazine

I read an article about my favorite band, the Volcanoes.

저는 제가 좋아하는 밴드인 볼케이노에 대한 기사를 읽었어요.

arouse
[əráuz]
v. 자극하다

to bring about or cause a feeling or idea in someone

It really aroused anger in me.

그것은 정말로 저를 화나게 했어요.

stir
[stə́ːr]
v. 감정을 자극하다

to make a person react with strong emotions

• stirring a. (감정을) 자극하는

It says they won't be on TV for some time and this stirs me

그들이 한동안 텔레비전에 나오지 않을 거라고 쓰여 있고 그것이 저의 감정을 자극해요.

censor
[sénsər]
v. 검열하다

to edit or cover up parts of something (art, music, etc.)

• censorship n. 검열

Some officials made a decision to censor the band.

몇몇 관계자들은 그 밴드를 검열하기로 결정했어요.

content
[kəntént]
n. 내용

substance or ideas in songs or books

They said there are some problems with the contents of some songs.

그들은 노래 몇 개의 내용에 문제가 있다고 말했어요.

uneducational
[ənèdʒukéiʃənəl]
a. 비교육적인

not educational, having no educational value

They said their songs are uneducational.

그들은 그 밴드의 노래가 비교육적이라고 말했어요.

ruin
[rúːin]
v. 망치다
n. 파멸

to damage or spoil something

• ruination n. 파괴, 황폐   • ruinous a. 파괴된, 황폐한

They claim the songs will ruin students.

그들은 그 노래들이 학생들을 망칠 거라고 주장해요.

criminal
[krímənəl]
n. 범죄자

a person who commits crimes and breaks laws
- crime n. 범죄

They seem to think that the Volcanoes are criminals.
그들은 볼케이노가 범죄자라고 생각하는 것 같아요.

outdated
[àutdéitid]
a. 시대에 뒤떨어진

not modern and not useful, obsolete

What an outdated idea!
정말 시대에 뒤떨어진 생각이에요!

criterion
[kraitíəriən]
n. 기준, 표준

a set of beliefs that someone uses to judge how good or bad something is; a standard
- criteria plural. criterion의 복수형

What criteria did they use to decide this?
이걸 결정하는 데 그들은 어떤 기준을 사용했나요?

rage
[réidʒ]
n. 성냄, 분노

strong anger, explosion
- in a rage 화가 난

I'm in a rage. 저는 화가 치밀어요.

undoubtedly
[ʌndáutidli]
ad. 의심할 여지 없이

definitely, surely, certainly

Undoubtedly, they don't know what art is.
의심할 여지 없이 그들은 예술이 무엇인지 몰라요.

absurd
[æbsə́:rd]
a. 불합리한, 어리석은

stupid, silly, foolish, not logical

Mom, you said it's an absurd decision.
엄마, 엄마는 그것이 불합리한 결정이라고 말씀하셨죠.

enrich
[enrítʃ]
v. 풍부하게 하다

to improve something, to make it better
- enrichment n. 풍부하게 함

Their songs enrich my mind.
그들의 노래는 제 마음을 풍성하게 해요.

democracy
[dimάkrəsi]
n. 민주주의

a society where everybody has the same rights
- democrat n. 민주주의자 - democratic a. 민주주의의

You said we live in a democracy.
엄마는 우리가 민주주의 사회에서 산다고 말했어요.

free speech
[frí: spí:tʃ]
언론의 자유

the right that people can say what they want

In a democracy, people have a right to free speech.
민주주의 사회에서 사람들은 언론의 자유에 대한 권리가 있어요.

check
[tʃék]
v. 확인하다

to look at something to make sure it is correct

Mom, you checked my text messages.
엄마, 엄마는 제 문자 메시지를 확인하셨어요.

deny
[dináí]
v. 부인하다

to say something is not true
- denial n. 부인

You can't deny it. 엄마는 그걸 부인할 수 없어요.

witness
[wítnis]
n. 목격자 v. 목격하다

a person who sees something and tells about it

Hoony is my witness.
후니가 증인이에요.

betray
[bitréi]
v. 배신하다, 등지다

to say or do something against one's beliefs
- betrayal n. 배신

Mom, are you going to betray your own beliefs?
엄마, 엄마는 자신의 믿음을 배신하실 건가요?

objective
[əbdʒéktiv]
a. 객관적인
n. 목표, 목적

making good and fair decisions
- objectivity n. 객관성

I want you to be objective.
저는 엄마가 객관적이면 좋겠어요.

confine
[kənfáin]
v. 가두다, 제한하다

to imprison; to limit someone, to stop someone doing a particular activity
- confinement n. 감금, 제한

Are you trying to confine me?
저를 가두려고 하시는 건가요?

violate
[váiəlèit]
v. 침해하다, 위반하다

to disturb someone's privacy or peace; to do something against someone's rights; to break a law or rule
- violation n. 침해, 위반

When you check my messages, you violate my freedom of speech.
엄마가 제 문자 메시지를 확인할 때, 엄마는 저의 언론의 자유를 침해하는 거예요.

prisoner
[príznər]
n. 죄수

a criminal who has broken the law and is in prison

Even prisoners have a right to say what they want.
죄수들조차도 자신이 원하는 것을 말할 권리가 있어요.

judge
[dʒʌdʒ]
n. 판사
v. 판단하다

a person who decides how a criminal will be punished
- judgment n. 판단

If I were a judge, I would order you not to do this.
제가 판사라면, 엄마에게 그런 행동을 하지 말라고 명령할 거예요.

allow
[əláu]
v. 허락하다

to let someone do something, to give permission

You're not allowed to touch my phone.
엄마는 제 전화를 만질 수 없어요.

objection
[əbdʒékʃən]
n. 반대

disagreement, counter-agreement
- object v. 반대하다 • objective n. 목적 a. 객관적인
- objectionable a. 반대할 만한

Any objections, mom? 이의 있으세요, 엄마?

Check Again!

A Translate each word into Korean.

1. article ....
2. stir ....
3. censor ....
4. confine ....
5. ruin ....
6. outdated ....
7. criterion ....
8. rage ....
9. absurd ....
10. enrich ....

B Translate each word into English.

1. 부인하다 ....
2. 목격자 ....
3. 배신하다 ....
4. 객관적인 ....
5. 침해하다 ....
6. 언론의 자유 ....
7. 자극하다 ....
8. 범죄자 ....
9. 판사 ....
10. 반대 ....

C Fill in the blank with the appropriate word. Refer to the Korean.

1. U_____, they don't know who the criminal is.

   의심할 여지없이 그들은 누가 범인인지 몰라요.

2. You're not a_____ to smoke in this room.

   이 방에서는 흡연이 금지되어 있어요.

3. All people deserve the right to live in a d_____.

   모든 사람들은 민주주의 사회에서 살 권리가 있다.

4. Some people say arranged marriages are an o_____ idea.

   어떤 사람들은 중매결혼이 시대에 뒤떨어진 생각이라고 말한다.

5. Do you think an a_____ decision is different from a wrong decision?

   당신은 불합리한 결정이 잘못된 결정과 다르다고 생각합니까?

(A), (B), (C) 각 밑줄 친 부분에 알맞은 어휘를 짝지은 것으로 가장 적절한 것을 고르시오.

Suppose a company realizes that it is not achieving its goals or **(A)** objectives / objections effectively. In this case, it can be useful to get an outside consultant to **(B)** analyze / finalize the company's performance and recommend changes to make it more efficient. This consultant can more **(C)** subjectively / objectively analyze the company's strengths and weaknesses as well as the opportunities and threats that face it. Then, the company can re-plan its strategy on the basis of the consultant's advice. In this way, the company will be able to get its intended results.

*consultant: 컨설턴트, 경영자문인

	(A)	(B)	(C)
①	objections	analyze	subjectively
②	objectives	analyze	objectively
③	objections	finalize	objectively
④	objectives	finalize	subjectively
⑤	objections	analyze	objectively

+ 복수형 -s와 접두사 ex- / pre-

복수형 -s가 명사 뒤에 붙어서 전혀 다른 뜻의 단어를 만들기도 한다. ex-는 'former'라는 뜻의 접두사로, '전에 어떤 지위나 신분에 있었던 자'를 뜻하는 단어를 만든다. pre-는 'before'라는 뜻의 접두사로, '어느 시점 이전'이라는 뜻의 단어를 만든다.

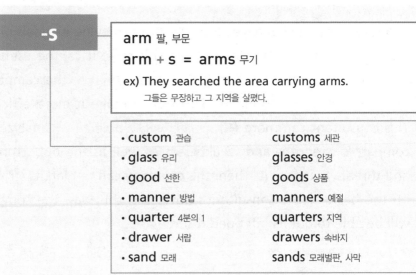

-s

arm 팔, 부문
arm + s = arms 무기
ex) They searched the area carrying arms.
　　그들은 무장하고 그 지역을 살폈다.

• **custom** 관습	**customs** 세관
• **glass** 유리	**glasses** 안경
• **good** 선한	**goods** 상품
• **manner** 방법	**manners** 예절
• **quarter** 4분의 1	**quarters** 지역
• **drawer** 서랍	**drawers** 속바지
• **sand** 모래	**sands** 모래벌판, 사막

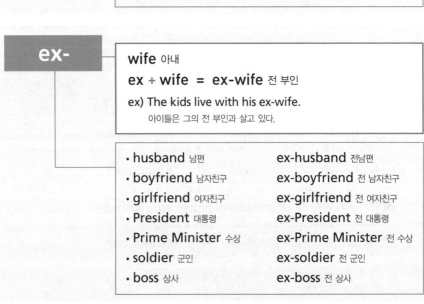

ex-

wife 아내
ex + wife = ex-wife 전 부인
ex) The kids live with his ex-wife.
　　아이들은 그의 전 부인과 살고 있다.

• **husband** 남편	**ex-husband** 전남편
• **boyfriend** 남자친구	**ex-boyfriend** 전 남자친구
• **girlfriend** 여자친구	**ex-girlfriend** 전 여자친구
• **President** 대통령	**ex-President** 전 대통령
• **Prime Minister** 수상	**ex-Prime Minister** 전 수상
• **soldier** 군인	**ex-soldier** 전 군인
• **boss** 상사	**ex-boss** 전 상사

pre-

caution 주의

pre + caution = precaution 예방

ex) Let's put it in the safe, just as a precaution.
예방 조치로 그것을 금고 안에 넣읍시다.

- **mature** 성숙한 **premature** 조숙한
- **determined** 결정된 **predetermined** 미리 결정된
- **meditate** 계획하다 **premeditate** 미리 계획하다
- **conception** 개념 **preconception** 선입견
- **occupy** 차지하다 **preoccupy** 선취하다
- **historic** 역사적인 **prehistoric** 선사의
- **monition** 충고, 권고 **premonition** 징조

Court 재판

+ plaintiff 원고 / + defendant 피고

+ jury 배심원

+ appeal 상소

+ verdict 판결

+ testify 증언하다

+ constitution 헌법

+ file a lawsuit 제소하다

VOCA EDGE
RED

oodbye, Sara. I learned about the earth. I went to a natural science museum. I had a
attends a community party. Mom's got a new hobby. Are they my bosses? Hoony is
ghter clinic. The Volcanoes are back. We have great brothers. What historical figures do
epathy between us! Sara goes to Turkey. Home decorating is not easy. Hoony thinks girls
war should be stopped. Mom, are you going to cut my allowance? Hoony is back from
ld have been more careful. Forgery should be stopped. Hoony wants to explore outer
icane hit the village. We're teens. I had my cell phone taken away. Goodbye, Brownie
e museum. I had a campus tour. If I were a judge,.... How can we survive in a jungle?
sses? Hoony is money-wise. Hoony goes to an herbal clinic. We became a rescue team
al figures do you want to meet? Are mom and dad compatible? I can't understand this
Hoony thinks girls have illusions about boys. I can't understand politicians. Wearing an
Hoony is back from an economics camp. construction a thriving business? How amazing
o explore outer space. I attended the Arbor Day ceremony. We can make the earth a
odbye, Brownie Life is full of contradictions. Goodbye, Sara. I learned about the earth.
a jungle? I became a Santa Claus. Sara attends a community party. Mom's got a new

Chapter 4. Trips and Entertainment

rescue team. Grandma goes to a laughter clinic. The Volcanoes are back. We ha

Unit 10. How can we survive in a jungle?

't understand this painting. There was telepathy between us! Sara goes to Turkey. Ho

Unit 11. I became a Santa Claus.

earing an electronic tag is horrible. The war should be stopped. Mom, are you going

Unit 12. Sara attends a community party.

ow amazing our life has become! I should have been more careful. Forgery should be
e the earth a better place. A super hurricane hit the village. We're teens. I had my ce
the earth. I went to a natural science museum. I had a campus tour. If I were a judge,..
got a new hobby. Are they my bosses? Hoony is money-wise. Hoony goes to an herba

Chapter 4
Trips and Entertainment

Unit 10. How can we survive in a jungle?

maintain **primitive** traditions and ceremonie

be bewildered

become **accustomed to** a lifestyle

Episode

Dear Diary,

Why do people try climbing to the **peaks** of mountains? • I recently watched a program **featuring** a movie star. • He climbed to the **summit** of a mountain in the Himalayas. • What **motivated** him? • I thought about what his **ultimate** goal could have been. • Maybe he wanted to test his **limits**. • It made me wonder, "Can we **survive** in a primitive society?" • I also watched a show where a man visited a **tribe** in the Amazon. • It was an **uncivilized** society. • They were like real **barbarians**. • However, they had an **orderly** society. • They still maintained **primitive** traditions and ceremonies. • For example, they **worshiped** crocodiles. • On special days, their **priest** held ceremonies. • They thought the ceremonies would drive away evil **spirits**. • They seemed very **superstitious**. • A few other things that surprised me were how **precious** fire was and that bugs were **edible** to them. • When they asked the man to eat bugs, he was **bewildered**. • Surprisingly, these people have **keen** senses and they use their **instincts** to hunt. • They **sharpen** sticks to make them into arrows. • With arrows, they hunt for food and protect themselves from **predators**. • After hunting, they have a big celebration. • They **distribute** food among each other. • They try to maintain **equality** among the whole tribe. • At the end of the program, the man seemed to have become **accustomed** to this primitive lifestyle. • I wonder, "Where's the **border** between civilization and barbarism?" • It seems difficult to draw a **boundary** between them.

다이어리에게,
사람들은 왜 산의 정상에 오르려 할까? 나는 최근에 어느 영화배우를 특집으로 한 프로그램을 보았어. 그는 히말라야 산맥에 있는 어떤 산의 정상에 올랐어. 무엇이 그에게 동기를 주었을까? 나는 그의 궁극적인 목표가 무엇이었을까에 대해 생각했어. 아마 그는 자신의 한계를 시험하고 싶었을지도 몰라. 그것이 나를 궁금하게 만들었어. "우리가 원시 사회에서 살아남을 수 있을까?" 또한 나는 한 남자가 아마존에 있는 어느 부족을 방문했던 쇼를 보았어. 그곳은 미개한 사회였어. 그들은 진짜 미개인 같았어. 그렇지만 그들 사회는 규율이 있었어. 그들은 여전히 원시적인 전통과 의식을 유지했어. 예를 들면, 그들은 악어를 숭배했어. 특별한 날에는 그들의 사제가 의식을 거행했어. 그들은 그 의식이 악령을 몰아낸다고 생각했어. 그들은 매우 미신적인 것처럼 보였어. 나를 놀라게 한 몇 가지 다른 사항은 불이 매우 귀중하다는 것과 그들에게는 벌레가 먹을 수 있는 것이라는 사실이었어. 그들이 그 남자에게 벌레를 먹으라고 요청했을 때, 그는 당황스러워했어. 놀랍게도, 이 사람들은 예리한 감각을 가지고 있으며 사냥할 때 본능을 사용해. 그들은 막대기를 날카롭게 해서 화살을 만들어. 화살을 가지고 그들은 먹을 것을 사냥하고 침략자들로부터 자신을 보호해. 사냥 후에는 큰 축하의식을 갖어. 그들은 음식을 서로에게 나누어 줘. 그들은 종종 전체에서 평등을 유지하려고 노력해. 프로그램의 마지막에, 그 남자는 이 원시적인 생활에 익숙해진 것 같았어. 나는 궁금해. "문명과 미개의 경계는 어디일까?" 둘 사이의 경계선을 표시하는 것은 어려울 것 같아.

peak
[píːk]
n. 정상

the highest level, top of something

Why do people try climbing to the peaks of mountains?
사람들은 왜 산의 정상에 오르려 할까?

feature
[fíːtʃər]
v. 특집으로 다루다
n. 특별기사, 특징

to give special attention to

I recently watched a program featuring a movie star.
나는 최근에 어느 영화배우를 특집으로 한 프로그램을 보았어.

summit
[sʌ́mit]
n. 정상

the highest point or part as of a hill

He climbed to the summit of a mountain in the Himalayas.
그는 히말라야 산맥에 있는 어떤 산의 정상에 올랐어.

motivate
[móutəvèit]
v. 동기부여하다,
   자극하다

to provide incentive for action; to stimulate

• **motivation** n. 동기부여, 자극   • **motive** n. 동기 a. 움직이게 하는

What motivated him?
무엇이 그에게 동기를 주었을까?

ultimate
[ʌ́ltəmit]
a. 궁극적인

final, last

• **ultimately** ad. 마침내

I thought about what his ultimate goal could have been.
나는 그의 궁극적인 목표가 무엇이었을까에 대해 생각했어.

limit
[límit]
n. 한계
v. 한정하다

the final, utmost, or furthest boundary

Maybe he wanted to test his limits.
아마 그는 자신의 한계를 시험하고 싶었을지도 몰라.

survive
[sərváiv]
v. 살아남다

to remain alive, to continue to live

• **survival** n. 생존   • **survivor** n. 생존자

It made me wonder, "Can we survive in a primitive society?"
그것이 나를 궁금하게 만들었어. "우리가 원시 사회에서 살아남을 수 있을까?"

tribe

[tráib]

n. 부족

a local division of an aboriginal people

I also watched a show where a man visited a tribe in the Amazon.

또한 나는 한 남자가 아마존에 있는 어느 부족을 방문했던 쇼를 보았어.

uncivilized

[ʌnsívəlàizd]

a. 미개한

not civilized or cultured; barbarous

It was an uncivilized society.

그곳은 미개한 사회였어.

barbarian

[bɑːrbɛ́əriən]

n. 미개인, 야만인

a person considered to have a primitive civilization

• barbarism n. 미개, 야만 • barbarous a. 야만스러운

They were like real barbarians.

그들은 진짜 미개인 같았어.

orderly

[ɔ́ːrdərli]

a. 규율이 있는

organized, opposite of chaotic

• order n. 질서, 규율

However, they had an orderly society.

그렇지만, 그들 사회는 규율이 있었어.

primitive

[prímətiv]

a. 원시적인, 초기의

of an early state of human development

They still maintained primitive traditions and ceremonies.

그들은 여전히 원시적인 전통과 의식을 유지했어.

worship

[wə́ːrʃip]

v. 숭배하다

n. 숭배, 예배

to pay homage to God or any sacred object

For example, they worshiped crocodiles.

예를 들면, 그들은 악어를 숭배했어.

priest

[príːst]

n. 사제

a person who performs religious rites, shaman, or holy person

On special days, their priest held ceremonies.

특별한 날에는 그들의 사제가 의식을 거행했어.

spirit
[spírit]
n. 영혼

a ghost or supernatural being

They thought the ceremonies would drive away evil spirits.

그들은 그 의식이 악령을 몰아낸다고 생각했어.

superstitious
[sùːpərstíʃəs]
a. 미신적인

believing in supernatural beings

• superstition n. 미신

They seemed very superstitious.

그들은 매우 미신적인 것처럼 보였어.

precious
[préʃəs]
a. 귀중한

valuable, important

A few other things that surprised me were how precious fire was and that bugs were edible to them.

나를 놀라게 한 몇 가지 다른 사항은 불이 매우 귀중하다는 것과 그들에게는 벌레가 먹을 수 있는 것이라는 사실이었어.

edible
[édəbəl]
a. 먹을 수 있는

able to be consumed or eaten, eatable

A few other things that surprised me were how precious fire was and that bugs were edible to them.

나를 놀라게 한 몇 가지 다른 사항은 불이 매우 귀중하다는 것과 그들에게는 벌레가 먹을 수 있는 것이라는 사실이었어.

bewildered
[biwíldərd]
a. 당황한

puzzled or confused

• bewilder v. 당황스럽게 하다 • bewilderment n. 당황스러움

When they asked the man to eat bugs, he was bewildered

그들이 그 남자에게 벌레를 먹으라고 요청했을 때, 그는 당황스러워했어.

keen
[kíːn]
a. 예리한

extremely sensitive or responsive

Surprisingly, these people have keen senses and they use their instincts to hunt.

놀랍게도, 이 사람들은 예리한 감각을 가지고 있으며 사냥할 때 본능을 사용해.

instinct
[ínstiŋkt]
n. 본능

an innate capability or aptitude, natural skill

Surprisingly, these people have keen senses and they use their instincts to hunt.

놀랍게도, 이 사람들은 예리한 감각을 가지고 있으며 사냥할 때 본능을 사용해.

sharpen
[ʃɑ́ːrpən]

v. 날카롭게 하다

to make or become sharp or sharper

• sharp a. 날카로운

They sharpen sticks to make them into arrows.

그들은 막대기를 날카롭게 해서 화살을 만들어.

predator
[prédətər]

n. 침략자, 약탈자

animals that hunt other animals for food; predatory people or organizations

• predatory a. 약탈하는

With arrows, they hunt for food and protect themselves from predators.

화살을 가지고 그들은 먹을 것을 사냥하고 침략자들로부터 자신을 보호해.

distribute
[distríbjuːt]

v. 나누다, 분배하다

to share things among the members of a group, to hand or deliver things

• distribution n. 분배   • distributor n. 분배자

They distribute food among each other.

그들은 음식을 서로에게 나누어 줘.

equality
[i(:)kwɑ́ləti]

n. 평등

the quality of being equal

• equal a. 평등한

They try to maintain equality among the whole tribe.

그들은 종족 전체에서 평등을 유지하려고 노력해.

accustomed
[əkʌ́stəmd]

a. 적응이 된, 익숙한

adjusted, experienced

• accustom v. ~을 적응시키다   • become accustomed to ~에 익숙해지다

At the end of the program, the man seemed to have become accustomed to this primitive lifestyle.

프로그램의 마지막에, 그 남자는 이 원시적인 생활에 익숙해진 것 같았어.

border
[bɔ́ːrdər]

n. 경계

the line that separates one province from another

I wonder, "Where's the border between civilization and barbarism?"

나는 궁금해. "문명과 미개의 경계는 어디일까?"

boundary
[báundəri]

n. 경계선

an imaginary line that separates one from another border

It seems difficult to draw a boundary between them.

둘 사이의 경계선을 표시하는 것은 어려울 것 같아.

Check Again!

A Translate each word into Korean.

1. peak ....

2. superstitious ....

3. summit ....

4. bewildered ....

5. sharpen ....

6. predator ....

7. distribute ....

8. motivate ....

9. uncivilized ....

10. barbarian ....

B Translate each word into English.

1. 숭배하다 ....

2. 규율이 있는 ....

3. 부족 ....

4. 한계 ....

5. 궁극적인 ....

6. 귀중한 ....

7. 평등 ....

8. 예리한 ....

9. 본능 ....

10. 적응이 된 ....

C Fill in the blank with the appropriate word. Refer to the Korean.

1. Can a small fish s   in a big pond?

   작은 물고기가 큰 연못에서 살아남을 수 있을까?

2. Some p   tribes have unusual culture and traditions.

   어떤 원시 부족들은 유별난 문화와 전통을 가지고 있다.

3. All species of the pine tree are e   to one extent or another.

   모든 종의 소나무는 어느 정도로는 식용으로 가능하다.

4. This tradition originated as a method of keeping evil s   away.

   이 전통은 악령을 물리치기 위한 방법에서 유래했다.

5. What was the b   between North Korea and South Korea in 1950?

   1950년에 북한과 남한간의 경계선은 어디였나요?

수능 기출 응용

(A), (B), (C) 각 밑줄 친 부분에 알맞은 어휘를 짝지은 것으로 가장 적절한 것을 고르시오.

Recently, I watched a program **(A)** featuring / capturing foreigners who were interested in Korean language. The number of foreigners interested in the Korean language has increased dramatically over the past few years. They say Korean language is easy because it's a systematic and **(B)** organic / orderly language. The total number of foreign students attending Korean language programs has increased to more than 30,000 in Seoul alone this year from about 4,700 at the end of last year. People speaking Korean have long been **(C)** limited / reduced mostly to those from the peninsula. It is no wonder few people ever imagined that the country's language might one day become popular in the international community.

(A)	(B)	(C)
① featuring	organic	reduced
② featuring	orderly	reduced
③ capturing	organic	limited
④ featuring	orderly	limited
⑤ capturing	orderly	limited

Chapter 4
Trips and Entertainment

Unit 11. I became a Santa Claus.

disguise oneself **as** a Santa Claus

volunteer and visit an orphanage

Episode

Dear Yuni,

Yuni, what are you going to do on Christmas Eve? • Dongjin ordered us to check everything. • Isn't he like a **dictator**? • He's always barking out **commands**. • Anyway, we're supposed to visit an **orphanage**. • We're going to **volunteer** there. • You need to **collect** games, CDs, and some toys, too. • Otherwise, the kids will be **dissatisfied**. • We also have some food being **donated**. • It's lucky those anonymous **donors** gave us so much stuff. • Thanks to them, this won't **cost** too much. • I'm going to **disguise** myself as a Santa Claus. • I'll wear **loose** pants and a fake beard and I'll **exaggerate** my voice. • Yuni, are you going to **assist** me as a reindeer? • Jungho has been **designated** as the coordinator. • He is going to **arrange** the show. • He'll organize the whole **process**. • But who is going to **entertain** them? • You **recommend** Jisu? • I think her music skills are **superior** to anyone else I know. • What else do we need to **confirm** before the event? • After we finish there, we are going to go to a **nursing home**. • Do you know what **senior citizens** like? • My grandma really likes sweets and **humorous** stories. • I have to **confess** that I'm good at making people laugh. • I can **improvise** interesting stories. • Our only **obstacle** is we don't have a car. • Can you ask your mom to **lend** us her jeep?

유니에게,

유니, 크리스마스 이브에 너는 뭘 할 거니? 동진이는 우리에게 모든 것을 확인하라고 지시했어. 독재자 같지 않아? 그는 항상 고함을 치면서 명령해. 어쨌든 우리는 고아원을 방문하기로 되어 있어. 우리는 그곳에서 자원봉사를 할 거야. 너는 게임, CD, 그리고 몇 가지 장난감도 모아야 해. 그렇지 않으면, 아이들이 실망할 거야. 우리는 또한 음식도 기부받고 있어. 그런 익명의 기부자들이 우리에게 그렇게 많은 물건을 주다니 행운이지. 그들 덕분에 이번 행사는 너무 많은 비용이 들지는 않을 거야. 나는 산타클로스로 변장할 거야. 나는 헐렁한 바지를 입고 가짜 턱수염을 달 거야. 그리고 내 목소리를 과장해서 말할 거야. 유니, 루돌프로 나를 도와 줄 거니? 정호는 코디네이터로 지명되었어. 그가 쇼를 준비할 거야. 그는 전체 과정을 진행할 거야. 그렇지만 누가 그들을 즐겁게 하지? 너는 지수를 추천하는 거니? 그녀의 음악적 기술은 내가 아는 다른 누구보다도 뛰어나다고 생각해. 행사 전에 우리는 그 외에 무엇을 확인해야 하지? 그곳에서 행사가 끝난 후에, 우리는 요양원으로 갈 거야. 노인들이 무엇을 좋아하는지 알고 있니? 우리 할머니는 단것과 우스운 이야기를 정말 좋아하셔. 나는 사람들을 웃게 만드는 재주가 있다는 걸 고백해야겠어. 나는 즉흥적으로 재미있는 이야기를 만들 수 있어. 우리의 유일한 장애물은 우리는 차가 없다는 거야. 엄마한테 지프를 빌려달라고 부탁할 수 있니?

order
[ɔ́ːrdər]

v. 명령하다, 지시하다

n. 명령

to give an order, direction, or command

Dongjin ordered us to check everything.

동진이는 우리에게 모든 것을 확인하라고 지시했어.

dictator
[díkteitər]

n. 독재자

an absolute ruler, an undemocratic leader, a tyrant

• dictate v. 명령하다 • dictatorial a. 독재자의

Isn't he like a dictator? 그는 독재자 같지 않아?

command
[kəmǽnd]

n. 명령 v. 명령하다

an order given with authority

He's always barking out commands.

그는 항상 고함을 치면서 명령해.

orphanage
[ɔ́ːrfənidʒ]

n. 고아원

an institution for the housing and care of orphans

• orphan n. 고아

Anyway, we're supposed to visit an orphanage.

어쨌든 우리는 고아원을 방문하기로 되어 있어.

volunteer
[vàləntíər]

v. 자원봉사하다

n. 자원봉사자

to do something without being forced to do it

We're going to volunteer there.

우리는 그곳에서 자원봉사를 할 거야.

collect
[kəlékt]

v. 모으다

to gather something together, to assemble

• collection n. 수집

You need to collect games, CDs, and some toys, too.

너는 게임과 CD와 몇 가지 장난감도 모아야 해.

dissatisfied
[dissǽtisfàid]

a. 불만스러운

not contented, disappointed

• dissatisfy v. 불만을 느끼게 하다

• dissatisfaction n. 불만, 불평

Otherwise, the kids will be dissatisfied.

그렇지 않으면, 아이들이 실망할 거야.

donate
[dóuneit]
v. 기부하다

to present as a gift, grant, or contribution
- donation n. 기부

We also have some food being donated.
우리는 또한 음식도 기부받고 있어.

donor
[dóunər]
n. 기부자

someone who makes a donation

It's lucky those anonymous donors gave us so much stuff.
그런 익명의 기부자들이 우리에게 그렇게 많은 물건을 주다니 행운이지.

cost
[kɔ́:st]
v. 돈이 들다   n. 비용

to require the payment of money
- costly a. 값비싼

Thanks to them, this won't cost too much.
그들 덕분에 이번 행사는 너무 많은 비용이 들지는 않을 거야.

disguise
[disgáiz]
v. 변장하다   n. 변장

to change one's appearance or identity

I'm going to disguise myself as a Santa Claus.
나는 산타클로스로 변장할 거야.

loose
[lú:s]
a. 헐렁한

big, baggy, opposite of tight

I'll wear loose pants and a fake beard and I'll exaggerate my voice.
나는 헐렁한 바지를 입고 가짜 턱수염을 달 거야. 그리고 내 목소리를 과장해서 말할 거야.

exaggerate
[igzǽdʒərèit]
v. 과장하다

to overstate, to embellish
- exaggeration n. 과장 • exaggerated a. 과장된

I'll wear loose pants and a fake beard and I'll exaggerate my voice.
나는 헐렁한 바지를 입고 가짜 턱수염을 달 거야. 그리고 내 목소리를 과장해서 말할 거야.

assist
[əsíst]
v. 돕다

to give aid or help
- assistant n. 조수 • assistance n. 조력, 원조

Yuni, are you going to assist me as a reindeer?
유니, 루돌프로 날 도와 줄 거니?

designate
[dézignèit]

v. 지명하다, 선정하다

to choose someone to do a particular job
- designation n. 임명, 지정

Jungho has been designated as the coordinator.
정호는 코디네이터로 지명되었어.

arrange
[əréindʒ]

v. 준비하다,
   예정을 세우다

to prepare or plan
- arrangement n. 정열, 정리

He is going to arrange the show.
그가 쇼를 준비할 거야.

process
[práses]

n. 과정

a systematic series of actions directed to some end

He'll organize the whole process.
그는 선제 과정을 신행할 거야.

entertain
[èntərtéin]

v. 즐겁게 하다

to amuse, to captivate
- entertainment n. 오락 - entertaining a. 재미있는

But who is going to entertain them?
그렇지만 누가 그들을 즐겁게 하지?

recommend
[rèkəménd]

v. 추천하다

to suggest, to represent something as positive
- recommendation n. 추천

You recommend Jisu? 너는 지수를 추천하는 거니?

superior
[səpíəriər]

a. 뛰어난

higher in rank or importance, opposite of inferior
- superior to ~보다 뛰어난

I think her music skills are superior to anyone else
I know.
그녀의 음악적 기술은 내가 아는 다른 누구보다도 뛰어나다고 생각해.

confirm
[kənfə́:rm]

v. 확인하다

to establish the truth, to verify
- confirmation n. 확인

What else do we need to confirm before the event?
행사 전에 우리는 그 외에 무엇을 확인해야 하지?

nursing home
[nə́:rsiŋ hòum]

양로원

a place where elderly and sickly people live and are taken care of

After we finish there, we are going to go to a nursing home.

그곳에서 행사가 끝난 후에, 우리는 요양원으로 갈 거야.

---

senior citizen
[síːnjər sítəzən]

노인

an elderly person

Do you know what senior citizens like?

노인들이 무엇을 좋아하는지 알고 있니?

---

humorous
[hjúːmərəs]

a. 우스운, 재미있는

funny, having a good sense of humor

• humor n. 유머, 익살

My grandma really likes sweets and humorous stories.

우리 할머니는 단것과 우스운 이야기를 정말 좋아하셔.

---

confess
[kənfés]

v. 고백하다, 인정하다

to admit that something is true

• confession n. 고백

I have to confess that I'm good at making people laugh.

나는 사람들을 웃게 만드는 재주가 있다는 걸 고백해야겠다.

---

improvise
[ímprəvàiz]

v. 즉흥적으로 만들다

to make something without planning

• improvisation n. 즉석에서 하기

I can improvise interesting stories.

나는 즉흥적으로 재미있는 이야기를 만들 수 있어.

---

obstacle
[ábstəkəl]

n. 장애물

something preventing someone from continuing

Our only obstacle is we don't have a car.

우리의 유일한 장애물은 우리는 차가 없다는 거야.

---

lend
[lénd]

v. 빌려주다

to allow someone to borrow something

Can you ask your mom to lend us her jeep?

엄마한테 지프를 빌려달라고 부탁할 수 있니?

Check Again!

A Translate each word into Korean.

1. obstacle ....
2. arrange ....
3. exaggerate ....
4. donate ....
5. designate ....
6. dictator ....
7. volunteer ....
8. orphanage ....
9. dissatisfied ....
10. donor ....

B Translate each word into English.

1. 힐링한 ....
2. 놉다 ....
3. 과정 ....
4. 추천하다 ....
5. 뛰어난 ....
6. 확인하다 ....
7. 빌려주다 ....
8. 고백하다 ....
9. 우스운 ....
10. 즉흥적으로 만들다 ....

C Fill in the blank with the appropriate word. Refer to the Korean.

1. Last Christmas I d   myself as a Santa Claus.

   지난 성탄절에 나는 산타클로스로 변장하였다.

2. People in the 65-and-over age group are often called s
   citizens.

   65세 이상의 사람들은 종종 노인이라고 불린다.

3. They are s   in number to us. In other words,
   they outnumber us.

   그들은 수적으로 우리보다 우세하다. 즉, 그들은 우리보다 숫자가 많다.

4. When you give out c   to your dog, keep your voice
   clear and composed.

   개에게 명령을 내릴 때는 목소리를 또렷하고 침착하게 유지해라.

5. The n   homes are required to have a licensed nurse
   on duty 24 hours a day.

   양로원에 면허증 있는 간호사를 하루 24시간 두도록 의무화하고 있다.

Check More!

다음 밑줄 친 부분에 알맞은 어휘를 골라 빈칸에 쓰시오. 아래의 영영 풀이를 참조하시오.

Peter Thompson, with whom I have a close working relationship, mentioned your name to me and strongly **(A)** surrendered / suggested I contact you. From what Peter tells me, you are very active in the toy industry and know a number of sales managers. Peter felt that you might be able to help me make **(B)** contracts / contacts. Because of new competition, we are **(C)** nervous / anxious to get our products into the market as soon as possible. Would it be convenient if I called you next Monday and we **(D)** arranged / arraigned a time to talk over lunch?

(A) to propose: ....

(B) a legal agreement usually between two companies or people:

....

(C) earnestly desirous; eager: ....

(D) to plan or prepare for: ....

Chapter 4
Trips and Entertainment

Unit 12. Sara attends a community party.

score a goal

perform the **commencement**

translate English for parents

Episode

Sara seems to **adjust** well. • Here is an e-mail from her.

Dear Bomi,

Hey, Bomi, our **community** is holding a special event. • It's a **biannual** event. • The city council **sponsors** it. • I met people from various **ethnic** backgrounds. • At the end, there was a **final** football match and a party. • Traditionally, there is an intense **rivalry** between the two teams, the Lions and the Bears. • Before the match, a man performed the **commencement**. • He also poured beer into a soccer ball-**shaped** trophy. • I felt as if I was watching a **commercial**. • Players on both teams made an **oath**. • They looked **serious**. • They looked **solemn**. • They reminded me of **warriors**. • They were there as a **delegation** from each community. • Carlos, a player from our team, **scored** two goals. • His play was **unmatchable**. • His skills were **sophisticated**. • While watching him play, the people were in **awe**. • People praised him as if he were a **legendary** soccer player. • His **opponents** could not touch him. • In the second half, Carlos **proceeded** to continue his excellent play. • He scored another goal and the people **applauded**. • The **spectators** were overwhelmed. • After the game, there was a **multinational** party. • People prepared a **variety** of food. • I was able to meet people who spoke English with various **accents**. • And I **translated** it for my parents.

사라는 잘 적응하는 것 같다. 여기 그녀에게서 온 이메일이 있다.

보미에게,

안녕, 보미, 우리 지역사회는 특별한 행사를 열고 있어. 1년에 두 번 있는 행사야. 시 의회가 그 행사를 후원해. 나는 다양한 민족의 사람들을 만났어. 마지막에 축구 경기 결승전과 파티가 열렸어. 전통적으로 라이온스와 베어스 두 팀 사이에 격렬한 경쟁이 있어. 경기 전에 한 남자가 시작을 알렸어. 그는 축구공 모양의 트로피에 맥주를 붓기도 했어. 나는 마치 내가 광고를 보는 것 같은 느낌이 들었어. 양팀의 선수들은 서서를 했어. 그들은 진지해 보였어. 그들은 엄숙해 보였어. 그들은 나에게 전사를 상기시켰어. 그들은 각 지역사회의 대표단으로 거기에 있었어. 우리 팀 선수인 카를로스는 두 골을 넣어서 점수를 올렸어. 그의 경기는 대항할 수 없는 것이었어. 그의 기술은 정교했어. 그가 경기하는 것을 보면서 사람들은 경외심을 가졌어. 사람들은 그가 마치 전설적인 축구 선수인 것처럼 그를 칭송했어. 그의 적들은 그와는 상대할 수가 없었어. 후반전에 카를로스는 앞서가면서 우수한 경기를 계속했어. 그는 또 한 골을 넣었고 사람들은 환호했어. 관중들은 압도되었어. 게임이 끝난 후에 다국적 파티가 열렸어. 사람들은 다양한 음식을 준비했어. 나는 다양한 악센트로 영어를 말하는 사람들을 만날 수 있었어. 그리고 나는 부모님을 위해 통역했어.

adjust
[ədʒ́ʌst]
v. 적응하다

to adapt, to change depending on one's environment
- adjustment n. 적응 • adjustable a. 적응할 수 있는

Sara seems to adjust well.
사라는 잘 적응하는 것 같다.

community
[kəmjú:nəti]
n. 지역사회

neighborhood

Hey, Bomi, our community is holding a special event.
안녕, 보미, 우리 지역사회는 특별한 행사를 열고 있어.

biannual
[baiǽnjuəl]
a. 1년에 두 번의

occurring twice a year

It's a biannual event.
1년에 두 번 있는 행사야.

sponsor
[spánsər]
v. 후원하다
n. 후원, 후원자

to provide money to pay for an event

The city council sponsors it.
시 의회가 그것을 후원해.

ethnic
[éθnik]
a. 민족의, 인종의

having to do with a particular race or ethnicity
- ethnicity n. 민족성

I met people from various ethnic backgrounds.
나는 다양한 민족의 사람들을 만났어.

final
[fáinəl]
a. 결승의

last, ultimate, end
- finalize v. 완성시키다, 끝내다

At the end, there was a final football match and a party.
마지막에 축구 경기 결승전과 파티가 열렸어.

rivalry
[ráivəlri]
n. 경쟁

intense competition between two teams
- rival v. 경쟁하다 n. 경쟁자 a. 경쟁하는

Traditionally, there is an intense rivalry between the two teams, the Lions and the Bears.
전통적으로 라이온스와 베어스 두 팀 사이에 격렬한 경쟁이 있어.

commencement
[kəménsmənt]
n. 개회식, 시작

a ceremony for the start of an event
- commence v. 시작하다

Before the match, a man performed the commencement.
경기 전에 한 남자가 시작을 알렸어.

shaped
[ʃéipt]
a. ~모양을 한

in the form of, having the same form or shape
- shape v. 형태를 취하다 n. 모양

He also poured beer into a soccer ball-shaped trophy.
그는 축구공 모양의 트로피에 맥주를 붓기도 했어.

commercial
[kəmə́:rʃəl]
n. 상업광고
a. 상업상의

an advertisement, a show for advertising products
- commerce n. 상업

I felt as if I was watching a commercial.
나는 마치 내가 광고를 보는 것 같은 느낌이 들었어.

oath
[óuθ]
n. 선서

a promise, a contract
- make an oath 선서를 하다

Players on both teams made an oath.
양팀의 선수들이 선서를 했어.

serious
[síəriəs]
a. 진지한

determined, without humor
- seriousness n. 진지함

They looked serious. 그들은 진지해 보였어.

solemn
[sáləm]
a. 엄숙한

quiet, serious

They looked solemn.
그들은 엄숙해 보였어.

warrior
[wɔ́(:)riər]
n. 전사

a fighter, a soldier

They reminded me of warriors.
그들은 나에게 전사를 상기시켰어.

delegation
[dèligéiʃən]
n. 대표단

a group of people in charge of representing people
- delegate v. 파견하다, 위임하다 n. 대표

They were there as a delegation from each community.
그들은 각 지역사회의 대표단으로 거기에 있었어.

score
[skɔ́ːr]
v. 득점하다

to make a goal, to gain a point or goal

Carlos, a player from our team, scored two goals.
우리 팀 선수인 카를로스는 두 골을 넣어서 점수를 올렸어.

unmatchable
[ʌnmǽtʃəbəl]
a. 대항할 수 없는

unbeatable, incomparable in skill or strength

His play was unmatchable.
그의 경기는 대항할 수 없는 것이었어.

sophisticated
[səfístəkèitid]
a. 정교한

experienced, refined, well-developed
- sophisticate v. 궤변을 부리다 n. 세련된 사람

His skills were sophisticated.
그의 기술은 정교했어.

awe
[ɔ́ː]
n. 경외, 경외심

admiration, astonishment
- in awe 경외하여

While watching him play, the people were in awe.
그가 경기하는 것을 보면서 사람들은 경외심을 가졌어.

legendary
[lédʒəndèri]
a. 전설의

fabulous, unreal, unforgettable
- legend n. 전설

People praised him as if he were a legendary soccer playe
사람들은 그가 마치 전설적인 축구 선수인 것처럼 그를 칭송했어.

opponent
[əpóunənt]
n. 적수, 상대

the other team or person you are playing against

His opponents could not touch him.
그의 적들은 그와는 상대할 수가 없었어.

proceed
[prousí:d]
v. 나아가다, 진행하다

to continue, to progress
- process n. 진행, 진전　• procedure n. 절차, 진행

In the second half, Carlos proceeded to continue his excellent play.
후반전에 카를로스는 앞서가면서 우수한 경기를 계속했어.

applaud
[əplɔ́:d]
v. 박수치다, 칭찬하다

to cheer, to clap
- applause n. 박수

He scored another goal and the people applauded.
그는 또 한 골을 넣었고 사람들은 환호했어.

spectator
[spékteitər]
n. 관중

audience

The spectators were overwhelmed.
관중들은 압도되었어.

multinational
[mʌltinǽʃənəl]
a. 다국적의

multiethnic, having many nationalities

After the game, there was a multinational party.
게임이 끝난 후에 다국적 파티가 열렸어.

variety
[vəráiəti]
n. 다양성

many different kinds or types
- various a. 다양한　• a variety of 다양한

People prepared a variety of food.
사람들은 다양한 음식을 준비했어.

accent
[ǽksent]
n. 악센트

a different pronunciation, different sound

I was able to meet people who spoke English with various accents.
나는 다양한 악센트로 영어를 말하는 사람들을 만날 수 있었어.

translate
[trænsléit]
v. 통역하다

to interpret, to change one language to another
- translation n. 통역　• translator n. 통역자

And I translated it for my parents.
그리고 나는 부모님을 위해 통역했어.

Check Again!

A Translate each word into Korean.

1. translate ....
2. solemn ....
3. warrior ....
4. biannual ....
5. sponsor ....
6. variety ....
7. opponent ....
8. rivalry ....
9. commencement ....
10. adjust ....

B Translate each word into English.

1. 관중 ....
2. 상업광고 ....
3. 대표단 ....
4. 득점하다 ....
5. 다국적인 ....
6. 정교한 ....
7. 전설의 ....
8. 박수치다 ....
9. 관중 ....
10. 대항할 수 없는 ....

C Fill in the blank with the appropriate word. Refer to the Korean.

1. Boot-s .... chocolate is available at the Little Farmers Market.
   장화 모양의 초코렛은 리틀파머스 마켓에서 구입할 수 있다.

2. We stood in a .... and amazement at what the Creator was doing.
   우리는 창조주가 하신 일을 경외하며 감탄하였다.

3. Students from different e .... backgrounds are studying in the same classroom.
   다양한 인종 출신의 학생들이 같은 교실에서 공부하고 있다.

4. He put some paper on the photocopier and p .... to make five copies.
   그는 복사기에 종이를 넣고 나아가 다섯 장의 복사를 했다.

5. Hippocrates, a wise Greek doctor, made an o .... of loyalty to his patients.
   그리스의 현명한 의사 히포크라테스는 환자들에 대한 충성을 선서했다.

Check More!

(A), (B), (C) 각 밑줄 친 부분에 알맞은 어휘를 짝지은 것으로 가장 적절한 것을 고르시오.

The United States remains an underdeveloped country when it comes to language skills. Immigrants are importing their mother tongues at record rates. Yet the vast majority of Americans remain stubbornly **(A)** bilingual / monolingual. Ignorance of other languages and **(B)** verification / variety of cultures handicaps the United States in dealing with the rest of the world. Today the language policies in the United States address this problem primarily with efforts to teach "foreign" languages to monolingual Americans. Meanwhile, the United States seeks to eliminate these same skills among **(C)** ethic / ethnic minorities by reducing existing bilingual programs, out of misplaced fears of diversity or haste to force their assimilation. Instead of focusing on immigrants' disabilities in English, why not encourage them to maintain their abilities in their mother tongues while they learn English?

(A)	(B)	(C)
① bilingual	variety	ethic
② monolingual	verification	ethic
③ monolingual	variety	ethnic
④ bilingual	verification	ethic
⑤ bilingual	variety	ethnic

+ 접두사 bi- / mono- / multi-

bi-는 'two' 라는 뜻의 접두사로, '둘(한 쌍) 또는 이중' 이라는 뜻의 단어를 만든다.
mono-는 'one' 이라는 뜻의 접두사로, '단일' 이라는 뜻의 단어를 만든다.
multi-는 'many' 라는 뜻의 접두사로, '많거나 여러 가지' 라는 뜻의 단어를 만든다.

bi-

weekly 매주
bi + weekly = biweekly 격주의
ex) Starting next month, the newsletter will be
printed biweekly.
다음 달부터 회보가 격주로 출간될 겁니다.

• **annual** 해마다의	**biannual** 연 2회의, 반년마다의
• **centennial** 100년마다의	**bicentennial** 200년마다의
• **-cycle** 바퀴	**bicycle** 자전거
• **lateral** 측면의	**bilateral** 양면이 있는
• **lingual** 언어의	**bilingual** 2개 국어의
• **-gamy** 결합	**bigamy** 중혼죄
• **partisan** 당파적인	**bipartisan** 두 정당의

mono-

rail 궤도
mono + rail = monorail 모노레일, 단궤 철도
ex) You can take the monorail to the pier.
부두까지 모노레일을 타고 갈 수 있습니다.

• **-logue** 담화, 연설	**monologue** 독백
• **-gamy** 결합	**monogamy** 일부일처
• **-chrome** 색소	**monochrome** 단색화, 흑백사진
• **syllable** 음절	**monosyllable** 단음절
• **tone** 음조	**monotone** 단조
• **molecular** 분자의	**monomolecular** 한 분자의
• **lingual** 언어의	**monolingual** 1개의 언어를 사용하는

multi-

national 국가의
multi + national = multinational 다국적의
ex) The multinational company has offices in 12 different countries.
그 다국적 기업은 12개국에 사무실이 있습니다.

- **facet** 한 면 **multifaceted** 다면체의
- **purpose** 목적 **multipurpose** 다목적의
- **lateral** 측면의 **multilateral** 다변의
- **cultural** 문화적인 **multicultural** 다문화의
- **media** 매체 **multimedia** 멀티미디어, 여러 매체를 사용한 커뮤니케이션
- **story** (건물) 층 **multistory** 여러 층의
- **channel** 채널 **multichannel** 다중 채널의

Culture Plus

Sports Game 운동 경기

+referee 심판
+spectator 관중
+amateur 아마추어
+professional 프로 선수
+preliminary game 예선 경기
+final game 본선 경기
+tournament 선수권 대회

VOCA EDGE

RED

Goodbye, Sara. I learned about the earth. I went to a natural science museum. I had a

ra attends a community party. Mom's got a new hobby. Are they my bosses? Hoony

ghter clinic. The Volcanoes are back. We have great brothers. What historical figures do

lepathy between us! Sara goes to Turkey. Home decorating is not easy. Hoony thinks girl

war should be stopped. Mom, are you going to cut my allowance? Hoony is back from

uld have been more careful. Forgery should be stopped. Hoony wants to explore oute

ricane hit the village. We're teens. I had my cell phone taken away. Goodbye, Brownie

e museum. I had a campus tour. If I were a judge,... How can we survive in a jungle?

osses? Hoony is money-wise. Hoony goes to an herbal clinic. We became a rescue team

cal figures do you want to meet? Are mom and dad compatible? I can't understand thi

Hoony thinks girls have illusions about boys. I can't understand politicians. Wearing a

Hoony is back from an economics camp. construction a thriving business? How amazing

to explore outer space. I attended the Arbor Day ceremony. We can make the earth

odbye, Brownie Life is full of contradictions. Goodbye, Sara. I learned about the earth.

n a jungle? I became a Santa Claus. Sara attends a community party. Mom's got a new

Chapter 5. Hobbies

a rescue team. Grandma goes to a laughter clinic. The Volcanoes are back. We ho

Unit 13. Mom's got a new hobby.

't understand this painting. There was telepathy between us! Sara goes to Turkey. Ho

Unit 14. Are they my bosses?

Wearing an electronic tag is horrible. The war should be stopped. Mom, are you going

Unit 15. Hoony is money-wise.

ow amazing our life has become! I should have been more careful. Forgery should be

e the earth a better place. A super hurricane hit the village. We're teens. I had my ce

the earth. I went to a natural science museum. I had a campus tour. If I were a judge,.

got a new hobby. Are they my bosses? Hoony is money-wise. Hoony goes to an herbo

Chapter 5
Hobbies

Unit 13. Mom's got a new hobby.

listen to meditation music

demonstrate some postures

stretch one's legs

Episode

Bomi: Mom, what's this music for? • It's so **monotonous**. • Why don't you listen to **lively** music?

Mom: Bomi, it's **meditation** music. • It's good for **mental** health. • It's also good for **purifying** our minds.

Bomi: Mom, you're not a **Buddhist** monk.

Mom: You don't know the real **value** of it.

Bomi: Do you think it's good for **relieving** stress? • Hip-hop music is a better **option** for stress relief.

My mom **registered** for yoga class. • Listening to meditation music is one of her **routines**. • She says yoga **benefits** us. • She **emphasizes** its health benefits. • Before she started yoga classes she had an **ulcer**, but now she's okay. • This made me **recall** a similar thing. • Mom once said tea has **healing** effects. • Now she stays healthy doing yoga. • My mom says it's good for **enlightening** people. • She also says it gives **insight** into life and it helps control our **emotions**. • She really **admires** people who are good at yoga. • This morning she **demonstrated** some unusual postures. • She also made me **stretch** my legs.

Bomi: Ouch, it's **torture**. • Mom, I can't **maintain** this posture. • Don't **press** my shoulders.

Mom: Bomi, you need more **tenacity**. • These exercises are effective in **strengthening** organs.

Bomi: Okay, mom. • I will try, but my body is too **stiff**.

보미 : 엄마, 이 음악은 뭐예요? 정말 단조롭네요. 경쾌한 음악을 들으시는 게 어때요?
엄마 : 보미, 이건 명상 음악이야. 정신 건강에 좋아. 마음을 정화하는 데에도 도움이 된단다.
보미 : 엄마, 엄마는 불교의 수도사가 아니잖아요.
엄마 : 너는 명상의 진정한 가치를 모르는구나.
보미 : 엄마는 명상이 스트레스를 줄이는 데 효과가 있다고 생각하세요? 스트레스 해소에는 힙합 음악이 더 나은 선택이에요.

우리 엄마는 요가 클래스에 등록하셨다. 명상 음악을 듣는 것이 엄마의 일과 중 하나이다. 엄마는 요가가 우리에게 이롭다고 말씀하신다. 엄마는 요가가 건강에 이롭다는 걸 강조하신다. 엄마는 요가 클래스를 시작하시기 전에는 궤양이 있으셨는데, 지금은 괜찮으시다. 이것 때문에 나는 비슷한 것을 생각하게 되었다. 엄마는 차가 치료 효과가 있다고 말씀하신 적이 있다. 요즘 엄마는 요가를 하면서 건강을 유지하신다. 우리 엄마는 요가가 사람을 가르치는 데 좋다고 말씀하신다. 엄마는 또한 요가가 인생에 대한 통찰력을 주고 우리의 감정을 통제하는 데 도움을 준다고 말씀하신다. 엄마는 요가에 정통한 사람들을 정말 동경하신다. 오늘 아침에 엄마는 몇 가지 기본 자세를 시범을 보이셨다. 엄마는 나보고 다리를 뻗어보라고 시키기도 하셨다.

보미 : 아야, 이건 고문이에요. 엄마, 저는 이 자세를 유지할 수 없어요. 제 어깨를 누르지 마세요.
엄마 : 보미, 좀 더 끈기가 있어야겠구나. 이 운동은 사람의 장기를 강화하는 데 효과가 있어.
보미 : 알았어요, 엄마. 해보겠지만 제 몸이 너무 뻣뻣해요.

monotonous
[mənátənəs]
a. 단조로운

boring and repetitive
- monotone n. 단조 a. 단조의 • monotony n. 단조로움

It's so monotonous. 정말 단조롭네요.

lively
[láivli]
a. 경쾌한

dynamic and full of energy
- liveliness n. 경쾌함

Why don't you listen to lively music?
경쾌한 음악을 들으시는 게 어때요?

meditation
[mèdətéiʃən]
n. 명상

being in a quiet, calm state
- meditate v. 명상하다, 숙고하다 • meditative a. 명상적인, 심사숙고하는

Bomi, it's meditation music. 보미, 이건 명상 음악이야.

mental
[méntl]
a. 정신의

relating to one's mind
- mentality n. 지력

It's good for mental health. 정신 건강에 좋아.

purify
[pjúərəfài]
v. 정화하다

to make something clean, to remove any bad things
- purification n. 정화 • pure a. 순수한

It's also good for purifying our minds.
마음을 정화하는 데에도 도움이 된단다.

Buddhist
[bú:dist]
n. 불교도

a member of the Buddhist religion
- Buddhism n. 불교

Mom, you're not a Buddhist monk.
엄마는 불교의 수도사가 아니잖아요.

value
[vǽlju:]
n. 가치

how much something is worth
- valuable a. 귀중한 • invaluable a. 매우 귀중한
- valueless a. 가치가 없는

You don't know the real value of it.
너는 그것의 진정한 가치를 모르는구나.

relieve
[rilíːv]
v. 줄이다

to make an unpleasant feeling less
- relief n. 경감

Do you think it's good for relieving stress?
명상이 스트레스를 줄이는 데 효과가 있다고 생각하세요?

option
[ápʃən]
n. 선택

a choice

Hip-hop music is a better option for stress relief.
스트레스 해소에는 힙합 음악이 더 나은 선택이에요.

register
[rédʒəstər]
v. 등록하다

to join a class
- registration n. 등록

My mom registered for yoga class.
우리 엄마는 요가 클래스에 등록하셨다.

routine
[ruːtíːn]
n. 일과

an activity someone does on a regular basis

Listening to meditation music is one of her routines.
명상 음악을 듣는 것이 그녀의 일과 중 하나이다.

benefit
[bénəfit]
v. 이익을 주다
n. 이익

to be good for someone
- beneficial a. 이로운

She says yoga benefits us.
그녀는 요가가 우리에게 이롭다고 말씀하신다.

emphasize
[émfəsàiz]
v. 강조하다

to strongly tell one's opinion to someone
- emphasis n. 강조

She emphasizes its health benefits.
그녀는 요가가 건강에 이롭다는 걸 강조하신다.

ulcer
[ʌ́lsər]
n. 궤양

a painful sore, often inside one's stomach

Before she started yoga classes she had an ulcer, but now she's okay.
그녀는 요가 클래스를 시작하시기 전에는 궤양이 있으셨는데, 지금은 괜찮으시다.

recall
[rikɔ́ːl]
v. 생각나게 하다,
상기시키다

to remember

This made me recall a similar thing.
이것 때문에 나는 비슷한 것을 생각하게 되었다.

healing
[híːliŋ]
a. 치료하는

making someone better and healthy
• heal v. 치료하다

Mom once said tea has healing effects.
엄마는 차가 치료 효과가 있다고 말씀하신 적이 있다.

enlighten
[enláitn]
v. 가르치다,
계몽시키다

to cause someone to understand, to civilize someone
• enlightenment n. 계몽

My mom says it's good for enlightening people.
우리 엄마는 요가가 사람을 가르치는 데 좋다고 말씀하신다.

insight
[ínsàit]
n. 통찰력

accurate and deep understanding
• insightful a. 통찰력 있는

She also says it gives insight into life and it helps control our emotions.
그녀는 또한 그것이 인생에 대한 통찰력을 주고 우리의 감정을 통제하는 데 도움을 준다고 말씀하신다.

emotion
[imóuʃən]
n. 감정

feelings such as love, anger, happiness, etc.
• emotional a. 감정적인

She also says it gives insight into life and it helps control our emotions.
그녀는 또한 그것이 인생에 대한 통찰력을 주고 우리의 감정을 통제하는 데 도움을 준다고 말씀하신다.

admire
[ædmáiər]
v. 동경하다, 감탄하다

to like and respect someone or something
• admiration n. 감탄 • admirable a. 감탄할 만한

She really admires people who are good at yoga.
그녀는 요가에 정통한 사람들을 정말 동경하신다.

demonstrate
[démənstrèit]
v. 시범을 보이다

to show someone how to do something
• demonstration n. 시범, 실연

This morning she demonstrated some unusual postures.
오늘 아침에 그녀는 몇 가지 기본 자세를 시범을 보이셨다.

stretch
[strétʃ]

v. 뻗다

to push one's arms or legs away from one's body
- stretchy a. 신축성 있는

She also made me stretch my legs.

그녀는 나보고 다리를 뻗어보라고 시키기도 하셨다.

torture
[tɔ́:rtʃər]

n. 고문

something which causes pain
- torturous a. 고통스러운

Ouch, it's torture. 아야, 이건 고문이에요.

maintain
[meintéin]

v. 유지하다

to continue doing something
- maintenance n. 유지

Mom, I can't maintain this posture.

엄마, 저는 이 자세를 유지할 수 없어요.

press
[prés]

v. 누르다

to push something

Don't press my shoulders.

제 어깨를 누르지 마세요.

tenacity
[tənǽsəti]

n. 끈기

diligence, firmness, perseverance
- tenacious a. 끈기 있는

Bomi, you need more tenacity.

보미, 좀 더 끈기가 있어야겠구나.

strengthen
[stréŋkθən]

v. 강화하다

to make someone or something stronger
- strength n. 힘 - strengthening a. 강화시키는

These exercises are effective in strengthening organs.

이 운동은 사람의 장기를 강화하는 데 효과가 있어.

stiff
[stíf]

a. 뻣뻣한

firm or not easily bent
- stiffen v. 근육 등이 경직되다

Okay, mom. I will try, but my body is too stiff.

알았어요, 엄마. 해보겠지만 제 몸이 너무 뻣뻣해요.

Check Again!

A Translate each word into Korean.

1. monotonous .... 2. ulcer ....

3. meditation .... 4. mental ....

5. routine .... 6. stiff ....

7. admire .... 8. enlighten ....

9. tenacity .... 10. torture ....

B Translate each word into English.

1. 유지하다 .... 2. 강조하다 ....

3. 가치 .... 4. 강화하다 ....

5. 이익을 주다 .... 6. 선택 ....

7. 치료하는 .... 8. 감정 ....

9. 생각나게 하다 .... 10. 시범을 보이다 ....

C Fill in the blank with the appropriate word. Refer to the Korean.

1. My friend and I r   for swimming class.

내 친구와 나는 수영 클래스에 등록했다.

2. Today's sociology class was very interesting with a l   discussic

오늘 사회학 수업은 활발한 토론으로 매우 재미있었다.

3. You may have some of your own ideas for r   stress.

스트레스를 줄이는 자신만의 방안이 있을 수도 있다.

4. The movie gives i   into the hardships these players had to endure.

그 영화는 이 배우들이 견뎌야 했던 시련을 통찰하게 해준다.

5. Self-reflection is essential for p   our minds and restoring our true nature.

자기 성찰은 마음을 정화하고 우리의 진정한 본성을 회복하는 데 필수적이다.

Check More!

수능 기출 응용

(A), (B), (C) 각 밑줄 친 부분에 알맞은 어휘를 짝지은 것으로 가장 적절한 것을 고르시오.

Some Korean artists suggest that the process of making hanji, hand-made Korean paper, **(A)** registers / reflects human life. In fact, you might say that people's day-to-day existence is shown in this paper-making process. The process starts when the branches of a tree are cut off. The branches then go through a complex process to become strong and **(B)** flexible / floatable paper. They are steamed, boiled, and then washed many times to remove any impure materials. They are also beaten for several hours. The more they are beaten, the stronger they actually become. This is similar to people getting wiser and more **(C)** struggled / strengthened by overcoming the difficulties and hardships they encounter day after day.

(A)	(B)	(C)
① registers	flexible	struggled
② reflects	flexible	strengthened
③ registers	flexible	strengthened
④ registers	floatable	struggled
⑤ reflects	floatable	struggled

Chapter 5
Hobbies

Unit 14. Are they my bosses?

be **exclusively** open to someone

have no **right** to say no

justify one's behavior

Episode

Dear Diary,

Today we had a rehearsal for the play, "A Midsummer Night's Dream." • The seniors gave me some difficult tasks. • Bomi, can you move this equipment downstairs? • Are they insane? • How can I carry such heavy things? • But I can't reject them. • It's obligatory to follow their orders. • I have no right to say no. • Why are they so inconsiderate? • How come thoughtful seniors have this kind of attitude? • Right before a performance, we receive special training. • There is tension between juniors and seniors. • All seniors become very strict and our relationship becomes like that of employees and employer. • Usually juniors are not allowed to enter the seniors' meeting room. • The meeting room is like a room for executives. • It is exclusively open to seniors. • They create a hierarchy between us. • The seniors monitor everything. • We need to get permission to do things. • We can't ask for pay or leave. • There is no paternity leave or maternity leave. • We literally become slaves. • Bomi, vacuum the floor. Be quick. • Okay, Bomi, be flexible, I said to myself. • You might think my reaction is too passive. • It's true I have an inner conflict about this. • The seniors always justify their behavior, saying it's for a better performance. • In two years, I will get the same privilege. • So I'm not so pessimistic about my future.

다이어리에게,

오늘 우리는 연극 "한 여름밤의 꿈"의 예행연습을 했어. 선배들은 나에게 어려운 일을 주었어. 보미, 이 장비를 아래층으로 옮겨 줄래? 선배들은 정신이 나간 것일까? 내가 어떻게 그렇게 무거운 걸 옮길 수 있지? 그렇지만 나는 거절할 수 없어. 선배의 명령을 따르는 것이 의무거든. 나는 안 된다고 말할 권리가 없어. 그들은 왜 그렇게 인정이 없을까? 사려 깊은 선배들이 왜 이런 태도를 보이는 걸까? 공연 바로 전에, 우리는 특별 훈련을 받아. 후배들과 선배들 사이에 긴장감이 감돌지. 모든 선배들은 매우 엄해지고 우리의 관계는 고용인과 고용주의 관계와 같이 되어가고 있어. 보통 후배들은 선배들의 회의실에 들어갈 수 없어. 회의실은 회사의 중역을 위한 방과 같은 거야. 그 방은 선배들에게만 개방되어 있어. 그들은 선후배 사이에 계급을 만드는 거야. 선배들은 모든 것을 감시해. 우리는 무언가를 하기 위해서는 허락을 받아야 해. 우리는 급여나 휴가를 달라고 요구할 수 없어. 아버지 출산 휴가나 어머니 출산 휴가는 없어. 우리는 완전히 노예가 되어가고 있어. 보미, 바닥을 청소해. 빨리 해. 좋아, 보미, 융통성을 발휘해 봐, 나는 혼잣말을 했어. 너는 내 반응이 너무 수동적이라고 생각할지도 몰라. 나는 이 문제에 대해 마음 속에 갈등이 있는 게 사실이야. 선배들은 그것이 더 나은 공연을 위한 것이라고 말하면서 항상 자신들의 행동을 정당화해. 2년 후에 나도 같은 특권을 갖게 되겠지. 그래서 나는 나의 미래에 대해 그렇게 비관적이지 않아.

rehearsal
[rihə́:rsəl]

n. 예행연습

a practice of a play or music in preparation for a performance
- rehearse v. 예행연습하다

Today we had a rehearsal for the play, "A Midsummer Night's Dream."

오늘 우리는 연극 "한 여름밤의 꿈"의 예행연습을 했어.

equipment
[ikwípmənt]

n. 장비

things that someone uses to do a task

Bomi, can you move this equipment downstairs?

보미, 이 장비를 아래층으로 옮겨줄래?

insane
[inséin]

a. 미친

crazy
- insanity n. 실성

Are they insane? 그들은 정신이 나간 것일까?

reject
[ridʒékt]

v. 거절하다

to say no, not to accept a proposal, a request, or an offer
- rejection n. 거절

But I can't reject them. 그렇지만 나는 거절할 수 없어.

obligatory
[əblígətɔ̀:ri]

a. 의무적인

necessary, compulsory, mandatory
- oblige v. 강요하다 - obligation n. 의무

It's obligatory to follow their orders.

그들의 명령을 따르는 것이 의무거든.

right
[ráit]

n. 권리

authority to do something
- have a right to + V ~할 권리가 있다

I have no right to say no. 나는 안 된다고 말할 권리가 없어.

inconsiderate
[ìnkənsídərit]

a. 인정 없는

careless, not caring about another person's feelings
- considerate a. 사려 깊은

Why are they so inconsiderate?

그들은 왜 그렇게 인정이 없을까?

thoughtful
[θɔ́ːtfəl]
a. 사려 깊은

being careful of another person's feelings, considerate

How come thoughtful seniors have this kind of attitude?
사려 깊은 선배들이 왜 이런 태도를 보이는 걸까?

training
[tréiniŋ]
n. 훈련

preparation, discipline
• train v. 훈련하다 • trainee n. 훈련생

Right before a performance, we receive special training.
공연 바로 전에, 우리는 특별 훈련을 받아.

tension
[ténʃən]
n. 긴장감, 긴장

an uncomfortable feeling
• tense a. 긴장한

There is tension between juniors and seniors.
후배들과 선배들 사이에 긴장감이 감돌지.

senior
[síːjər]
n. 선배

someone who is older or has more power than you
• seniority n. 손위임, 손위

All seniors become very strict and our relationship becomes like that of employees and employer.
모든 선배들은 매우 엄해지고 우리의 관계는 고용인와 고용주의 관계와 같이 되어가고 있어.

employer
[emplɔ́iər]
n. 고용주

a person who hires someone to do a job
• employee n. 고용인

All seniors become very strict and our relationship becomes like that of employees and employer.
모든 선배들은 매우 엄해지고 우리의 관계는 고용인와 고용주의 관계와 같이 되어가고 있어.

junior
[dʒúːnjər]
n. 후배

someone who is younger and has less power than you

Usually juniors are not allowed to enter the seniors' meeting room.
보통 후배들은 선배들의 회의실에 들어갈 수 없어.

executive
[igzékjətiv]
n. 중역

a powerful businessman

The meeting room is like a room for executives.
회의실은 회사의 중역을 위한 방과 같은 거야.

exclusively
[iksklú:sivli]
ad. 배타적으로

available to only one person or one group
- exclusive a. 배타적인, 독점적인

It is exclusively open to seniors.
그 방은 선배들에게만 개방되어 있어.

hierarchy
[háiərà:rki]
n. 계급제

a system of separating people into different levels, grouping
- hierarchical a. 계급제의

They create a hierarchy between us.
그들은 우리들 사이에 계급을 만드는 거야.

monitor
[mánitər]
v. 감시하다

to supervise, to watch people carefully

The seniors monitor everything.
선배들은 모든 것을 감시해.

permission
[pə:rmíʃən]
n. 허가

agreement, approval, consent
- permit v. 허가하다

We need to get permission to do things.
우리는 무언가를 하기 위해서는 허락을 받아야 해.

leave
[lí:v]
n. 휴가

vacation time

We can't ask for pay or leave.
우리는 급여나 휴가를 달라고 요구할 수 없어.

maternity leave
[mətə́:rnəti lì:v]
출산 휴가

vacation time a mother is allowed to take off work when she gives birth
- maternity n. 모성, 모계 • maternal a. 어머니의
- paternity n. 부성, 부계 • paternal a. 아버지의

There is no paternity leave or maternity leave.
아버지 출산 휴가나 어머니 출산 휴가는 없어.

literally
[lítərəli]
ad. 완전히,
글자 뜻대로

completely, really, exactly
- literal a. 글자 그대로의

We literally become slaves. 우리는 완전히 노예가 되어가고 있어.

vacuum
[vǽkjuəm]

v. 진공청소기로 청소하다

to clean the floor with a vacuum cleaner

Bomi, vacuum the floor. Be quick.

보미, 바닥을 청소해. 빨리 해.

flexible
[fléksəbəl]

a. 융통성이 있는

being adaptable, changing easily when a situation changes

• flexibility n. 융통성

Okay, Bomi, be flexible, I said to myself.

좋아, 보미, 융통성을 발휘해 봐, 나는 혼잣말을 했어.

passive
[pǽsiv]

a. 수동적인

quiet, not reacting aggressively

• passivity n. 수동성

You might think my reaction is too passive.

너는 내 반응이 너무 수동적이라고 생각할지도 몰라.

conflict
[kánflikt]

n. 갈등 v. 충돌하다

serious disagreement and argument

It's true I have an inner conflict about this.

나는 이 문제에 대해 마음 속에 갈등이 있는 게 사실이야.

justify
[dʒʌ́stəfài]

v. 정당화하다

to show that something is reasonable or necessary

• justification n. 정당화

The seniors always justify their behavior, saying it's for a better performance.

선배들은 그것이 더 나은 공연을 위한 것이라고 말하면서 항상 자신들의 행동을 정당화해.

privilege
[prívəlidʒ]

n. 특권

a special advantage that is given to some people

• privileged a. 특권이 있는

In two years, I will get the same privilege.

2년 후에 나도 같은 특권을 갖게 되겠지.

pessimistic
[pèsəmístik]

a. 비관적인

expecting a bad outcome, cynical

• pessimism n. 비관론 • pessimist n. 비관론자

So I'm not so pessimistic about my future.

그래서 나는 나의 미래에 대해 그렇게 비관적이지 않아.

Check Again!

A Translate each word into Korean.

1. literally ....   2. vacuum ....

3. reject ....   4. hierarchy ....

5. tension ....   6. training ....

7. insane ....   8. inconsiderate ....

9. thoughtful ....   10. equipment ....

B Translate each word into English.

1. 고용주 ....   2. 중역 ....

3. 감시하다 ....   4. 후배 ....

5. 휴가 ....   6. 융통성이 있는 ....

7. 수동적인 ....   8. 정당화하다 ....

9. 특권 ....   10. 비관적인 ....

C Fill in the blank with the appropriate word. Refer to the Korean.

1. It's o   to learn English in school.

   학교에서 영어를 배우는 것은 의무적이다.

2. You need to get p   to take a trip to certain areas.

   특정 지역으로 여행을 하려면 허가를 받아야 한다.

3. Many couples have a r   for the wedding ceremony.

   많은 커플들이 결혼식 예행연습을 가진다.

4. Identify the most important area in your life where you feel inner

   c   .

   여러분이 내적 갈등을 느끼는 인생의 가장 중요한 부분을 찾아내라.

5. More and more Korean mothers are coming back to work after

   three-month m   leave.

   더욱 많은 한국 엄마들이 3개월의 출산 휴가 후에 직장으로 되돌아오고 있다.

Check More!

다음 밑줄 친 부분에 알맞은 어휘를 고르시오. 아래의 영영 풀이를 참조하시오.

What **(A)** equipment / equivalent did Newton use to point out that light is colorless, and that consequently color has to occur inside our brains? He wrote, "The waves themselves are not colored." In those days people might have thought him **(B)** considerate / insane. However, since his time, we have learned that light waves are **(C)** characterized / characteristics by different frequencies of vibration. When they enter the eye of an observer, they set off a chain of neurochemical events, the end product of which is an internal mental image that we call color. The essential point here is: what we **(D)** perceive / proceed as color is not made up of color. Although an apple may appear red, its atoms are not themselves red.

*neurochemical: 신경화학의

(A) things that we use to do a task: ....

(B) crazy, not normal: ....

(C) to be distinguished; to be marked: ....

(D) to notice; to identify; to recognize: ....

Chapter 5
Hobbies

Unit 15. Hoony is money-wise.

be obsessed with something

know how the **barter system** works

sign a **contract**

Episode

Bomi: Hoony, look. Your cards are everywhere. ● Please dispose of your cards.

Hoony: Don't worry. I know the best disposal method. ● Bomi, don't give me such a suspicious look.

For two months, Hoony purchased strange cards every day. ● He seemed to be obsessed with these useless things. ● When I asked him about it, he just grinned at me. ● What's your purpose for collecting these cards? ● Then he divulged his plan to me. ● He triumphantly pulled a video game out of his bag. ● He had exchanged his cards for his friend Brian's brand-new video game. ● Wow, he seems to know how the economy works. ● He knows how he can make a surplus. ● He's acquired the basic theory already. ● I mean, he knows how the barter system works. ● Hoony, what if Brian changes his mind? ● Hoony showed me a written document. ● He said they signed a contract. ● It states certain conditions. ● For example, the contract is valid until September 21st. ● Then the contract will expire. ● He must be a good negotiator. ● It seems it's too good a deal. ● How did he convince Brian to exchange his brand-new game for these old cards? ● How did he make such a profitable deal? ● He said he showed Brian a few samples of his cards and Brian really liked them. ● Hoony's homeschooling is really working out well. ● Our dad told Hoony to keep an account book. ● Dad taught him what expenditure and income mean. ● Hoony already knows how to spend money.

보미 : 후니, 봐. 네 카드가 사방에 널려 있어. 카드 좀 버려.
후니 : 걱정하지 마. 가장 좋은 폐기 방법을 알고 있어. 보미, 날 그렇게 의심스러운 눈초리로 쳐다보지 마.

두 달 동안, 후니는 매일 이상한 카드를 샀어. 후니는 마치 이 쓸모 없는 것들에 사로잡힌 것 같았어. 내가 카드에 대해서 물어보면 후니는 나를 보고 그냥 웃기만 했어. 이 카드를 모으는 목적이 뭐야? 그러면 후니는 자신의 계획을 나에게 말해주었어. 후니는 의기양양하게 가방에서 비디오 게임을 꺼냈어. 후니는 자신의 카드를 친구인 브라이언의 새 비디오 게임과 바꿨어. 와, 후니는 경제가 어떻게 움직이는지 알고 있는 것 같아. 후니는 어떻게 이익을 남길 수 있을지를 알아. 후니는 이미 기본적인 이론을 습득하고 있어. 내 말은, 후니가 물물교환 시스템이 어떻게 돌아가는지 안다는 거야. 후니, 브라이언이 마음을 바꾸면 어떻게 할 거니? 후니는 글로 쓴 서류를 나에게 보여주었어. 그들은 계약서에 서명을 했다고 말했어. 계약서에는 특정 조건이 언급되어 있어. 예를 들면, 계약은 9월 21일까지 유효하다. 그리고 나서 계약은 만기가 된다. 후니는 틀림없이 훌륭한 협상가야. 거래를 너무 잘하는 것 같아. 후니는 브라이언이 이런 낡은 카드와 새 비디오 게임을 바꿀 수 있도록 어떻게 설득했을까? 후니는 그렇게 이익이 많이 남는 거래를 어떻게 성사시켰을까? 후니는 자신이 브라이언에게 몇 가지 카드 샘플을 보여주었고 브라이언이 그걸 정말 좋아했다고 말했어. 후니의 자택 학습은 정말 잘 되어가고 있어. 우리 아빠는 후니에게 금전출납부를 쓰라고 말씀하셨어. 아빠는 후니에게 수입과 지출의 의미를 가르쳐주셨어. 후니는 이미 돈 쓰는 방법을 알고 있어.

dispose
[dispóuz]
v. 처분하다

to throw away
- disposable a. 일회용의 • dispose of ~을 처분하다

Please dispose of your cards.
카드 좀 버려.

disposal
[dispóuzəl]
n. 폐기

a way to throw something away

Don't worry. I know the best disposal method.
걱정하지 마. 가장 좋은 폐기 방법을 알고 있어.

suspicious
[səspíʃəs]
a. 의심스러운

not trusting someone, distrustful
- suspicion n. 의심

Bomi, don't give me such a suspicious look.
보미, 날 그렇게 의심스러운 눈초리로 쳐다보지 마.

purchase
[pə́:rtʃəs]
v. 사다 n. 구입

to buy something

For two months, Hoony purchased strange cards every day.
두 달 동안, 후니는 매일 이상한 카드를 샀어.

obsess
[əbsés]
v. 사로잡다

to think about something all the time
- obsession n. 강박관념 • be obsessed with ~에 사로잡히다

He seemed to be obsessed with these useless things.
그는 마치 이 쓸모 없는 것들에 사로잡힌 것 같았어.

grin
[grín]
v. 이를 드러내고
싱긋 웃다

to smile widely and show one's teeth

When I asked him about it, he just grinned at me.
내가 카드에 대해서 물어보면 그는 나를 보고 그냥 웃기만 했어.

purpose
[pə́:rpəs]
n. 목적

a reason or goal for doing something

What's your purpose for collecting these cards?
이 카드를 모으는 목적이 뭐야?

divulge
[daivʌ́ldʒ]
v. 누설하다, 폭로하다

to tell a person something that was a secret

Then he divulged his plan to me.
그러면 그는 자신의 계획을 나에게 말해주었어.

triumphantly
[traiʌ́mfəntli]
ad. 의기양양해서

happily, boastfully
• triumphant a. 의기양양한

He triumphantly pulled a video game out of his bag.
그는 의기양양하게 가방에서 비디오 게임을 꺼냈어.

brand-new
[brǽndnjú:]
a. 아주 새로운

completely new

He had exchanged his cards for his friend Brian's brand-new video game.
그는 자신의 카드를 친구인 브라이언의 새 비디오 게임과 바꿨어.

economy
[ikánəmi]
n. 경제

the way that business is organized
• economic a. 경제의 • economical a. 경제적인, 절약이 되는

Wow, he seems to know how the economy works.
와, 그는 경제가 어떻게 움직이는지 알고 있는 것 같아.

surplus
[sə́:rplʌs]
n. 흑자

extra material balance, something extra, opposite of deficit

He knows how he can make a surplus.
그는 어떻게 이익을 남길 수 있을지를 알아.

acquire
[əkwáiər]
v. 습득하다

to get or learn something
• acquisition n. 획득, 습득

He's acquired the basic theory already.
그는 이미 기본적인 이론을 습득하고 있어.

barter
[bá:rtər]
n. 물물교환
v. 물물교환하다

exchange of goods for other goods

I mean, he knows how the barter system works.
내 말은, 그가 물물교환 시스템이 어떻게 돌아가는지 안다는 거야.

document
[dákjəmənt]
n. 서류

a piece of paper with writing on it
• documentation n. 문서 분류 시스템
Hoony showed me a written document.
후니는 글로 쓴 서류를 나에게 보여주었어.

contract
[kántrækt]
n. 계약서, 계약

a formal written agreement
He said they signed a contract.
그들은 계약서에 서명을 했다고 말했어.

state
[stéit]
v. 언급하다

to say something in a formal way
• statement n. 언급
It states certain conditions.
계약서에는 특정 조건이 언급되어 있어.

valid
[vælid]
a. 유효한

able to be used; legally or officially acceptable
• validate v. 유효하게 하다 • validity n. 유효함, 타당성
For example, the contract is valid until September 21st.
예를 들면, 계약은 9월 21일까지 유효하다.

expire
[ikspáiər]
v. 만기가 되다

to come to an end
• expiry n. 만기
Then the contract will expire.
그리고 나서 계약은 만기가 된다.

negotiator
[nigóuʃièitər]
n. 협상가

a person who bargains, a middleperson
• negotiate v. 협상하다 • negotiation n. 협상
He must be a good negotiator.
그는 틀림없이 훌륭한 협상가야.

deal
[díːl]
n. 거래 v. 거래하다

a bargain

It seems it's too good a deal.
거래를 너무 잘하는 것 같아.

convince
[kənvíns]
v. 설득하다,
확신시키다

to make someone agree with you
• conviction n. 확신 • convincing a. 설득력 있는

How did he convince Brian to exchange his brand-new game for these old cards?
그는 브라이언이 이런 낡은 카드와 새 비디오 게임을 바꿀 수 있도록 어떻게 설득했을까?

profitable
[práfitəbəl]
a. 이익이 되는

making a profit
• profit n. 이익

How did he make such a profitable deal?
그는 그렇게 이익이 많이 남는 거래를 어떻게 성사시켰을까?

homeschooling
[hóumskùːliŋ]
n. 자택 학습

teaching a child at home instead of at school
• homeschool v. 자택에서 교육하다

Hoony's homeschooling is really working out well.
후니의 자택 학습은 정말 잘 되어가고 있어.

account
[əkáunt]
n. 회계, 계산

a detailed record of all the money one earns and spends
• accountant n. 회계사

Our dad told Hoony to keep an account book.
우리 아빠는 후니에게 금전출납부를 쓰라고 말씀하셨어.

expenditure
[ikspéndit∫ər]
n. 지출

money that one spends to buy things, opposite of income

Dad taught him what expenditure and income mean.
아빠는 그에게 수입과 지출의 의미를 가르쳐주셨어.

Check Again!

A Translate each word into Korean.

1. valid ....
2. account ....
3. expenditure ....
4. expire ....
5. negotiator ....
6. disposal ....
7. state ....
8. purchase ....
9. divulge ....
10. triumphantly ....

B Translate each word into English.

1. 목적 ....
2. 흑자 ....
3. 습득하다 ....
4. 물물교환 ....
5. 서류 ....
6. 계약서 ....
7. 아주 새로운 ....
8. 거래 ....
9. 설득하다 ....
10. 이익이 되는 ....

C Fill in the blank with the appropriate word. Refer to the Korean.

1. The old lady gave the young man a s_____ look.
   그 나이든 부인이 젊은이를 의심스러운 눈초리로 쳐다봤다.

2. He confessed that he seemed to be o_____ with gambling.
   그는 자신이 도박에 사로잡혀 있는 것 같다고 고백했다.

3. The gentleman nodded and g_____ at Amy when she offered him some tea.
   에이미가 차를 권하자 그 신사는 고개를 끄덕이며 그녀에게 싱긋 웃어주었다.

4. Please d_____ of recyclable materials in the blue container at the back of the kitchen.
   재활용 물건은 부엌 뒤에 있는 파란색 통에 버리세요.

5. There are three ways to make a p_____ deal in the real estate investment industry.
   부동산 투자업계에는 수익성 있는 거래를 하는 3가지 방법이 있다.

Check More!

다음 밑줄 친 부분에 알맞은 어휘를 고르시오. 아래의 영영 풀이를 참조하시오.

Many people seem to be **(A)** obliged / obsessed with the Internet, believing that all the information provided to us is trustworthy. Flooded by cellphones, the Internet, and television, we incorrectly imagine that our ancestors inhabited an innocent world where the news did not travel far beyond the village. It may not be **(B)** valid / invalid to assume that the media makes our time distinct from the past, because we know relatively little about how information was shared in the past.

In fact, the Olympics celebrate the memory of the Greek soldier who brought the news of the Athenian victory over the Persians. Most of us could come up with many other examples – message drums, smoke signals, church bells, ship flags. But their primitiveness would only **(C)** confirm / conform our sense that we live in a fundamentally different world, one of constant, instant access to information.

(A) thinking about something all the time:

(B) useful, reasonable:

(C) to prove, to certify:

Chapter 5. Hobbies **145**

+ 접두사 anti- / contra- / pro-

anti-와 contra-는 둘 다 'against'라는 뜻의 접두사이다. anti-는 '적대 또는 배척'이라는 뜻의 단어를 만들고, contra-는 '역(逆) 또는 반대'라는 뜻의 단어를 만든다. pro-는 'for'라는 뜻의 접두사로, '무언가를 지지하다'라는 뜻의 단어를 만든다.

anti-

government 정부
anti + government = antigovernment 반 정부의
ex) Another antigovernment protest took place on Saturday.
토요일에 또 다른 반 정부 시위가 발생했다.

- -biotic 생명의   antibiotic 항생 물질의
- aging 노화   anti-aging 노화 방지의
- septic 부패성의   antiseptic 살균의
- -pathy 감정   antipathy 반감
- -onym 단어, 이름   antonym 반의어
- freeze 결빙   antifreeze 부동액
- social 사회적인, 사교적인   antisocial 반 사회적인, 반 사교적인

contra-

seasonal 계절의
contra + seasonal = contraseasonal 시기에 벗어난, 계절에 벗어난
ex) The recent rise in corn prices is contraseasonal.
최근 옥수수 가격의 인상은 계절에 맞지 않다.

- contraband 금지품
- contraception 피임
- contradict 반박하다
- contraflow 역행, 역류
- contravene 위반 행위를 범하다
- contralateral 몸의 반대쪽에서 일어나는
- contraindicate (증후가 약에 대한) 금기를 나타내다

pro-

abortion 임신 중절
pro + abortion = proabortion 임신 중절 지지의
ex) I am proabortion in cases of sexual violence.
　　성폭력의 경우에 나는 임신 중절을 지지한다.

• choice 선택	pro-choice 임신 중절 지지의
• life 생명	pro-life 임신 중절 반대의
• government 정부	progovernment 정부를 지지하는
• republican 공화당의	pro-republican 공화당을 지지하는
• democrat 민주당의	pro-democrat 민주당을 지지하는
• liberal 진보적인	pro-liberal 진보주의 정책을 지지하는
• conservative 보수적인	pro-conservative 보수주의 정책을 지지하는

Culture Plus

Religion 종교
⁺Buddhism 불교
⁺Christianity 기독교
⁺Catholicism 천주교
⁺Islamism 이슬람교
⁺Judaism 유대교
⁺Hinduism 힌두교
⁺Atheism 무신론

VOCA EDGE
RED

Goodbye, Sara. I learned about the earth. I went to a natural science museum. I had a
ra attends a community party. Mom's got a new hobby. Are they my bosses? Hoony
ghter clinic. The Volcanoes are back. We have great brothers. What historical figures do
lepathy between us! Sara goes to Turkey. Home decorating is not easy. Hoony thinks girl
war should be stopped. Mom, are you going to cut my allowance? Hoony is back from
uld have been more careful. Forgery should be stopped. Hoony wants to explore outer
ricane hit the village. We're teens. I had my cell phone taken away. Goodbye, Brownie
e museum. I had a campus tour. If I were a judge,... How can we survive in a jungle?
osses? Hoony is money-wise. Hoony goes to an herbal clinic. We became a rescue team
cal figures do you want to meet? Are mom and dad compatible? I can't understand th
Hoony thinks girls have illusions about boys. I can't understand politicians. Wearing an
Hoony is back from an economics camp. construction a thriving business? How amazing
to explore outer space. I attended the Arbor Day ceremony. We can make the earth
odbye, Brownie Life is full of contradictions. Goodbye, Sara. I learned about the earth.
n a jungle? I became a Santa Claus. Sara attends a community party. Mom's got a new

Chapter 6. Health

a rescue team. Grandma goes to a laughter clinic. The Volcanoes are back. We ha

ow amazing our life has become! I should have been more careful. Forgery should be

e the earth a better place. A super hurricane hit the village. We're teens. I had my ce

the earth. I went to a natural science museum. I had a campus tour. If I were a judge,.

got a new hobby. Are they my bosses? Hoony is money-wise. Hoony goes to an herba

taste bitter

become a **hostage**

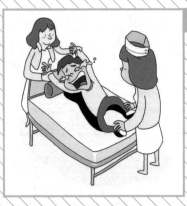

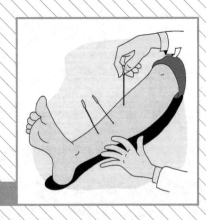

stimulate blood circulation

Episode

Bomi: Mom, are you going to see a **physician** for grandma? • And you are going to see a **pediatrician** for Hoony, right?

Mom: No, they're going to an **oriental** clinic with me.

Bomi: Do you mean an **herbal** doctor? • Hoony has a **sprained** ankle. • And grandma has high **blood pressure**. • Are you thinking of **acupuncture**?

Mom: Sure, it is good for their **circulation**.

Mom always says acupuncture **stimulates** blood circulation. • She seems to be **addicted** to acupuncture. • Once when I had food **poisoning**, she **abruptly** took me to the herbal clinic. • At the herbal clinic, the doctor took my **pulse**. • Then, can you just **imagine**? • I had to drink a black **liquid**. • At first **glance**, I could see that it was going to taste bitter. • I really wanted to stop, but it was **compulsory**. • Today Hoony is going to **experience** the same thing. • Mom says fear of needles is **hereditary**. • She says dad has a **phobia** of needles and so do Hoony and me. • But how can mom **soothe** him? • Won't he **hesitate** to enter the examination room? • He is going to cry **frantically**. • The nurse will hold him tightly and Hoony will become a **hostage**. • My poor brother, mom, you're **inhumane**. • Don't you think it's child **abuse**? • Why don't you **acknowledge** that I'm right?

보미: 엄마, 할머니 치료하는 의사를 만나실 거예요? 그리고 후니의 담당의사도 만나실 거죠, 그렇죠?
엄마: 아니, 나와 함께 한의원에 갈 거야.
보미: 한의사를 말씀하시는 거예요? 후니는 발목이 삐었고 할머니는 혈압이 높으시잖아요. 침술을 생각하시는 건가요?
엄마: 물론이야, 그게 혈액순환에 좋거든.

엄마는 항상 침술이 혈액 순환을 원활하게 한다고 말씀하신다. 엄마는 침술에 중독되신 것 같다. 언젠가 내가 식중독에 걸렸을 때, 엄마는 나를 갑자기 한의원에 데려가셨다. 한의원에서 의사는 내 맥박을 짚었다. 그리고 나서 상상할 수 있어? 나는 검정색 액체를 마셔야 했다. 첫눈에도 그건 맛이 쓸 것 같았다. 나는 정말 마시고 싶지 않았지만, 그건 강제적이었다. 오늘은 후니가 같은 경험을 할 것이다. 엄마는 주사를 무서워하는 것은 유전이라고 하신다. 엄마는 아빠가 주사에 대한 공포증이 있어서 후니와 나도 그렇다고 말씀하신다. 그렇지만 엄마가 어떻게 후니를 안심시킬 수 있을까? 후니가 진료실에 들어가지 않으려고 하지 않을까? 후니는 미친 듯이 울어댈 것이다. 간호사는 후니를 단단히 붙들 것이고 후니는 인질이 되겠지. 불쌍한 내 동생, 엄마, 엄마는 잔인해요. 그것이 아동 학대라고 생각하지 않으세요? 제 말이 맞다고 인정하시는 것이 어떠세요?

physician
[fizíʃən]
n. 내과의사

a doctor

Mom, are you going to see a physician for grandma?

엄마, 할머니 치료하는 의사를 만나실 거예요?

pediatrician
[pìːdiətríʃən]
n. 소아과 의사

a doctor for children

And you are going to see a pediatrician for Hoony, right?

그리고 후니의 담당의사도 만나실 거죠, 그렇죠?

oriental
[ɔːriéntl]
a. 동양의

having to do with Asian culture and/or history

• orient n. 동양

No, they're going to an oriental clinic with me.

아니, 그들은 나와 함께 한의원에 갈 거야.

herbal
[hə́rbəl]
a. 약초의, 식물의

natural, made from plants and natural sources

• herb n. 허브, 약초

Do you mean an herbal doctor?

한의사를 말씀하시는 거예요?

sprained
[spréind]
a. 접지른, 삔

having an injury of a joint

• sprain v. ~을 접지르다

Hoony has a sprained ankle.

후니는 발목이 삐었어요.

blood pressure
[blʌd préʃər]
혈압

a measure of how strongly one's blood flows

And grandma has high blood pressure.

그리고 할머니는 혈압이 높으시잖아요.

acupuncture
[ǽkjupʌ̀ŋktʃər]
n. 침술

a type of medical treatment where needles are stuck into the body

• acupuncturist n. 침술사

Are you thinking of acupuncture?

침술을 생각하시는 건가요?

circulation
[sə́:rkjəléiʃən]

n. 순환

the flow of blood through one's body
- circulate v. 순환하다 • circular a. 원형의
- circulating a. 순환하는, 순회하는

Sure, it is good for their circulation.
물론이야, 그게 혈액순환에 좋거든.

stimulate
[stímjəlèit]

v. 자극하다

to arouse or cause to become active
- stimulation n. 자극

Mom always says acupuncture stimulates blood circulation.
엄마는 항상 침술이 혈액 순환을 원활하게 한다고 말씀하신다.

addicted
[ədíktid]

a. 중독된

hooked, unable to stop doing something
- addict v. 중독시키다 n. 중독자 • addiction n. 중독
- be addicted to ~에 중독되다

She seems to be addicted to acupuncture.
그녀는 침술에 중독되신 것 같다.

poisoning
[pɔ́izəniŋ]

n. 중독

a type of sickness caused by having a toxic substance in the body
- poison n. 독 • food poisoning n. 식중독

Once when I had food poisoning, she abruptly took me to the herbal clinic.
언젠가 내가 식중독에 걸렸을 때, 그녀는 나를 갑자기 한의원에 데려가셨다.

abruptly
[əbrʌ́ptli]

ad. 갑작스럽게

suddenly, hurriedly
- abrupt a. 갑작스런

Once when I had food poisoning, she abruptly took me to the herbal clinic.
언젠가 내가 식중독에 걸렸을 때, 그녀는 나를 갑자기 한의원에 데려가셨다.

pulse
[pʌ́ls]

n. 맥박

heartbeat, the rate at which one's heart is beating

At the herbal clinic, the doctor took my pulse.
한의원에서 의사는 내 맥박을 짚었다.

imagine
[imǽdʒin]
v. 상상하다

to think creatively
- imagination n. 상상   - imaginary a. 상상의
- imaginative a. 상상력이 풍부한

Then, can you just imagine? 그리고 나서 상상할 수 있어?

liquid
[líkwid]
n. 액체

a fluid, a state of matter between solid and gas

I had to drink a black liquid.
나는 검정색 액체를 마셔야 했다.

glance
[glǽns]
n. 흘긋 봄
v. 흘긋 보다

looking quickly at something
- at first glance   첫눈에

At first glance, I could see that it was going to taste bitter.
첫눈에도 그건 맛이 쓸 것 같았다.

compulsory
[kəmpʌ́lsəri]
a. 강제적인, 의무의

mandatory, necessary
- compulsion n. 강제   - compulsive a. 강제적인, 강박관념에 사로잡힌

I really wanted to stop, but it was compulsory.
나는 정말 마시고 싶지 않았지만, 그건 강제적이었다.

experience
[ikspíəriəns]
v. 경험하다
n. 경험

to go through a situation or event
- experienced a. 경험이 있는

Today Hoony is going to experience the same thing.
오늘은 후니가 같은 경험을 할 것이다.

hereditary
[hirédətèri]
a. 유전성의

genetic, received from one's parents
- heredity n. 유전

Mom says fear of needles is hereditary.
엄마는 주사를 무서워하는 것은 유전이라고 하신다.

phobia
[fóubiə]
n. 공포증

an intense fear of something
- phobic a. 공포증이 있는

She says dad has a phobia of needles and so do Hoony and me.
그녀는 아빠가 주사에 대한 공포증이 있어서 후니와 나도 그렇다고 말씀하신다.

soothe
[súːð]
v. 진정시키다

to calm or relax someone or something
- soothing a. 진정시키는

But how can mom soothe him?
그렇지만 엄마가 어떻게 그를 안심시킬 수 있을까?

hesitate
[hézətèit]
v. 망설이다, 주저하다

to wait a moment before acting, to act slowly because of uncertainty
- hesitation n. 망설임

Won't he hesitate to enter the examination room?
그는 진료실에 들어가지 않으려고 하지 않을까?

frantically
[frǽntikəli]
ad. 미친 듯이

wildly and uncontrollably
- frantic a. 미친

He is going to cry frantically. 그는 미친 듯이 울어댈 것이다.

hostage
[hɑ́stidʒ]
n. 인질

a person being held

The nurse will hold him tightly and Hoony will become a hostage.
간호사는 그를 단단히 붙들 것이고 후니는 인질이 되겠지.

inhumane
[ìnhjuːméin]
a. 잔인한, 무자비한

cruel, not ethical or caring
- inhumanity n. 무자비함, 비인간적임

My poor brother, mom, you're inhumane.
불쌍한 내 동생, 엄마, 엄마는 잔인해요.

abuse
[əbjúːz]
n. 학대, 남용
v. 학대하다, 남용하다

punishment or unethical physical treatment
- abusive a. 학대하는, 남용의

Don't you think it's child abuse?
그것이 아동 학대라고 생각하지 않으세요?

acknowledge
[æknɑ́lidʒ]
v. 인정하다

to accept or admit that something is true
- acknowledgement n. 승인, 인정

Why don't you acknowledge that I'm right?
제 말이 맞다고 인정하시는 것이 어떠세요?

Check Again!

A Translate each word into Korean.

1. pediatrician ....
2. stimulate ....
3. soothe ....
4. acupuncture ....
5. hereditary ....
6. imagine ....
7. poisoning ....
8. herbal ....
9. compulsory ....
10. hostage ....

B Translate each word into English.

1. 학대 ....
2. 순환 ....
3. 공포증 ....
4. 인정하다 ....
5. 내과의사 ....
6. 잔인한 ....
7. 갑작스럽게 ....
8. 망설이다 ....
9. 미친 듯이 ....
10. 경험하다 ....

C Fill in the blank with the appropriate word. Refer to the Korean.

1. One in three adults has high blood p_____ .
   성인 3명 중 1명이 고혈압이다.

2. What should I do when my cat has a s_____ paw?
   고양이가 발을 삐었을 때 어떻게 해야 할까요?

3. At first g_____, I thought they were identical twins.
   첫눈에 나는 그들이 일란성 쌍둥이라고 생각했다.

4. These days lots of children seem to be a_____ to the Internet.
   요즘 많은 어린이들이 인터넷에 중독되어 있는 것 같다.

5. The doctor took my p_____, and it was well over a 100 beats per minute.
   의사가 내 맥박을 쟀는데, 1분에 100회가 훨씬 넘었다.

(A), (B), (C) 각 밑줄 친 부분에 알맞은 어휘를 짝지은 것으로 가장 적절한 것을 고르시오.

Someone who reads only newspapers and books by contemporary authors looks to me like a near-sighted person. He is completely dependent on the prejudices of his times. And what a person thinks on his own without being **(A)** simulated / stimulated by the thoughts and experiences of other people is at best insignificant and monotonous. There are only a few **(B)** enlightened / enlarged people with a clear mind and with good taste within a century. What has been **(C)** perceived / preserved of their work belongs among the most precious possessions of mankind. We owe it to a few writers of old times that the people in the Middle Ages could slowly free themselves from ignorance.

	(A)	(B)	(C)
①	stimulated	enlightened	preserved
②	simulated	enlarged	perceived
③	stimulated	enlarged	preserved
④	simulated	enlightened	preserved
⑤	stimulated	enlarged	perceived

Chapter 6
Health

Unit 17. We became a rescue team.

be **cautious** when traveling

cope with emergencies

experiment on a dummy

Episode

Dear Sara,

Sara, is your friend okay now? • I didn't know that rattle snakes were so **poisonous**. • Your teacher was wise for taking **prompt** action. • Otherwise he could have become **paralyzed**. • He could have been in a **critical** condition. • Sara, are there many **casualties** from snake bites in the desert? • Tourists need to be **cautious** when traveling through deserts. • Snakes there have natural **camouflage**. • People can hardly **distinguish** between snakes and sand. • Your video clips about that **biologist** surprised me. • How could he just grab such **lethal** snakes? • He even **simultaneously** explained about snakes while handling them. • He seemed to ignore the fact that their poison could harm his **nervous** system. • Or did he carry an **antidote**? • In order to survive, we need to be able to **cope** with emergencies. • They come to us **unexpectedly**. • Today the whole class **experimented** on a dummy. • We became a **rescue** team. • Sara, suppose a little boy **swallowed** a small Lego block. • His **respiratory** system wouldn't be able to function properly. • Before he is sent to the **emergency** room, something must be done. • Otherwise he will **suffocate**. • Our teacher demonstrated some **essential** techniques to us. • He showed us how to **eliminate** things blocking a person's airway. • He also showed us how to **inhale**. • We were also **instructed** to press on the dummy. • "Hey, press on the chest not on the **abdomen**," teacher said to me. • Playing with the dummy was not fun at all, but I will **keep** these instructions in **mind**. • Who knows I may have to use them in the near future?

사라에게,

사라, 너의 친구는 이제 괜찮니? 나는 방울뱀이 그렇게 독이 있는 줄 몰랐어. 너의 선생님이 신속한 조치를 취한 건 현명한 행동 이었어. 그렇지 않았으면 네 친구는 몸이 마비되었을 수도 있었어. 위독한 상태에 빠질 수도 있었어. 사라, 사막에서 뱀에게 물리 는 사상자들이 많이 있어? 여행객들은 사막을 지날 때 조심해야만 해. 그곳에 사는 뱀은 타고난 위장술을 가지고 있어. 사람들은 뱀과 모래를 거의 구별할 수 없어. 그 생물학자에 대한 너의 비디오는 나를 놀라게 했어. 그는 그렇게 치명적인 뱀을 어떻게 잡을 수 있었을까? 그는 뱀을 다루면서 동시에 뱀에 대해 설명하기도 했어. 그는 뱀의 독이 자신의 신경계를 해칠 수도 있다는 사실을 무시하는 것처럼 보였어. 아니면 그는 해독제를 들고 다녔나? 살아남기 위해서 우리는 위급한 상황에 대처할 수 있어야 해. 그런 상황은 우리에게 갑자기 오니까. 오늘은 모든 학생들이 인체 모형을 놓고 실험했어. 우리는 구조팀이 되었어. 사라, 어린 소년이 작은 레고 블록을 삼켰다고 상상해봐. 그의 호흡기관이 제대로 기능을 다 하지 못하게 될 거야. 그 소년이 응급실로 보내어지기 전에 뭔가 조치를 취해야 해. 그렇지 않으면 그 소년은 질식할 거야. 우리 선생님은 우리에게 몇 가지 필요한 기술을 시범 보이셨 어. 그는 사람의 기도를 막고 있는 것을 제거하는 방법을 가르쳐주셨어. 그는 또한 숨을 들이쉬는 방법도 보여주셨어. 우리는 인 형을 누르는 것도 배웠어. "이봐, 배가 아니라 가슴을 눌러" 선생님은 나에게 말씀하셨어. 인체 모형을 가지고 노는 것은 전혀 재 미가 없었지만, 나는 이 가르침을 기억할 거야. 가까운 미래에 내가 그 방법들을 사용하게 될지 누가 알겠어?

poisonous
[pɔ́izənəs]
a. 독이 있는, 독성의

causing poisoning, deadly, harmful
- poison n. 독

I didn't know that rattle snakes were so poisonous.
나는 방울뱀이 그렇게 독이 있는 줄 몰랐어.

prompt
[prámpt]
a. 신속한

quick, done quickly, done right away
- promptly ad. 신속하게

Your teacher was wise for taking prompt action.
너의 선생님이 신속한 조치를 취한 건 현명한 행동이었어.

paralyzed
[pǽrəlàizd]
a. 마비된

unable to move one's body
- paralyze v. 마비시키다 - paralysis n. 마비

Otherwise he could have become paralyzed.
그렇지 않았으면 그는 몸이 마비되었을 수도 있었어.

critical
[krítikəl]
a. 위독한, 위기의

being in danger of death

He could have been in a critical condition.
그는 위독한 상태에 빠질 수도 있었어.

casualty
[kǽʒuəlti]
n. 사상자

a person who is injured or killed in an incident

Sara, are there many casualties from snake bites in the desert?
사라, 사막에서 뱀에게 물리는 사상자들이 많이 있어?

cautious
[kɔ́:ʃəs]
a. 조심성 있는

careful, not reckless
- caution n. 조심

Tourists need to be cautious when traveling through deserts.
여행객들은 사막을 지날 때 조심해야만 해.

camouflage
[kǽmuflà:ʒ]
n. 위장, 위장 수단

disguise that keeps something hidden

Snakes there have natural camouflage.
그곳에 사는 뱀은 타고난 위장술을 가지고 있어.

distinguish
[distíŋgwiʃ]

v. 구별하다

to tell something apart from something different
- distinguished a. 구별되는

People can hardly distinguish between snakes and sand.
사람들은 뱀과 모래를 거의 구별할 수 없어.

biologist
[baiálədʒist]

n. 생물학자

a person who specializes in biology
- biology n. 생물학

Your video clips about that biologist surprised me.
그 생물학자에 대한 너의 비디오는 나를 놀라게 했어.

lethal
[líːθəl]

a. 치명적인

deadly, causing death

How could he just grab such lethal snakes?
그는 그렇게 치명적인 뱀을 어떻게 잡을 수 있었을까?

simultaneously
[sàiməltéiniəsli]

ad. 동시에

at the same time
- simultaneous a. 동시에 일어나는

He even simultaneously explained about snakes while handling them.
그는 뱀을 다루면서 동시에 뱀에 대해 설명하기도 했어.

nervous system
[nə́ːrvəs sístəm]

신경계

the system of the human body that controls organs

He seemed to ignore the fact that their poison could harm his nervous system.
그는 그들의 독이 자신의 신경계를 해칠 수도 있다는 사실을 무시하는 것처럼 보였어.

antidote
[ǽntidòut]

n. 해독제

anti-poison, a substance that can cure poison

Or did he carry an antidote?
아니면 그는 해독제를 들고 다녔나?

cope
[kóup]

v. 대처하다, 극복하다

to deal with, to attempt to overcome problems and difficulties
- cope with ~에 대처하다

In order to survive, we need to be able to cope with emergencies.
살아남기 위해서 우리는 위급한 상황에 대처할 수 있어야 해.

unexpectedly
[ʌ̀nikspéktədli]

ad. 갑자기

surprisingly, abruptly

They come to us unexpectedly.

그런 상황은 우리에게 갑자기 오니까.

experiment
[ikspérəmənt]

v. 실험하다 n. 실험

to test or perform experiments

Today the whole class experimented on a dummy.

오늘은 모든 학생들이 인체 모형을 놓고 실험했어.

rescue
[réskjuː]

n. 구조
v. 구조하다

an attempt to save someone from a dangerous situation

• rescuer n. 구조하는 사람

We became a rescue team.

우리는 구조팀이 되었어.

swallow
[swάlou]

v. 삼키다

to take something through the mouth and into the stomach

Sara, suppose a little boy swallowed a small Lego block.

사라, 어린 소년이 작은 레고 블록을 삼켰다고 상상해봐.

respiratory
[réspərətɔ̀ːri]

a. 호흡의

relating to breathing

• respiration n. 호흡   • respirator n. 인공호흡장치

His respiratory system wouldn't be able to function properly.

그의 호흡기관이 제대로 기능을 다 하지 못하게 될 거야.

emergency
[imə́ːrdʒənsi]

n. 응급상황

a situation that requires immediate help or assistance

• emergent a. 긴급한, 뜻밖의

Before he is sent to the emergency room, something must be done.

그가 응급실로 보내어지기 전에 뭔가 조치를 취해야 해.

suffocate
[sʌ́fəkèit]

v. 질식하다,
   질식시키다

to die because of an inability to breathe

• suffocation n. 질식

Otherwise he will suffocate.

그렇지 않으면 그는 질식할 거야.

essential
[isénʃəl]

a. 필요한

necessary, needed, required

• essence n. 본질, 요소

Our teacher demonstrated some essential techniques to us.
우리 선생님은 우리에게 몇 가지 필요한 기술을 시범 보이셨어.

eliminate
[ilímənèit]

v. 제거하다

to get rid of, to remove

• elimination n. 제거

He showed us how to eliminate things blocking a person's airway.
그는 사람의 기도를 막고 있는 것을 제거하는 방법을 가르쳐주셨어.

inhale
[inhéil]

v. 숨을 들이쉬다

to breath in

He also showed us how to inhale.
그는 또한 숨을 들이쉬는 방법도 보여주셨어.

instruct
[instrʌ́kt]

v. 지도하다

to give information, to teach something

• instruction n. 지도 • instructive a. 교훈적인

We were also instructed to press on the dummy.
우리는 인체 모형을 누르는 것도 배웠어.

abdomen
[ǽbdəmən]

n. 복부

part of the human body above the waist and below the chest

"Hey, press on the chest not on the abdomen," teacher said to me.
"이봐, 배가 아니라 가슴을 눌러" 선생님은 나에게 말씀하셨어.

keep in mind
[kíːp in máind]

기억해 두다

to remember, to think about

Playing with the dummy was not fun at all, but I will keep these instructions in mind.
인체 모형을 가지고 노는 것은 전혀 재미가 없었지만, 나는 이 가르침을 기억할 거야.

Check Again!

A Translate each word into Korean.

1. poisonous ....
2. paralyzed ....
3. eliminate ....
4. antidote ....
5. lethal ....
6. abdomen ....
7. swallow ....
8. inhale ....
9. suffocate ....
10. cautious ....

B Translate each word into English.

1. 사상자 ....
2. 생물학자 ....
3. 신속한 ....
4. 갑자기 ....
5. 위장 ....
6. 구조 ....
7. 호흡의 ....
8. 응급상황 ....
9. 필요한 ....
10. 지도하다 ....

C Fill in the blank with the appropriate word. Refer to the Korean.

1. This gas can harm your n   system.

   이 가스는 신경계를 손상시킬 수 있다.

2. I am color-blind, so I can't d   between green and red.

   나는 색맹이어서 초록색과 빨간색을 구분할 수 없다.

3. Children imitate the way adults c   with emergencies.

   어린이는 어른들이 위급한 상황에 대처하는 방식을 모방한다.

4. Meanwhile, a two-year-old toddler is reported to be in c
   condition.

   한편, 두 살짜리 걸음마 단계의 아이가 위독한 상태라는 보도입니다.

5. The first woman to win a Nobel Prize, Marie Curie, e
   with radioactivity.

   최초의 노벨상 수상 여성인 마리 퀴리는 방사능을 실험했다.

Check More!

다음 밑줄 친 부분에 알맞은 어휘를 골라 빈칸에 쓰시오. 아래의 영영 풀이를 참조하시오.

My wife and I were at a friend's house recently. We noticed our friend talking on the phone while **(A)** simultaneously / stimulatively answering the door, checking on dinner, and changing her baby's diaper. Many of us do the same when we are speaking to someone and our mind is elsewhere. When this happens, we not only lose much of the **(B)** encouragement / enjoyment of what we are doing, but we also become far less focused and effective. To take this to an **(C)** extreme / exclamation, imagine yourself driving down the highway while shaving, drinking coffee, or reading the newspaper. You may be inviting an accident. Just **(D)** keep in mind / keep your head that when doing anything, just focus on what you are doing.

*diaper: 기저귀

(A) at the same instant: ....

(B) the act or state of enjoying: ....

(C) the utmost or highest degree, or a very high degree:

....

(D) to remember, to think about: ....

Chapter 6
Health

Unit 18. Grandma goes to a laughter clinic.

combine exercise and laughter therapy

create **antibodies**

motivate someone to laugh

Episode

Dear Diary,

Do you know how great laughter is? • Laughter works like a miracle and its impact on life is great. • Ha ha ha... My grandma's been combining exercise and laughter therapy for 2 months. • Can you believe she once suffered from depression? • Last year her close friend was diagnosed with Alzheimer's disease. • After hearing the news, she lost her appetite. • She even collapsed. • The doctor said her bone density was decreasing. • She said her hearing was deteriorating. • She concluded that she was aging. • She said that she didn't feel intellectual anymore. • She wasn't willing to interact with anyone. • But now, nothing can impede her. • She is energetic and always motivates us to laugh. • She tries to consume more vegetables than meat.

"Where is my anti-aging cream?" • "Where is my sweatsuit?" • "Can you give me a decaffeinated drink?" she says. • Now all my family is sure that laughter creates antibodies. • Her life expectancy should be increasing. • Even her wrinkles seem to be gone. • She doesn't even have to apply anti-aging cream on her face. • Apparently laughter is the best medicine. • Moreover it's contagious. • So it affects us and spreads like an infectious disease. • If you laugh, who wouldn't laugh along?

다이어리에게,

웃음이 얼마나 대단한지 아니? 웃음은 기적과 같은 효과가 있고 인생에 미치는 영향은 대단해. 하하하… 우리 할머니는 운동과 웃음을 결합시킨 치료를 두 달 동안 받으셨어. 한때 할머니가 우울증에 시달렸다는 걸 믿을 수 있니? 작년에 할머니의 친한 친구 분이 알츠하이머병이라는 진단을 받으셨어. 그 소식을 듣고 할머니는 입맛을 잃으셨어. 할머니는 심지어 쓰러지셨어. 의사는 할머니의 골밀도가 낮아지고 있다고 말했어. 할머니는 청력도 악화되고 있다고 말씀하셨어. 할머니는 자신이 늙고 있다고 결론 내리셨어. 할머니는 자신이 더 이상 지적인 것 같지 않다고 말씀하셨어. 할머니는 더 이상 사람들과 말하려고 하지 않으셨어. 그렇지만 지금은 아무것도 할머니를 막을 수 없어. 할머니는 활기차시고 항상 우리를 웃게 하셔. 할머니는 고기보다는 야채를 더 많이 드시려고 하셔.

"내 노화방지 크림이 어디에 있니?" "내 운동복은 어디에 있니?" "나에게 카페인이 들어 있지 않은 음료수를 줄래?" 말씀하셔. 이제 우리 가족 모두는 웃음이 항체를 만들어 낸다는 걸 확실히 알아. 할머니의 수명은 분명히 연장되었을 거야. 주름조차도 없어진 것 같아. 할머니는 얼굴에 노화방지 크림을 바를 필요조차 없으셔. 분명히 웃음은 최고의 약이야. 더군다나 전염성이 있어. 그래서 웃음은 우리에게 영향을 미치고 전염병처럼 퍼져. 네가 웃는데 누가 따라 웃지 않겠어?

laughter
[læftər]
n. 웃음

the act of laughing
- laugh v. 웃다

Do you know how great laughter is?
웃음이 얼마나 대단한지 아니?

miracle
[mírəkəl]
n. 기적

something amazing or unbelievable
- miraculous a. 기적의

Laughter works like a miracle and its impact on life is great.
웃음은 기적과 같은 효과가 있고 인생에 미치는 영향은 대단해.

impact
[ímpækt]
n. 영향
v. 영향을 주다

powerful effect or influence

Laughter works like a miracle and its impact on life is great.
웃음은 기적과 같은 효과가 있고 인생에 미치는 영향은 대단해.

combine
[kəmbáin]
v. 결합하다

to put one or more things together at the same time
- combination n. 조합

My grandma's been combining exercise and laughter therapy for 2 months.
우리 할머니는 운동과 웃음을 결합시킨 치료를 두 달 동안 받으셨어.

depression
[dipréʃən]
n. 우울증

a mental disease where a person is very sad
- depress v. ~을 우울하게 하다   - depressed a. 우울한

Can you believe she once suffered from depression?
한때 그녀가 우울증에 시달렸다는 걸 믿을 수 있니?

diagnose
[dáiəgnòus]
v. 진단하다

to recognize a disease by its signs and symptoms
- diagnosis n. 진단

Last year her close friend was diagnosed with Alzheimer's disease.
작년에 그녀의 친한 친구분이 알츠하이머병이라는 진단을 받으셨어.

appetite
[æpitàit]
n. 식욕, 입맛

desire to eat food
- appetizer n. 애피타이저

After hearing the news, she lost her appetite.
그 소식을 듣고 그녀는 입맛을 잃으셨어.

collapse
[kəlǽps]
v. 쓰러지다

to fall down completely

She even collapsed.
그녀는 심지어 쓰러지셨어.

density
[dénsəti]
n. 밀도

thickness, amount of mass per area
• dense a. 조밀한

The doctor said her bone density was decreasing.
의사는 그녀의 골밀도가 낮아지고 있다고 말했어.

deteriorate
[ditíəriərèit]
v. 악화되다

to become less in quality or amount, to gradually break down
• deterioration n. 악화 • deteriorating a. 악화되고 있는

She said her hearing was deteriorating.
그녀는 청력도 악화되고 있다고 말씀하셨어.

aging
[éidʒiŋ]
n. 나이 먹음, 노화

the process of becoming older
• age v. 나이를 먹다, 늙다 n. 나이

She concluded that she was aging.
그녀는 자신이 늙고 있다고 결론 내리셨어.

intellectual
[ìntəléktʃuəl]
a. 지적인
n. 지식인

intelligent, able to think and reason well
• intellect n. 지성

She said that she didn't feel intellectual anymore.
그녀는 자신이 더 이상 지적인 것 같지 않다고 말씀하셨어.

interact
[ìntərǽkt]
v. 상호작용하다

to participate in actions with other people
• interaction n. 상호작용 • interactive a. 상호작용하는

She wasn't willing to interact with anyone.
그녀는 더 이상 사람들과 말하려고 하지 않으셨어.

impede
[impíːd]
v. 방해하다,
   지연시키다

to prevent or disrupt the ability to do something
• impediment n. 방해, 지연

But now, nothing can impede her.
그렇지만 지금은 아무것도 그녀를 막을 수 없어.

energetic
[ènərdʒétik]
a. 활기에 찬

having lots of energy and vigor
- energy n. 에너지

She is energetic and always motivates us to laugh.
그녀는 활기차시고 항상 우리를 웃게 하셔.

motivate
[móutəvèit]
v. 동기부여하다,
자극하다

to encourage, to provide a reason to act
- motivation n. 동기부여, 자극 • motive n. 동기 a. 움직이게 하는

She is energetic and always motivates us to laugh.
그녀는 활기차시고 항상 우리를 웃게 하셔.

consume
[kənsú:m]
v. 먹다, 소비하다

to eat or drink something
- consumption n. 소비

She tries to consume more vegetables than meat.
그녀는 고기보다는 야채를 더 많이 드시려고 하셔.

anti-aging
[æntiéidʒiŋ]
a. 노화방지의

slowing down the aging process

Where is my anti-aging cream?
내 노화방지 크림이 어디에 있니?

sweatsuit
[swétsù:t]
n. 운동복

an outfit worn for exercise and activity

Where is my sweatsuit?
내 운동복은 어디에 있니?

decaffeinated
[di:kǽfiənèitid]
a. 카페인이 없는

not containing any caffeine

"Can you give me a decaffeinated drink?" she says.
"나에게 카페인이 들어 있지 않은 음료수를 줄래?" 말씀하셔.

antibody
[ǽntibàdi]
n. 항체

part of one's body that fights against disease

Now all my family is sure that laughter creates antibodies.
이제 우리 가족 모두는 웃음이 항체를 만들어 낸다는 걸 확실히 알아.

life expectancy
[láif iklspéktənsi]
평균 수명

how long a person is expected to live for

Her life expectancy should be increasing.

그녀의 수명은 분명히 연장되었을 거야.

wrinkle
[ríŋkəl]
n. 주름

a line in the skin usually due to old age

Even her wrinkles seem to be gone.

그녀의 주름조차도 없어진 것 같아.

apply
[əplái]
v. 바르다, 적용하다

to put something on, to use

• application n. (연고, 화장품 등을) 바름, 적용

She doesn't even have to apply anti-aging cream on her face.

그녀는 얼굴에 노화방지 크림을 바를 필요조차 없으셔.

apparently
[əpǽrəntli]
ad. 분명히

seemingly, outwardly

• apparent a. 명백한

Apparently laughter is the best medicine.

분명히 웃음은 최고의 악이야.

contagious
[kəntéidʒəs]
a. 전염성의

spreading easily to cause similar action in others

• contagion n. 전염, 감염

Moreover it's contagious.

더군다나 그것은 전염성이 있어.

infectious
[infékʃəs]
a. 전염성의

contagious, capable of spreading rapidly

• infect v. 전염시키다 • infection n. 전염, 감염

So it affects us and spreads like an infectious disease.

그래서 그것은 우리에게 영향을 미치고 전염병처럼 퍼져.

Check Again!

A Translate each word into Korean.

1. apparently ....
2. contagious ....
3. density ....
4. impede ....
5. depression ....
6. diagnose ....
7. consume ....
8. collapse ....
9. wrinkle ....
10. deteriorate ....

B Translate each word into English.

1. 동기부여하다 ....
2. 노화방지의 ....
3. 웃음 ....
4. 카페인이 없는 ....
5. 항체 ....
6. 평균 수명 ....
7. 결합하다 ....
8. 바르다 ....
9. 식욕 ....
10. 지적인 ....

C Fill in the blank with the appropriate word. Refer to the Korean.

1. TV has a great i   on our lives.

   TV는 우리 삶에 대단한 영향을 끼친다.

2. My niece is two years old and she was d   with autism.

   내 조카딸은 두 살인데 자폐증 진단을 받았다.

3. A person's life e   depends on a lot of factors.

   사람의 평균 수명은 많은 요인에 달려 있다.

4. Young children develop social skills as they i   with people around them.

   어린 아이들은 주변에 있는 사람들과 상호작용하면서 사회성을 키운다.

5. Tuberculosis remains one of the most deadly i   diseases in the world today.

   결핵은 오늘날도 여전히 세계에서 가장 무서운 전염병의 하나로 남아 있다.

Check More!

수능 기출 응용

(A), (B), (C) 각 밑줄 친 부분에 알맞은 어휘를 짝지은 것으로 가장 적절한 것을 고르시오.

There are few people who do not react to music to some degree. The power of music is **(A)** contaminating / contagious. People respond in different ways. To some it is mainly an instinctive, exciting sound to which they dance or move their bodies. Other people listen for its message, or take an **(B)** intellectual / infectious approach to its form and construction, appreciating its formal patterns or originality. Above all, however, there can be hardly anyone who is not moved by some kind of music. Music **(C)** covers / curves the whole range of emotions: it can make us feel happy or sad, helpless or energetic, and some music is capable of overtaking the mind until it forgets all else. It works on the subconscious, creating or enhancing mood and unlocking deep memories.

(A)	(B)	(C)
① contagious	intellectual	covers
② contaminating	intellectual	curves
③ contagious	intellectual	curves
④ contaminating	infectious	covers
⑤ contagious	infectious	curves

+ 접두사 ex- / in- / inter-

ex-는 'out'이라는 뜻의 접두사로, '~로부터,' '~밖으로'라는 뜻의 단어를 만든다. in-은 'in'이라는 뜻의 접두사로, '안으로'라는 뜻의 단어를 만든다. inter-는 'between'이라는 뜻의 접두사로, '~의 사이에'라는 뜻의 단어를 만든다.

ex-

halare 숨을 쉬다
ex + halare = exhale 숨을 내쉬다
ex) The yoga instructor told us to exhale slowly.
요가 강사는 우리에게 숨을 천천히 내쉬라고 했다.

- **exit** 나가다, 퇴장하다
- **export** 수출하다   cf) **import** 수입하다
- **exclude** 제외하다   cf) **include** 포함하다
- **extract** ~을 빼내다
- **excavate** 발굴하다
- **explicit** 명시적인, 노골적인   cf) **implicit** 암시적인
- **external** 외부의   cf) **internal** 내부의

in-

put 넣다
in + put = input 투입하다, 입력하다
ex) He quickly inputted the new data into the computer.
그는 서둘러서 새 정보를 컴퓨터에 입력하였다.

- **inhale** 숨을 들이마시다   cf) **exhale** 숨을 내쉬다
- **include** 포함하다   cf) **exclude** 제외하다
- **income** 수입
- **import** 수입하다   cf) **export** 수출하다
- **inbound** 본국행의   cf) **outbound** 외국행의
- **involve** 포함시키다, 관계시키다
- **inseam** 안쪽 솔기

inter-

racial 인종의

inter + racial = interracial 인종간의

ex) Interracial marriages are becoming more common.
다른 인종간의 결혼이 점점 흔해지고 있다.

- **international** 국제의
- **intermediate** 중재자, 중간의
- **intervene** 사이에 끼다
- **interrupt** 도중에 방해하다
- **interrogate** 심문하다
- **intercept** 가로채다
- **interject** 불쑥 끼워 넣다

Internal Organs 장기

+ brain 뇌

+ lungs 폐 / + stomach 위

+ liver 간 / + heart 심장

+ kidneys 신장

+ intestines 창자

+ bladder 방광

+ tonsils 편도선

VOCA EDGE
RED

Chapter 7. People

Unit 19. The Volcanoes are back.

Unit 20. We have great brothers.

Unit 21. What historical figures do you want to meet?

Unit 22. Are mom and dad compatible?

Chapter 7
People

Unit 19. The Volcanoes are back.

have fame all over the world

make an attempt at hypnosis

become more **receptive**

Episode

Dear Diary,
Finally, the Volcanoes has returned from their Asia tour. • I bought their new album **released** last week. • Today I am going to their concert at the **grand** concert hall. • My mom is supposed to **give** me **a ride** there.

Mom: Bomi, pack your **banner**. • You'd better hurry. • What if the streets are **congested**? • You need to get there early to get a good seat. • What if someone **blocks** your view? • Bomi, this song is **familiar**.
Bomi: Actually, they **revived** a few Korean pop songs.
Mom: What **genre** of music do they cover other than hip-hop?
Bomi: They cover a wide **range** of music.

As a fan of the Beatles, she says their music **inspires** her. • She is not interested in **contemporary** music. • She thinks there is something **negative** about hip-hop music. • Every morning I **insert** the Volcanoes' CDs into my player. • And my attempt at **hypnosis** is starting to work out. • Now she seems to be becoming more **receptive** to their music. • She knows that there are many Volcanoes' **fanatics** all over the world. • Now she knows that they have **fame** all over the world. • She also knows that they are **renowned** even in Japan.

I always tell my mom that my hero, Youngwoong, attracts people like a **magnet**. • Youngwoong is **passionate** about music. • He always says, "Music **sustains** me." • Doesn't he sound like a **specialist**? • If mom saw him playing the **electric** guitar, she would be **speechless**. • Today's concert is **meaningful**. • The profit is going to be used to help the kids with **leukemia**. • It will also be used to help the kids suffering from **famine**.

다이어리에게,
마침내, 볼케이노가 아시아 순회공연을 마치고 돌아왔어. 나는 지난주에 발매된 그들의 새 앨범을 샀어. 나는 오늘 대형 경기장에서 열리는 그들의 콘서트를 보러 갈 거야. 우리 엄마가 나를 거기까지 태워주기로 하셨어.

엄마: 보미, 현수막 잘 챙겨라. 서둘러야겠다. 길이 막히면 어떻게 하니? 좋은 자리 맡으려면 일찍 가야 해. 다른 사람이 네 시야를 막으면 어떻게 하니? 보미, 이 노래는 친숙하구나.
보미: 실은 그들이 몇몇 한국 가요를 다시 불렀어요.
엄마: 힙합 말고 그들은 어떤 장르의 음악을 하고 있니?
보미: 광범위한 음악을 다루고 있어요.

비틀즈의 팬인 엄마는 비틀즈의 음악이 그녀에게 영감을 주었다고 말해. 엄마는 요즘 음악에는 별로 관심이 없으셔. 힙합 음악에는 뭔가 부정적인 것들이 있다고 생각하셔. 매일 아침 나는 볼케이노의 시디를 플레이어에 넣어. 그리고 최면을 걸려는 나의 시도가 효과를 발휘하기 시작해. 이제 엄마는 그들의 음악을 좀 더 받아들이기 시작하는 것 같아. 전 세계적으로 볼케이노의 열혈팬들이 많다는 것을 알고 계셔. 이제 엄마는 그들이 전 세계에서 명성을 떨치고 있다는 것을 알고 계셔. 심지어 일본에서도 유명하다는 것을 알고 계셔.

나는 늘 우리 엄마에게 나의 영웅인 영웅이 사람들을 자석처럼 끌어당긴다고 말해. 그는 음악에 열정적이야. 그는 늘 "음악이 나를 지탱한다"라고 말해. 정말 전문가다운 소리 아닌가? 만일 엄마가 그가 전자기타 연주하는 모습을 보신다면, 감탄하실 거야. 오늘의 콘서트는 의미 있어. 수익금은 백혈병 어린이들을 돕는 데 사용될 거야. 그것은 또한 기아로 고통 받는 아이들을 돕는 데에도 쓰일 거야.

release
[rilíːs]
v. (앨범, 영화) 등을
발매하다
n. 발매, 출시

to become available

I bought their new album released last week.
나는 지난주에 발매된 그들의 새 앨범을 샀어.

grand
[grǽnd]
a. 커다란, 장관의

great, spectacular
• grandeur n. 웅장함, 장대함

Today I am going to their concert at the grand concert hall.
나는 오늘 대형 경기장에서 열리는 그들의 콘서트를 보러 갈 거야.

give a ride
[gív ə ráid]
태워주다

to take someone somewhere, usually in a car or other vehicle

My mom is supposed to give me a ride there.
우리 엄마가 나를 거기까지 태워주기로 하셨어.

banner
[bǽnər]
n. 현수막, 기치, 주장

a large sign written on cloth or paper

Bomi, pack your banner.
보미, 현수막 잘 챙겨라.

congested
[kəndʒéstid]
a. 정체된, 막힌

overly crowded, packed, full
• congest v. 정체시키다 • congestion n. 정체, 혼잡

You'd better hurry. What if the streets are congested?
서둘러야겠다. 길이 막히면 어떻게 하니?

block
[blɔ́k]
v. 막다, 차단하다
n. 블록

to prevent from going or seeing, to get in the way

You need to get there early to get a good seat. What if someone blocks your view?
좋은 자리 맡으려면 일찍 가야 해. 다른 사람이 네 시야를 막으면 어떻게 하니?

familiar
[fəmíljər]
a. 익숙한, 친숙한

well acquainted, well-known
• familiarize v. 친숙하게 하다 • familiarity n. 친함, 잘 앎

Bomi, this song is familiar.
보미, 이 노래는 친숙하구나.

revive
[riváiv]

v. 되살리다,
   재공연하다

to bring back to life; to present a new production of a song, a play, or an opera
- revival n. 부활, 재생, 리바이벌

Actually, they revived a few Korean pop songs.
실은 그들이 몇몇 한국 가요를 다시 불렀어요.

genre
[ʒɑ́:nrə]

n. 장르

a type, a category

What genre of music do they cover other than hip-hop?
힙합 말고 그들은 어떤 장르의 음악을 하고 있니?

range
[réindʒ]

n. 범주, 범위

the total area or amount covered by something

They cover a wide range of music.
그들은 광범위한 음악을 다루고 있어요.

inspire
[inspáiər]

v. 영감을 주다,
   고무시키다

to influence someone to do something in a positive way
- inspiration n. 영감 - inspirational a. 고무적인, 영감을 주는

As a fan of the Beatles, she says their music inspires her.
비틀즈의 팬인 그녀는 비틀즈의 음악이 그녀에게 영감을 주었다고 말해.

contemporary
[kəntémpərèri]

a. 동시대의, 현대의

modern, current, of today

She is not interested in contemporary music.
그녀는 요즘 음악에는 별로 관심이 없으셔.

negative
[négətiv]

a. 부정적인

bad, not positive

She thinks there is something negative about hip-hop music.
그녀는 힙합 음악에는 뭔가 부정적인 것들이 있다고 생각하셔.

insert
[insə́:rt]

v. 넣다, 삽입하다

to put something into something else
- insertion n. 삽입, 끼워넣음

Every morning I insert the Volcanoes' CDs into my player.
매일 아침 나는 볼케이노의 시디를 플레이어에 넣어.

hypnosis
[hipnóusis]
n. 최면

a form of mind control
• hypnotize v. 최면을 걸다 • hypnotism n. 최면술, 최면상태

And my attempt at hypnosis is starting to work out.
그리고 최면을 걸려는 나의 시도가 효과를 발휘하기 시작해.

receptive
[riséptiv]
a. 수용적인,
받아들이는

open and responsive to ideas
• reception n. 수용

Now she seems to be becoming more receptive to their music.
이제 그녀는 그들의 음악을 좀 더 받아들이기 시작하는 것 같아.

fanatic
[fənǽtik]
n. 열광자, 광신자

a person who is crazy or who has a strong interest in something
• fanatical a. 광적인, 열중한

She knows that there are many Volcanoes' fanatics all over the world.
그녀는 전 세계적으로 볼케이노의 열혈팬들이 많다는 것을 알고 계셔.

fame
[féim]
n. 명성

a measure of being famous, renown
• famous a. 유명한

Now she knows that they have fame all over the world.
이제 그녀는 그들이 전 세계에서 명성을 떨치고 있다는 것을 알고 계셔.

renowned
[rináund]
a. 유명한

very famous
• renown n. 명성

She also knows that they are renowned even in Japan.
그녀는 그들이 심지어 일본에서도 유명하다는 것을 알고 계셔.

magnet
[mǽgnit]
n. 자석

something that attracts or draws other things
• magnetic a. 자석의

I always tell my mom that my hero, Youngwoong, attracts people like a magnet.
나는 늘 우리 엄마에게 나의 영웅인 영웅이 사람들을 자석처럼 끌어당긴다고 말해.

passionate
[pǽʃənit]
a. 열정적인

capable of expressing intense feeling or caring greatly
• passion n. 열정

Youngwoong is passionate about music.
그는 음악에 열정적이야.

sustain
[səstéin]
v. 지탱하다, 기운내게 하다

to keep alive, to support

• sustenance n. 지탱, 유지　• sustainable a. 지탱할 수 있는

He always says, "Music sustains me."
그는 늘 "음악이 나를 지탱한다"라고 말해.

specialist
[spéʃəlist]
n. 전문가

a person who is extremely skilled in a particular thing

• specialize v. 전문으로 하다

Doesn't he sound like a specialist?
정말 전문가다운 소리 아닌가?

electric
[iléktrik]
a. 전기의

powered by electricity

• electricity n. 전기　• electrical a. 전기에 관한

If mom saw him playing the electric guitar, she would be speechless.
만일 엄마가 그가 전자기타 연주하는 모습을 보신다면, 감탄하실 거야.

speechless
[spíːtʃlis]
a. 감탄한, 말문이 막힐 정도로 놀란

amazed, astounded

If mom saw him playing the electric guitar, she would be speechless.
만일 엄마가 그가 전자기타 연주하는 모습을 보신다면, 감탄하실 거야.

meaningful
[míːniŋfəl]
a. 의미 있는

having a purpose or reason

Today's concert is meaningful.
오늘의 콘서트는 의미 있어.

leukemia
[luːkíːmiə]
n. 백혈병

a deadly form of cancer (characterized by an abnormal increase in the number of white blood cells in one's body)

The profit is going to be used to help the kids with leukemia.
수익금은 백혈병 어린이들을 돕는 데 사용될 거야.

famine
[fǽmin]
n. 기아

hunger, poverty

It will also be used to help the kids suffering from famine.
그것은 또한 기아로 고통 받는 아이들을 돕는 데에도 쓰일 거야.

Check Again!

A Translate each word into Korean.

1. banner ....
2. congested ....
3. inspire ....
4. contemporary ....
5. negative ....
6. hypnosis ....
7. leukemia ....
8. speechless ....
9. renowned ....
10. sustain ....

B Translate each word into English.

1. 커다란 ....
2. 전문가 ....
3. 전기의 ....
4. 막다 ....
5. 자석 ....
6. 명성 ....
7. 되살리다 ....
8. 장르 ....
9. 열광자 ....
10. 의미 있는 ....

C Fill in the blank with the appropriate word. Refer to the Korean.

1. This magazine covers a wide r   of topics.
   이 잡지는 다양한 주제를 다룬다.

2. After a few minutes, a white van pulled over to give us a
   r   .
   몇 분 후에 흰색 밴이 우리를 태워주기 위해 섰다.

3. When you are p   about your work, it's not really work
   anymore.
   자신의 일에 열정이 있으면, 그것은 더 이상 일이 아니다.

4. U.S. consumers may be becoming more r   to text messaging
   ads.
   미국 소비자들이 점점 문자 광고를 받아들이고 있는지도 모른다.

5. If you are paying for others, tell the driver before you i
   your card into the reader.
   다른 사람의 것을 지불할 거라면, 카드를 리더기에 넣기 전에 운전사에게 말하세요.

Check More!

(A), (B), (C) 각 밑줄 친 부분에 알맞은 어휘를 짝지은 것으로 가장 적절한 것을 고르시오.

Would a modern music composer be your first choice for a hero? Or would you think of the painter of a **(A)** contemporary / contemplative masterpiece? If you are like most people, the answer to both questions is "no." More likely, a sports hero or a movie star would be your first choice. It seems that the worlds of contemporary art and music have failed to offer people works that **(B)** despise / inspire them. Moreover they also fail to reflect human achievements. People, therefore, have lost interest in modern arts and have turned to sports stars and other popular **(C)** formulas / figures to find their role models.

(A)	(B)	(C)
① contemplative	despise	formulas
② contemporary	inspire	figures
③ contemplative	inspire	formulas
④ contemporary	despise	formulas
⑤ contemplative	inspire	figures

make a strenuous **effort**

know the **fundamental principles**

Stop the War!

advocate a halt to the war

Episode

Dear Sara,

What **induced** Hoony to change like that? • He has been **subscribing** to a science magazine. • He even read the **biography** of Albert Einstein. • He thinks it is important to know the **fundamental** principles of physics. • Today he showed me a strange **formula**. • It was Einstein's theory of **relativity**. • Hoony wants to be the first Korean **physicist** to win the Nobel Prize. • He's becoming very **patriotic**. • He is also making a **strenuous** effort to improve his water rocket. • He spends **entirely** too much time experimenting with his rocket. • Then he puts it on the shelf to keep it **intact**. • He **polishes** it with wax every morning.

Bomi: Why are you pasting the **metal** pieces on its body?
Hoony: I'm trying to make my rocket fly for the longest **period** of time.
• I will make this **extraordinary**. • Finally, it will **surpass** Minsu's.

Sara, does your brother still enjoy making **presidential** speeches? • I hope he gets **elected** school president, competing with 5 other **candidates**. • Once he makes his **pledges** to do well in front of the students, they will vote for him. • He will **attain** his goal of being elected. • I remember him being quite an **eloquent** speaker. • He demonstrated his abilities in front of the American **Embassy**. • At that time he was **advocating** a **halt** to the war. • He tried to emphasize **non-violence**. • I'm sure your brother will be a good **statesman**.

사라에게,
무엇이 후니를 그렇게 변하게 했을까? 후니는 과학 잡지를 정기구독하고 있어. 심지어 알버트 아인슈타인의 전기도 읽었어. 후니는 물리학의 근본 원리를 아는 것이 중요하다고 생각해. 오늘 후니는 내게 이상한 공식을 보여주었어. 그것은 아인슈타인의 상대성 이론이었어. 후니는 노벨상을 타는 최초의 한국 물리학자가 되기를 바래. 후니는 아주 애국심이 많아지고 있어. 후니는 또 물로켓의 성능을 나아지게 하려고 부단한 노력을 하고 있어. 로켓을 가지고 실험하는 데 아주 많은 시간을 보내. 그리고는 후니는 로켓이 손상되지 않도록 선반에 올려놓아. 매일 아침 왁스로 광택까지 내.

보미: 몸체에 왜 쇳조각을 붙이고 있는 거야?
후니: 내 로켓이 가장 오랜 시간 동안 날도록 만들고 있어. 나는 이것을 특별하게 만들 거야. 결국에는 민수의 로켓을 이길 거야.

사라, 네 남동생은 여전히 회장연설하는 걸 좋아하니? 나는 네 남동생이 다섯 명의 다른 후보들과 경쟁해서 학교회장에 당선되길 바래. 일단 네 남동생이 학생들 앞에서 잘하겠다고 공약하면, 학생들이 그에게 투표할 거야. 네 남동생은 회장으로 뽑히는 목표를 달성할 수 있을 거야. 나는 네 남동생이 말재주가 있는 것으로 기억하고 있어. 네 남동생은 미국 대사관 앞에서 자신의 능력을 보여주었잖아. 그 당시에 네 남동생은 전쟁 중지를 주장하고 있었어. 네 남동생은 비폭력을 강조하려고 했어. 네 남동생은 분명히 훌륭한 정치인이 될 거야.

induce
[indjú:s]
v. 유도하다, 권유하다

to cause to happen
- inducement n. 유도, 권유

What induced Hoony to change like that?
무엇이 후니를 그렇게 변하게 했을까?

subscribe
[sʌ́bskraib]
v. 정기구독하다

to sign up in order to receive something periodically
- subscription n. 정기구독 - subscribe to ~을 정기구독하다

He has been subscribing to a science magazine.
그는 과학 잡지를 정기구독하고 있어.

biography
[baiágrəfi]
n. 전기

a book written about a person
- autobiography n. 자서전 - biographical a. 전기적인, 전기문의

He even read the biography of Albert Einstein.
그는 심지어 알버트 아인슈타인의 전기도 읽었어.

fundamental
[fʌ̀ndəméntl]
a. 근본적인

of central importance
- fundamentally ad. 근본적으로

He thinks it is important to know the fundamental principles of physics.
그는 물리학의 근본 원리를 아는 것이 중요하다고 생각해.

formula
[fɔ́:rmjələ]
n. 공식

a set of numbers and characters expressing a scientific rule

Today he showed me a strange formula.
오늘 그는 내게 이상한 공식을 보여주었어.

relativity
[rèlətívəti]
n. 상대성

a scientific law discovered by Einstein that is fundamental to physics
- relative a. 상대적인 - relatively ad. 상대적으로

It was Einstein's theory of relativity.
그것은 아인슈타인의 상대성 이론이었어.

physicist
[fízisist]
n. 물리학자

a person who studies and researches the science of physics
- physics n. 물리학

Hoony wants to be the first Korean physicist to win the Nobel Prize.

후니는 노벨상을 타는 최초의 한국 물리학자가 되기를 바래.

patriotic
[pèitriátik]
a. 애국심이 강한,
   애국적인

strongly supporting one's own country
- patriot n. 애국자 • patriotism n. 애국심

He's becoming very patriotic.

그는 아주 애국심이 많아지고 있어.

strenuous
[strénjuəs]
a. 부단한,
   분투를 요하는

demanding or requiring vigorous exertion, laborious

He is also making a strenuous effort to improve his water rocket.

그는 또 물로켓의 성능을 나아지게 하려고 부단한 노력을 하고 있어.

entirely
[entáiərli]
ad. 아주, 전적으로

completely, absolutely
- entire a. 전적인

He spends entirely too much time experimenting with his rocket.

그는 로켓을 가지고 실험하는 데 아주 많은 시간을 보내.

intact
[intǽkt]
a. 손상되지 않은,
   손대지 않은

undamaged, uninjured

Then he puts it on the shelf to keep it intact.

그리고는 그는 로켓이 손상되지 않도록 선반에 올려놓아.

polish
[páliʃ]
v. 광을 내다

to rub something to make it shiny
- polished a. 광을 낸

He polishes it with wax every morning.

그는 매일 아침 왁스로 광택까지 내.

metal
[métl]
n. 금속

a hard substance such as iron and steel

Why are you pasting the metal pieces on its body?

몸체에 왜 쇳조각을 붙이고 있는 거야?

period
[píəriəd]
n. 기간

the amount of time between two points
• periodical n. 정기간행물 • periodic a. 주기적인
I'm trying to make my rocket fly for the longest period of time.
내 로켓이 가장 오랜 시간 동안 날도록 만들고 있어.

extraordinary
[ikstrɔ́ːrdənèri]
a. 비범한, 우수한

exceptional, marvelous
• extraordinarily ad. 비범하게, 특별히
I will make this extraordinary.
나는 이것을 특별하게 만들 거야.

surpass
[sərpǽs]
v. 능가하다

to outdo someone or something
Finally, it will surpass Minsu's.
결국에는 민수의 로켓을 이길 거야.

presidential
[prèzidénʃəl]
a. 회장의, 대통령의

having to do with the president
• president n. 회장, 대통령
Sara, does your brother still enjoy making presidential speeches?
사라, 네 남동생은 여전히 회장연설하는 걸 좋아하니?

elect
[ilékt]
v. 선출하다

to choose someone by voting for them
• election n. 선출, 선거
I hope he gets elected school president, competing with 5 other candidates.
나는 그가 다섯 명의 다른 후보들과 경쟁해서 학교회장에 당선되길 바래.

candidate
[kǽndədèit]
n. 후보자

a person attempting to be hired, elected, etc. for a position
I hope he gets elected school president, competing with 5 other candidates.
나는 그가 다섯 명의 다른 후보들과 경쟁해서 학교회장에 당선되길 바래.

pledge
[plédʒ]

n. 공약, 서약
v. 서약하다, 공약하다

a promise to do something
- make a pledge 공약하다

Once he makes his pledges to do well in front of the students, they will vote for him.
일단 그가 학생들 앞에서 잘하겠다고 공약하면, 학생들이 그에게 투표할 거야.

attain
[ətéin]

v. 달성하다

to achieve something, to accomplish
- attainment n. 달성, 성취 • attainable a. 성취할 수 있는

He will attain his goal of being elected.
그는 회장으로 뽑히는 목표를 달성할 수 있을 거야.

eloquent
[éləkwənt]

a. 말재주 있는,
웅변의

very well-spoken and well-mannered
- eloquence n. 웅변, 호소력 • eloquently ad. 호소력 있게, 웅변력 있게

I remember him being quite an eloquent speaker.
나는 그가 말재주가 있는 것으로 기억하고 있어.

embassy
[émbəsi]

n. 대사관

the official residence and office of an ambassador

He demonstrated his abilities in front of the American Embassy.
그는 미국 대사관 앞에서 자신의 능력을 보여주었잖아.

advocate
[ǽdvəkèit]

v. 주장하다, 옹호하다

to recommend a particular action or plan publicly

At that time he was advocating a halt to the war.
그 당시에 그는 전쟁 중지를 주장하고 있었어.

halt
[hɔ́:lt]

n. 정지 v. 멈추다

the end, stoppage

At that time he was advocating a halt to the war.
그 당시에 그는 전쟁 중지를 주장하고 있었어.

non-violence
[nɔ́nvàiələns]

n. 비폭력

abstention from violence, nonaggression
- non-violent a. 비폭력의

He tried to emphasize non-violence.
그는 비폭력을 강조하려고 했어.

statesman
[stéitsmən]

n. 정치인

a politician; a person well-educated in politics and government

I'm sure your brother will be a good statesman.
네 남동생은 분명히 훌륭한 정치인이 될 거야.

Check Again!

A Translate each word into Korean.

1. induce ....
2. intact ....
3. eloquent ....
4. attain ....
5. extraordinary ....
6. period ....
7. relativity ....
8. surpass ....
9. entirely ....
10. biography ....

B Translate each word into English.

1. 공식 ....
2. 정치인 ....
3. 물리학자 ....
4. 애국심이 강한 ....
5. 광을 내다 ....
6. 근본적인 ....
7. 후보자 ....
8. 정지 ....
9. 대사관 ....
10. 비폭력 ....

C Fill in the blank with the appropriate word. Refer to the Korean.

1. I'd like to s   to a science magazine.

   나는 과학 잡지를 정기구독하고 싶다.

2. We hoped she would get e   mayor of our town.

   우리는 그녀가 우리 시의 시장으로 당선되길 바랐다.

3. Janet has been making a s   effort to lose weight.

   자넷은 살을 빼기 위해 부단한 노력을 기울여왔다.

4. He made his p   to rescue the poor and the suffering.

   그는 가난한 사람들과 고통받는 사람들을 구제하겠다고 공약했다.

5. Stricken with polio, F. D. Roosevelt made P   speeches from a seated position.

   소아마비에 걸려서 F.D. 루즈벨트는 앉은 자세로 대통령 연설을 하였다.

Check More!

다음 밑줄 친 부분에 알맞은 어휘를 골라 빈칸에 쓰시오. 아래의 영영 풀이를 참조하시오.

A small number of people have recognized the value of wild plants in Korea. They are fascinated by the beauty of these plants.

Their beauty **(A)** introduced / induced them to conserve them after discovering the tragic realities these plants face. Because of indifference to and **(B)** destruction / destroy of their natural habitats, some wild plants face an uncertain future. Given this situation, these people have striven to conserve the wild plants growing in Korea. They have taught the public to value plant species and **(C)** launched / reached efforts to preserve wild plants for generations to come. Thanks to their efforts, more Koreans now understand the full value of their precious wild plants.

(A) to cause to happen: ....

(B) the act of destroying: ....

(C) to set going; to initiate: ....

Chapter 7
People

make a commitment to help society

make a historic **voyage**

long for eternal life

be one's **subordinate**

Episode

Bomi: Sara, who do you think are some of the world's most **influential** people? • And what **qualities** distinguish them? • How did Bill Gates earn such an **astronomical** amount of money? • Does he have some kind of **intuition** that allows him to see the future in business? • Or is he just a **money-oriented** person?

Sara: I don't think he is money-oriented. • He is a **philanthropist**. • His **foundation** benefits many people.

Bomi: Really? So he does have some **mercy**. • What's the **primary** goal of his foundation? • Does it support **prodigies**?

Sara: Exactly. It supports future scientists **throughout** the world.

Bomi: It **nurtures** future Bill Gates.

Sara: Right. He's made a **commitment** to help society.

Bomi: Are there any historical **figures** you are interested in?

Sara: I'd like to meet an **adventurer** like Columbus. • I'd like to ask why he **ventured** out into the unknown world. • I wonder how he could have made such a historic **voyage**.

Bomi: I'd like to ask if spices such as pepper were so **priceless**. • And I'd like to ask him, "If I brought you a crate of pepper, would you be my **subordinate**?"

Sara: Interesting. If you met the Chinese **Emperor**, Shin Huang-di, what would you say?

Bomi: The emperor who longed for **eternal** life? • I'd say, "Hey, why don't you stop drinking **toxic** liquids?" or "Why don't you stop **disciplining** your army so cruelly?"

Sara: If you said that, you'd be **exiled**.

Bomi: He should know that he is a **tyrant**. • His people were suffering under his **regime**.

Sara: Right. If he hadn't died early, he could have **fled** his own country.

Bomi: Exactly. He could have been **assassinated**.

....

보미: 사라, 세상에서 가장 영향력 있는 사람들은 누구라고 생각해? 그리고 어떤 자질이 그들을 유명하게 만들지? 빌 게이츠는 어떻게 그런 천문학적인 양의 돈을 벌었을까? 그는 일종의 직관력 같은 것이 있어서 비즈니스의 미래를 볼 수 있는 것일까? 아니면 그냥 금전만능주의자일 뿐일까?
사라: 그는 금전만능주의자는 아니라고 생각해. 그는 박애주의자야. 그의 재단은 많은 사람들에게 혜택을 주고 있어.
보미: 정말이니? 그렇다면 그는 자비심이 있는 거네. 그의 재단의 일차적인 목표는 뭐야? 천재들을 지원하는 거야?
사라: 맞아. 전 세계에 있는 미래의 과학자들을 지원하고 있어.
보미: 미래의 빌 게이츠를 길러내는구나.
사라: 그래. 그는 사회를 돕겠다고 공약했어.
보미: 네가 관심을 가지고 있는 역사적인 인물들이 있니?
사라: 나는 콜럼버스 같은 탐험가를 만나고 싶어. 그가 왜 미지의 세계를 향해 모험을 나섰는지 물어보고 싶어. 그가 어떻게 그렇게 대단한 역사적인 항해를 해냈는지 궁금해.
보미: 나는 후추 같은 향신료가 그렇게 귀했는지 묻고 싶어. 그리고 "후추 한 상자 가져오면, 제 부하가 되어주겠어요?"라고 물어보고 싶어.
사라: 재밌네. 만일 네가 중국의 진시황제를 만난다면, 뭐라고 할래?
보미: 영원히 살고 싶어 했던 그 황제? "이보게, 독한 액체 좀 그만 마시지 그래?" 아니면 "그렇게 잔인하게 군대를 훈련시키는 것 좀 그만두는 게 어때?"라고 말할 거야.
사라: 그렇게 말하면, 너는 추방당할 거야.
보미: 그는 자기가 폭군인 걸 알아야 해. 백성들이 그의 정권 하에 고통받고 있었잖아.
사라: 맞아. 그가 일찍 죽지 않았다면, 자기 나라에서 도망쳐야 했을 수도 있어.
보미: 맞아. 그는 암살당할 수도 있었을 거야.

influential
[ìnfluénʃəl]
a. 영향력 있는

having a strong influence over somebody or something
- influence v. 영향을 미치다 n. 영향(력)

Sara, who do you think are some of the world's most influential people?
사라, 세상에서 가장 영향력 있는 사람들은 누구라고 생각해?

quality
[kwáləti]
n. 자질

good characteristic, feature

And what qualities distinguish them?
그리고 어떤 자질이 그들을 유명하게 만들지?

astronomical
[æ̀strənámikəl]
a. 천문학적인,
   천문학의

extremely huge, of cosmic proportions
- astronomy n. 천문학

How did Bill Gates earn such an astronomical amount of money?
빌 게이츠는 어떻게 그런 천문학적인 양의 돈을 벌었을까?

intuition
[ìntʃuíʃən]
n. 직관, 직감

immediate understanding, ability to think ahead
- intuitive a. 직관의, 직관력 있는

Does he have some kind of intuition that allows him to see the future in business?
그는 일종의 직관력 같은 것이 있어서 비즈니스의 미래를 볼 수 있는 것일까?

money-oriented
[mʌ́ni-ɔ́:riəntid]
a. 금전만능의

mainly concerned with money

Or is he just a money-oriented person?
아니면 그는 그냥 금전만능주의자일 뿐일까?

philanthropist
[filǽnθrəpist]
n. 박애주의자

a person who tries to help people in trouble and improve the world
- philanthropy n. 박애주의, 자선

I don't think he is money-oriented. He is a philanthropist
그는 금전만능주의자는 아니라고 생각해. 그는 박애주의자야.

foundation
[faundéiʃən]
n. 재단

an organization supported by a large amount of money

His foundation benefits many people.
그의 재단은 많은 사람들에게 혜택을 주고 있어.

mercy
[mə́:rsi]
n. 자비심

pity, compassion shown to others

• merciful a. 자비로운 • merciless a. 무자비한

So he does have some mercy.
그렇다면 그는 자비심이 있는 거네.

primary
[práimèri]
a. 일차적인,
   가장 중요한

most important, most essential

• primarily ad. 첫째로, 우선

What's the primary goal of his foundation?
그의 재단의 일차적인 목표는 뭐야?

prodigy
[prádədʒi]
n. 천재, 신동

a person who is extremely gifted at doing something

• prodigious a. 비범한, 놀라운

Does it support prodigies?
천재들을 지원하는 거야?

throughout
[θru:áut]
prep. ~도처에

all through, in every part

Exactly. It supports future scientists throughout the world.
맞아. 전 세계에 있는 미래의 과학자들을 지원하고 있어.

nurture
[nə́:rtʃər]
v. 키우다, 돌보다

to take care of, to nourish

It nurtures future Bill Gates.
미래의 빌 게이츠를 길러내는구나.

commitment
[kəmítmənt]
n. 공약, 헌신

a promise to do something, dedication

• make a commitment 공약하다, 헌신하다

Right. He's made a commitment to help society.
그래. 그는 사회를 돕겠다고 공약했어.

figure
[fígjər]
n. 인물

a person, especially a well-known one

Are there any historical figures you are interested in?
네가 관심을 가지고 있는 역사적인 인물들이 있니?

adventurer
[ædvéntʃərər]
n. 모험가

a person who goes on adventures and explorations
• adventure n. 모험   • adventurous a. 모험을 좋아하는, 대담한

I'd like to meet an adventurer like Columbus.
나는 콜럼버스 같은 탐험가를 만나고 싶어.

venture
[véntʃər]
v. 탐험하다
n. 모험

to travel, to explore

I'd like to ask why he ventured out into the unknown world.
그가 왜 미지의 세계를 향해 모험을 나섰는지 물어보고 싶어.

voyage
[vɔ́iidʒ]
n. 항해
v. 항해하다

a long trip over the sea
• voyager n. 항해가

I wonder how he could have made such a historic voyage.
그가 어떻게 그렇게 대단한 역사적인 항해를 해냈는지 궁금해.

priceless
[práislis]
a. 매우 귀한

extremely valuable

I'd like to ask if spices such as pepper were so priceless.
나는 후추 같은 향신료가 그렇게 귀했는지 묻고 싶어.

subordinate
[səbɔ́:rdənit]
n. 부하
a. 부하의, 종속의

a person who must obey another

And I'd like to ask him, "If I brought you a crate of pepper, would you be my subordinate?"
"제가 후추 한 상자 가져오면, 제 부하가 되어주겠어요?"라고 물어보고 싶어.

emperor
[émpərər]
n. 황제

a ruler of an empire
• empire n. 제국

Interesting. If you met the Chinese Emperor, Shin Huang-di, what would you say?
재밌네. 만일 네가 중국의 진시황제를 만난다면, 뭐라고 할래?

eternal
[itə́:rnəl]
a. 영원한

forever, never-ending
• eternity n. 영원함

The emperor who longed for eternal life?
영원히 살고 싶어 했던 그 황제?

toxic
[táksik]

a. 유독한, 독(성)의

poisonous, very harmful

• toxin n. 독소

I'd say, "Hey, why don't you stop drinking toxic liquids?"

"이보게, 독한 액체 좀 그만 마시지 그래?"라고 말할 거야.

discipline
[dísəplin]

v. 훈련시키다,
단련시키다

n. 훈련, 기강, 징계

to drill, to train to act in accordance with rules

• disciplinary a. 훈련상의, 훈육의 • disciplined a. 훈련받은

Why don't you stop disciplining your army so cruelly?

그렇게 잔인하게 군대를 훈련시키는 것 좀 그만두는 게 어때?

exile
[égzail]

v. 추방하다

n. 추방, 망명자

to cast someone out from a place

If you said that, you'd be exiled.

그렇게 말하면, 너는 추방당할 거야.

tyrant
[táiərənt]

n. 폭군

a cruel ruler who rules with fear and strength

• tyranny n. 폭정 • tyrannical a. 압제적인, 폭정의

He should know that he is a tyrant.

그는 자기가 폭군인 걸 알아야 해.

regime
[reiʒíːm]

n. 정권, 통치기간

a form of government, a specific government group

His people were suffering under his regime.

백성들이 그의 정권 하에 고통받고 있었잖이.

flee
[flíː]

v. 도피하다

to run away, to escape

Right. If he hadn't died early, he could have fled his own country.

맞아. 그가 일찍 죽지 않았다면, 자기 나라에서 도망쳐야 했을 수도 있어.

assassinate
[əsǽsənèit]

v. 암살하다

to kill an important person on purpose

• assassination n. 암살 • assassinator n. 암살자

Exactly. He could have been assassinated.

맞아. 그는 암살당할 수도 있었을 거야.

Check Again!

A Translate each word into Korean.

1. influential ....
2. voyage ....
3. quality ....
4. intuition ....
5. philanthropist ....
6. exile ....
7. tyrant ....
8. figure ....
9. flee ....
10. assassinate ....

B Translate each word into English.

1. 재단 ....
2. 일차적인 ....
3. 키우다 ....
4. 모험가 ....
5. 천재 ....
6. 자비심 ....
7. 매우 귀한 ....
8. 부하 ....
9. 영원한 ....
10. 유독한 ....

C Fill in the blank with the appropriate word. Refer to the Korean.

1. Corruption under his r   has reached the zenith.

   그의 정권 하에서 부패가 절정에 달했다.

2. We live in a m   society.

   우리는 금전만능주의 사회에 산다.

3. NASA has an a   amount of information on its many web sites.

   미국항공우주국(NASA)은 많은 웹사이트에 천문학적인 양의 정보를 가지고 있다.

4. President Obama made a c   to change the way Washington does business.

   오바마 대통령은 미국이 경제를 하는 방식을 바꾸겠다고 공약했다.

5. I'm not the kind of person who v   out into the unknown world.

   나는 미지의 세계를 향해 모험을 나서는 종류의 사람이 아니다.

Check More!

(A), (B), (C) 각 밑줄 친 부분에 알맞은 어휘를 짝지은 것으로 가장 적절한 것을 고르시오.

Mathematics definitely **(A)** influenced / infected Renaissance art. Renaissance art was different from the art in the Middle Ages in many ways. Prior to the Renaissance, objects in paintings were flat and symbolic rather than real in appearance. Artists during the Renaissance reformed painting. They wanted objects in paintings to be represented with accuracy. Mathematics was used to **(B)** portray / poetry the essential form of objects in perspective, as they appeared to the human eye. Renaissance artists achieved perspective using geometry, which resulted in a naturalistic, precise, three-dimensional representation of the real world. The application of mathematics to art, particularly in paintings, was one of the **(C)** primitive / primary characteristics of Renaissance art.

(A)	(B)	(C)
① influenced	poetry	primary
② infected	poetry	primary
③ influenced	portray	primary
④ infected	portray	primitive
⑤ influenced	portray	primitive

Chapter 7
People

be late for an appointment

have to pay **overdue charges**

be upset by reckless driver

Episode

Dear Diary,

Is it possible to find our ideal spouse? • My mom and dad are not similar at all; in fact, their behaviors contrast in many ways. • My dad is very punctual. • He is almost never late for his appointments. • But mom is always tardy when she goes to meet him. • Dad thinks it's because she lingers over coffee with her acquaintances. • If I were my dad, I would be late purposely in revenge. • Usually my dad is more prudent than my mom, except while driving. • It's dad who carefully checks all our outgoings. • It's mom who often has to pay overdue charges for her cell phone. • She complains that due dates should be extended. • Consequently, they have arguments over these matters.

This morning my dad declared he is going to apply for auto banking services for her. • Mom remarked that ideal couples should have a close bond. • I wonder why so many couples have more contrasts than similarities. • My grandparents say that a husband and wife should complement each other. • In some respects, I agree with them. • My dad is a bit temperamental. • While driving, he is easily upset by reckless drivers. • Then he accelerates, trying to frighten them. • He even wants verbal confirmation that they are wrong. • It's mom who always persuades dad to calm down. • She has a talent for soothing him.

다이어리에게,

이상적인 배우자를 찾는 게 가능할까? 우리 엄마와 아빠는 비슷한 구석이 전혀 없어; 사실, 두 분의 행동은 여러 가지 면에서 대조가 돼. 아빠는 상당히 시간을 잘 지키셔. 아빠는 약속에 늦으시는 법이 거의 없어. 그렇지만 엄마는 아빠를 만나러 가실 때 항상 늦으셔. 아빠는 엄마가 아는 사람들과 커피를 마시며 꾸물거리기 때문이라고 생각하셔. 내가 아빠라면, 나는 복수를 하기 위해서 일부러 늦게 갈 거야. 보통 아빠는 운전할 때를 제외하고는 엄마보다 더 조심스러워. 지출에 관해 조심스럽게 챙기는 사람은 아빠야. 종종 휴대전화 연체 요금을 내야 하는 사람은 엄마야. 엄마는 요금 납부 기한이 연장되어야 한다고 불평하셔. 그래서 엄마와 아빠는 이런 문제에 대해서 말다툼하셔.

오늘 아침에 아빠는 엄마를 위해서 자동 이체 서비스를 신청할 거라고 말씀하셨어. 엄마는 이상적인 커플은 친밀한 유대감이 있어야 한다고 말씀하셨어. 나는 왜 많은 커플들이 비슷한 점보다 다른 점이 더 많은지 궁금해. 조부모님은 부부는 서로를 보완해야 한다고 말씀하셔. 어떤 면에서 나는 그분들의 의견에 동의해. 아빠는 약간 변덕스러워. 운전할 때 아빠는 무모한 운전자들 때문에 쉽게 화를 내셔. 그리고 나서 아빠는 속도를 높여서 그들을 겁주려고 하셔. 아빠는 심지어 그들이 틀렸다고 말로 확인해주고 싶어하셔. 엄마는 항상 아빠가 침착하시도록 설득하셔. 엄마는 아빠를 진정시키는 소질이 있어.

spouse
[spáus]

n. 배우자

a person one is married to, partner, husband or wife

Is it possible to find our ideal spouse?

이상적인 배우자를 찾는 게 가능할까?

contrast
[kəntrǽst]

v. 대조되다 n. 대조

to be very different

• contrastive a. 대조적인

My mom and dad are not similar at all; in fact, their behaviors contrast in many ways.

우리 엄마와 아빠는 비슷한 구석이 전혀 없어; 사실, 두 분의 행동은 여러 가지 면에서 대조가 돼.

punctual
[pʌ́ŋktʃuəl]

a. 시간을 잘 지키는

being prompt and on time

• punctuality n. 시간 엄수

My dad is very punctual.

우리 아빠는 상당히 시간을 잘 지키셔.

appointment
[əpɔ́intmənt]

n. 약속

a meeting with one or more people

He is almost never late for his appointments.

그는 약속에 늦으시는 법이 거의 없어.

tardy
[tá:rdi]

a. 늦은, 지각하는

late, doing something later than one should

• tardiness n. 지각 • tardily ad. 늦게

But mom is always tardy when she goes to meet him.

그러나 엄마는 그를 만나러 가실 때 항상 늦으셔.

linger
[líŋgər]

v. 꾸물거리다

to take a longer time to do something than one should

• lingering a. 우물쭈물하는

Dad thinks it's because she lingers over coffee with her acquaintances.

아빠는 그녀가 아는 사람들과 커피를 마시며 꾸물거리기 때문이라고 생각하셔.

acquaintance
[əkwéintəns]
n. 아는 사람

a person that you have met and know slightly, but not well
- acquaint v. 알게 하다 • acquainted a. 안면이 있는, ~에 정통한

Dad thinks it's because she lingers over coffee with her acquaintances.
아빠는 그녀가 아는 사람들과 커피를 마시며 꾸물거리기 때문이라고 생각하셔.

revenge
[rivéndʒ]
n. 복수

punishment done to a person who has done something bad to you
- revengeful a. 복수심에 불타는 • in revenge 복수로

If I were my dad, I would be late purposely in revenge.
내가 우리 아빠라면, 나는 복수를 하기 위해서 일부러 늦게 갈 거야.

prudent
[prú:dənt]
a. 신중한

sensible and careful
- prudence n. 신중함

Usually my dad is more prudent than my mom, except while driving.
보통 우리 아빠는 운전할 때를 제외하고는 엄마보다 더 조심스러워.

outgoings
[áutgòuiŋz]
n. 지출

all the money that a person or family spends

It's dad who carefully checks all our outgoings.
지출에 관해 조심스럽게 챙기는 사람은 아빠야.

overdue
[òuvərdjú:]
a. 지불 기한이 넘은

late, not paid for on time

It's mom who often has to pay overdue charges for her cell phone.
종종 휴대 전화 연체 요금을 내야 하는 사람은 엄마야.

complain
[kəmpléin]
v. 불평하다

to express one's dissatisfaction, to grumble
- complaint n. 불평

She complains that due dates should be extended.
그녀는 요금 납부 기한이 연장되어야 한다고 불평하셔.

extend
[iksténd]
v. 연장하다

to give extra time
- extension n. 연장

She complains that due dates should be extended.
그녀는 요금 납부 기한이 연장되어야 한다고 불평하셔.

consequently
[kánsikwəntli]
ad. 결과적으로, 따라서

as a result of something
• consequence n. 결과 • consequent a. 결과의
Consequently, they have arguments over these matters.
그래서 그들은 이런 문제에 대해서 말다툼하셔.

auto banking
[ɔ́:tou bǽŋkiŋ]
자동 이체

the system that has the bank pay one's bills on the same day each month
This morning my dad declared he is going to apply for auto banking services for her.
오늘 아침에 그는 그녀를 위해서 자동 이체 서비스를 신청할 거라고 말씀하셨어.

bond
[bánd]
n. 유대, 유대감

a feeling of friendship and love between people
Mom remarked that ideal couples should have a close bond.
엄마는 이상적인 커플은 친밀한 유대감이 있어야 한다고 말씀하셨어.

similarity
[sìmǝlǽrǝti]
n. 유사점, 비슷한 점

alikeness, closeness
• similar a. 유사한, 비슷한
I wonder why so many couples have more contrasts than similarities.
나는 왜 많은 커플들이 비슷한 점보다 다른 점이 더 많은지 궁금해.

complement
[kámplǝmǝnt]
v. 보완하다

to make a good combination
• complementary a. 보완하는, 보완적인
My grandparents say that a husband and wife should complement each other.
조부모님은 부부는 서로를 보완해야 한다고 말씀하셔.

respect
[rispékt]
n. 측면

an aspect, a way
• in some respects 어떤 면에서
In some respects, I agree with them.
어떤 면에서 나는 그분들의 의견에 동의해.

temperamental
[tèmpǝrǝméntl]
a. 변덕스러운,
   기질상의

moody, changing quickly from happiness to anger
• temperament n. 성격, 기질
My dad is a bit temperamental.
우리 아빠는 약간 변덕스러워.

reckless
[réklis]
a. 무모한

careless and dangerous, not careful
- recklessly ad. 무모하게

While driving, he is easily upset by reckless drivers.
운전할 때 그는 무모한 운전자들 때문에 쉽게 화를 내셔.

accelerate
[æksélərèit]
v. 가속하다

to go faster
- acceleration n. 가속 - accelerator n. 가속장치

Then he accelerates, trying to frighten them.
그리고 나서 그는 속도를 높여서 그들을 겁주려고 하셔.

frighten
[fráitn]
v. 놀라게 하다,
두려워지게 하다

to scare someone
- fright n. 공포 - frightened a. 놀란

Then he accelerates, trying to frighten them.
그리고 나서 그는 속도를 높여서 그들을 겁주려고 하셔.

verbal
[vɔ́:rbəl]
a. 말의, 구두의

spoken, oral
- verbally ad. 말로, 구두로

He even wants verbal confirmation that they are wrong.
그는 심지어 그들이 틀렸다고 말로 확인해주고 싶어하셔.

confirmation
[kɑ̀nfərméiʃən]
n. 확인, 승인

verification, approval of something
- confirm v. 확인하다

He even wants verbal confirmation that they are wrong.
그는 심지어 그들이 틀렸다고 말로 확인해주고 싶어하셔.

persuade
[pə:rswéid]
v. 설득하다

to give someone a good reason to do something
- persuasion n. 설득 - persuasive a. 설득력 있는

It's mom who always persuades dad to calm down.
엄마는 항상 아빠가 침착하시도록 설득하셔.

soothe
[sú:ð]
v. 진정시키다

to make an angry or upset person feel better
- soothing a. 진정시키는, 달래는

She has a talent for soothing him.
그녀는 그를 진정시키는 소질이 있어.

Check Again!

A Translate each word into Korean.

1. temperamental ....
2. verbal ....
3. accelerate ....
4. soothe ....
5. complement ....
6. punctual ....
7. tardy ....
8. linger ....
9. acquaintance ....
10. prudent ....

B Translate each word into English.

1. 불평하다 ....
2. 연장하다 ....
3. 유사점 ....
4. 확인 ....
5. 배우자 ....
6. 대조되다 ....
7. 약속 ....
8. 무모한 ....
9. 놀라게 하다 ....
10. 설득하다 ....

C Fill in the blank with the appropriate word. Refer to the Korean.

1. His design is too confusing in some r_____.
   어떤 면에서 그의 디자인은 너무 혼란스럽다.

2. Do you have a close b_____ with your siblings?
   너는 형제들과 긴밀한 유대감을 가지고 있니?

3. If you do not return your loans on time, you will have to pay o_____ charges.
   제때에 대출금을 상환하지 못하면, 당신은 연체료를 내야 할 것이다.

4. He is the most popular candidate; c_____ he will be elected the next president.
   그는 가장 인기 있는 후보자이다; 따라서 다음 대통령으로 선출될 것이다.

5. I broke his mug and he hid my cellphone in r_____.
   나는 그의 머그잔을 망가뜨렸고 그는 복수로 내 휴대 전화를 숨겼다.

Check More!

다음 밑줄 친 부분에 알맞은 어휘를 고르시오. 아래의 영영 풀이를 참조하시오.

Sailors in the 1800s had a hard life. They found rare **(A)** comfort / compete in the simple songs that they sang aboard their ships. **(B)** Consequently / Likewise, these songs were valuable friends to sailors, helping them work as a team. Many of these songs have lasted through the years. Some chanteys broke up the **(C)** bosom / boredom of long trips. Others helped them express their feelings of longing and loneliness. Still, chanteys let sailors **(D)** complain / compliment about their hard lives. All in all, the sea chanteys made their stay aboard less difficult.

*chantey: 뱃노래

(A) ease; well-being: ....

(B) as a result: ....

(C) the state of being bored; tedium: ....

(D) to find a fault; to grumble: ....

+ 접두사 extra- / de- 와 접미사 -less

extra-는 'outside'라는 뜻의 접두사로, '어떤 범위 이외 혹은 이상'이라는 뜻의 단어를 만든다. de-는 'un-'과 같은 뜻으로, 단어 앞에 붙어 '반대'의 의미를 나타낸다. -less는 'without'이라는 뜻의 접미사로, 명사 뒤에 붙어 '~없이는'이라는 뜻의 형용사를 만든다.

extra-

curricular 교과과정의
extra + curricular = extracurricular 과외활동의
ex) Fencing is now a part of the school's extracurricular activities.
이제는 펜싱이 학교 과외활동에 포함된다.

• **literary** 문학의	**extraliterary** 문학밖의
• **ordinary** 평범한	**extraordinary** 비상한
• **marital** 결혼의, 부부의	**extramarital** 혼외의, 불륜의
• **judicial** 재판의	**extrajudicial** 사법 관할 밖의
• **terrestrial** 지구의	**extraterrestrial** 지구 밖의
• **cellular** 세포의	**extracellular** 세포 밖의
• **legal** 법적인	**extralegal** 법률의 지배를 받지 않는

de-

code 암호화하다
de + code = decode 암호문을 풀다
ex) The teacher couldn't decode the student's note.
선생님은 암호화된 학생의 쪽지를 풀 수 없었다.

• **compose** 조립하다	**decompose** 분해시키다
• **certify** 인증하다	**decertify** 인가를 취소하다
• **caffeinated** 카페인을 함유한	**decaffeinated** 카페인을 제거한
• **frost** 얼리다	**defrost** 녹이다
• **centralize** 집중시키다	**decentralize** 분산시키다
• **hydrated** 함수의	**dehydrated** 탈수한
• **forestation** 조림	**deforestation** 삼림 벌채

-less

speech 말, 담화

speech + less = speechless 말문이 막힌

ex) She stood speechless when he suddenly proposed.
그 남자가 갑자기 청혼하자 그녀는 말문이 막혀 서 있었다.

- **ground** 지면, 땅
- **fruit** 열매
- **odor** 냄새, 악취
- **price** 가격
- **value** 가치
- **faith** 믿음
- **power** 힘

groundless 기초가 없는, 사실무근의
fruitless 열매를 맺지 않는, 결실이 없는
odorless 무취의
priceless 값을 매길 수 없는, 매우 소중한
valueless 가치가 없는
faithless 신의가 없는, 믿지 못할
powerless 무력한, 무능한

At a Music Concert 음악회에서

⁺ opera singer 성악가

⁺ symphony orchestra 교향악단

⁺ conductor / maestro 지휘자

⁺ company / troupe 공연단

⁺ intermission 휴식 시간

⁺ give a standing ovation 기립 박수를 치다

⁺ call for an encore 앙코르를 청하다

VOCA EDGE
RED

We're teens. I had my cell phone taken away. Goodbye, Brownie Life is full of contrad
campus tour. If I were a judge,... How can we survive in a jungle? I became a Santa C
money-wise. Hoony goes to an herbal clinic. We became a rescue team. Grandma goe
you want to meet? Are mom and dad compatible? I can't understand this painting. The
have illusions about boys. I can't understand politicians. Wearing an electronic tag is ho
economics camp. construction a thriving business? How amazing our life has beco
space. I attended the Arbor Day ceremony. We can make the earth a better place. A
Life is full of contradictions. Goodbye, Sara. I learned about the earth. I went to a natu
became a Santa Claus. Sara attends a community party. Mom's got a new hobby. Are t
Grandma goes to a laughter clinic. The Volcanoes are back. We have great brothers. W
painting. There was telepathy between us! Sara goes to Turkey. Home decorating is r
electronic tag is horrible. The war should be stopped. Mom, are you going to cut my all
our life has become! I should have been more careful. Forgery should be stopped. Hoc
better place. A super hurricane hit the village. We're teens. I had my cell phone taken
went to a natural science museum. I had a campus tour. If I were a judge,... How can w
hobby. Are they my bosses? Hoony is money-wise. Hoony goes to an herbal clinic. We
great brothers. What historical figures do you want to meet? Are mom and dad compa
decorating is not easy. Hoony thinks girls have illusions about boys. I can't understand p
cut my allowance? Hoony is back from an economics camp. construction a thriving
stopped. Hoony wants to explore outer space. I attended the Arbor Day ceremony. W
phone taken away. Goodbye, Brownie Life is full of contradictions. Goodbye, Sara. I lea
How can we survive in a jungle? I became a Santa Claus. Sara attends a community p

oodbye, Sara. I learned about the earth. I went to a natural science museum. I had a
attends a community party. Mom's got a new hobby. Are they my bosses? Hoony is
ghter clinic. The Volcanoes are back. We have great brothers. What historical figures do
epathy between us! Sara goes to Turkey. Home decorating is not easy. Hoony thinks girls
war should be stopped. Mom, are you going to cut my allowance? Hoony is back from
ld have been more careful. Forgery should be stopped. Hoony wants to explore oute
icane hit the village. We're teens. I had my cell phone taken away. Goodbye, Brownie
e museum. I had a campus tour. If I were a judge,... How can we survive in a jungle?
sses? Hoony is money-wise. Hoony goes to an herbal clinic. We became a rescue team
al figures do you want to meet? Are mom and dad compatible? I can't understand this
Hoony thinks girls have illusions about boys. I can't understand politicians. Wearing an
Hoony is back from an economics camp. construction a thriving business? How amazing
o explore outer space. I attended the Arbor Day ceremony. We can make the earth a
odbye, Brownie Life is full of contradictions. Goodbye, Sara. I learned about the earth.
n a jungle? I became a Santa Claus. Sara attends a community party. Mom's got a new

Chapter 8. History, Art, and Culture

a rescue team. Grandma goes to a laughter clinic. The Volcanoes are back. We ha

e the earth a better place. A super hurricane hit the village. We're teens. I had my ce

the earth. I went to a natural science museum. I had a campus tour. If I were a judge,...

got a new hobby. Are they my bosses? Hoony is money-wise. Hoony goes to an herba

Chapter 8
History, Art, and Culture

Unit 23. I can't understand this painting.

portray a **contemplative** person

figure out the underlying meaning

give someone **concrete** concepts

Episode

Dear Sara,

Sara, how do you **appreciate** pieces of art? • My class went to a **gallery**. • I saw a **sculpture**, *The thinker*, by Rodin. • What did Rodin try to **portray**? • What made this work, *The thinker*, his **masterpiece**? • Did he want to portray a **contemplative** person? • *The thinker* looked **uncomfortable**. • I guess *The thinker* symbolizes a **vulnerable** person. • I can't judge whether the sculpture has perfect **proportions** or not. • Once I **molded** a tiny artwork with mud. • It was not **symmetrical** at all. • There were many **cracks** in it. • The mud didn't have enough **moisture**. • I had to spend a few days **completing** the ugly piece. • Rodin must have worked **vigorously** to finish his great artwork.

Later I stood in front of some **abstract** paintings. • Hmmm, how can I **evaluate** them? • I tried to figure out their **underlying** meaning, but they were really **ambiguous**. • Some paintings were really hard to **comprehend**. • Our teacher said they depicted our **subconscious**. • How can I grasp **invisible** things? • "These paintings are **vague**," I said to myself.

Finally, I moved to where there were paintings with **vivid** colors. • They were **comparatively** easy to understand. • They gave me **concrete** concepts. • They were different from the **preceding** artworks. • Now I was able to have a **mutual** understanding with the painters.

사라에게,

사라, 너는 미술작품을 어떻게 감상하니? 우리 반은 미술관에 갔어. 로댕의 '생각하는 사람' 이라는 조각상을 봤어. 로댕은 무엇을 표현하려고 했던 것일까? 무엇이 이 작품, '생각하는 사람' 을 그의 걸작으로 만들었을까? 그는 사색하는 사람을 표현하고 싶었던 것일까? '생각하는 사람' 은 불편한 듯 보였어. 내 짐작에는 '생각하는 사람' 이 상처입기 쉬운 사람을 상징하는 것 같아. 나는 그 조각상이 완벽한 비율인지 아닌지는 판단할 수 없어. 언젠가 나는 진흙으로 조그마한 작품을 만든 적이 있어. 전혀 대칭이 맞지 않았어. 그 안에 균열도 많았어. 진흙에 수분이 충분하지 않았어. 나는 그 형편없는 작품을 완성하느라 며칠을 보내야 했어. 로댕은 자신의 위대한 작품을 끝내기 위해 틀림없이 왕성하게 작업했을 거야.

나중에 나는 몇몇 추상화 앞에 서게 되었어. 흠, 내가 그것들을 어떻게 평가할 수 있겠니? 나는 그것들의 저변에 깔린 의미를 찾아내려고 애를 썼지만, 정말 애매했어. 어떤 그림들은 정말 이해하기가 어려웠어. 우리 선생님은 그것들이 우리의 잠재의식을 표현한 것이라고 하셨어. 내가 눈에 보이지 않는 것을 어떻게 파악할 수 있겠니? "이 그림들은 모호해"라고 혼잣말을 했어.

마지막으로, 나는 선명한 색채로 그려진 그림이 있는 곳으로 자리를 옮겼어. 그것들은 비교적 이해하기 쉬웠어. 그것들은 내게 구체적인 개념을 전달해줬어. 그것들은 이전 작품들과는 달랐어. 나는 그제서야 화가들과 상호 이해할 수가 있었어.

appreciate
[əprí:ʃièit]

v. 감상하다, 평가하다, 감사하다

to recognize good qualities or worth
- appreciation n. 감상, 평가, 감사

Sara, how do you appreciate pieces of art?
사라, 너는 미술작품을 어떻게 감상하니?

gallery
[gǽləri]

n. 미술관, 화랑

a building where artworks are displayed

My class went to a gallery.
우리 반은 미술관에 갔어.

sculpture
[skʌ́lptʃər]

n. 조각품

an artwork made from solid materials (not paint)
- sculpt v. 조각하다   - sculptor n. 조각가

I saw a sculpture, *The thinker*, by Rodin.
로댕의 '생각하는 사람' 이라는 조각상을 봤어.

portray
[pɔːrtréi]

v. 표현하다, 그리다

to explain something using art instead of words
- portrayal n. 그리기, 묘사   - portrait n. 초상화

What did Rodin try to portray?
로댕은 무엇을 표현하려고 했던 것일까?

masterpiece
[mǽstərpìːs]

n. 걸작

the best piece of work made by an artist

What made this work, *The Thinker*, his masterpiece?
무엇이 이 작품, '생각하는 사람' 을 그의 걸작으로 만들었을까?

contemplative
[kəntémplətiv]

a. 사색하는

thinking very hard and deeply
- contemplate v. 묵상하다, 사색하다   - contemplation n. 묵상, 사색

Did he want to portray a contemplative person?
그는 사색하는 사람을 표현하고 싶었던 것일까?

uncomfortable
[ʌnkʌ́mfərtəbəl]

a. 불편한, 마음이 편치 못한

not relaxed, opposite of comfortable

The thinker looked uncomfortable.
'생각하는 사람' 은 불편한 듯 보였어.

vulnerable
[vʌ́lnərəbəl]

a. 상처입기 쉬운, 연약한

can be easily harmed, weak and unprotected
- vulnerability n. 취약성, 상처 받기 쉬움

I guess *the Thinker* symbolizes a vulnerable person.
내 짐작에는 '생각하는 사람'이 상처입기 쉬운 사람을 상징하는 것 같아.

proportion
[prəpɔ́ːrʃən]

n. 비율

the balance between parts of the whole
- proportional a. 비례하는, 비례의 • proportionate a. 비례하는, 균형 잡힌

I can't judge whether the sculpture has perfect proportions or not.
나는 그 조각상이 완벽한 비율인지 아닌지는 판단할 수 없어.

mold
[móuld]

v. 형태를 만들다, 주조하다

to use a material and shape it with one's hands

Once I molded a tiny artwork with mud.
언젠가 나는 진흙으로 조그마한 작품을 만든 적이 있어.

symmetrical
[simétrikəl]

a. 대칭의

matching perfectly on both sides
- symmetry n. 대칭

It was not symmetrical at all.
그것은 전혀 대칭이 맞지 않았어.

crack
[kræk]

n. 균열 v. 금이 가다

a thin gap or split in an object, damage

There were many cracks in it.
그 안에 균열도 많았어.

moisture
[mɔ́istʃər]

n. 수분

dampness, wateriness
- moist a. 습한, 습기 있는

The mud didn't have enough moisture.
진흙에 수분이 충분하지 않았어.

complete
[kəmplíːt]

v. 완성하다, 완수하다

to finish
- completion n. 완성, 완료

I had to spend a few days completing the ugly piece.
나는 그 형편없는 작품을 완성하느라 며칠을 보내야 했어.

vigorously
[vígərəsli]
ad. 원기 왕성하게

energetically, powerfully
- vigor n. 원기 • vigorous a. 원기 왕성한

Rodin must have worked vigorously to finish his great artwork.
로댕은 자신의 위대한 작품을 끝내기 위해 틀림없이 왕성하게 작업했을 거야.

abstract
[æbstrǽkt]
a. 추상적인

conceptual, not concrete
- abstraction n. 추상, 추상주의 작품

Later I stood in front of some abstract paintings.
나중에 나는 몇몇 추상화 앞에 서게 되었어.

evaluate
[ivǽljuèit]
v. 평가하다

to decide if something is good or bad
- evaluation n. 평가

Hmmm, how can I evaluate them?
흠음, 내가 그것들을 어떻게 평가할 수 있겠니?

underlying
[ʌndərláiiŋ]
a. 저변에 깔린,
기초(근본)적인

basic, fundamental and concealed
- underlie v. 기초가 되다

I tried to figure out their underlying meaning, but they were really ambiguous.
나는 그것들의 저변에 깔린 의미를 찾아내려고 애를 썼지만, 정말 애매했어.

ambiguous
[æmbígjuəs]
a. 애매한, 중의적인

confusing and not clear, vague
- ambiguity n. 애매함

I tried to figure out their underlying meaning, but they were really ambiguous.
나는 그것들의 저변에 깔린 의미를 찾아내려고 애를 썼지만, 정말 애매했어.

comprehend
[kàmprihénd]
v. 이해하다

to understand
- comprehension n. 이해 • comprehensive a. 이해력이 있는, 포괄적인

Some paintings were really hard to comprehend.
어떤 그림들은 정말 이해하기가 어려웠어.

subconscious
[sʌbkánʃəs]
n. 잠재의식
a. 잠재의식의

inner thoughts that one has but they are not aware of
- subconsciousness n. 잠재의식 • subconsciously ad. 잠재의식으로

Our teacher said they depicted our subconscious.
우리 선생님은 그것들이 우리의 잠재의식을 표현한 것이라고 하셨어.

invisible
[invízəbəl]
a. 보이지 않는

unable to be seen
- invisibility n. 눈에 보이지 않음

How can I grasp invisible things?
내가 눈에 보이지 않는 것을 어떻게 파악할 수 있겠니?

vague
[véig]
a. 모호한, 애매한

difficult to understand because the meaning is not explained well

"These paintings are vague," I said to myself.
"이 그림들은 모호해"라고 혼잣말을 했어.

vivid
[vívid]
a. 생생한

bright and colorful
- vividness n. 생생함

Finally, I moved to where there were paintings with vivid colors.
마지막으로, 나는 선명한 색채로 그려진 그림이 있는 곳으로 자리를 옮겼어.

comparatively
[kəmpǽrətivli]
ad. 비교적

relatively, rather
- compare v. 비교하다 • comparison n. 비교

They were comparatively easy to understand.
그것들은 비교적 이해하기 쉬웠어.

concrete
[kánkri:t]
a. 구체적인

real, definite, specific, opposite of abstract

They gave me concrete concepts.
그것들은 내게 구체적인 개념을 전달해줬어.

preceding
[pri:sí:diŋ]
a. 이전의

earlier, former
- precede v. 앞서다, 먼저 일어나다 • precedent n. 선례

They were different from the preceding artworks.
그것들은 이전 작품들과는 달랐어.

mutual
[mjú:tʃuəl]
a. 상호의

shared by both of two people
- mutuality n. 상호관계, 상관

Now I was able to have a mutual understanding with the painters.
나는 그제서야 화가들과 상호 이해할 수가 있었어.

Check Again!

A Translate each word into Korean.

1. appreciate ....   2. ambiguous ....

3. portray ....   4. comprehend ....

5. contemplative ....   6. moisture ....

7. vulnerable ....   8. proportion ....

9. vigorously ....   10. symmetrical ....

B Translate each word into English.

1. 걸작 ....   2. 균열 ....

3. 평가하다 ....   4. 조각품 ....

5. 잠재의식(의) ....   6. 보이지 않는 ....

7. 생생한 ....   8. 비교적 ....

9. 완성하다 ....   10. 이전의 ....

C Fill in the blank with the appropriate word. Refer to the Korean.

1. A c   object is a real, physical object.

   구체적인 사물은 실재하는 물리적인 사물이다.

2. His description was so v   that none of us could understand.

   그의 설명은 너무 모호해서, 우리 모두 이해할 수 없었다.

3. Can we have m   communication with the subconscious?

   우리가 잠재의식과 상호 소통할 수 있을까?

4. I can't figure out the u   meaning of the sentence.

   나는 그 문장의 저변에 깔린 의미를 이해할 수가 없다.

5. Piet Mondrian was a famous a   painter, born in the Netherlands in 1872.

   삐에트 몬드리안은 1872년 네덜란드에서 태어난 유명한 추상화가였다.

(A), (B), (C) 각 밑줄 친 부분에 알맞은 어휘를 짝지은 것으로 가장 적절한 것을 고르시오.

Poetry moves us to sympathize with the emotions of the poet himself or with those of the persons whom his **(A)** imagination / imagine has created. We witness their struggles, **(B)** vulnerabilities / vulnerable, and failures. We feel their loves and losses, joys and sorrows, hopes and fears, somewhat as if they were our own. Though we sometimes suffer along with their anxieties and sorrows, we receive pleasure from the experience. Poetry provides us with what is missing in our own lives — the experience of imaginative pleasure. That is why we **(C)** appreciate / depreciate poetry in everyday life.

	(A)	(B)	(C)
①	imagination	vulnerable	depreciate
②	imagine	vulnerabilities	appreciate
③	imagination	vulnerabilities	appreciate
④	imagine	vulnerable	appreciate
⑤	imagination	vulnerabilities	depreciate

see **a herd of** cows

be compared to a meek person

intuit one's thoughts

Episode

Dear Diary,

Our family visited a farm full of **pastureland**. • The **meadow** was located in a **rural** area. • When we arrived, we saw a **herd** of cows on the grass. • And there were many **livestock** animals.

"I'm going to watch the lambs **graze**," Hoony said. • Maybe he was thinking of a **fable**. • In the fable, the lamb is always **innocent** while the wolf is **vicious**. • In other stories, the lamb is often **naive**. • But sometimes it is compared to a **meek** person.

Seri and I milked the cows to **extract** their milk. • Looking into their eyes, I felt a kind of **intimacy**. • I felt as if I were **identifying** myself with the cows. • I felt as if there was **telepathy** between us. • I felt that I could **intuit** their thoughts. • Why do we have to **provide** humans with milk? • Why do we have to be **harnessed**? • Are we **destined** to serve them? • We have been companions of **peasants** for a long time. • They should **honor** us. • We have been used for **plowing**. • We've been **exploited** for **harvesting**. • We've been used for **manual** labor. • We've been living in **wretched** conditions. • We've **consistently** given our labor to humans. • Don't you think we're **essential** to human's success at farming? • They seemed to **urge** me to tell their story. • What a strange feeling!

다이어리에게,

우리 가족은 목초지로 가득한 한 농장을 방문했어. 그 목초지는 시골에 있었어. 우리가 도착했을 때, 한 무리의 소들이 풀밭에 있는 것을 보았어. 그리고 거기에는 가축들도 많았어.

"나는 양들이 풀 뜯어먹는 것을 지켜볼래"라고 후니가 말했어. 아마 우화가 생각난 모양이야. 우화에서 양은 늘 순수하고 반면에 늑대는 사악해. 또 다른 이야기들에서 양은 종종 단순해. 하지만 때로 온순한 사람에 비유되기도 해.

세리와 나는 우유를 짜내기 위해 소의 젖을 짰어. 그들의 눈을 보면서, 나는 일종의 친밀감을 느꼈어. 마치 내가 젖소와 동일시되는 기분이었어. 우리 사이에 텔레파시가 있는 것 같은 느낌이었어. 나는 소들의 생각을 직관으로 알 수 있을 것 같았어. 왜 우리가 인간에게 우유를 제공해줘야 하지? 왜 우리가 인간에게 이용되어야 하지? 그들을 섬겨야 할 운명인가? 우리는 오랫동안 농부들의 동무가 되어줬어. 그들은 우리를 귀하게 여겨야 해. 우리는 밭을 가는 데 이용되어 왔어. 추수하는 데에도 이용되어 왔어. 우리는 육체노동에 이용되어 왔어. 비참한 조건에서 살아왔어. 우리는 인간에게 일관되게 노동력을 주고 있어. 인간들이 농사를 성공적으로 짓는 데 우리가 필수적이라고 생각하지 않니? 소들이 나에게 자신들의 이야기를 해달라고 요구하는 것 같았어. 정말 묘한 기분이었어!

pastureland
[pǽstʃərlənd]
n. 목초지

a grass field where animals can eat the grass

Our family visited a farm full of pastureland.
우리 가족은 목초지로 가득한 한 농장을 방문했어.

meadow
[médou]
n. 목초지, 초원

a field where plants and flowers are growing

The meadow was located in a rural area.
그 목초지는 시골에 있었어.

rural
[rúərəl]
a. 시골의

countryside, not in the city

The meadow was located in a rural area.
그 목초지는 시골에 있었어.

herd
[hə́:rd]
n. 무리, 떼

a group of animals

• a herd of 한 무리의

When we arrived, we saw a herd of cows on the grass.
우리가 도착했을 때, 한 무리의 소들이 풀밭에 있는 것을 보았어.

livestock
[láivstὰk]
n. 가축

farm animals such as cows, pigs and sheep

And there were many livestock animals.
그리고 거기에는 가축들도 많았어.

graze
[gréiz]
v. 풀을 뜯어먹다

to eat grass

"I'm going to watch the lambs graze," Hoony said.
"나는 양들이 풀 뜯어먹는 것을 지켜볼래"라고 후니가 말했어.

fable
[féibəl]
n. 우화

a story that teaches a moral lesson

Maybe he was thinking of a fable.
아마 그는 우화가 생각난 모양이야.

innocent
[ínəsnt]
a. 순수한, 죄없는

angelic, crimeless, not guilty of any wrong

• innocence n. 순수, 무죄

In the fable, the lamb is always innocent while the wolf is vicious.
우화에서 양은 늘 순수하고 반면에 늑대는 사악해.

vicious
[víʃəs]
a. 사악한

corrupt and cruel, wrong
- vice n. 악, 부패

In the fable, the lamb is always innocent while the wolf is vicious.

우화에서 양은 늘 순수하고 반면에 늑대는 사악해.

naive
[nɑːíːv]
a. 순진한, 단순한

childlike, frank, innocent, simple

In other stories, the lamb is often naive.

또 다른 이야기들에서 양은 종종 단순해.

meek
[míːk]
a. 온순한

humble and not proud
- meekness n. 온순함

But sometimes it is compared to a meek person.

하지만 때로 온순한 사람에 비유되기도 해.

extract
[ikstrǽkt]
v. 뽑다, 짜다
n. 추출물

to take or remove something
- extraction n. 뽑아냄, 추출 • extractor n. 추출자, 추출 장치

Seri and I milked the cows to extract their milk.

세리와 나는 우유를 짜내기 위해 소의 젖을 짰어.

intimacy
[íntəməsi]
n. 친밀감

closeness between people
- intimate a. 친밀한

Looking into their eyes, I felt a kind of intimacy.

그들의 눈을 보면서 나는 일종의 친밀감을 느꼈어.

identify
[aidéntəfài]
v. 동일시하다,
   구별하다

to think someone or something is closely associated with you
- identification n. 동일함, 동화 • identity n. 동일함, 신원
- identify A with B   A를 B와 동일시하다

I felt as if I were identifying myself with the cows.

마치 내가 젖소와 동일시되는 기분이었어.

telepathy
[təlépəθi]
n. 텔레파시

the direct communication of thoughts and feelings between people's minds
- telepathic a. 텔레파시의

I felt as if there was telepathy between us.

우리 사이에 텔레파시가 있는 것 같은 느낌이었어.

intuit
[intʃú(:)it]

v. 직관으로 알다

to feel or know something even though nobody tells you
- intuition n. 직관력 • intuitive a. 직관력 있는, 직관적인

I felt like I could intuit their thoughts.
나는 그들의 생각을 직관으로 알 수 있을 것 같았어.

provide
[prəváid]

v. 제공하다

to give something to someone else
- provide A with B A에게 B를 공급하다

Why do we have to provide humans with milk?
왜 우리가 인간에게 우유를 제공해줘야 하지?

harness
[háːrnis]

v. 마구를 채우다,
이용하다 n. 마구

to put leather ropes around an animal so that one can attach things to it

Why do we have to be harnessed?
왜 우리가 이용되어야 하지?

destined
[déstind]

a. 예정된,
운명 지어진

planned, predetermined
- destiny n. 운명 • be destined to+ V ~할 운명이다

Are we destined to serve them?
우리는 그들을 섬겨야 할 운명인가?

peasant
[pézənt]

n. 농부

a person who works on a farm
- peasantry n. 영세농민, 소작인 〈집합적〉

We have been companions of peasants for a long time.
우리는 오랫동안 농부들의 동무가 되어줬어.

honor
[ánər]

v. 존중하다

to respect someone
- honorable a. 존경할 만한

They should honor us.
그들은 우리를 귀하게 여겨야 해.

plow
[pláu]

v. 갈다, 경작하다
n. 쟁기

to dig up ground for cultivation

We have been used for plowing.
우리는 밭을 가는 데 이용되어 왔어.

exploit
[iksplɔ́it]

v. 이용하다, 착취하다

to take advantage of something for oneself

• exploitation n. 이용, 착취

We've been exploited for harvesting.

우리는 추수하는 데에도 이용되어 왔어.

harvest
[háːrvist]

v. 추수하다   n. 추수

to take the ripe crop out of the fields

We've been exploited for harvesting.

우리는 추수하는 데에도 이용되어 왔어.

manual
[mǽnjuəl]

a. 손으로 하는

n. 소책자, 안내서

done by hand, not automatic

• manual labor 육체노동

We've been used for manual labor.

우리는 육체노동에 이용되어 왔어.

wretched
[rétʃit]

a. 비참한

terrible, very bad

We've been living in wretched conditions.

우리는 비참한 조건에서 살아왔어.

consistently
[kənsístəntli]

ad. 일관되게

constantly, invariably

• consistency n. 일관성   • consistent a. 시종 일관된

We've consistently given our labor to humans.

우리는 인간에게 일관되게 노동력을 주고 있어.

essential
[isénʃəl]

a. 필수적인

necessary, being needed

• essence n. 본질, 진수

Don't you think we're essential to human's success at farming?

인간들이 농사를 성공적으로 짓는 데 우리가 필수적이라고 생각하지 않니?

urge
[ɔ́ːrdʒ]

v. 요구하다, 촉구하다

to forcefully ask someone to do something

They seemed to urge me to tell their story.

그들이 나에게 자신들의 이야기를 해달라고 요구하는 것 같았어.

Check Again!

A Translate each word into Korean.

1. pastureland ....   2. intuit ....

3. harness ....   4. extract ....

5. intimacy ....   6. peasant ....

7. exploit ....   8. livestock ....

9. graze ....   10. consistently ....

B Translate each word into English.

1. 필수적인 ....   2. 순수한 ....

3. 온순한 ....   4. 시골의 ....

5. 추수하다 ....   6. 존중하다 ....

7. (밭을) 갈다 ....   8. 사악한 ....

9. 비참한 ....   10. 요구하다 ....

C Fill in the blank with the appropriate word. Refer to the Korean.

1. M   labor is physical work done with the hands.

   육체노동은 손으로 하는 신체 노동이다.

2. The couple was d   to meet on the bridge.

   그 커플은 다리 위에서 만나기로 운명이 정해져 있었다.

3. When she watches the play, she i   herself with one of the characters.

   그녀는 연극을 볼 때, 등장인물 중 한 명과 자신을 동일시한다.

4. The federal government will p   some aid to flood victims.

   연방정부는 홍수 피해자들에게 도움을 제공할 것이다.

5. There's a cowboy tending a h   of cattle grazing in an open field.

   카우보이가 탁 트인 들판에서 풀을 뜯는 소떼들을 돌보고 있다.

Check More!

다음 밑줄 친 부분에 알맞은 어휘를 고르시오. 아래의 영영 풀이를 참조하시오.

When you begin noticing yourself interrupting others, you'll see that this is nothing more than an **(A)** innocent / innovative habit. To correct it, all you have to do is to begin catching yourself when you forget. Remind yourself to be patient and wait. Allow the other person to finish speaking before you take your turn. You'll notice by **(B)** intuition / intrigue how much the **(C)** interruptions / interactions with the people in your life will improve as a direct result of this simple act. The people you **(D)** communicate / communalize with will feel much more relaxed around you when they feel heard and listened to.

(A) free from evil or guilt; not harmful:

(B) unexplained feelings:

(C) a mutual or reciprocal action:

(D) to interchange thoughts, feelings, information:

Chapter 8. History, Art, and Culture **229**

Chapter 8
History, Art, and Culture

Unit 25. Sara goes to Turkey.

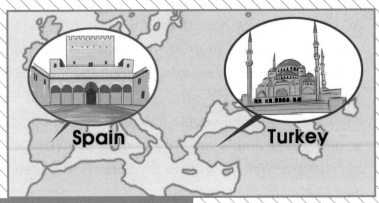

experience both Oriental and Western cultures

show geometric patterns

Episode

Dear Bomi,
What a splendid culture Turkey has! • Turkey is an integrated place. • It is a great place to experience both Oriental and Western cultures. • It has also been influenced by Islamic culture. • Islamic culture has really flourished in Turkey. • The Turkish people are religious. • During Ramadan, they fast. • They pray five times a day. • There are many mosques, which are sacred places like churches. • The mosques are aesthetically beautiful. • The tiles of the mosques show geometric patterns.

Bomi, what do you think about Islamic culture? • Don't you have any prejudices about it? • Before my trip, I only had superficial knowledge. • I just knew that pork is taboo there. • I just overlooked their culture. • I didn't know that Muslims had established many trading routes. • In terms of trading, they were real pioneers. • I'm sure many people have underestimated their majestic culture.

Isn't it a great pity that information about their cultural legacies are not shown accurately? • Their history seems to have been distorted. • I didn't know that films and TV programs just provide insufficient information. • For example, Muslims were often depicted as terrorists. • Some programs just focused on the terrorists' invasion. • Or they even feature places with unsanitary conditions, not beautiful palaces or their culture. • Do they encourage us to be biased about Islamic culture?

Tomorrow we will go to Spain. • We will visit the famous Islamic architecture, the Alhambra. • It's one of the great tourist attractions. • I won't forget to send you the pictures of it.

보미에게,
터키는 정말 찬란한 문화를 가지고 있어. 터키는 여러 가지가 통합된 곳이야. 그곳은 동양과 서양의 문화를 모두 경험할 수 있는 좋은 곳이야. 또한 그곳은 이슬람 문화의 영향을 받아왔어. 이슬람 문화는 터키에서 정말 융성했어. 터키 사람들은 종교적이야. 라마단 기간 동안 금식을 해. 그들은 하루에 다섯 번 기도해. 모스크가 많은데, 그곳은 교회처럼 성스러운 장소야. 모스크는 미적으로 아름다워. 모스크의 타일은 기하학 무늬를 보여줘.

보미, 너는 이슬람 문화에 대해 어떻게 생각하니? 이슬람 문화에 대해 편견을 가지고 있지는 않니? 여행 전에 나는 피상적인 지식밖에 없었어. 돼지고기가 금기라는 것 정도만 알고 있었어. 나는 그들의 문화를 간과했던 거야. 나는 이슬람교도들이 많은 무역로를 확립했다는 것을 몰랐어. 무역에 있어서 그들은 정말 개척자였어. 나는 많은 사람들이 그들의 웅장한 문화를 과소평가했다고 확신해.

그들의 문화 유산에 관한 정보가 정확하게 보여지지 않는다는 사실이 안타깝지 않니? 그들의 역사는 왜곡된 것 같아. 나는 영화와 TV 프로그램에서 충분한 정보를 주고 있지 않다는 것을 몰랐어. 예를 들어, 이슬람교도들은 종종 테러리스트로 묘사되잖아. 어떤 프로그램에서는 테러리스트들의 침략에 초점을 맞추기도 해. 아니면 아름다운 궁전이나 문화가 아니라 비위생적인 장소를 집중적으로 다루기도 해. 그런 것이 우리가 이슬람 문화에 대해 편견을 갖도록 유도하는 것은 아닐까?

내일 우리는 스페인으로 갈 거야. 우리는 유명한 이슬람 건축물인 알람브라를 가 볼 거야. 그곳은 아주 유명한 관광지 중 하나야. 너에게 사진 보내는 것 잊지 않을게.

splendid
[spléndid]
a. 찬란한

very impressive and excellent
- splendor n. 훌륭함 • splendidly ad. 찬란하게

What a splendid culture Turkey has!
터키는 정말 찬란한 문화를 가지고 있어.

integrated
[íntəgrèitid]
a. 통합된

mixed, blended, merged
- integrate v. 통합하다 • integration n. 통합

Turkey is an integrated place.
터키는 여러 가지가 통합된 곳이야.

Western
[wéstərn]
a. 서양의

coming from or associated with Western countries

It is a great place to experience both Oriental and Western cultures.
그곳은 동양과 서양의 문화를 모두 경험할 수 있는 좋은 곳이야.

Islamic
[islámik]
a. 이슬람교의

associated with the religion of Islam
- Islam n. 이슬람교

It has also been influenced by Islamic culture.
또한 그곳은 이슬람 문화의 영향을 받아왔어.

flourish
[fláːriʃ]
v. 번창하다, 융성하다

to be very successful
- flourishing a. 번창하는, 융성한

Islamic culture has really flourished in Turkey.
이슬람 문화는 터키에서 정말 융성했어.

religious
[rilídʒəs]
a. 종교적인

connected with religion
- religion n. 종교

The Turkish people are religious.
터키 사람들은 종교적이야.

fast
[fæst]
v. 금식하다
n. 금식

to stop eating for several days or longer
- fasting n. 금식

During Ramadan, they fast.
라마단 기간 동안 그들은 금식을 해.

pray
[préi]

v. 기도하다

to speak to God
- prayer n. 기도

They pray five times a day. 그들은 하루에 다섯 번 기도해.

sacred
[séikrid]

a. 성스러운

holy, divine

There are many mosques, which are sacred places like churches.

모스크가 많은데, 그곳은 교회처럼 성스러운 장소야.

aesthetically
[esθétikəli]

ad. 미적으로

artistically
- aesthetic a. 미의, 미적인 • aestheticism n. 탐미주의

The mosques are aesthetically beautiful.

모스크는 미적으로 아름다워.

geometric
[dʒìːəmétrik]

a. 기하학의,
   기하학적인

consisting of regular shaped patterns and lines
- geometry n. 기하학 • geometrically ad. 기하학적으로

The tiles of the mosques show geometric patterns.

모스크의 타일은 기하학 무늬를 보여줘.

prejudice
[prédʒədis]

n. 편견

an unreasonable dislike or preference
- prejudiced a. 편견을 가진

Don't you have any prejudices about it?

그것에 대해 편견을 가지고 있지는 않니?

superficial
[sùːpərfíʃəl]

a. 피상적인

without depth, having little understanding of something
- superficially ad. 피상적으로

Before my trip, I only had superficial knowledge.

여행 전에 나는 피상적인 지식밖에 없었어.

taboo
[təbúː]

n. 금기 a. 금기의

a subject or activity which is not allowed or not permitted

I just knew that pork is taboo there.

돼지고기가 금기라는 것 정도만 알고 있었어.

overlook
[òuvərlúk]

v. 간과하다

to neglect, to disregard

I just overlooked their culture.

나는 그들의 문화를 간과했던 거야.

establish
[istǽbliʃ]
v. 확립하다

to create something and make it last
- establishment n. 확립

I didn't know that Muslims had established many trading routes.
나는 이슬람교도들이 많은 무역로를 확립했다는 것을 몰랐어.

pioneer
[pàiəníər]
n. 개척자, 선구자

a person who is first involved in an activity

In terms of trading, they were real pioneers.
무역에 있어서 그들은 정말 개척자였어.

underestimate
[ʌndəréstəmèit]
v. 과소평가하다

not to appreciate value of something properly
- underestimation n. 과소평가

I'm sure many people have underestimated their majestic culture.
나는 많은 사람들이 그들의 웅장한 문화를 과소평가했다고 확신해.

majestic
[mədʒéstik]
a. 웅장한

impressive, splendid
- majesty n. 웅장함, 장엄함

I'm sure many people have underestimated their majestic culture.
나는 많은 사람들이 그들의 웅장한 문화를 과소평가했다고 확신해.

legacy
[légəsi]
n. 유산

something that is handed down from someone else, heritage

Isn't it a great pity that information about their cultural legacies are not shown accurately?
그들의 문화 유산에 관한 정보가 정확하게 보여지지 않는다는 사실이 안타깝지 않니?

accurately
[ǽkjərətli]
ad. 정확하게

correctly, exactly
- accuracy n. 정확(성) - accurate a. 정확한

Isn't it a great pity that information about their cultural legacies are not shown accurately?
그들의 문화 유산에 관한 정보가 정확하게 보여지지 않는다는 사실이 안타깝지 않니?

distort
[distɔ́:rt]
v. 왜곡하다

to change something to make it look bad
- distortion n. 왜곡

Their history seems to have been distorted.
그들의 역사는 왜곡된 것 같아.

insufficient
[ìnsəfíʃənt]
a. 불충분한

not having enough of something
- insufficiency n. 불충분 • insufficiently ad. 불충분하게

I didn't know that films and TV programs just provide insufficient information.

나는 영화와 TV 프로그램에서 충분한 정보를 주고 있지 않는다는 것을 몰랐어.

depict
[dipíkt]
v. 묘사하다

to describe something
- depiction n. 묘사 • depictive 묘사적인

For example, Muslims are often depicted as terrorists.

예를 들어, 이슬람교도들은 종종 테러리스트로 묘사되잖아.

invasion
[invéiʒən]
n. 침략

an action of taking an army into another country
- invade v. 침략하다

Some programs just focused on the terrorists' invasion.

어떤 프로그램에서는 테러리스트들의 침략에 초점을 맞추기도 해.

unsanitary
[ʌnsǽnətèri]
a. 비위생적인

dirty, unclean
- sanitary a. 위생적인 • sanitation n. 위생

Or they even feature places with unsanitary conditions, not beautiful palaces or their culture.

아니면 아름다운 궁전이나 문화가 아니라 비위생적인 장소를 집중적으로 다루기도 해.

biased
[báiəst]
a. 편견을 가진

judging something unfairly, prejudiced
- bias v. 편견을 갖게 하다 n. 편견, 선입견

Do they encourage us to be biased about Islamic culture?

그런 것이 우리가 이슬람 문화에 대해 편견을 갖도록 유도하는 것은 아닐까?

architecture
[á:rkətèktʃər]
n. 건축물

the design and style of a building
- architect n. 건축가 • architectural a. 건축의

We will visit the famous Islamic architecture, the Alhambra.

우리는 유명한 이슬람 건축물인 알람브라를 가 볼 거야.

attraction
[ətrǽkʃən]
n. 관광지, 매력

a famous thing that people come to see
- attract v. 주의를 끌다 • attractive a. 매력적인

It's one of the great tourist attractions.

그곳은 아주 유명한 관광지 중 하나야.

Check Again!

A Translate each word into Korean.

1. splendid ....
2. underestimate ....
3. superficial ....
4. flourish ....
5. integrated ....
6. overlook ....
7. religious ....
8. unsanitary ....
9. majestic ....
10. geometric ....

B Translate each word into English.

1. 성스러운 ....
2. 기도하다 ....
3. 금기 ....
4. 불충분한 ....
5. 금식하다 ....
6. 왜곡하다 ....
7. 확립하다 ....
8. 개척자 ....
9. 건축물 ....
10. 관광지 ....

C Fill in the blank with the appropriate word. Refer to the Korean.

1. We need to preserve our cultural l   .
   우리는 우리의 문화 유산들을 보존해야 한다.

2. This children's book d   caterpillars as lovable animals.
   이 아동 도서는 애벌레를 사랑스러운 동물로 묘사한다.

3. His art is known for being a   beautiful.
   그의 예술은 미적으로 아름답다고 알려져 있다.

4. Not a few foreigners have had p   against Korean traditional medicine.
   적지 않은 외국인들이 한국의 전통 의학에 대해 선입견을 가져왔다.

5. Some of my friends were b   about this book from the moment they saw the cover.
   나의 몇몇 친구들은 책 표지를 보는 순간 이 책에 대해 편견을 가졌다.

Check More!

(A), (B), (C) 각 밑줄 친 부분에 알맞은 어휘를 짝지은 것으로 가장 적절한 것을 고르시오.

Since the mid-1990s, teaching Korean to foreigners has made quiet and steady **(A)** progress / process. Many universities now offer Korean language programs in Korea and abroad, and many textbooks have been produced for learners of Korean. Only a small number of foreigners, however, have benefited from this progress. Still, the importance of teaching Korean to foreigners seems to be **(B)** overestimated / underestimated. Therefore, most foreign workers are being taught by Korean coworkers or volunteers who have no or little teaching experience. Thus, it is necessary to **(C)** establish / estimate better educational programs for teaching the Korean language to foreign workers.

(A)	(B)	(C)
① progress	underestimated	establish
② progress	overestimated	establish
③ process	underestimated	estimate
④ progress	underestimated	estimate
⑤ process	overestimated	establish

Chapter 8
History, Art, and Culture

Unit 26. Home decorating is not easy.

have a **career** as a designer

make a room more **decorative**

choose a color scheme that **typifies** someon

Episode

Seri: Why don't we change our home decor? • We can relocate the furniture. • I can show you how to rearrange your room. • We can change the wallpaper and make the room more decorative.

Bomi: You look self-confident. • But I'm not sure I like your design concept.

Seri thinks herself very artistic. • She believes she is very versatile. • She likes making crafts. • She once designed a jewelry box and won a prize. • She said her jewelry box was designed elaborately. • She also said it fascinated all the girls. • She thought her box was sensational. • I can easily imagine her having a career as a designer. • For one design contest, she created a bandage with beads attached to it. • I perceived that it would be totally impractical. • But she expected that she would get a substantial amount of prize money. • She said that her bandage would be prominent.

Bomi: Seri, what's your wallpaper color scheme? Would you think of pink?

Seri: What a coincidence! • How come you came up with the same idea as me? • This pink fabric will be the best fit for the pink wallpaper, too.

Bomi: But our color scheme can be selective, right? • I'm very skeptical about your color scheme. • Why don't you modify your plan?

Then Hoony interjected with his own idea. • He chose a blue color scheme that typifies him. • Maybe he was thinking of Superman. • Hey, Seri and Hoony, maybe we should postpone changing our home decor.

세리: 우리 집안 장식 좀 바꾸어볼까? 가구 위치를 좀 바꿔볼 수 있잖아. 내가 언니 방을 어떻게 다시 정리할 수 있는지 보여줄게. 벽지를 바꾸어 방을 좀 더 화사하게 할 수 있어.
보미: 너는 자신 있어 보이는구나. 하지만 나는 네 디자인 컨셉이 맘에 드는지 잘 모르겠다.

세리는 자신이 아주 예술감각이 있다고 생각한다. 자신이 다재다능하다고 믿는다. 공예품 만드는 것을 좋아한다. 세리는 한때 보석함을 만들어 상을 타기도 했다. 자기의 보석함이 정교하게 디자인 되었다고 말했다. 또한 자신의 보석함이 모든 소녀들을 사로잡았다고 했다. 그녀는 자신의 보석함이 선풍적이라고 생각했다. 나는 그녀가 디자이너로서 직업을 갖는 것을 쉽게 상상할 수 있다. 한 디자인 경시대회에서 그녀는 구슬을 단 일회용 반창고를 만들었다. 나는 그것이 정말 비실용적일 거라고 생각했다. 하지만 세리는 상당한 금액의 상금을 받을 것이라고 기대했다. 세리는 자기의 일회용 반창고가 두드러질 것이라고 말했다.

보미: 세리, 벽지 색깔은 뭐로 할 거야? 분홍색으로 할 거야?
세리: 정말 우연의 일치네! 어떻게 나와 같은 생각을 했어? 이 핑크색 천도 핑크 벽지와 잘 어울릴 거야.
보미: 하지만 우리가 색깔을 고르는 건 선택의 여지가 있어, 그렇지? 나는 네가 생각하는 색깔에 매우 회의적이야. 계획을 바꾸는 것이 어때?

그때 후니가 자신의 생각을 가지고 불쑥 끼어들었다. 그는 자신을 상징하는 파란색을 골랐다. 아마 그는 슈퍼맨에 대해 생각하고 있었던 것 같다. 이봐, 세리와 후니, 우리 집안 장식을 바꾸는 것은 좀 뒤로 미루어야겠다.

decor
[deikɔ́ːr]

n. 장식

the style of a house's furnishing and decoration such as wallpaper

Why don't we change our home decor?

우리 집안 장식 좀 바꾸어볼까?

relocate
[riːlóukeit]

v. 위치를 바꾸다

to move something

• relocation n. 위치 변경, 재배치

We can relocate the furniture. 가구 위치를 좀 바꿔볼 수 있잖아.

rearrange
[rìːəréindʒ]

v. 재배치하다,
재배열하다

to change the positions of things

• rearrangement n. 재배치

I can show you how to rearrange your room.

내가 네 방을 어떻게 다시 정리할 수 있는지 보여줄게.

wallpaper
[wɔ́ːlpèipər]

n. 벽지

the decorative paper on the walls of a room

We can change the wallpaper and make the room more decorative.

벽지를 바꾸어 방을 좀 더 화사하게 할 수 있어.

decorative
[dékərèitiv]

a. 장식적인

looking pretty and attractive

• decorate v. 장식하다   • decoration n. 장식

We can change the wallpaper and make the room more decorative.

벽지를 바꾸어 방을 좀 더 화사하게 할 수 있어.

self-confident
[sélfkánfədənt]

a. 자신 있는

believing that you can do something well

• self-confidence n. 자신감

You look self-confident. 너는 자신 있어 보이는구나.

concept
[kánsept]

n. 개념

an idea or theme

But I'm not sure I like your design concept.

하지만 나는 네 디자인 컨셉이 맘에 드는지 잘 모르겠다.

artistic
[ɑːrtístik]

a. 예술적인

good at drawing, painting, or designing things in a beautiful way

• artist n. 예술가

Seri thinks herself very artistic.

세리는 자신이 아주 예술감각이 있다고 생각한다.

versatile
[və́:rsətl]

a. 다재다능한,
   다용도의

having the ability to do many different things well
- versatility n. 다재다능, 다용도

She believes she is very versatile.
그녀는 자신이 다재다능하다고 믿는다.

craft
[kræft]

n. 공예품, 수공품

a thing that is made by hand such as pottery or toys
- craftwork n. 공예 • craftsman n. 장인, 기능공

She likes making crafts. 그녀는 공예품 만드는 것을 좋아한다.

jewelry
[dʒú:əlri]

n. 보석류

precious stones and metals
- jewel n. 보석 • jeweled a. 보석으로 장식한

She once designed a jewelry box and won a prize.
그녀는 한때 보석함을 만들어 상을 타기도 했다.

elaborately
[ilǽbərèitli]

ad. 정교하게,
    공들여서

intricately, elegantly
- elaborate a. 공들인, 정교한

She said her jewelry box was designed elaborately.
그녀는 자기의 보석함이 정교하게 디자인 되었다고 말했다.

fascinate
[fǽsənèit]

v. 마음을 사로잡다,
   황홀하게 하다

to get people's attention
- fascination n. 매혹, 매료 • fascinating a. 매혹적인

She also said it fascinated all the girls.
그녀는 또한 그것이 모든 소녀들을 사로잡았다고 했다.

sensational
[senséiʃənəl]

a. 선풍적인

remarkable, causing great excitement and interest
- sensation n. 세상을 떠들썩하게 함 • sensationally ad. 선풍적으로

She thought her box was sensational.
그녀는 자신의 보석함이 선풍적이라고 생각했다.

career
[kəríər]

n. 직업, 경력

a job that one has for a long time

I can easily imagine her having a career as a designer.
나는 그녀가 디자이너로서 직업을 갖는 것을 쉽게 상상할 수 있다.

bead
[bíːd]
n. 구슬

a small piece of colored glass, plastic or stone
• beading n. 구슬 세공 • beaded a. 구슬 장식한

For one design contest, she created a bandage with beads attached to it.
한 디자인 경시대회에서 그녀는 구슬을 단 일회용 반창고를 만들었다.

perceive
[pərsíːv]
v. 알아차리다, 인지하다

to be aware of something
• perception n. 인지 • perceptible a. 인지할 수 있는

I perceived that it would be totally impractical.
나는 그것이 실용성이 전혀 없을 것이라고 생각했다.

impractical
[impræktikəl]
a. 비실용적인

unrealistic, absurd, opposite of practical

I perceived that it would be totally impractical.
나는 그것이 정말 비실용적일 거라고 생각했다.

substantial
[səbstǽnʃəl]
a. 상당한

abundant, ample
• substantially ad. 상당히

But she expected that she would get a substantial amount of prize money.
하지만 그녀는 상당한 금액의 상금을 받을 것이라고 기대했다.

prominent
[prάmənənt]
a. 두드러진, 눈길을 끄는

easily seen, eye-catching
• prominence n. 두드러짐, 탁월함

She said that her bandage would be prominent.
그녀는 자기의 일회용 반창고가 두드러질 것이라고 말했다.

color scheme
[kʌ́lər skìːm]
색 배합

a combination of several colors that one chooses to decorate something with

Seri, what's your wallpaper color scheme?
세리, 벽지 색깔은 뭐로 할 거야?

coincidence
[kouínsədəns]
n. 우연의 일치

a situation in which related events happen at the same time
• coincidental a. 일치하는, 동시에 일어나는 • coincidentally ad. 우연의 일치로

What a coincidence! 정말 우연의 일치네!

come up with
[kʌ́m ʌp wið]
생각해내다

to suggest, to think

How come you came up with the same idea as me?
어떻게 나와 같은 생각을 했어?

fabric
[fǽbrik]
n. 천, 헝겊

cloth

This pink fabric will be the best fit for the pink wallpaper, too.
이 핑크색 천도 핑크 벽지와 잘 어울릴 거야.

selective
[siléktiv]
a. 선택안이 있는, 고르는

choicy, choosy
• selectively ad. 선택적으로

But our color scheme can be selective, right?
하지만 우리 색깔 고르는 건 선택의 여지가 있어, 그렇지?

skeptical
[sképtikəl]
a. 회의적인

having doubts about something, unsure of something
• skeptic n. 회의론자 • skepticism n. 회의론

I'm very skeptical about your color scheme.
나는 네가 생각하는 색깔에 매우 회의적이야.

modify
[mɑ́dəfài]
v. 수정하다

to change something slightly
• modification n. 수정

Why don't you modify your plan? 계획을 바꾸는 것이 어때?

interject
[ìntərdʒékt]
v. 끼어들다

to stop someone talking so that you can talk
• interjection n. 끼어들기

Then Hoony interjected with his own idea.
그때 후니가 자신의 생각을 가지고 불쑥 끼어들었다.

typify
[típəfài]
v. 상징하다, 대표하다

to represent something, to characterize
• typical a. 전형적인

He chose a blue color scheme that typifies him.
그는 자신을 상징하는 파란색을 골랐다.

postpone
[poustpóun]
v. 연기하다

to put off till later time
• postponement n. 연기

Hey, Seri and Hoony, maybe we should postpone changing our home decor.
이봐, 세리와 후니, 우리 집안 장식을 바꾸는 것은 좀 뒤로 미루어야겠다.

Check Again!

A Translate each word into Korean.

1. versatile ....
2. craft ....
3. rearrange ....
4. decor ....
5. sensational ....
6. relocate ....
7. rearrange ....
8. impractical ....
9. prominent ....
10. career ....

B Translate each word into English.

1. 예술적인 ....
2. 연기하다 ....
3. 정교하게 ....
4. 알아차리다 ....
5. 장식적인 ....
6. 수정하다 ....
7. 자신 있는 ....
8. 개념 ....
9. 우연의 일치 ....
10. 선택안이 있는 ....

C Fill in the blank with the appropriate word. Refer to the Korean.

1. Personally, I am very s   about what they claim they can do.
   개인적으로 나는 그들이 할 수 있다고 주장하는 것에 대해 아주 회의적이다.

2. The Bank of America Tower is lit with the red, white and blue color
   s   .
   뱅크 오브 아메리카 타워가 빨간색, 흰색, 파란색의 색 배합으로 조명을 밝히고 있다.

3. Americans get a s   amount of news and information from
   blogs.
   미국인들은 상당한 양의 뉴스와 정보를 블로그에서 얻는다.

4. "That's not how it was," she i   with a strong voice,
   somewhat angry.
   "그건 그런 게 아니에요"라고 그녀가 강한 어조로 다소 화가 나서 끼어 들었다.

5. People will be more likely to believe you when you look s
   네가 자신 있어 보이면 사람들은 너의 말을 좀 더 믿을 것이다.

수능 기출 응용

다음 밑줄 친 부분에 알맞은 어휘를 고르시오. 아래의 영영 풀이를 참조하시오.

Fueled by a lifelong love of literature, Gonzales has **(A)** devised / devoted himself to providing people with more access to literature. When he moved to Marysville, Kansas, after a successful **(B)** carrier / career as a barber in Los Angeles, he noticed a widespread hunger for reading in the community. He helped customers read books by opening a library with a collection of 500 books inside his barbershop in 1990. "Even though many people wanted to read books, they had nowhere to turn," said Gonzales. At first some people were very **(C)** skeptical / fascinated about his idea, but his efforts came to be recognized nationwide and he won the Livingstone Award in 2003. "Mr. Gonzales has helped people find a **(D)** shelve / shelter for their spirits," wrote the Livingstone Committee.

(A) to dedicate; to give; to commit: ....

(B) occupation; life's work; vocation: ....

(C) having doubts: ....

(D) protection; safety; cover: ....

+ 접두사 post-와 어근 -pos / -spect / cre-

-pos는 'to put'이라는 뜻의 어근으로, '어떤 위치나 상태에 놓다'는 뜻의 단어를 만든다.
post-는 behind라는 뜻의 접두사로, '어떤 시점 후에 발생하다'는 뜻의 단어를 만든다.
-spect는 'look'이라는 뜻의 어근으로, '바라보거나 주의를 기울이다'는 뜻의 단어를 만든다. cre-는 'believe'라는 뜻의 어근으로, '신뢰나 믿음'과 관련된 단어를 만든다.

-pos/post-

de- 반대의(un-)
de + pose = depose 물러나게 하다
ex) Soon, the king was deposed from the throne.
곧 왕은 왕위에서 물러나게 되었다.

- **ex-** ~밖으로 — **expose** 드러내다, 노출시키다
- **in-** ~안으로 — **impose** 의무를 부과하다, 강요하다
- **trans-** 횡단 — **transposition** 위치를 바꾸어 넣기
- **war** 전쟁 — **postwar** 전후
- **position** 위치 — **postposition** 후치, 뒤에 둠
- **graduate** 졸업생 — **postgraduate** 대학원 학생
- **modernism** 모더니즘 — **postmodernism** 포스트모더니즘

-spect

retro 뒤
retro + spect = retrospect 회상
ex) In retrospect, I wish I'd been nicer to her.
돌이켜 생각해보면, 그녀에게 더 잘해줄 걸 그랬어요.

- **in-** ~안으로 — **inspect** 면밀히 살피다
- **ex-** 외부의 — **expect** 기대하다
- **pro-** 앞으로 — **prospect** 전망
- **re-** 뒤 — **respect** 관심, 고려
- **intro-** 안의 — **introspection** 자기 관찰
- **ad-** ~를 향하여 — **aspect** 관점, 양상
- **circum-** 주위에 — **circumspect** 조심성 있는, 용의주도한

cre-

credere 믿다
credit 신뢰, 신용
ex) He is a fine man of credit.
그는 믿을 만한 훌륭한 사람이에요.

- **creditor** 채권자
- **credible** 신뢰할 수 있는, 확실한
- **creditable** 칭찬할 만한
- **accredit** ~의 공적으로 치다
- **incredible** 신뢰할 수 없는
- **discreditable** 신용을 떨어뜨리는
- **creed** 신조, 신념

Culture Plus

Art Movements 미술 사조

+Classicism 고전주의

+Romanticism 낭만주의

+Impressionism 인상주의

+Cubism 입체파

+Abstract Art 추상 미술

+Realism 사실주의

+Surrealism 초현실주의

We're teens. I had my cell phone taken away. Goodbye, Brownie Life is full of contrad
campus tour. If I were a judge,.... How can we survive in a jungle? I became a Santa C
oney-wise. oony goes to an erbal clinic. We ecame a rescue team. Grandma goes
u want to meet? A and c mp ible? I n't understand this painting. The
ve ill sions abo t boys can't nderst nd po ticians. Wearing an electronic tag is hor
econ mics c mp. con ruc on a thriving b siness? How amazing our life has becor
pace. I attended the Arbor Day ceremony. We can make the earth a better place. A

VOCA
EDGE
RED

ife is full of contradictions. Goodbye, Sara. I learned about the earth. I went to a natu

ecame a Santa Claus. Sara attends a community party. Mom's got a new hobby. Are t

Grandma goes to a laughter clinic. The Volcanoes are back. We have great brothers. W

ainting. There was telepathy between us! Sara goes to Turkey. Home decorating is r

electronic tag is horrible. The war should be stopped. Mom, are you going to cut my allc

ur life has become! I should have been more careful. Forgery should be stopped. Hoo

etter place. A super hurricane hit the village. We're teens. I had my cell phone taken

vent to a natural science museum. I had a campus tour. If I were a judge,... How can w

hobby. Are they my bosses? Hoony is money-wise. Hoony goes to an herbal clinic. We

great brothers. What historical figures do you want to meet? Are mom and dad compa

decorating is not easy. Hoony thinks girls have illusions about boys. I can't understand p

cut my allowance? Hoony is back from an economics camp. construction a thriving b

topped. Hoony wants to explore outer space. I attended the Arbor Day ceremony. W

phone taken away. Goodbye, Brownie Life is full of contradictions. Goodbye, Sara. I lea

low can we survive in a jungle? I became a Santa Claus. Sara attends a community po

oodbye, Sara. I learned about the earth. I went to a natural science museum. I had a

a attends a community party. Mom's got a new hobby. Are they my bosses? Hoony i

ghter clinic. The Volcanoes are back. We have great brothers. What historical figures do

epathy between us! Sara goes to Turkey. Home decorating is not easy. Hoony thinks girl

war should be stopped. Mom, are you going to cut my allowance? Hoony is back from

ld have been more careful. Forgery should be stopped. Hoony wants to explore oute

ricane hit the village. We're teens. I had my cell phone taken away. Goodbye, Brownie

e museum. I had a campus tour. If I were a judge,... How can we survive in a jungle?

osses? Hoony is money-wise. Hoony goes to an herbal clinic. We became a rescue team

cal figures do you want to meet? Are mom and dad compatible? I can't understand thi

Hoony thinks girls have illusions about boys. I can't understand politicians. Wearing ar

Hoony is back from an economics camp. construction a thriving business? How amazing

o explore outer space. I attended the Arbor Day ceremony. We can make the earth a

odbye, Brownie Life is full of contradictions. Goodbye, Sara. I learned about the earth.

a jungle? I became a Santa Claus. Sara attends a community party. Mom's got a new

Chapter 9. Politics and Social Issues

a rescue team. Grandma goes to a laughter clinic. The Volcanoes are back. We ha

Unit 27. Hoony thinks girls have illusions about boys.

't understand this painting. There was telepathy between us! Sara goes to Turkey. Ho

Unit 28. I can't understand politicians.

earing an electronic tag is horrible. The war should be stopped. Mom, are you going

Unit 29. Wearing an electronic tag is horrible.

ow amazing our life has become! I should have been more careful. Forgery should

Unit 30. The war should be stopped.

e the earth a better place. A super hurricane hit the village. We're teens. I had my ce

the earth. I went to a natural science museum. I had a campus tour. If I were a judge,...

got a new hobby. Are they my bosses? Hoony is money-wise. Hoony goes to an herba

Chapter 9
Politics and Social Issues

Unit 27. Hoony thinks girls have illusions about boys.

be victims of **gender discrimination**

pass specific **rites of passage**

wear very **feminine** clothing

Episode

Dear Diary,
I **inferred** from Hoony's behavior that something was wrong.

Bomi: What's wrong, Hoony?
Hoony: Why do girls have **illusions** about boys? • I didn't realize that gender discrimination is **prevalent** among girls. • Why do they think boys should be better at math problems like **fractions**? • They think it should be boys who carry heavy objects like **recycling** bins. • Why should boys do that? • We are **victims** of **gender discrimination**. • Sometimes girls treat us like **slaves**. • Girls are **irresponsible**. • They just pretend that such work is **exhausting** for them.

I know why Hoony is so sensitive about this **issue**. • He is **concealing** his feelings. • Hoony is afraid that his new classmate, Taeji, is more **appealing** to girls. • Taeji is good at **martial arts**. • Before Taeji came to school, Hoony was the most **popular** boy. • He doesn't want to **surrender** his position. • He wants to **secure** his position. • Now he is **attributing** the girls' attitude to discrimination. • Sometimes boys have to pass specific **rites of passage** to prove their physical power. • They fight because they think that strength is a **virtue** that boys have. • They think weak boys are often **despised**. • Hoony thinks Taeji has more **masculine** characteristics than him.
Hoony, girls are **inclined** to like boys who have tender hearts, not big muscles. • Girls like **warm-hearted** boys. • I think you're the **ideal** type of man. • Now, he is getting more **agitated**. • I always thought that girls were victims of **sexism**. • I thought I should always wear very **feminine** clothing. • Now I see that boys and girls are **equal** victims of gender discrimination. • Hoony made me realize that boys feel **social pressure**, too.

다이어리에게,
후니의 행동으로 보아 나는 뭔가 잘못되었다고 추론했어.

보미: 왜 그래, 후니?
후니: 왜 여자아이들은 남자아이들에 대해 환상을 갖는 거야? 여자아이들 사이에 성차별이 그렇게 만연해 있는 줄 몰랐어. 왜 분수 같은 수학 문제는 남자아이들이 더 잘할 거라고 생각해? 여자아이들은 재활용통 같은 무거운 물건은 남자아이들이 날라야 한다고 생각해. 왜 남자아이들이 그것을 해야 해? 우리가 성차별의 피해자야. 이따금 여자아이들은 우리를 노예 취급해. 여자아이들은 무책임해. 그들은 그런 일이 자기들한테 아주 힘든 척하잖아.

후니가 이 문제에 그렇게 민감한 이유를 나는 알고 있어. 자신의 감정을 감추고 있어. 후니는 새로운 반 친구 태지가 여자아이들한테 더 인기가 있을까 봐 두려워하는 거야. 태지는 무술을 잘해. 태지가 학교에 전학 오기 전에는, 후니가 가장 인기 있는 남학생이었어. 그 자리를 내주고 싶지 않을 거야. 그는 그 자리를 지키고 싶어해. 이제 그는 여자아이들의 태도를 차별 탓으로 돌리고 있어. 남자아이들은 가끔 자신들의 신체적 힘을 증명하기 위해 특정한 통과의례를 거쳐야 해. 남자아이들은 힘을 자신들이 가진 미덕이라고 생각하기 때문에 싸워. 그들은 약한 남자아이들은 자주 무시당한다고 생각해. 후니는 태지가 자기보다 더 남자다운 특징을 많이 가졌다고 생각하는 거야.
후니, 여자아이들은 커다란 근육이 아니라 따뜻한 가슴을 가진 남자아이들을 좋아하는 경향이 있어. 여자아이들은 따뜻한 마음을 가진 남자아이들을 좋아해. 나는 네가 이상적인 타입의 남자라고 생각해. 이제 그가 더욱 동요하고 있어. 나는 늘 여자아이들이 성차별의 피해자라고 생각했었어. 나는 아주 여성스러운 옷을 항상 입어야 된다고 생각했었어. 이제 보니 남자아이들과 여자아이들 모두가 성차별의 똑같은 피해자라는 걸 알겠어. 후니때문에 남자아이들도 사회적 압력을 느낀다는 것을 깨닫게 되었어.

infer
[infə́:r]
v. 추론하다

to guess something; to decide that something is probably true
• inference n. 추론

I inferred from Hoony's behavior that something was wrong.
후니의 행동으로 보아 나는 뭔가 잘못되었다고 추론했어.

illusion
[ilú:ʒən]
n. 환상, 착각

a false belief or idea
• illusory a. 착각의, 착각을 일으키는

Why do girls have illusions about boys?
왜 여자아이들은 남자아이들에 대해 환상을 갖는 거야?

prevalent
[prévələnt]
a. 널리 퍼진, 보급된

widespread, commonly occurring
• prevail v. 우세하다, 만연하다   • prevalence n. 우세함, 만연함

I didn't realize that gender discrimination is prevalent among girls.
여자아이들 사이에 성차별이 그렇게 만연해 있는 줄 몰랐어.

fraction
[frǽkʃən]
n. 분수

a number which is expressed as a proportion of two whole numbers

Why do they think boys should be better at math problems like fractions?
왜 분수 같은 수학 문제는 남자아이들이 더 잘할 거라고 생각해?

recycling
[rì:sáikliŋ]
n. 재활용

using something again instead of throwing it away
• recycle v. 재활용하다

They think it should be boys who carry heavy objects like recycling bins.
그들은 재활용 통 같은 무거운 물건은 남자아이들이 날라야 한다고 생각해.

victim
[víktim]
n. 피해자, 희생자

someone who has been hurt or killed by another person
• victimize v. 희생시키다

We are victims of gender discrimination.
우리는 성차별의 피해자야.

gender discrimination
[dʒéndər diskrìmənéiʃən]
성차별

giving a disadvantage to someone because of their gender

We are victims of gender discrimination.
우리는 성차별의 피해자야.

slave
[sléiv]

n. 노예

someone who is forced to work without pay
- slavery n. 노예제도

Sometimes girls treat us like slaves.
이따금 여자아이들은 우리를 노예 취급해.

irresponsible
[ìrispánsəbəl]

a. 무책임한

untrustworthy, careless
- irresponsibility n. 무책임

Girls are irresponsible. 여자아이들은 무책임해.

exhausting
[igzɔ́ːstiŋ]

a. 피로하게 하는

difficult and making one tired

They just pretend that such work is exhausting for them.
그들은 그런 일이 자기들한테 아주 힘든 척하잖아.

issue
[íʃuː]

n. 논제, 이슈

a fact or important subject that many people discuss

I know why Hoony is so sensitive about this issue.
후니가 이 문제에 그렇게 민감한 이유를 나는 알고 있어.

conceal
[kənsíːl]

v. 숨기다, 은폐하다

to hide something
- concealment n. 은폐

He is concealing his feelings. 그는 자신의 감정을 감추고 있어.

appealing
[əpíːliŋ]

a. 마음을 끄는,
   관심을 끄는

attractive to other people
- appeal v. 마음을 끌다 n. 마음을 움직이는 힘, 매력

Hoony is afraid that his new classmate, Taeji, is more appealing to girls.
후니는 새로운 반 친구 태지가 여자아이들한테 더 인기가 있을까 봐 두려워하는 거야.

martial art
[máːrʃəl áːrt]

무술

one of the techniques of self-defense such as kung fu or taekwondo
- martial artist n. 무술가

Taeji is good at martial arts. 태지는 무술을 잘해.

popular
[pápjələr]

a. 인기 있는

being liked by many people
- popularity n. 인기

Before Taeji came to school, Hoony was the most popular boy.
태지가 학교에 전학 오기 전에는, 후니가 가장 인기 있는 남학생이었어.

surrender
[səréndər]
v. 내주다, 포기하다

to give up something or lose status

He doesn't want to surrender his position.
그는 그 자리를 내주고 싶지 않은 거야.

secure
[sikjúər]
v. 지키다, 확보하다

to keep one's status, to make something safe from attack

• security n. 보호, 보장, 안전

He wants to secure his position. 그는 그 자리를 지키고 싶어해.

attribute
[ətríbju:t]
v. ~의 탓으로 돌리다
n. 속성, 특징

to think that a situation is caused by a particular thing

• attribution n. 귀착시킴, 귀속 • attributable a. ~에 돌릴 수 있는, ~에 기인하는
• attribute A to B   A를 B의 탓으로 돌리다

Now he is attributing the girls' attitude to discrimination.
이제 그는 여자아이들의 태도를 차별 탓으로 돌리고 있어.

rite of passage
[ráit ɔv pǽsidʒ]
통과의례

a tradition or custom that one must follow to gain something

Sometimes boys have to pass specific rites of passage
to prove their physical power.
남자아이들은 가끔 자신들의 신체적 힘을 증명하기 위해 특정한 통과의례를 거쳐야 해.

virtue
[və́:rtʃu:]
n. 미덕

a behavior or characteristic that people believe is good

• virtuous a. 덕 있는, 고결한

They fight because they think that strength is a virtue
that boys have.
그들은 힘을 자신들이 가진 미덕이라고 생각하기 때문에 싸워.

despise
[dispáiz]
v. 무시하다, 얕보다

to have a low opinion of someone or something

They think weak boys are often despised.
그들은 약한 남자아이들은 자주 무시당한다고 생각해.

masculine
[mǽskjəlin]
a. 남자다운, 힘센

manly, opposite of feminine

• masculinity n. 남성다움

Hoony thinks Taeji has more masculine characteristics
than him.
후니는 태지가 자기보다 더 남자다운 특징을 많이 가졌다고 생각하는 거야.

inclined
[inkláind]

a. ~의 경향이 있는,
~하고 싶어하는

being likely to do something in one way, disposed
- incline v. ~한 경향이 생기게 하다 - inclination n. 경향, 기질
- be inclined to+ V ~하는 경향이 있다

Hoony, girls are inclined to like boys who have tender hearts, not big muscles.
후니, 여자아이들은 커다란 근육이 아니라 따뜻한 가슴을 가진 남자아이들을 좋아하는 경향이 있어.

warm-hearted
[wɔ́ːrmháːrtid]

a. 마음이 따뜻한

kind and generous to other people

Girls like warm-hearted boys.
여자아이들은 따뜻한 마음을 가진 남자아이들을 좋아해.

ideal
[aidíːəl]

a. 이상적인
n. 이상

the best, perfect
- ideally ad. 이상적으로

I think you're the ideal type of man.
나는 네가 이상적인 타입의 남자라고 생각해.

agitated
[ǽdʒətèitid]

a. 흥분된, 동요한

angry and upset
- agitate v. 흥분시키다 - agitation n. 흥분, 동요

Now, he is getting more agitated. 이제 그가 더욱 동요하고 있어.

sexism
[séksizəm]

n. 성차별

gender discrimination
- sexist n. 성차별주의자

I always thought that girls were victims of sexism.
나는 늘 여자아이들이 성차별의 피해자라고 생각했어.

feminine
[fémənin]

a. 여성스러운

womanish, opposite of masculine
- femininity n. 여성다움, 여성임

I thought I should always wear very feminine clothing.
나는 아주 여성스러운 옷을 항상 입어야 된다고 생각했어.

equal
[íːkwəl]

a. 같은, 동등한

alike, the same, fair
- equality n. 동등함

Now I see that boys and girls are equal victims of gender discrimination.
이제 보니 남자아이들과 여자아이들 모두가 성차별의 똑같은 피해자라는 걸 알겠어.

social pressure
[sóuʃəl préʃər]

사회적 압력

rules and guidelines that other people want you to follow

Hoony made me realize that boys feel social pressure, too.
후니때문에 남자아이들도 사회적 압력을 느낀다는 것을 깨닫게 되었어.

Check Again!

A Translate each word into Korean.

1. infer ....
2. despise ....
3. equal ....
4. fraction ....
5. conceal ....
6. attribute ....
7. surrender ....
8. agitated ....
9. inclined ....
10. masculine ....

B Translate each word into English.

1. 이상적인 ....
2. 무책임한 ....
3. 미덕 ....
4. 마음을 끄는 ....
5. 인기 있는 ....
6. 지키다 ....
7. 피로하게 하는 ....
8. 피해자 ....
9. 마음이 따뜻한 ....
10. 여성스러운 ....

C Fill in the blank with the appropriate word. Refer to the Korean.

1. He a_____ his failure to a bad luck.

   그는 자신의 실패를 불운때문이라고 탓했다.

2. Young people are likely to have i_____ about TV stars.

   어린 아이들은 TV스타에 대한 환상을 가질 가능성이 있다.

3. Body image dissatisfaction is p_____ among girls and women.

   소녀들과 여자들 사이에 자기 신체에 대한 불만족이 만연해 있다.

4. "Gender d_____" is unequal treatment of a person based on gender.

   "성차별"이란 성에 따라 불평등한 대우를 하는 것이다.

5. Hapkido is a type of Korean m_____ art, which focuses on defense rather than offense.

   합기도는 공격보다는 방어에 집중하는 한국의 무술 중 하나이다.

Check More!

다음 밑줄 친 부분에 알맞은 어휘를 고르시오. 아래의 영영 풀이를 참조하시오.

The number of hunting accidents has increased sharply this year. The **(A)** victims / virtues were mostly hunters and hikers who were mistaken for game. Questions have arisen from victims and their families about who is **(B)** responsible / irresponsible for these avoidable accidents. They blame police for not taking proper measures. In fact, police do issue permits to qualified hunters and advise hikers to wear bright, colorful clothing during hunting season. Of course, police should **(C)** investigate / issue some additional warnings or take other preventive actions. It is the victims themselves, however, who are responsible for guaranteeing their own safety. They should not **(D)** lack / risk their own lives in deep forests when they are alone in plain clothes.

(A) someone who has been hurt or killed:

....

(B) in charge; in control: ....

(C) to make it known formally or publicly:

....

(D) to expose to the chance of injury or loss:

....

Chapter 9
Politics and Social Issues

Unit 28. I can't understand politicians.

pretend to be courteous

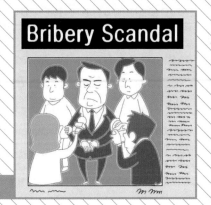

be involved in bribery scandal

be interested in satirical games

Episode

Dear Sara,

What are **politicians** like? • What are the **requirements** to enter parliament? • What **qualifications** do they need? • People who want to become politicians should be given a **rigorous** interview. • During the interview, we should check carefully to see if they are **two-faced**. • Many politicians seem to have some **traits** in common. • They pretend to be **courteous**. • They even promise voters that their actions will be **transparent**. • But, once they are elected, their **policies** change. • Recently, some politicians were involved in **bribery** scandals. • Grandpa said that people shouldn't have voted for those **nominees**. • Their **corrupt** actions are very serious. • I think they should **resign** immediately. • When will the **Supreme Court** intervene in these cases? • Are the police going to **investigate** them thoroughly?

In cyberspace, we can **mock** these people in funny ways. • My friends like writing **satirical** jokes about them on their webpages. • These things sweep through our country like an **epidemic**. • They **illustrate** how people feel about corrupt politicians. • Sometimes government **officials** at the highest rank are described as animals. • They are sentenced to **life-long imprisonment**. • They have to **crawl** around like bugs, making apologies. • We can make them **vanish** from our view. • If you're also interested in satirical games and jokes, please let me know.

Sara, I heard America has a **two-party** system, the Democrats and Republicans. • Which party shows more support for the rights of **minorities** such as the **handicapped**? • Are both parties strongly against **racism**? • I heard the Democrats are more **liberal**, while Republicans are more **conservative**. • Anyway, I hope both parties work for the people.

사라에게,

정치인들은 어떤 사람들이야? 의회에 들어가기 위한 요건은 무엇일까? 어떤 자격이 필요한 것일까? 정치인이 되고 싶은 사람들은 엄격한 면접을 받아야 해. 면접 중에 그들이 표리부동한 사람인지 세심하게 조사해야 해. 많은 정치인들은 공통적인 특성이 있어. 그들은 정중한 척해. 그들은 유권자들에게 자신들의 행동이 투명할 것이라고 약속을 해. 하지만 일단 당선되면 정책이 바뀌어. 최근에 몇몇 정치인들이 뇌물수수 스캔들에 연루되었어. 할아버지께서는 사람들이 그 후보자들에게 투표하지 말았어야 했다고 말씀하셨어. 그들의 부패한 행동은 아주 심각해. 나는 그들이 즉시 사임해야 한다고 생각해. 대법원이 언제 이 사건에 개입할까? 경찰은 그들을 철저하게 수사할까?

사이버 공간에서 우리는 정치인들을 재미있는 방법으로 조롱할 수 있어. 내 친구들은 그들에 관한 풍자적인 글을 웹페이지에 올리는 것을 좋아해. 이러한 것들이 유행병처럼 전국을 휩쓸고 있어. 그것들은 사람들이 부패한 정치인들을 어떻게 생각하는지 잘 보여줘. 이따금 최고위급 정부 관리들은 동물로 묘사돼. 그들은 종신형을 선고받아. 그들은 벌레처럼 기며 사죄를 해. 우리는 그들을 시야에서 사라지게 할 수도 있어. 너도 풍자 게임이나 조크에 관해 관심이 있으면 알려줘.

사라, 미국은 민주당과 공화당의 양당제라고 들었어. 어느 당이 장애인과 같은 소수 사람들의 권리를 더 지지하니? 양쪽 당 모두 인종주의에 강하게 반대하니? 나는 민주당은 더 진보적이고 공화당은 더 보수적이라고 들었어. 어쨌든, 두 당이 다 국민들을 위해 일했으면 해.

politician
[pəlitíʃən]
n. 정치인

a person who is part of the government of a country
- politics n. 정치, 정치학 - political a. 정치적인

What are politicians like? 정치인들은 어떤 사람들이야?

requirement
[rikwáiərmənt]
n. 요건

a quality or qualification that people need to have
- require v. 필요로 하다

What are the requirements to enter parliament?
의회에 들어가기 위한 요건은 무엇일까?

qualification
[kwàləfəkéiʃən]
n. 자격

a special skill
- qualify v. 자격을 주다, 자격을 얻다 - qualified a. 자격을 갖춘

What qualifications do they need? 그들은 어떤 자격이 필요한 것일까?

rigorous
[rígərəs]
a. 엄격한

very thorough, severe
- rigor n. 엄격, 준엄 - rigorously ad. 엄격하게

People who want to become politicians should be given a rigorous interview.
정치인이 되고 싶은 사람들은 엄격한 면접을 받아야 해.

two-faced
[tú:fèist]
a. 표리부동한,
   위선적인

deceitful, cunning

During the interview, we should check carefully to see if they are two-faced.
면접 중에 그들이 표리부동한 사람인지 세심하게 조사해야 해.

trait
[tréit]
n. 특성

a particular characteristic that someone has
- have (traits) in common ~라는 공통점이 있다(공통적인 특성을 가지고 있다

Many politicians seem to have some traits in common.
많은 정치인들은 공통적인 특성이 있어.

courteous
[kə́:rtiəs]
a. 정중한

well-mannered, polite
- courteously ad. 정중하게

They pretend to be courteous. 그들은 정중한 척해.

transparent
[trænspέərənt]
a. 투명한, 정직한

understandable, apparent, easily understood or recognized
- transparency n. 투명성

They even promise voters that their actions will be transparent.
그들은 유권자들에게 자신들의 행동이 투명할 것이라고 약속을 해.

policy
[pάləsi]
n. 정책

a set of plans used as a basis for an organization

But, once they are elected, their policies change.

하지만 일단 당선되면 정책이 바뀌어.

bribery
[bráibəri]
n. 뇌물수수

the act of giving money to people so that they will do what you want

• bribe v. 뇌물을 주다 n. 뇌물

Recently, some politicians were involved in bribery scandals.

최근에 몇몇 정치인들이 뇌물수수 스캔들에 연루되었어.

nominee
[nàməní:]
n. 지명자

a person who other people recommend for a job

• nominate v. 지명하다 • nomination n. 지명

Grandpa said that people shouldn't have voted for those nominees.

할아버지께서는 사람들이 그 후보자들에게 투표하지 말았어야 했다고 말씀하셨어.

corrupt
[kərʌ́pt]
a. 부패한, 타락한
v. 타락시키다

morally wrong, dishonest

• corruption n. 타락, 부패 • corruptible a. 타락하기 쉬운

Their corrupt actions are very serious.

그들의 부패한 행동은 아주 심각해.

resign
[rizáin]
v. 사임하다, 사직하다

to announce that one is leaving a job or position

• resignation n. 사임, 사직

I think they should resign immediately.

나는 그들이 즉시 사임해야 한다고 생각해.

Supreme Court
[səprí:m kɔ́:rt]
대법원

the highest level court where criminals go to trial

When will the Supreme Court intervene in these cases?

대법원이 언제 이 사건에 개입할까?

investigate
[invéstəgèit]
v. 수사하다

to ask questions and examine a situation in order to decide what is true

• investigation n. 수사, 조사

Are the police going to investigate them thoroughly?

경찰은 그들을 철저하게 수사할까?

mock
[mák]
v. 조롱하다

to ridicule someone

In cyberspace, we can mock these people in funny ways.

사이버 공간에서 우리는 이 사람들을 재미있는 방법으로 조롱할 수 있어.

satirical
[sətírikəl]
a. 풍자의, 비꼬는

criticizing something, mocking

• satire n. 풍자 • satirically ad. 풍자적으로

My friends like writing satirical jokes about them on their webpages.

내 친구들은 그들에 관한 풍자적인 글들을 웹페이지에 올리는 것을 좋아해.

epidemic
[èpədémik]
n. 유행병, 유행

a particular disease that spreads very quickly

These things sweep through our country like an epidemic

이러한 것들이 유행병처럼 전국을 휩쓸고 있어.

illustrate
[íləstrèit]
v. 설명하다

to explain; to let people understand

• illustration n. 설명

They illustrate how people feel about corrupt politicians.

그것들은 사람들이 부패한 정치인들을 어떻게 생각하는지 잘 보여줘.

official
[əfíʃəl]
n. 공무원, 관리
a. 관리의, 공식의

a person who has authority in an organization

• officially ad. 공식적으로

Sometimes government officials at the highest rank are described as animals.

이따금 최고위급 정부 관리들은 동물로 묘사돼.

life-long imprisonment
[láiflɔ̀:ŋ imprízənmənt]
종신형

being put in prison for the rest of one's life

They are sentenced to life-long imprisonment.

그들은 종신형을 선고받아.

crawl
[krɔ́:l]
v. 기다, 아첨하다

to move on hands and knees

They have to crawl around like bugs, making apologies.

그들은 벌레처럼 기며 사죄를 해.

vanish
[vǽniʃ]

v. 사라지다

to disappear; not to be seen

We can make them vanish from our view.

우리는 그들을 시야에서 사라지게 할 수도 있어.

two-party system
[tuːpáːrti sístəm]

양당제

a political system which consists of two different groups of politicians

Sara, I heard America has a two-party system, the Democrats and Republicans.

사라, 미국은 민주당과 공화당의 양당제라고 들었어.

minority
[minɔ́ːriti]

n. 소수

a number of people forming less than half in a larger group

Which party shows more support for the rights of minorities such as the handicapped?

어느 당이 장애인과 같은 소수 사람들의 권리를 더 지지하니?

handicapped
[hǽndikæpt]

a. 장애를 가진

having a physical or mental disability

Which party shows more support for the rights of minorities such as the handicapped?

어느 당이 장애인과 같은 소수 사람들의 권리를 더 지지하니?

racism
[réisizəm]

n. 인종차별주의

prejudice against an ethnic group; unfair treatment against a different race

• race n. 인종 a. 인종의, 인종적인   • racist n. 인종차별주의자

Are both parties strongly against racism?

양쪽 당 모두 인종차별주의에 강하게 반대하니?

liberal
[líbərəl]

a. 진보적인,
   자유주의의

progressive, broad-minded

• liberate v. 해방시키다   • liberty n. 해방, 자유
• liberalism n. 자유주의, 진보주의

I heard the Democrats are more liberal, while Republicans are more conservative.

나는 민주당은 더 진보적이고 공화당은 더 보수적이라고 들었어.

conservative
[kənsə́ːrvətiv]

a. 보수적인

preserving the status, cautious

• conserve v. 보존하다   • conservation n. 보존
• conservatism n. 보수주의

I heard the Democrats are more liberal, while Republicans are more conservative.

나는 민주당은 더 진보적이고 공화당은 더 보수적이라고 들었어.

Check Again!

A Translate each word into Korean.

1. racism ....
2. satirical ....
3. epidemic ....
4. requirement ....
5. qualification ....
6. rigorous ....
7. courteous ....
8. conservative ....
9. minority ....
10. trait ....

B Translate each word into English.

1. 지명자 ....
2. 부패한 ....
3. 정책 ....
4. 수사하다 ....
5. 정치인 ....
6. 사라지다 ....
7. 투명한 ....
8. 진보적인 ....
9. 공무원 ....
10. 장애를 가진 ....

C Fill in the blank with the appropriate word. Refer to the Korean.

1. Let's wait for the S _____ Court to make a decision.

   대법원이 결정을 내릴 때까지 기다리자.

2. Now that you know these people are t _____ , just avoid them.

   이제 이 사람들이 위선적이라는 것을 알았으니 그냥 피해라.

3. The serial killer was arrested and sentenced to life-long i _____ .

   그 연쇄살인범이 체포되어 종신형을 선고받았다.

4. This article i _____ the basic mechanism of photosynthesis in plain terms.

   이 기사는 광합성의 기본 원리를 쉬운 말로 설명한다.

5. Being involved in b _____ scandals can bring serious harm to your reputation and credibility.

   뇌물수수 스캔들에 연루되면 평판과 신뢰도에 심각한 해를 가져올 수 있다.

Check More!

(A), (B), (C) 각 밑줄 친 부분에 알맞은 어휘를 짝지은 것으로 가장 적절한 것을 고르시오.

It is my great pleasure to inform you that your sons and daughters have completed all the academic **(A)** requirements / qualifications over the last three years of study at Hutt High School. We feel as if the day they entered our school was yesterday, and now they will proudly receive their graduation certificates. Not unlike many successful graduates in our long history, your children will go out into the world, and successfully participate in the fields of **(B)** politics / politicians, economics, culture, and education. The graduation ceremony will be held next Friday in Hutt High School's Assembly Hall. On behalf of the school, I would like to **(C)** expand / extend our invitation to you and your family. I look forward to seeing you there.

	(A)	(B)	(C)
①	requirements	politicians	extend
②	requirements	politics	expand
③	qualifications	politicians	extend
④	qualifications	politics	expand
⑤	requirements	politics	extend

Chapter 9
Politics and Social Issues

Unit 29. Wearing an electronic tag is horrible.

wear an **electronic** tag

pros and cons about the punishment

have to **defend oneself**

Episode

Dear Diary,

Sara's story about the **sex offender** was horrible. • How can he live wearing an **electronic** tag all his life? • People can spot him so easily, so how can he get along with the other **residents**? • What about his **self-esteem**? • He might feel **humiliated** whenever people look at him. • Then he may not be able to **assimilate** into his new neighborhood. • There are some **pros and cons** about this punishment. • It's such a **controversial** issue. • **Proponents** say this punishment is effective. • They argue that **crime** rates will fall. • But **opponents** have some concerns about this type of punishment. • **Human rights activists** are strongly against the idea.

This week the newspapers are full of stories about **kidnapping**. • Two kids were found **murdered** after they were kidnapped. • Most people are in a **panic** over these things and it **provokes** debate. • The issue of the **death penalty** has come up again. • Some people say public safety is our **priority**. • I read some **editorials** in the papers, where many **journalists** expressed their opinions on these issues. • I think the death penalty should be **abolished**.

Seri carries hair spray instead of **perfume**. • She says she is going to use it if someone tries to **harass** her. • She believes the spray **emission** will stop the person. • Seri has always been brave when she **confronts** bullies. • She never compromises when someone **bullies** her. • She says she has to **defend** herself because her life is **worth** defending.

....

다이어리에게,

성범죄자에 대한 사라의 이야기는 끔찍했어. 어떻게 전자발찌를 평생 차고 살 수 있을까? 사람들이 쉽게 알아볼 텐데, 어떻게 다른 주민들과 어울릴 수 있을까? 그의 자존심은 어떻게 될까? 사람들이 쳐다볼 때마다 굴욕감을 느낄 텐데. 그러면 그는 새로운 동네 사람들과 동화될 수 없을 거야. 이런 처벌에는 찬반양론이 있어. 아주 논란이 되는 쟁점이야. 찬성론자들은 이 처벌이 효과적이라고 말해. 범죄율이 감소할 것이라고 주장해. 하지만 반대론자들은 이러한 형태의 처벌에 관해 우려를 나타내고 있어. 인권운동가들은 이러한 생각에 강력히 반대해.

이번 주 신문들은 유괴에 대한 기사로 가득해. 어린이 두 명이 납치된 후에 살해되어 발견되었어. 대부분의 사람들이 이것 때문에 공포에 떨게 되고, 그것이 논쟁을 유발시키고 있어. 사형제도에 대한 문제가 다시 불거지고 있어. 어떤 사람들은 국민의 안전이 우선이라고 주장해. 신문에서 사설 몇 개를 읽어보았는데, 많은 언론인들이 이 문제에 관해 자신들의 견해를 표현했어. 나는 사형제도가 폐지되어야 한다고 생각해.

세리는 향수 대신 헤어 스프레이를 가지고 다녀. 세리는 누군가가 자신을 괴롭히려고 하면 그것을 사용할 것이라고 해. 스프레이 분사가 그 사람의 행동을 막아줄 것이라고 믿고 있어. 세리는 남을 괴롭히는 사람들을 만났을 때 늘 용감했어. 세리는 누군가가 자신을 위협해도 절대 타협하지 않았어. 세리는 자신의 생명은 지킬 만한 가치가 있으니까 자신을 지켜야 한다고 주장해.

sex offender
[séks əfèndər]
성범죄자

a criminal who does crimes that involve sex or sexual behavior
- sex offence 성범죄

Sara's story about the sex offender was horrible.
성범죄자에 대한 사라의 이야기는 끔찍했어.

electronic
[ilèktránik]
a. 전자의

involving the use of an electronic device
- electronics n. 전자공학 - electronically ad. 전자공학적으로

How can he live wearing an electronic tag all his life?
그는 어떻게 전자발찌를 평생 차고 살 수 있을까?

resident
[rézidənt]
n. 주민

a person who lives in a particular area
- residential a. 주거의, 거주에 관한 - residentially ad. 거주지역에 관해

People can spot him so easily, so how can he get along with the other residents?
사람들이 쉽게 알아볼 텐데, 그는 어떻게 다른 주민들과 어울릴 수 있을까?

self-esteem
[sélfistíːm]
n. 자존심, 자부심

how one feels about oneself

What about his self-esteem?
그의 자존심은 어떻게 될까?

humiliated
[hjuːmílièitid]
a. 굴욕감을 느끼는, 창피한

embarrassed and ashamed
- humiliate v. 굴욕감을 느끼게 하다, 창피하게 하다 - humiliation n. 굴욕, 창피

He might feel humiliated whenever people look at him.
사람들이 쳐다볼 때마다 그는 굴욕감을 느낄 텐데.

assimilate
[əsíməlèit]
v. 동화되다

to become adjusted, to blend in
- assimilation n. 동화

Then he may not be able to assimilate into his new neighborhood.
그러면 그는 새로운 동네 사람들과 동화될 수 없을 거야.

pros and cons
[prás ænd káns]
찬반양론

the good points (pros) and bad points (cons)

There are some pros and cons about this punishment.
이런 처벌에는 찬반양론이 있어.

controversial
[kàntrəvə́:rʃəl]

a. 논쟁의,
논란의 여지가 있는

causing a lot of discussion and argument
• controversy n. 논란 • controversially ad. 논쟁적으로

It's such a controversial issue.
그것은 아주 논란이 되는 쟁점이야.

proponent
[prəpóunənt]

n. 찬성론자

someone who supports an idea, opposite of opponent

Proponents say this punishment is effective.
찬성론자들은 이 처벌이 효과적이라고 말해.

crime
[kràim]

n. 범죄

an illegal action or activity
• criminal n. 범인

They argue that crime rates will fall.
그들은 범죄율이 감소할 것이라고 주장해.

opponent
[əpóunənt]

n. 반대론자

someone who does not support an idea, opposite of proponent
• oppose v. 반대하다 • opposition n. 반대

But opponents have some concerns about this type of punishment.
하지만 반대론자들은 이러한 형태의 처벌에 관해 우려를 나타내고 있어.

human rights activist
[hjú:mən ràits ǽktəvist]

인권 운동가

someone who tries to protect other people who are underprivileged

Human rights activists are strongly against the idea.
인권 운동가들은 이러한 생각에 강력히 반대해.

kidnapping
[kídnæ̀piŋ]

n. 유괴

an act of taking someone away illegally and by force usually in order to get money
• kidnap v. 유괴하다, 납치하다 • kidnapper n. 유괴범

This week the newspapers are full of stories about kidnapping.
이번 주 신문들은 유괴에 대한 기사로 가득해.

murder
[mə́:rdər]

v. 살해하다 n. 살해

to kill another person
• murderous a. 살인의, 살인적인

Two kids were found murdered after they were kidnapped.
어린이 두 명이 납치된 후에 살해되어 발견되었어.

panic
[pǽnik]
n. 돌연한 공포, 공황
a. 허둥대는

extreme fright
- panicky a. 공포스러운 • in a panic 공포에 질린

Most people are in a panic over these things and it provokes debate.

대부분의 사람들이 이것 때문에 공포에 떨게 되고, 그것이 논쟁을 유발시키고 있어.

provoke
[prəvóuk]
v. 도발하다

to cause something, to stimulate
- provocation n. 도발 • provocative a. 도발적인

Most people are in a panic over these things and it provokes debate.

대부분의 사람들이 이것 때문에 공포에 떨게 되고, 그것이 논쟁을 유발시키고 있어.

death penalty
[déθ pènəlti]
사형(제도)

killing a criminal instead of putting them in prison

The issue of the death penalty has come up again.

사형제도에 대한 문제가 다시 불거지고 있어.

priority
[praiɔ́(:)rəti]
n. 우선순위

a thing that is more important than other things
- prioritize v. 우선순위를 매기다

Some people say public safety is our priority.

어떤 사람들은 국민의 안전이 우선이라고 주장해.

editorial
[èdətɔ́:riəl]
n. 사설

a newspaper article written by an editor
- editorialize v. 사설로 논하다

I read some editorials in the papers, where many journalists expressed their opinions on these issues.

신문에서 사설 몇 개를 읽어보았는데, 많은 언론인들이 이 문제에 관해 자신들의 견해를 표현했어.

journalist
[dʒə́ːrnəlist]
n. 언론인

a person who reports or writes news stories for TV and newspapers
- journalism n. 언론 • journal n. 신문, 잡지

I read some editorials in the papers, where many journalists expressed their opinions on these issues.

신문에서 사설 몇 개를 읽어보았는데, 많은 언론인들이 이 문제에 관해 자신들의 견해를 표현했어.

abolish
[əbáliʃ]
v. 폐지하다

to do away with a system or practice
- abolishment n. 폐지

I think the death penalty should be abolished.

나는 사형제도가 폐지되어야 한다고 생각해.

perfume
[pə́:rfju:m]

n. 향수
v. 향수를 뿌리다

a nice smelling liquid
• perfumed a. 향수를 뿌린

Seri carries hair spray instead of perfume.
세리는 향수 대신 헤어 스프레이를 가지고 다녀.

harass
[hərǽs]

v. 괴롭히다,
  귀찮게 굴다

to annoy someone and make them angry
• harassment n. 괴롭힘, 희롱

She says she is going to use it if someone tries to harass her.
그녀는 누군가가 자신을 괴롭히려고 하면 그것을 사용할 것이라고 해.

emission
[imíʃən]

n. 분사, 내뿜음

the release of gas or liquid into the atmosphere
• emit v. 내뿜다, 분사하다

She believes the spray emission will stop the person.
그녀는 스프레이 분사가 그 사람의 행동을 막아줄 것이라고 믿고 있어.

confront
[kənfrʌ́nt]

v. 직면하다, 마주하다

to encounter someone or something
• confrontation n. 직면, 대립

Seri has always been brave when she confronts bullies.
세리는 남을 괴롭히는 사람들을 만났을 때 늘 용감했어.

bully
[búli]

v. 위협하다, 괴롭히다
n. 위협하는 사람

to frighten someone

She never compromises when someone bullies her.
그녀는 누군가가 자신을 위협해도 절대 타협하지 않았어.

defend
[difénd]

v. 방어하다

to take action to protect someone or something
• defense n. 방어 • defensive a. 방어적인

She says she has to defend herself because her life is worth defending.
그녀는 자신의 생명은 지킬 만한 가치가 있으니까 자신을 지켜야 한다고 주장해.

worth
[wə́:rθ]

a. 가치가 있는
n. 가치, 중요성

important enough for a particular action
• worthless a. 가치 없는 • be worth ~ing ~할 만한 가치가 있다

She says she has to defend herself because her life is worth defending.
그녀는 자신의 생명은 지킬 만한 가치가 있으니까 자신을 지켜야 한다고 주장해.

Check Again!

A Translate each word into Korean.

1. editorial ....
2. self-esteem ....
3. provoke ....
4. assimilate ....
5. pros and cons ....
6. confront ....
7. controversial ....
8. proponent ....
9. opponent ....
10. kidnapping ....

B Translate each word into English.

1. 살해하다 ....
2. 전자의 ....
3. 가치가 있는 ....
4. 주민 ....
5. 방어하다 ....
6. 우선순위 ....
7. 언론인 ....
8. 위협하다 ....
9. 괴롭히다 ....
10. 분사 ....

C Fill in the blank with the appropriate word. Refer to the Korean.

1. The kids were in a p　　　　　　 when they were trapped in an elevator.

   아이들은 엘리베이터에 갇혀 있는 동안 공포에 사로잡혔다.

2. I felt he might feel h　　　　　　 if I spoke of his bad grades.

   나는 내가 그의 형편없는 성적에 대해 얘기하면 그가 굴욕감을 느낄지도 모른다고 느꼈다.

3. The c　　　　　　 rates in this city have risen for the first time since 19〔

   이 도시의 범죄율은 1980년 이래 처음으로 높아졌다.

4. Why don't you go to the cathedral? It is w　　　　　　 a visit.

   그 대성당에 가보지 그러니? 그곳은 가볼 만해.

5. A sex o　　　　　　 is a person who has been criminally charged and convicted of a sex crime.

   성범죄자란 성범죄로 형사 기소되어 유죄를 받은 사람이다.

Check More!

수능 기출 응용

다음 밑줄 친 부분에 알맞은 어휘를 고르시오. 아래의 영영 풀이를 참조하시오.

Environmental psychologists have long known about the harmful effects of unpredictable, high-volume noise. It can **(A)** provide / provoke negative feelings such as anger. In laboratory **(B)** entertainments / experiments, people exposed to 110-decibel bursts of noise experienced a decrease in their ability to solve problems. However, when subjects either could predict when the bursts of noise would occur or had the ability to terminate the noise with a "**(C)** panic / panicked button," the negative effects disappeared.

We are not always fortunate enough to enjoy a work environment free of noise pollution. But when we feel we are in charge of our noisy environments, we may no longer suffer from anxiety and poor performance.

(A) to cause something: ....

(B) a scientific test: ....

(C) a very strong feeling of anxiety or fear:

....

Chapter 9. Politics and Social Issues **273**

Politics and Social Issues

Unit 30. The war should be stopped.

have one's own **strategy**

make a **treaty**

Episode

Dear Diary,

Hoony and his friend are playing computer games. • They call each other the **enemy**. • They each refer to themselves as a **mighty army**. • They each have their own **strategy**. • They **dispatch** warships. • They also dispatch **troops**. • Each has its own **allies**. • They use many **assault** weapons. • They attack each other by dropping **atomic bombs**. • They try to **occupy** each other's **territory**. • And the winner is the one who **displaces** his opponents. • Finally, a message pops up, "**Mission completed.**" • Why do boys like such **violent** games? • Hoony says it's not real, just **imaginary**. • Recently, a war **broke out** in the Middle East. • The authorities are meeting to make a **treaty**. • When are they going to **declare** an end to war? • Isn't it **feasible**? • Why is it so hard to declare a **cease-fire**? • One president said they started this war for **justice**. • But both sides still **blame** each other. • Innocent people are becoming **refugees**. • They **lack** medicine and food. • All their facilities are **demolished**. • And their **infrastructure** has been destroyed. • Some people say both sides fight over natural **resources**. • Do the leaders even have a **conscience**? • They even say in **explicit terms** that they want peace and justice. • How can we **ascertain** their intentions? • I doubt they think life is valuable.

다이어리에게,

후니와 그의 친구가 컴퓨터 게임을 하고 있어. 그들은 서로를 적이라고 불러. 각자는 자기 자신을 강력한 군대라고 불러. 각자 전략이 있어. 그들은 전함을 급파해. 그들은 군대도 파병해. 각각은 동맹국도 있어. 그들은 많은 공격용 무기를 사용해. 그들은 원자탄을 투하해 서로를 공격해. 그들은 서로의 영토를 점령하기 위해 애써. 그리고 승자는 상대를 몰아내는 사람이야. 마침내 "임무 완수"라는 메시지가 떠. 왜 남자아이들은 이런 폭력적인 게임을 좋아할까? 후니는 그것이 실제가 아니라 가상일 뿐이라고 말해. 최근에 중동에서 전쟁이 발발했어. 관계 당국들이 조약을 맺기 위해 만나고 있어. 그들은 언제 전쟁 종식을 선언할까? 가능성이 없는 것일까? 정전을 선언하는 것이 그렇게 어려울까? 정의를 위해 이 전쟁을 시작했다고 어떤 대통령이 말했어. 하지만 양쪽 다 아직도 서로를 비난해. 선량한 사람들이 난민이 되어가고 있어. 그들은 의약품과 음식이 부족해. 모든 시설들이 파괴되었어. 그들은 기간시설이 파괴되었어. 어떤 사람들은 양쪽이 천연자원을 놓고 싸운다고 말해. 지도자들은 양심이 있을까? 그들은 심지어 분명하게 그들이 평화와 정의를 원한다고 말해. 우리가 어떻게 그들의 의중을 확인할 수 있을까? 나는 그들이 생명이 귀하다고 생각하는지가 의심스러워.

enemy
[énəmi]
n. 적

someone who hates you and wants to argue or fight with you

They call each other the enemy.
그들은 서로를 적이라고 불러.

mighty
[máiti]
a. 강력한

strong, powerful, hardy
- mightiness n. 위대, 강대

They each refer to themselves as a mighty army.
그들 각자는 자기 자신을 강력한 군대라고 불러.

strategy
[strǽtədʒi]
n. 전략

a plan, an idea of the best way to do something
- strategize v. 전략을 짜다   • strategist n. 전략가
- strategic a. 전략의, 전략상 중요한

They each have their own strategy.
그들은 각자 전략이 있어.

dispatch
[dispǽtʃ]
v. 파견하다, 발송하다

to send something to do a particular job or task

They dispatch warships.
그들은 전함을 급파해.

troop
[trúːp]
n. 군대

a group of soldiers

They also dispatch troops.
그들은 군대도 파병해.

ally
[ǽlai]
n. 동맹국

a country that supports another country and will fight its enemies
- alliance n. 동맹   • allied a. 연합된

Each has its own allies. 각각은 동맹국도 있어.

assault
[əsɔ́ːlt]
n. 공격 v. 공격하다

a strong attack made by an army
- assault weapon 공격용 무기

They use many assault weapons. 그들은 많은 공격용 무기를 사용해.

atomic bomb
[ətámik bám]
원자폭탄

a bomb that causes an explosion by energy resulting from splitting atoms

They attack each other by dropping atomic bombs.
그들은 원자탄을 투하해 서로를 공격해.

occupy
[ákjəpài]
v. 점령하다

to take another person's land or country
- occupation n. 점령 - occupied a. 점령된

They try to occupy each other's territory.
그들은 서로의 영토를 점령하기 위해 애써.

territory
[térətɔ̀:ri]
n. 영토

the area controlled by a particular country

They try to occupy each other's territory.
그들은 서로의 영토를 점령하기 위해 애써.

displace
[displéis]
v. 내쫓다, 내몰다

to make people leave their land or country
- displacement n. 바꾸어 놓기, 퇴거

And the winner is the one who displaces his opponents.
그리고 승자는 상대를 몰아내는 사람이야.

mission
[míʃən]
n. 임무

an important task or goal that one has to do
- missionary n. 선교사 a. 전도의

Finally, a message pops up, "Mission completed."
마침내 "임무 완수"라는 메시지가 떠.

violent
[váiələnt]
a. 폭력적인

using physical force, destructive
- violence n. 폭력 - violently ad. 폭력적으로

Why do boys like such violent games?
왜 남자아이들은 이런 폭력적인 게임을 좋아할까?

imaginary
[imǽdʒənèri]
a. 상상의, 가상의

not real and only existing in one's mind
- imagination n. 상상 - imaginative a. 상상력이 풍부한

Hoony says it's not real, just imaginary.
후니는 그것이 실제가 아니라 가상일 뿐이라고 말해.

break out
[bréik aut]
발발하다, 일어나다

to begin very quickly instead of over a long period of time

Recently, a war broke out in the Middle East.
최근에 중동에서 전쟁이 발발했어.

treaty
[trí:ti]
n. 조약

a contract that people write when they agree to make peace

The authorities are meeting to make a treaty.
관계 당국들이 조약을 맺기 위해 만나고 있어.

declare
[diklɛ́ər]

v. 선언하다

to announce, to tell many people

• declaration n. 선언

When are they going to declare an end to war?

그들은 언제 전쟁 종식을 선언할까?

feasible
[fíːzəbəl]

a. 가능한, 있음직한

possible, achievable

• feasibility n. 가능성, 타당성   • feasibly ad. 가능하게

Isn't it feasible? 가능성이 없는 것일까?

cease-fire
[síːsfàiər]

n. 정전, 휴전

stop in fighting

Why is it so hard to declare a cease-fire?

정전을 선언하는 것이 그렇게 어려울까?

justice
[dʒʌ́stis]

n. 정의

good and fair behavior towards other people

• justify v. 정당화하다   • justification n. 정당화

One president said they started this war for justice.

정의를 위해 이 전쟁을 시작했다고 어떤 대통령이 말했어.

blame
[bléim]

v. 비난하다, 탓하다

to say that other people are wrong or a situation is someone else's fault

But both sides still blame each other.

하지만 양쪽 다 아직도 서로를 비난해.

refugee
[rèfjudʒíː]

n. 난민

a person who has to leave their city or country because of war

Innocent people are becoming refugees.

선량한 사람들이 난민이 되어가고 있어.

lack
[lǽk]

v. 부족하다, 결핍되다
n. 부족, 결핍

not to have enough of something

• lacking a. 부족한

They lack medicine and food.

그들은 의약품과 음식이 부족해.

demolish
[dimáliʃ]
v. 파괴하다

to destroy something; to smash something to pieces
- demolition n. 파괴, 폭파 • demolished a. 파괴된

All their facilities are demolished.
모든 시설들이 파괴되었어.

infrastructure
[ínfrəstrʌktʃər]
n. 기간시설

the framework that allows a country to function, work and exist

And their infrastructure has been destroyed.
그리고 그들의 기간시설이 파괴되었어.

resources
[risɔ́:rsiz]
n. 자원

things such as food and materials that people can use to make things

Some people say both sides fight over natural resources.
어떤 사람들은 양쪽이 천연자원을 놓고 싸운다고 말해.

conscience
[kánʃəns]
n. 양심

moral sense, a feeling of guilt
- conscientious a. 양심적인 • conscientiously ad. 양심적으로

Do the leaders even have a conscience?
지도자들은 양심이 있을까?

explicit
[iksplísit]
a. 분명한, 명백한

expressed clearly and openly
- explicitly ad. 분명히, 분명하게

They even say in explicit terms that they want peace and justice.
그들은 심지어 분명하게 그들이 평화와 정의를 원한다고 말해.

term
[tə́:rm]
n. 용어

a description of a concept, a word or expression

They even say in explicit terms that they want peace and justice.
그들은 심지어 분명하게 그들이 평화와 정의를 원한다고 말해.

ascertain
[æsərtéin]
v. 확인하다

to make sure, to confirm
- ascertainment n. 확인 • ascertainable a. 확인할 수 있는

How can we ascertain their intentions?
우리가 어떻게 그들의 의중을 확인할 수 있을까?

Check Again!

A Translate each word into Korean.

1. conscience ....
2. mighty ....
3. dispatch ....
4. refugee ....
5. territory ....
6. atomic bomb ....
7. occupy ....
8. displace ....
9. imaginary ....
10. treaty ....

B Translate each word into English.

1. 전략 ....
2. 정의 ....
3. 비난하다 ....
4. 부족하다 ....
5. 파괴하다 ....
6. 기간시설 ....
7. 분명한 ....
8. 선언하다 ....
9. 폭력적인 ....
10. 가능한 ....

C Fill in the blank with the appropriate word. Refer to the Korean.

1. A _____ weapons refer to a broad category of firearms.

   공격용 무기는 광범위한 범주의 화기를 지칭한다.

2. Mongolia is abundant in natural r _____.

   몽고는 천연자원이 풍부하다.

3. He said in explicit t _____ that he would leave the country.

   그는 명백하게 나라를 떠날 것이라고 말했다.

4. I strongly urge them to declare a c _____ unilaterally.

   나는 그들이 일방적으로 종전을 선언할 것을 강력히 촉구한다.

5. Lots of teenagers do not know when the Korean War b _____ out or who started it.

   많은 10대들이 한국전쟁이 언제 일어났고, 누가 일으켰는지 모른다.

수능 기출 응용

(A), (B), (C) 각 밑줄 친 부분에 알맞은 어휘를 짝지은 것으로 가장 적절한 것을 고르시오.

The introduction of unique products alone does not guarantee market success. Another vital factor is increasing one's **(A)** responsiveness / responsibility to the markets by providing products suited for the local communities that make up the market. This means understanding that each country, community and individual has unique characteristics and needs; it requires **(B)** sensitivity / sensibility to regional and individual differences. In other words, one of the challenges is to avoid a one-size-fits-all **(C)** strategy / system that places too much emphasis on the "global" aspect alone. Even categorizing countries as "developed" or "emerging" is dangerous. Upon closer analysis, "emerging" countries are not only vastly different from one another, they are also composed of numerous unique individuals and communities.

	(A)	(B)	(C)
①	responsibility	sensitivity	system
②	responsiveness	sensibility	system
③	responsiveness	sensitivity	strategy
④	responsibility	sensibility	strategy
⑤	responsiveness	sensibility	strategy

+ 접두사 sym-/syn- / uni- / sub-

sym-/syn-은 'together,' 'with'라는 뜻의 접두사로, '함께 또는 동시에 존재하다'는 뜻의 단어를 만든다. uni-는 'one'이라는 뜻의 접두사로, '유일한 또는 공동'이라는 뜻의 단어를 만든다. sub-는 'under'라는 뜻의 접두사로, '무언가 아래에 있다'라는 뜻의 단어를 만든다.

sym-/syn-

-pathy 고통, 감정
sym + pathy = sympathy 공감, 동정
ex) My heart was filled with sympathy for the poor kid.
내 마음 속에 그 불쌍한 아이에 대한 동정심이 가득했다.

- **symphony** 교향곡, 연주회
- **symbiosis** 공생
- **symbiotic** 공생하는
- **synchronous** 동시에 일어나는
- **synchronize** 동시에 일어나다
- **synonym** 동의어
- **synthesis** 종합, 통합

uni-

-cycle 바퀴
uni + cycle = unicycle 외바퀴 자전거
ex) The clown on the unicycle waved to the audience.
외바퀴 자전거를 탄 광대가 관중을 향해 손을 흔들었다.

- **unicorn** 일각수
- **uniform** 한결같은, 동형의
- **unisex** 남녀 공용의
- **unilateral** 일면인, 일방적인
- **unify** 단일화하다
- **unicameral** 단원제의
- **unison** 동음, 화합

sub-

standard 표준, 기준

sub + standard = substandard 표준 이하의

ex) The hotel room turned out to be in substandard conditions.
알고 봤더니 호텔방은 수준 이하의 상태였다.

• culture 문화	subculture 하위 문화
• divide 나누다	subdivide 다시 나누다
• continent 대륙	subcontinent 아대륙
• committee 위원회	subcommittee 소위원회
• terrain 지역, 지대	subterranean 지하의
• marine 바다의	submarine 해저의
• merge 병합하다	submerge 물 속에 잠그다, 몰두시키다

Culture Plus

U.S. Politics 미국 정치

+ the two-party system 양당제
+ the Republican Party 공화당
+ the Democratic Party 민주당
+ the Senate 상원
+ the House of Representatives 하원
+ primary election 예비 선거
+ ballot 투표 용지

We're teens. I had my cell phone taken away. Goodbye, Brownie Life is full of contrad

campus tour. If I were a judge,.... How can we survive in a jungle? I became a Santa C

ney-wise. oony goes to an herbal clinic. We became a rescue team. Grandma goe

want to meet? A... and ... mpatible? I can't understand this painting. The

ve illusions about boys. can't understand politicians. Wearing an electronic tag is hor

economics camp. construction a thriving business? How amazing our life has becor

pace. I attended the Arbor Day ceremony. We can make the earth a better place. A

ife is full of contradictions. Goodbye, Sara. I learned about the earth. I went to a natu

became a Santa Claus. Sara attends a community party. Mom's got a new hobby. Are t

Grandma goes to a laughter clinic. The Volcanoes are back. We have great brothers. Wh

painting. There was telepathy between us! Sara goes to Turkey. Home decorating is n

electronic tag is horrible. The war should be stopped. Mom, are you going to cut my allo

our life has become! I should have been more careful. Forgery should be stopped. Hoo

better place. A super hurricane hit the village. We're teens. I had my cell phone taken

went to a natural science museum. I had a campus tour. If I were a judge,... How can w

obby. Are they my bosses? Hoony is money-wise. Hoony goes to an herbal clinic. We

great brothers. What historical figures do you want to meet? Are mom and dad compat

decorating is not easy. Hoony thinks girls have illusions about boys. I can't understand po

cut my allowance? Hoony is back from an economics camp. construction a thriving b

topped. Hoony wants to explore outer space. I attended the Arbor Day ceremony. We

phone taken away. Goodbye, Brownie Life is full of contradictions. Goodbye, Sara. I lear

How can we survive in a jungle? I became a Santa Claus. Sara attends a community

VOCA
EDGE
RED

Chapter 10. Economy

Unit 31. Mom, are you going to cut my allowance?

Unit 32. Hoony is back from an economics camp.

Unit 33. Is construction a thriving business?

Chapter 10
Economy

Unit 31. Mom, are you going to cut my allowance?

restrain consumer spending

use the subway to **commute** to work

have to **be thrifty**

Episode

Dear Diary,
The world's markets don't seem to be **stable**. • And what does **deflation** mean? • The newspaper says the **unemployment** rate keeps increasing. • **Entrepreneurs** can't hire many employees. • And some employees are being **laid off**. • Companies say they are having **financial** difficulties. • Why don't we ask the government to make an **amendment** to the laws to help them? • Then the banks will have to **comply** with it. • I mean, the bank can just print out **abundant** amounts of cash for all of us. • But, some economists say that will just cause **inflation**. • These days farmers are holding **rallies** downtown. • They even burned their own **agricultural** products. • Why do they **protest**? • Are they expressing their anti-government **sentiment**? • Farmers say that they are victims of **globalization**. • They claim local products can't compete with **imported** goods because of their low prices. • They demand that the government **take some measures** to help them. • What if we were **imposing** heavy taxes on imported goods? • I mean imposing a heavy import **tariff**. • Oil prices have **soared**, too. • These rising prices **restrain** consumer spending. • The rising prices will bring the market into a deep **recession**. • Dad will have to start using the subway to **commute** to work. • The price of **commodities** is going up, too. • Mom says we have to be **thrifty**. • She **intends** to cut my allowance.

Mom: Bomi, the President is on TV saying we have to work hard to overcome this **adversity**.
Bomi: Mom, do you think your plan is **adequate**? • What if I go **bankrupt**? • I don't want to be in **debt**.

다이어리에게,
세계 시장이 안정적이지 못한 것 같아. 그렇다면 디플레이션은 뭐지? 신문에 의하면 실업률은 계속해서 높아지고 있어. 기업가들은 직원들을 많이 고용할 수가 없어. 어떤 직원들은 정리해고 당하고 있어. 회사들은 자금난을 겪고 있다고 말해. 그들을 돕기 위해 정부에게 법을 개정하도록 요구하면 어떨까? 그러면 은행들은 그것에 따라야 할 거야. 내 말은, 은행은 그냥 우리 모두를 위해 현금을 충분히 찍어내면 돼. 그러나 어떤 경제학자들은 그것이 인플레이션만 유발시킬 것이라고 말해. 요즈음 농부들이 시내에서 집회를 하고 있어. 그들은 심지어 자신들의 농산물을 태워버리기도 했어. 그들은 왜 항의하는 것일까? 자신들의 반정부 감정을 표출하는 걸까? 농부들은 자신들이 세계화의 피해자라고 주장해. 그들은 국산품이 수입상품의 낮은 가격 때문에 수입상품과 경쟁할 수 없다고 주장해. 정부가 자신들을 도와줄 조치를 취해줄 것을 요구해. 우리가 수입품에 무거운 관세를 붙인다면 어떨까? 내 말은 무거운 수입관세 부과 말야. 유가도 치솟았어. 이런 오름세 물가가 소비자 지출을 억제해. 오름세 물가는 시장을 크게 침체시킬 거야. 아빠는 출퇴근할 때 지하철을 이용하셔야 할 거야. 상품들의 가격도 오르고 있어. 엄마는 우리가 절약해야 한다고 하셔. 엄마는 내 용돈도 깎을 작정이야.

엄마: 보미, 대통령이 TV에 나와서 이 역경을 극복하려면 열심히 일해야 한대.
보미: 엄마, 엄마의 계획이 적절하다고 생각해요? 내가 파산하면 어떻게 돼요? 난 빚지고 싶지 않아요.

stable
[stéibl]
a. 안정된

not easily moved or disturbed
- stabilize v. 안정화하다 • stability n. 안정, 안정성

The world's markets don't seem to be stable.
세계 시장이 안정적이지 못한 것 같아.

deflation
[difléiʃən]
n. 디플레이션

a persistent decrease in the level of consumer prices
- deflate v. (가격, 통화를) 수축시키다, 수축하다

And what does deflation mean?
그렇다면 디플레이션은 뭐지?

unemployment
[ʌnimplɔ́imənt]
n. 실업

a condition of not having a job
- unemployed a. 실직한

The newspaper says the unemployment rate keeps increasing.
신문에 의하면 실업률은 계속해서 높아지고 있어.

entrepreneur
[ɑ̀:ntrəprəné:r]
n. 기업가

a person who runs his or her own business, a businessman
- entrepreneurship n. 기업 운영, 기업가 정신

Entrepreneurs can't hire many employees.
기업가들은 직원들을 많이 고용할 수가 없어.

lay off
[léi ɔ̀:f]
정리해고하다

to temporarily remove employees from working at a particular job

And some employees are being laid off.
어떤 직원들은 정리해고 당하고 있어.

financial
[finǽnʃəl]
a. 재정의, 금융의

having to do with finance, money management, investments, etc.
- finance n. 금융, 재정

Companies say they are having financial difficulties.
회사들은 자금난을 겪고 있다고 말해.

amendment
[əméndmənt]
n. 개정, 수정

a change made to a constitution or law
- amend v. 개정하다

Why don't we ask the government to make an amendmen to the laws to help them?
그들을 돕기 위해 정부에게 법을 개정하도록 요구하면 어떨까?

comply
[kəmplái]

v. 따르다, 준수하다

to perform what someone has asked or ordered

• compliance n. (명령에 관한) 순응, 이행

Then the banks will have to comply with it.

그러면 은행들은 그것에 따라야 할 거야.

abundant
[əbʌ́ndənt]

a. 풍부한

existing in plentiful amounts, affluent

• abound v. 많이 있다, 풍부하다 • abundance n. 풍부

I mean, the bank can just print out abundant amounts of cash for all of us.

내 말은, 은행은 그냥 우리 모두를 위해 현금을 충분히 찍어내면 돼.

inflation
[infléiʃən]

n. 인플레이션

a continuing rise in the general level of prices of goods and services

• inflate v. 팽창하다

But, some economists say that will just cause inflation.

그러나 어떤 경제학자들은 그것이 인플레이션만 유발시킬 것이라고 말해.

rally
[rǽli]

n. 집회

v. 규합하다, 단결하다

a mass meeting intended to arouse group enthusiasm and support

These days farmers are holding rallies downtown.

요즘 농부들이 시내에서 집회를 하고 있어.

agricultural
[æ̀grikʌ́ltʃərəl]

a. 농업의

having to do with or related to farming

• agriculture n. 농업

They even burned their own agricultural products.

그들은 심지어 자신들의 농산물을 태워버리기도 했어.

protest
[prətést]

v. 항의하다 n. 항의

to make a gesture or statement against something

Why do they protest?

그들은 왜 항의하는 것일까?

sentiment
[séntəmənt]

n. 감정

an attitude based on one's thoughts and feelings, an idea or feeling expressed in words

• sentimental a. 감상적인, 감정적인

Are they expressing their anti-government sentiment?

그들은 자신들의 반정부 감정을 표출하는 걸까?

globalization
[glóubəlizéʃən]

n. 세계화

the development of an increasingly global economy

• globalize v. 세계화하다 • global a. 세계적인

Farmers say that they are victims of globalization.

농부들은 자신들이 세계화의 피해자라고 주장해.

---

imported
[impɔ́ːrtid]

a. 수입된

brought from a foreign country

• import v. 수입하다 n. 수입

They claim local products can't compete with imported goods because of their low prices.

그들은 국산품이 수입상품의 낮은 가격 때문에 수입상품과 경쟁할 수 없다고 주장해.

---

take some measures
[téik sʌm méʒərz]

몇몇 조치를 취하다

to take action in order to prevent something from happening

They demand that the government take some measures to help them.

그들은 정부가 자신들을 도와줄 조치를 취해줄 것을 요구해.

---

impose
[impóuz]

v. 부과하다

to establish or apply by authority

• imposition n. 부과 • impose A on B A를 B에 부과하다

What if we were imposing heavy taxes on imported goods?

우리가 수입품에 무거운 관세를 붙인다면 어떨까?

---

tariff
[tǽrif]

n. 관세

a tax placed on imported goods

I mean imposing a heavy import tariff.

내 말은 무거운 수입관세 부과 말야.

---

soar
[sɔ́ːr]

v. 치솟다

to ascend, to go higher and higher

Oil prices have soared, too.

유가도 치솟았어.

---

restrain
[riːstréin]

v. 억제하다

to prevent, to hold back, to make it difficult to do something

• restraint n. 억제, 제지

These rising prices restrain consumer spending.

이런 오름세 물가가 소비자 지출을 억제해.

---

recession
[riséʃən]
n. 침체, 불경기

a period when the economy is doing badly
- recede v. 나빠지다, 후퇴하다

The rising prices will bring the market into a deep recession.
오름세 물가는 시장을 크게 침체시킬 거야.

commute
[kəmjú:t]
v. 통근하다
n. 통근, 통학

to travel to work
- commuter n. 통근자 a. 통근(자)의

Dad will have to start using the subway to commute to work.
아빠는 출퇴근할 때 지하철을 이용하셔야 할 거야.

commodity
[kəmádəti]
n. 상품

a thing that is sold, goods

The price of commodities is going up, too.
상품들의 가격도 오르고 있어.

thrifty
[θrífti]
a. 절약하는, 검소한

being good at money management
- thrift n. 검약, 절약

Mom says we have to be thrifty. 엄마는 우리가 절약해야 한다고 하셔.

intend
[inténd]
v. 의도하다, 작정하다

to have a purpose or goal in mind
- intention n. 의도, 작정

She intends to cut my allowance. 엄마는 내 용돈도 깎을 작정이야.

adversity
[ædvə́:rsəti]
n. 역경

a state of serious or continued difficulties
- adverse a. 불리한, 반대의

Bomi, the President is on TV saying we have to work hard to overcome this adversity.
보미, 대통령이 TV에 나와서 이 역경을 극복하려면 열심히 일해야 한대.

adequate
[ǽdikwit]
a. 적절한, 충분한

acceptable, good enough, sufficient
- adequacy n. 적절함, 타당성

Mom, do you think your plan is adequate?
엄마, 엄마의 계획이 적절하다고 생각해요?

bankrupt
[bǽŋkrʌpt]
a. 파산한

being completely out of money, broke
- bankruptcy n. 파산

What if I go bankrupt? 내가 파산하면 어떻게 돼요?

Check Again!

A Translate each word into Korean.

1. stable ....
2. entrepreneur ....
3. commodity ....
4. rally ....
5. abundant ....
6. globalization ....
7. adversity ....
8. adequate ....
9. thrifty ....
10. impose ....

B Translate each word into English.

1. 치솟다 ....
2. 파산한 ....
3. 농업의 ....
4. 항의하다 ....
5. 재정의 ....
6. 침체 ....
7. 감정 ....
8. 수입된 ....
9. 억제하다 ....
10. 통근하다 ....

C Fill in the blank with the appropriate word. Refer to the Korean.

1. The government made an a   to the law last year.
   정부는 작년에 그 법을 개정하였다.

2. The government must take every m   to end this war.
   정부는 이 전쟁을 끝내기 위해 모든 조치를 취해야 한다.

3. Lots of people are concerned about the possibility of being
   l   off.
   많은 사람들이 정리해고될 가능성에 대해 걱정하고 있다.

4. As of 6:00 a.m. this morning, all supermarkets had to c
   with the new rules.
   오늘 아침 6시를 기해, 모든 슈퍼마켓들은 새로운 규정을 따라야 한다.

5. The u   rate for the month of May was 5.1%, down from
   5.2% in April.
   5월 실업률이 5.1퍼센트로 4월 5.2퍼센트에서 감소되었다.

Check More!

(A), (B), (C) 각 밑줄 친 부분에 알맞은 어휘를 짝지은 것으로 가장 적절한 것을 고르시오.

Allen Pearson, who headed a forecast center for years, tells about a lady who was not pleased with the warning system. "She called me up to **(A)** protest / protect that the tornado watch had kept her in her basement for five hours, and nothing happened," says Allen Pearson. "I tried to explain that we did not want to **(B)** alarm / allude her; we just wanted her to be aware. Unfortunately, the same thing happened again five months later. She was really angry and complained to the weather bureau, 'Some **(C)** measures / miseries should have been taken.' "

*tornado: 회오리바람

	(A)	(B)	(C)
①	protest	alarm	measures
②	protect	alarm	measures
③	protect	allude	miseries
④	protest	alarm	miseries
⑤	protest	allude	measures

Chapter 10
Economy

Unit 32. Hoony is back from an economics camp.

finish a course **with honors**

pretend to be a financial analyst

Episode

Dear Diary,

Dad, what is today's **stock index** like? • "I think this particular item is **undervalued**," says Hoony. • He is just **quoting** comments by an expert. • Hoony received his **certificate** from an economics camp. • He is boasting that he finished the course with honors. • He really **cherishes** his certificate. • "What's this **graph** for?" I asked Hoony. • **Presumably**, he is trying to figure out some basic principles of economics. • He keeps saying people's desires are **infinite** while resources are finite. • Hoony is talking like a **scholar**. • He pretends to have gained a **profound** knowledge of economics. • He also likes pretending to be a financial **analyst**.

Hoony: Dad, is animation a **prosperous** business? • I learned at the camp that the **prospects** of success for a business are important. • And are we **insured** against fire?
Dad: No, but we have car **insurance**.
Hoony: Dad, where is the **warranty** of my new computer CD?
Dad: In the drawer, I guess.
Bomi: Hoony, can you help with my **investment** plans?
Hoony: Sure. Why don't you **deposit** more money in the bank? • Or why don't you invest money in **real estate**?

I have **approximately** 50,000 won in my bank account. • About 20 won worth of **interest** has been added. • If interest is added at these amounts, when can I **accumulate** a fortune and become a **millionaire**?

다이어리에게,

아빠, 오늘 주가지수 어때요? "이 품목이 가치가 저평가된 것 같아요" 라고 후니가 말해. 그는 한 전문가의 설명을 인용하고 있을 뿐이야. 후니는 경제캠프에서 수료증을 받았어. 그는 그 코스를 우등으로 수료했다고 자랑하고 있어. 그는 자신의 수료증을 정말 소중히 간직하고 있어. "이 그래프는 뭐야?"라고 후니에게 물었어. 아마도 그는 경제학의 몇몇 기본원리를 생각해내려고 하는 것 같아. 그는 자원은 제한되어 있는데 인간의 욕망은 끝이 없다는 말을 계속해서 해. 후니는 마치 학자처럼 말하고 있어. 그는 경제학에 대해 심오한 지식을 얻은 척해. 그는 또한 금융 분석가인 척하기를 정말 좋아해.

후니: 아빠, 만화영화는 잘 나가는 업종인가요? 저는 캠프에서 어떤 업종의 성공 가능성이 중요하다는 것을 배웠어요. 그리고 우리 화재 보험 들었어요?
아빠: 아니, 하지만 자동차 보험은 있단다.
후니: 아빠, 새로 산 컴퓨터 CD의 품질보증서 어디 있어요?
아빠: 아마 서랍에 있을 거야.
보미: 후니, 내 투자 계획 좀 도와줄래?
후니: 물론. 은행에 더 많은 돈을 예치하지 그래? 아니면 부동산에 투자하는 게 어때?

내 은행 계좌에 대략 5만원 정도 있어. 약 20원 정도의 이자가 붙었어. 만일 이 정도로 이자가 붙으면, 나는 언제쯤 돈을 모아서 백만장자가 될 수 있을까?

stock index
[stɔ́k índeks]
주가지수

a measure of the current values of stock in a market

Dad, what is today's stock index like?

아빠, 오늘 주가지수 어때요?

undervalue
[ʌ̀ndərvǽljuː]
v. 저평가하다

to treat something as having less value than it does

• undervalued a. 저평가된

"I think this particular item is undervalued," says Hoony.

"이 품목이 가치가 저평가된 것 같아요"라고 후니가 말해.

quote
[kwóut]
v. 인용하다
n. 인용문

to speak or write something already stated by another person

• quotation n. 인용

He is just quoting comments by an expert.

그는 한 전문가의 설명을 인용하고 있을 뿐이야.

certificate
[sərtífəkit]
n. 수료증, 증명서
v. 증명하다

a document stating that someone has made certain accomplishments

• certify v. (서명 날인한 문서로) 증명하다, 인증하다

Hoony received his certificate from an economics camp.

후니는 경제캠프에서 수료증을 받았어.

with honors
[wið ánərz]
우등으로

with extremely high scores, at a high level, worthy of honorary status

He is boasting that he finished the course with honors.

그는 그 코스를 우등으로 수료했다고 자랑하고 있어.

cherish
[tʃériʃ]
v. 소중히 여기다

to hold dear, to feel affection for, to care about deeply

He really cherishes his certificate.

그는 자신의 수료증을 정말 소중히 간직하고 있어.

graph
[grǽf]
n. 그래프, 도표
v. 그래프로 나타내다

a diagram or chart used for measuring the differences among things

"What's this graph for?" I asked Hoony.

"이 그래프는 뭐야?"라고 후니에게 물었어.

presumably
[prizú:məbli]
ad. 아마도

likely, reasonably, by reasonable assumption
- presume v. 추정하다 • presumption n. 추정

Presumably, he is trying to figure out some basic principles of economics.

아마도 그는 경제학의 몇몇 기본원리를 생각해내려고 하는 것 같아.

infinite
[ínfənit]
a. 무한한

unending, eternal, something that goes on forever
- infinity n. 무한

He keeps saying people's desires are infinite while resources are finite.

그는 자원은 제한되어 있는데 인간의 욕망은 끝이 없다는 말을 계속해서 해.

finite
[fáinait]
a. 제한된

limited

He keeps saying people's desires are infinite while resources are finite.

그는 자원은 제한되어 있는데 인간의 욕망은 끝이 없다는 말을 계속해서 해.

scholar
[skálər]
n. 학자

an academic person who is very involved in learning
- scholarly a. 학자의, 학자다운

Hoony is talking like a scholar.

후니는 마치 학자처럼 말하고 있어.

profound
[prəfáund]
a. 심오한, 깊이 있는

intellectual, deep

He pretends to have gained a profound knowledge of economics.

그는 경제학에 대해 심오한 지식을 얻은 척해.

analyst
[ǽnəlist]
n. 분석가

a person who examines and determines, an examiner
- analyze v. 분석하다 • analysis n. 분석

He also likes pretending to be a financial analyst.

그는 또한 금융 분석가인 척하기를 정말 좋아해.

prosperous
[práspərəs]
a. 번영하는, 성공한

affluent, booming, successful, thriving
- prosper v. 번영하다   - prosperity n. 번영, 번창

Dad, is animation a prosperous business?
아빠, 만화영화는 잘 나가는 업종인가요?

prospect
[práspekt]
n. 가능성, 전망

an outlook on the future
- prospective a. 예상된, 가망 있는

I learned at the camp that the prospects of success for a business are important.
저는 캠프에서 어떤 업종의 성공 가능성이 중요하다는 것을 배웠어요.

insured
[inʃúərd]
a. 보험에 든

safeguarded, protected against
- insure v. 보험에 들다

And are we insured against fire?
그리고 우리 화재 보험 들었어요?

insurance
[inʃúərəns]
n. 보험

security allowance

No, but we have car insurance.
아니, 하지만 자동차 보험은 있단다.

warranty
[wɔ́(:)rənti]
n. 품질보증서

an assurance of security, a promise of replacement for broken products

Dad, where is the warranty of my new computer CD?
아빠, 새로 산 컴퓨터 CD의 품질보증서 어디 있어요?

investment
[invéstmənt]
n. 투자

money given with an expectation of more money received later
- invest v. 투자하다   - investor n. 투자자

Hoony, can you help with my investment plans?
후니, 내 투자 계획 좀 도와줄래?

deposit
[dipázit]

v. 예치하다

n. 예치

to put money into a bank account

Sure. Why don't you deposit more money in the bank?

물론. 은행에 더 많은 돈을 예치하지 그래?

---

real estate
[ríːəl istèit]

부동산

property in the form of land and buildings

Or why don't you invest money in real estate?

아니면 부동산에 투자하는 게 어때?

---

approximately
[əpráksəmitli]

ad. 대략

about, nearly, around

I have approximately 50,000 won in my bank account.

내 은행 계좌에 대략 5만원 정도 있어.

---

interest
[íntərist]

n. 이자

money earned on an investment or deposit

About 20 won worth of interest has been added.

약 20원 정도의 이자가 붙었어.

---

accumulate
[əkjúːmjəlèit]

v. 모으다, 축척하다

to collect or gather something

• accumulation n. 축척

If interest is added at these amounts, when can I accumulate a fortune and become a millionaire?

만일 이 정도로 이자가 붙으면, 나는 언제쯤 돈을 모아서 백만장자가 될 수 있을까?

---

millionaire
[mìljənέər]

n. 백만장자

a person with more than one million dollars

If interest is added at these amounts, when can I accumulate a fortune and become a millionaire?

만일 이 정도로 이자가 붙으면, 나는 언제쯤 돈을 모아서 백만장자가 될 수 있을까?

Check Again!

A Translate each word into Korean.

1. undervalue ....
2. scholar ....
3. quote ....
4. accumulate ....
5. approximately ....
6. profound ....
7. warranty ....
8. deposit ....
9. certificate ....
10. cherish ....

B Translate each word into English.

1. 무한한 ....
2. 이자 ....
3. 그래프 ....
4. 가능성 ....
5. 보험 ....
6. 투자 ....
7. 부동산 ....
8. 제한된 ....
9. 백만장자 ....
10. 분석가 ....

C Fill in the blank with the appropriate word. Refer to the Korean.

1. To my surprise, she graduated with h   .
   놀랍게도, 그녀는 우등으로 졸업했다.

2. The main Chinese s   index rose to a record on Monday.
   주요 중국 주가지수가 월요일 최고치로 올랐다.

3. At the end of 1996, I had a p   business and everything was going great.
   1996년 말, 나는 잘 나가는 사업체를 가지고 있었고 모든 일이 잘 되고 있었다.

4. The building owner has his building i   against fire for one billion won.
   그 건물 주인이 그 건물을 10억 원의 화재보험에 가입해 두었다.

5. P   , they crossed the Atlantic Ocean as passengers in the cargo ship.
   아마도 그들은 화물선의 승객으로 대서양을 횡단했던 것 같다.

Check More!

다음 밑줄 친 부분에 알맞은 어휘를 골라 빈칸에 쓰시오. 아래의 영영 풀이를 참조하시오.

Ever since the coming of television, there has been a rumor that the novel is dying, if not already dead. **(A)** Presumably / Precisely, print-oriented novelists seem doomed to disappear, as **(B)** electrical / electronic media and computer games are becoming more influential. Nowadays, many young people seem to prefer surfing the Internet to reading books. And often what they seek is not so much **(C)** profound / propound knowledge as quick information. One may wonder if literary fiction is destined to become an old-fashioned genre to be preserved in a museum like an **(D)** extinct / extent species.

(A) likely, reasonably: ....

(B) of or relating to electrons: ....

(C) deep; great: ....

(D) no longer existing; dead: ....

Chapter 10
Economy

Unit 33. Is construction a thriving business?

read **how to transplant**

be replaced by modernized buildings

transform the landscape

Episode

Dear Sara,

Sara, how many people do you think live in the Seoul **metropolitan** area? • Our sociology teacher said about a quarter of the whole population **dwells** here. • I also learned that a lot of people **migrate** here from rural areas. • Now I can understand why dad complains that the subway is **overcrowded**. • He isn't satisfied with the **quality** of life in Seoul. • He sometimes says he will leave Seoul after **retirement**. • He says he will buy a few **acres** of land in a remote area. • Like a **botanist**, he reads books on growing plants. • He read a book about growing **organic** fruit. • And he is reading how to t**ransplant** grape trees. • I don't know if he can **discern** which grapes are **ripe**. • Does he know what to do to increase his **yield**? • Can mom **adapt** to farming?

Bomi: Where is the **vacant** lot where you were playing with Kite?
Hoony: It's gone. It has become a **construction** site.

Construction must be a **thriving** business. • It has been **booming**. • The **blueprint** of our neighborhood is changing rapidly. • Most old houses have been replaced by **modernized** buildings. • Apartment buildings are **multiplying**. • It's like new buildings are just being **replicated, transforming** the landscape. • Our neighborhood has **altered** a lot since Sara left. • Hoony and Kite used to play in that empty space. • Now it is **restricted** to construction workers. • My mom expects the **land price** to go up. • But Hoony and Kite miss their playground.

사라에게,
사라, 서울 수도권에 몇 명이나 산다고 생각하니? 우리 사회학 선생님이 그러시는데 전체 인구의 4분의 1이 이 지역에 산대. 많은 사람들이 시골에서 여기로 이주한다는 것도 배웠어. 이젠 왜 아빠가 지하철이 만원이라고 불평하시는지 이해할 수 있어. 아빠는 서울에서의 삶의 질에 만족하지 못하셔. 은퇴하면 서울을 떠나시겠다고 가끔 말씀하셔. 외딴 곳에 땅을 조금 사시겠대. 식물학자처럼 아빠는 식물을 재배하는 방법에 관한 책을 읽으셔. 아빠는 유기농 과일 재배에 관한 책을 읽으셨어. 그리고 지금은 포도나무 이식하는 방법에 관해 읽고 계셔. 나는 아빠가 어느 포도가 익었는지 구별하실지 모르겠어. 수확을 늘리기 위해 무엇을 해야 할지 아실까? 엄마가 농사에 적응하실까?

보미: 네가 카이트랑 놀던 빈터가 어디니?
후니: 없어졌어. 지금은 공사 부지가 되어버렸어.

건설이 번창하는 업종인 것은 분명하다. 그것은 성황 중이다. 우리 동네 청사진이 빠르게 바뀌고 있다. 대부분의 낡은 집이 현대식 건물로 바뀌었다. 아파트가 계속 늘어나고 있다. 그것은 마치 새로운 건물들이 주변의 모습을 바꾸면서 계속 복제되는 것만 같다. 우리 동네는 사라가 떠난 후로 많이 달라졌다. 후니와 카이트는 빈터에서 놀곤 했다. 이제 그곳은 건설 근로자 외에는 출입금지이다. 우리 엄마는 땅값이 오르기를 기대하신다. 하지만 후니와 카이트는 놀이터를 그리워한다.

metropolitan

[mètrəpálitən]

a. 수도의, 대도시의

urban, main area of a city

• **metropolis** n. 주요 도시, 대도시

Sara, how many people do you think live in the Seoul metropolitan area?

사라, 서울 수도권에 몇 명이나 산다고 생각하니?

dwell

[dwél]

v. 거주하다

to live in or at, to reside

• **dwelling** n. 거주

Our sociology teacher said about a quarter of the whole population dwells here.

우리 사회학 선생님이 그러시는데 전체 인구의 4분의 1이 이 지역에 산대.

migrate

[máigreit]

v. 이주하다

to move, to emigrate or immigrate

• **migration** n. 이주 • **migratory** a. 이주하는, 이주성의

I also learned that a lot of people migrate here from rural areas.

많은 사람들이 시골에서 여기로 이주한다는 것도 배웠어.

overcrowded

[òuvərkráudid]

a. 만원인

jammed, packed, having too many people

Now I can understand why dad complains that the subway is overcrowded.

이젠 왜 아빠가 지하철이 만원이라고 불평하시는지 이해할 수 있어.

quality

[kwáləti]

n. 질, 품질

a. 훌륭한

the value of something, opposite of quantity

He isn't satisfied with the quality of life in Seoul.

그는 서울에서의 삶의 질에 만족하지 못하셔.

retirement

[ritáiərmənt]

n. 은퇴, 퇴직

leaving one's job and usually stopping working completely

• **retire** v. 은퇴하다

He sometimes says he will leave Seoul after retirement.

그는 은퇴하면 서울을 떠나시겠다고 가끔 말씀하셔.

acre
[éikər]
n. 에이커

a piece of land, a measure of an area of land

He says he will buy a few acres of land in a remote area.

그는 외딴 곳에 땅을 조금 사시겠대.

---

botanist
[bátənist]
n. 식물학자

a person who studies plants

• botany n. 식물학

Like a botanist, he reads books on growing plants.

식물학자처럼 그는 식물을 재배하는 방법에 관한 책을 읽으셔.

---

organic
[ɔːrgǽnik]
a. 유기농의

not using chemicals in growing animals or plants

He read a book about growing organic fruit.

그는 유기농 과일 재배에 관한 책을 읽으셨어.

---

transplant
[trænsplǽnt]
v. 이식하다
n. 이식

to relocate, to move from one location to another

• transplanter n. 이식자   • transplantation n. 이식

And he is reading how to transplant grape trees.

그리고 지금은 포도나무 이식하는 방법에 관해 읽고 계셔.

---

discern
[disə́ːrn]
v. 구별하다

to recognize and understand something

• discernment n. 구별, 식별

I don't know if he can discern which grapes are ripe.

나는 그가 어느 포도가 익었는지 구별하실지 모르겠어.

---

ripe
[ráip]
a. 익은

fully developed, ready to be picked

• ripen v. 익다, 익히다

I don't know if he can discern which grapes are ripe.

나는 그가 어느 포도가 익었는지 구별하실지 모르겠어.

---

yield
[jíːld]
n. 소출, 수확
v. 산출하다

product of labor, amount of crops produced

Does he know what to do to increase his yield?

그는 수확을 늘리기 위해 무엇을 해야 할지 아실까?

adapt
[ədǽpt]
v. 적응하다

to change or adjust to a different situation
- adaptability n. 적응성, 순응성 • adaptation n. 적응, 개조
- adaptable a. 적응할 수 있는, 융통성 있는 • adapt to ~에 적응하다

Can mom adapt to farming?
엄마가 농사에 적응하실까?

vacant
[véikənt]
a. 비어 있는

empty, unoccupied, abandoned
- vacate v. 비우다 • vacancy n. 공허, 빈터

Where is the vacant lot where you were playing with Kite?
네가 카이트랑 놀던 빈터가 어디니?

construction
[kənstrʌ́kʃən]
n. 건설, 건축

building, a creation of new buildings
- construct v. 건설하다 • constructive a. 건설적인

It's gone. It has become a construction site.
없어졌어. 지금은 공사 부지가 되어버렸어.

thriving
[θráiviŋ]
a. 번창하는, 성공하는

successful, prosperous, flourishing
- thrive v. 번창하다

Construction must be a thriving business.
건설이 번창하는 업종인 것은 분명하다.

booming
[búːmiŋ]
a. 급속히 발전하는

improving, growing or succeeding steadily
- boom v. 경기가 좋아지다 n. 성황, 인기

It has been booming. 그것은 성황 중이다.

blueprint
[blúːprint]
n. 청사진, 계획

an architectural plan; a project

The blueprint of our neighborhood is changing rapidly.
우리 동네 청사진이 빠르게 바뀌고 있다.

modernized
[mádərnàizd]
a. 현대화된

improved, up to date, remodeled
- modernize v. 현대화하다 • modernization n. 현대화

Most old houses have been replaced by modernized buildings.
대부분의 낡은 집이 현대식 건물로 바뀌었다.

multiply
[mʌ́ltəplài]
v. 늘다, 증가하다

to increase, to reproduce
- multiplication n. 증가, 배가

Apartment buildings are multiplying.
아파트가 계속 늘어나고 있다.

replicate
[répləkèit]
v. 복제하다

to duplicate, to reproduce
- replication n. 복제, 모사 - replicated a. 복제된

It's like new buildings are just being replicated,
transforming the landscape.
그것은 마치 새로운 건물들이 주변의 모습을 바꾸면서 계속 복제되는 것만 같다.

transform
[trænsfɔ́ːrm]
v. 변형시키다

to change completely, to alter
- transformation n. 변형 - transformative a. 변형시키는, 변형의

It's like new buildings are just being replicated,
transforming the landscape.
그것은 마치 새로운 건물들이 주변의 모습을 바꾸면서 계속 복제되는 것만 같다.

alter
[ɔ́ːltər]
v. 달라지다, 바꾸다

to change, to adjust
- alteration n. 변경

Our neighborhood has altered a lot since Sara left.
우리 동네는 사라가 떠난 후로 많이 달라졌다.

restricted
[ristríktid]
a. 제한된

allowed to only people with special permission; limited
- restrict v. 제한하다 - restriction n. 제한

Now it is restricted to construction workers.
이제 그곳은 건설 근로자 외에는 출입 금지이다.

land price
[lǽnd práis]
땅값

the cost of a piece of land

My mom expects the land price to go up.
우리 엄마는 땅값이 오르기를 기대하신다.

Check Again!

A Translate each word into Korean.

1. metropolitan ....
2. discern ....
3. replicate ....
4. alter ....
5. organic ....
6. transplant ....
7. ripe ....
8. yield ....
9. vacant ....
10. quality ....

B Translate each word into English.

1. 식물학자 ....
2. 만원인 ....
3. 변형시키다 ....
4. 은퇴 ....
5. 늘다 ....
6. 번창하는 ....
7. 급속히 발전하는 ....
8. 현대화된 ....
9. 청사진 ....
10. 건설 ....

C Fill in the blank with the appropriate word. Refer to the Korean.

1. Abundant wildlife d _____ in this area.

   풍부한 야생생물이 이 지역에 거주한다.

2. This area is r _____ to bank personal use only.

   이곳은 은행직원들만 사용하는 곳이다.

3. But the two allies will be able to a _____ to these changing conditions.

   하지만 두 동맹국은 이러한 변화하는 상황에 적응할 수 있을 것이다.

4. The finding suggests that Asian turtles m _____ from Asia to North America.

   그 조사결과는 아시아 거북이 아시아에서 북아메리카로 이주했음을 시사한다.

5. An unused building will be t _____ into the new home of the City Art Center.

   사용 안하는 건물이 시티예술센터의 새 보금자리로 변신하게 될 것이다.

Check More!

(A), (B), (C) 각 밑줄 친 부분에 알맞은 어휘를 짝지은 것으로 가장 적절한 것을 고르시오.

Like all other industries, the rose business must **(A)** adapt / adopt to changing conditions in the marketplace. In the past, a florist shop was most likely a local, independently owned business that bought roses from a wholesaler who purchased them from a farmer. As a result of high demand, on special days like Valentine's Day, the cost of a dozen roses rose nearly doubles regardless of their **(B)** quantity / quality.

Today, suppliers of roses include large supermarket chains, wholesalers who sell directly at many locations, and direct telephone marketers. The romance of roses has been **(C)** replaced / misplaced by economic realities.

(A)	(B)	(C)
① adopt	quantity	misplaced
② adapt	quality	replaced
③ adopt	quality	misplaced
④ adopt	quality	replaced
⑤ adapt	quantity	replaced

+ 접두사 trans- / sur-와 어근 struct-

trans-는 'across'라는 뜻의 접두사로, '넘거나 가로지르다'라는 뜻의 단어를 만든다. sur-는 'over'라는 뜻의 접두사로, '어떤 기준 이상'이라는 뜻의 단어를 만든다. struct-는 'to build'라는 뜻의 어근으로, '무언가를 세우다'라는 뜻의 단어를 만든다.

trans-

portare 들다
trans + port = transport 운송하다
ex) Your mission is to secretly transport the documents to his office.
당신의 임무는 비밀리에 서류를 그의 사무실까지 운반하는 것이다.

- transplant 이식하다
- transcribe 베끼다
- transform 변형시키다
- transcontinental 대륙 저편의
- transpolar 극지를 넘는
- transparent 투명한
- transparency 투명함

sur-

pass 지나가다
sur + pass = surpass 능가하다
ex) The experience surpassed my wildest dreams.
그 경험은 나의 가장 극단적인 상상을 초월했다.

- surplus 나머지, 잔여
- surcharge 추가 요금
- surmount 넘어 오르다, 극복하다
- surface 표면
- surreal 비현실의
- surtax 부가세
- survive 살아남다

struct-

struere 쌓다, 세우다

structure 구조, 건물

ex) The artist was fascinated by the structure of the human body.
그 화가는 인체의 구조에 매료되었다.

- **infra-** 아래에   **infrastructure** 하부 조직
- **re-** 다시   **restructure** 재구성하다, 개혁하다
- **in-** ~위에   **instruct** 가르치다
- **de-** un–   **destruct** 파괴하다
- **self-** 자기자신   **self-destruct** 스스로 파괴하다
- **ob-** ~에 반대하여   **obstruct** 가로막다, 방해하다
- **com-** 함께   **construct** 조립하다

Investments 투자

⁺financial products   금융 상품

⁺stocks   주식

⁺bonds   채권

⁺trust fund   신탁 자금

⁺securities   유가 증권

⁺high risk   고위험

⁺high return   고수익

VOCA EDGE
RED

We're teens. I had my cell phone taken away. Goodbye, Brownie Life is full of contrad

campus tour. If I were a judge,... How can we survive in a jungle? I became a Santa C

money-wise. Hoony goes to an herbal clinic. We became a rescue team. Grandma goe

you want to meet? Are mom and dad compatible? I can't understand this painting. The

have illusions about boys. I can't understand politicians. Wearing an electronic tag is hor

economics camp. construction a thriving business? How amazing our life has becor

space. I attended the Arbor Day ceremony. We can make the earth a better place. A

life is full of contradictions. Goodbye, Sara. I learned about the earth. I went to a natu

became a Santa Claus. Sara attends a community party. Mom's got a new hobby. Are t

Grandma goes to a laughter clinic. The Volcanoes are back. We have great brothers. Wh

painting. There was telepathy between us! Sara goes to Turkey. Home decorating is n

electronic tag is horrible. The war should be stopped. Mom, are you going to cut my allo

our life has become! I should have been more careful. Forgery should be stopped. Hoor

better place. A super hurricane hit the village. We're teens. I had my cell phone taken

went to a natural science museum. I had a campus tour. If I were a judge,... How can w

hobby. Are they my bosses? Hoony is money-wise. Hoony goes to an herbal clinic. We

great brothers. What historical figures do you want to meet? Are mom and dad compat

decorating is not easy. Hoony thinks girls have illusions about boys. I can't understand po

cut my allowance? Hoony is back from an economics camp. construction a thriving b

stopped. Hoony wants to explore outer space. I attended the Arbor Day ceremony. We

phone taken away. Goodbye, Brownie Life is full of contradictions. Goodbye, Sara. I lear

How can we survive in a jungle? I became a Santa Claus. Sara attends a community pc

Goodbye, Sara. I learned about the earth. I went to a natural science museum. I had
ra attends a community party. Mom's got a new hobby. Are they my bosses? Hoony
ghter clinic. The Volcanoes are back. We have great brothers. What historical figures d
lepathy between us! Sara goes to Turkey. Home decorating is not easy. Hoony thinks gir
war should be stopped. Mom, are you going to cut my allowance? Hoony is back from
uld have been more careful. Forgery should be stopped. Hoony wants to explore oute
ricane hit the village. We're teens. I had my cell phone taken away. Goodbye, Brownie
e museum. I had a campus tour. If I were a judge,... How can we survive in a jungle?
osses? Hoony is money-wise. Hoony goes to an herbal clinic. We became a rescue team
cal figures do you want to meet? Are mom and dad compatible? I can't understand th
Hoony thinks girls have illusions about boys. I can't understand politicians. Wearing a
Hoony is back from an economics camp. construction a thriving business? How amazing
to explore outer space. I attended the Arbor Day ceremony. We can make the earth
odbye, Brownie Life is full of contradictions. Goodbye, Sara. I learned about the earth.
a jungle? I became a Santa Claus. Sara attends a community party. Mom's got a new

Chapter 11. Technology

a rescue team. Grandma goes to a laughter clinic. The Volcanoes are back. We ha

Unit 34. How amazing our life has become!

't understand this painting. There was telepathy between us! Sara goes to Turkey. Ho

Unit 35. I should have been more careful.

Wearing an electronic tag is horrible. The war should be stopped. Mom, are you going

Unit 36. Forgery should be stopped.

ow amazing our life has become! I should have been more careful. Forgery should be
e the earth a better place. A super hurricane hit the village. We're teens. I had my ce
the earth. I went to a natural science museum. I had a campus tour. If I were a judge,...
got a new hobby. Are they my bosses? Hoony is money-wise. Hoony goes to an herb

Chapter 11
Technology

Unit 34. How amazing our life has become!

have video **conferences**

pay utilities by using Internet banking

become **three-dimensional**

be **converted into** an interactive disp

Episode

Dear Diary,

High-tech products can be applied in various ways. ● Because of our new technology, location and time are no longer **barriers**. ● It has brought about **drastic** changes in our lives. ● It really enables us to experience things that were **inconceivable** in the past. ● My dad doesn't have to go abroad to have international **conferences**. ● Once a week he has video conferences instead of **conventional** meetings. ● He can talk with **clients** anywhere in the world at any time. ● If our ancestors came to life, they would call our technology **revolutionary**.

Diary, my mom is never early to **adopt** new technology. ● She prefers her **analog watch** to a digital one. ● A few months ago, she didn't use the **Internet banking** services. ● She was worried that they would **malfunction**. ● But after she paid our **utilities** by using Internet banking, she realized how convenient it was. ● Now, every month she **transfers** my allowance into my bank account. ● She even **transmits** photos to my grandparents via the Internet.

Sara emailed me about an interesting museum. ● If you touch art pieces, they are instantly **converted** into **interactive** displays. ● When she touched the paintings, the **subjects** in the paintings danced and even answered her questions. ● For example, *The Mona Lisa*, by Leonardo da Vinci, talked about the lives of **aristocrats** during the 15th century. ● *Mona Lisa* also explained their **unique** customs. ● She said that drawing **portraits** was in fashion during those days.

Diary, can you **conceive** of a huge 10 dollar bill about the size of a house? ● Sounds **weird**, doesn't it? ● But try to imagine a **specimen** of a 10 dollar bill multiplied in size by 100 times. ● When Sara touched a part of the bill, it became **three-dimensional**. ● Interestingly, a **referee** appeared on the screen and threw a ball to her. ● I'm curious who **devised** this system. ● The **graphics** are really amazing.

다이어리에게,

첨단기술 제품은 다양한 방법으로 적용될 수 있어. 우리의 새로운 기술 덕분에, 장소와 시간은 더 이상 장애가 되지 않아. 새로운 기술은 우리의 생활에 엄청난 변화를 가져왔어. 우리는 새로운 기술 덕분에 과거에는 상상할 수 없었던 것들을 경험할 수 있어. 우리 아빠는 국제 회의를 하기 위해 해외로 가실 필요가 없어. 아빠는 전통적인 방법으로 회의를 하는 대신에 일주일에 한 번 화상 회의를 하셔. 어느 때든지 세계 어디에 있는 고객들과도 이야기를 할 수 있어. 만약 우리 조상들이 살아온다면, 그들은 우리의 기술을 혁신적인 것이라고 부를 거야.

다이어리, 우리 엄마는 절대로 첨단 기술을 빨리 받아들이는 분이 아니셔. 디지털 시계보다는 아날로그 시계를 더 좋아하셔. 몇 달 전에 엄마는 인터넷뱅킹 서비스를 사용하지 않으셨어. 엄마는 제대로 되지 않을 것이라고 걱정하셨던 거야. 그렇지만 공공요금을 인터넷뱅킹으로 지불하신 후에는, 그것이 얼마나 간편한지 알게 되셨어. 요즘 엄마는 매달 내 용돈을 내 은행 계좌로 송금하셔. 엄마는 인터넷으로 우리 조부모님께 사진도 전송하셔.

사라는 흥미로운 박물관에 대해 나에게 이메일을 보냈어. 만일 미술 작품을 만지면, 즉시 상호작용이 가능한 작품으로 변해. 사라가 그림을 만졌을 때, 그림 속의 피사체가 춤을 추고 사라의 질문에 대답도 했어. 예를 들면, 레오나르도 다빈치의 모나리자가 15세기의 귀족들의 삶에 대해 설명했어. 모나리자는 그들의 독특한 풍습에 대해서도 설명했어. 그녀는 또한 초상화를 그리는 것이 그 시대의 유행이었다고 말했어.

다이어리, 집 한 채 크기만한 거대한 10달러짜리 지폐를 상상할 수 있니? 이상하게 들리지 않니? 하지만 100배 확대된 10달러짜리의 견본을 상상해 봐. 사라가 그 지폐의 일부분에 손을 댔을 때 그것은 입체적이 되었어. 흥미롭게도 화면에 심판이 나타나서 그녀에게 공을 던졌어. 나는 이 시스템을 누가 생각해냈는지 궁금해. 그 그래픽은 정말 놀라워.

high-tech
[hàiték]

a. 첨단 기술의

the newest and most advanced

High-tech products can be applied in various ways.

첨단기술 제품은 다양한 방법으로 적용될 수 있어.

barrier
[bǽriər]

n. 장애

something that stops one from doing something, an obstacle

Because of our new technology, location and time are no longer barriers.

우리의 새로운 기술 덕분에, 장소와 시간은 더 이상 장애가 되지 않아.

drastic
[drǽstik]

a. 엄청난, 격렬한

severe, extreme and sudden

• drastically ad. 엄청나게, 격렬하게

It has brought about drastic changes in our lives.

그것은 우리의 생활에 엄청난 변화를 가져왔어.

inconceivable
[ìnkənsíːvəbəl]

a. 상상할 수 없는

difficult to believe, very unlikely to happen or be true

• inconceivably ad. 상상할 수 없게

It really enables us to experience things that were inconceivable in the past.

우리는 그것 덕분에 과거에는 상상할 수 없었던 것들을 경험할 수 있어.

conference
[kɑ́nfərəns]

n. 회의

a formal meeting

My dad doesn't have to go abroad to have international conferences.

우리 아빠는 국제 회의를 하기 위해 해외로 가실 필요가 없어.

conventional
[kənvénʃənəl]

a. 전통적인, 재래식의

normal, traditional

• convention n. 관습, 풍습 • conventionally ad. 전통적으로, 의례적으로

Once a week he has video conferences instead of conventional meetings.

그는 전통적인 방법으로 회의를 하는 대신에 일주일에 한 번 화상 회의를 하셔.

client
[klɑ́iənt]

n. 고객

a customer or a person who one does business with

He can talk with clients anywhere in the world at any time.

어느 때든지 세계 어디에 있는 고객들과도 이야기를 할 수 있어.

revolutionary
[rèvəlúːʃənèri]

a. 혁신적인

innovative, progressive
- revolution n. 혁명

If our ancestors came to life, they would call our technology revolutionary.

만약 우리 조상들이 살아온다면, 그들은 우리의 기술을 혁신적인 것이라고 부를 거야.

adopt
[ədápt]

v. 채택하다,
양자로 삼다

to take something; to accept something
- adoption n. 채택, 입양

Diary, my mom is never early to adopt new technology.

다이어리, 우리 엄마는 절대로 첨단 기술을 빨리 받아들이는 분이 아니셔.

analog watch
[ǽnəlɔ̀ːg wátʃ]

아날로그 시계

a watch that uses pointers that move around a dial, opposite of digital watch

She prefers her analog watch to a digital one.

그녀는 디지털 시계보다는 아날로그 시계를 더 좋아하셔.

Internet banking
[íntərnèt bǽŋkiŋ]

인터넷뱅킹

doing your banking by using the Internet

A few months ago, she didn't use the Internet banking services.

몇 달 전에 그녀는 인터넷뱅킹 서비스를 사용하지 않으셨어.

malfunction
[mælfʌ́ŋkʃən]

v. 제대로 작동하지 않다
n. 고장

not to work properly

She was worried that they would malfunction.

그녀는 제대로 되지 않을 것이라고 걱정하셨던 거야.

utility
[juːtíləti]

n. 공공 설비

an important service such as electricity, gas and water

But after she paid our utilities by using Internet banking, she realized how convenient it was.

그렇지만 공공요금을 인터넷뱅킹으로 지불하신 후에는, 그것이 얼마나 간편한지 알게 되셨어.

transfer
[trænsfə́ːr]

v. 송금하다, 전달하다

to move something from one location to another
- transference n. 이동, 전송

Now, every month she transfers my allowance into my bank account.

요즘 그녀는 매달 내 용돈을 내 은행 계좌로 송금하셔.

transmit
[trænsmít]

v. 전송하다

to send something by using a computer or electronic device
- transmission n. 전송

She even transmits photos to my grandparents via the Internet.

그녀는 인터넷으로 우리 조부모님께 사진도 전송하셔.

convert
[kənvə́ːrt]

v. 변하게 하다,
전환하다

to change something into a different form
- conversion n. 전환

If you touch art pieces, they are instantly converted into interactive displays.

만일 미술 작품을 만지면, 즉시 상호작용이 가능한 작품으로 변해.

interactive
[ìntərǽktiv]

a. 상호작용을 하는

allowing people to be involved with something
- interact v. 상호작용하다 · interaction n. 상호작용

If you touch art pieces, they are instantly converted into interactive displays.

만일 미술 작품을 만지면, 즉시 상호작용이 가능한 작품으로 변해.

subject
[sʌ́bdʒikt]

n. 피사체, 대상

a person or object in a painting

When she touched the paintings, the subjects in the paintings danced and even answered her questions.

그녀가 그림을 만졌을 때, 그림 속의 피사체가 춤을 추고 그녀의 질문에 대답도 했어.

aristocrat
[ərístəkræt]

n. 귀족

a person of high status, for example a duchess or marquis
- aristocracy n. 귀족정치 · aristocratic a. 귀족의

For example, *the Mona Lisa*, by Leonardo da Vinci, talked about the lives of aristocrats during the 15th century.

예를 들면, 레오나르도 다빈치의 모나리자가 15세기의 귀족들의 삶에 대해 설명했어.

unique
[juːníːk]

a. 독특한

very unusual and special
- uniqueness n. 독특함

Mona Lisa also explained their unique customs.

모나리자는 그들의 독특한 풍습에 대해서도 설명했어.

portrait
[pɔ́:rtrit]
n. 초상화

a picture of a person's face

• portray v. (초상을) 그리다   • portraiture n. 초상화법
• portrayal n. 그리기, 묘사

She said that drawing portraits was in fashion during those days.
그녀는 초상화를 그리는 것이 그 시대의 유행이었다고 말했어.

conceive
[kənsí:v]
v. 상상하다

to imagine

• conceivable a. 상상할 수 있는

Diary, can you conceive of a huge 10 dollar bill about the size of a house?
다이어리, 집 한 채 크기만한 거대한 10달러짜리 지폐를 상상할 수 있니?

weird
[wíərd]
a. 이상한

strange and peculiar

Sounds weird, doesn't it? 이상하게 들리지 않니?

specimen
[spésəmən]
n. 견본

one example of an object, a sample

But try to imagine a specimen of a 10 dollar bill multiplied in size by 100 times.
하지만 100배 확대된 10달러짜리의 견본을 상상해 봐.

three-dimensional
[θri: diménʃənəl]
a. 입체적인

having depth instead of looking like a flat picture

When Sara touched a part of the bill, it became three-dimensional.
사라가 그 지폐의 일부분에 손을 댔을 때, 그것은 입체적이 되었어.

referee
[rèfərí:]
n. 심판
v. 심판하다

a person who controls the players in a sports match

Interestingly, a referee appeared on the screen and threw a ball to her.
흥미롭게도 화면에 심판이 나타나서 그녀에게 공을 던졌어.

devise
[diváiz]
v. 고안하다, 발명하다

to make something, to invent something

• device n. 장치

I'm curious who devised this system.
나는 이 시스템을 누가 생각해냈는지 궁금해.

graphics
[grǽfiks]
n. 그래픽

pictures - usually created on a computer

The graphics are really amazing.
그 그래픽은 정말 놀라워.

Check Again!

A Translate each word into Korean.

1. barrier ....

2. high-tech ....

3. inconceivable ....

4. adopt ....

5. revolutionary ....

6. weird ....

7. subject ....

8. convert ....

9. malfunction ....

10. unique ....

B Translate each word into English.

1. 고객 ....

2. 회의 ....

3. 공공 설비 ....

4. 초상화 ....

5. 심판 ....

6. 고안하다 ....

7. 입체의 ....

8. 견본 ....

9. 상호작용을 하는 ....

10. 상상하다 ....

C Fill in the blank with the appropriate word. Refer to the Korean.

1. I would call this r .... It's a huge step.

   나는 이것을 혁명적인 것이라고 하겠다. 그건 엄청난 진보이다.

2. How do I t .... my money into an overseas account?

   내 돈을 해외 계좌로 어떻게 송금하죠?

3. Automatically t .... files to the bank via the Internet.

   인터넷을 통해 은행으로 파일을 자동으로 전송하세요.

4. Use a pressure cooker instead of c .... pots and pans.

   재래식 냄비나 팬 대신에 압력 조리기구를 사용하세요.

5. The twentieth century brought about d .... changes in the way classical music was written.

   20세기는 클래식 음악의 작곡 방식에 엄청난 변화를 가져왔다.

Check More!

다음 밑줄 친 부분에 알맞은 어휘를 고르시오. 아래의 영영 풀이를 참조하시오.

The first true piece of sports equipment that man invented was the ball. In ancient Egypt, pitching stones was children's favorite game, but a badly thrown rock could hurt a child. Egyptians were therefore looking for something less dangerous to throw. And they developed **(A)** conventional / unique playthings, which were probably the first balls. They were first made of grass or leaves held together by strings, and later of pieces of animal skin **(B)** sewn / sown together and stuffed with feathers or hay. Even though the Egyptians were warlike, they found time for peaceful games. Before long they **(C)** revised / devised a number of ball games. Perhaps they played ball more for **(D)** instruction / construction than for fun. Ball playing was thought of mainly as a way to teach young men the speed and skill they would need for war.

(A) unusual, special: ....

(B) fastened with stitches: ....

(C) to form, plan, or arrange in the mind:

....

(D) teaching; training; education: ....

Chapter 11
Technology

Unit 35. I should have been more careful.

update one's own blog with music and photos

infringe on one's copyright

Episode

Dear Diary,

Blogging is an **outlet** for my creative ideas. • For a few weeks, I **updated** my own blog with music and photos. • I **downloaded** music and the Volcanoes' photos. • Then I paired the two **components**, music and photos. • Sometimes I matched **classical** music with the Volcanoes' photos. • I spent a few hours combining the best pairs. • The results were **phenomenal**. • Every day over 400 people visited my blog. • They left quite **positive** and **complimentary** messages. • Someone wrote that my materials were **ingenious**. • I was **delighted** to read the messages. • It was **gratifying** to entertain others. • Today I found a **warning** message. • Some music files had been **deleted**. • I was very **confused**. • There was a written message, "You're not allowed to use these **materials**."

Bomi: What's wrong? • Am I going to be arrested by **cybercops**? • Are there any **defects** in my materials? • Mom, why do they think my materials are **illegal**?

Mom: It's related to **copyright** laws.

Bomi: But I didn't **utilize** the materials for anything other than my personal interest.

Mom: Other people's creations should be treated like personal **property**. • If you used the materials without the owner's permission, it's like **theft**. • If someone **asserts** copyright properties of their materials, you have to give it back to them. • The owner may try to **sue** you for money.

Bomi: I didn't know I was **infringing** on their copyright. • From now on, I'll obtain their **consent** before I use someone else's materials.

다이어리에게,

블로그를 하는 것은 나의 창의적인 아이디어를 표현하는 수단이야. 몇 주 동안 나는 내 블로그의 음악과 사진을 업데이트했어. 나는 음악과 볼케이노의 사진을 다운로드했어. 그리고 나서 나는 음악과 사진이라는 두 구성요소의 짝을 맞추었어. 가끔 나는 고전 음악과 그에 어울리는 볼케이노의 사진을 맞추었어. 나는 최고의 쌍을 결합시키는 데 몇 시간이 걸렸어. 결과는 놀랄 만한 것이었어. 매일 400명 이상의 사람들이 나의 블로그를 방문했어. 그들은 꽤 긍정적이고 칭찬하는 메시지를 남겼어. 어떤 사람은 내가 사용한 자료들이 독창적이라고 썼어. 나는 메시지를 읽는 것이 즐거웠어. 다른 사람들을 즐겁게 하는 것이 만족스러웠어. 오늘 난 경고 메시지를 발견했어. 어떤 음악 파일은 삭제되어 있었어. 나는 매우 혼란스러웠어. 메시지에는 "당신은 이 자료를 사용할 수 없습니다"라고 쓰여 있었어.

보미: 뭐가 잘못됐나요? 제가 사이버 경찰에게 체포될까요? 제 자료에 뭔가 결함이 있나요? 엄마, 왜 그 사람들은 제 자료가 불법이라고 생각할까요?

엄마: 그건 저작권법에 관련된 거야.

보미: 하지만 저는 그 자료들을 제 개인적인 관심 이외의 다른 용도로는 사용하지 않았어요.

엄마: 다른 사람들의 창작물은 개인적인 재산으로 취급되어야 해. 네가 자료를 주인의 허가 없이 사용했다면, 그건 절도와 같은 거야. 만약 누군가가 자신의 자료에 관해 저작권을 주장한다면, 너는 그걸 그들에게 돌려주어야 해. 자료의 주인은 돈을 받으려고 너를 고소하려고 할지도 몰라.

보미: 저는 제가 저작권을 침해한 줄 몰랐어요. 지금부터는 다른 사람의 자료를 사용하기 전에 동의를 얻을 거예요.

outlet
[áutlet]
n. 표현 수단, 배출구

a means of expressing some feelings

Blogging is an outlet for my creative ideas.
블로그를 하는 것은 나의 창의적인 아이디어를 표현하는 수단이야.

update
[ʌpdéit]
v. 새롭게 하다
n. 새롭게 함, 갱신

to improve something by adding new material

For a few weeks, I updated my own blog with music and photos.
몇 주 동안 나는 내 블로그의 음악과 사진을 업데이트했어.

download
[dáunlòud]
v. 다운로드하다

to take something from the Internet and keep it on one's computer

I downloaded music and the Volcanoes' photos.
나는 음악과 볼케이노의 사진을 다운로드했어.

component
[kəmpóunənt]
n. 구성요소
a. 구성하는

one piece of an object made of several pieces

Then I paired the two components, music and photos.
그리고 나서 나는 음악과 사진이라는 두 구성요소의 짝을 맞추었어.

classical
[klǽsikəl]
a. 고전의, 클래식의

traditional in style

• classical music 고전 음악

Sometimes I matched classical music with the Volcanoes' photos.
가끔 나는 고전 음악과 그에 어울리는 볼케이노의 사진을 맞추었어.

combine
[kəmbáin]
v. 결합하다

to put two or more things together

• combination n. 결합

I spent a few hours combining the best pairs.
나는 최고의 쌍을 결합시키는 데 몇 시간이 걸렸어.

phenomenal
[finámənəl]
a. 놀랄 만한

extremely good, amazing

• phenomenon n. 현상

The results were phenomenal. 결과는 놀랄 만한 것이었어.

blog
[blɑ́ːg]
n. 블로그

a personal website that one writes about oneself

Every day over 400 people visited my blog.

매일 400명 이상의 사람들이 나의 블로그를 방문했어.

---

positive
[pɑ́zətiv]
a. 긍정적인

good and pleasant

They left quite positive and complimentary messages.

그들은 꽤 긍정적이고 칭찬하는 메시지를 남겼어.

---

complimentary
[kàmpləméntəri]
a. 칭찬하는, 무료의

expressing nice things to somebody, expressing admiration for something

• compliment n. 칭찬

They left quite positive and complimentary messages.

그들은 꽤 긍정적이고 칭찬하는 메시지를 남겼어.

---

ingenious
[indʒíːnjəs]
a. 독창적인

extremely clever, creative

• ingenuity n. 독창성

Someone wrote that my materials were ingenious.

어떤 사람은 내가 사용한 자료들이 독창적이라고 썼어.

---

delighted
[diláitid]
a. 즐거운

very pleased and happy

• delight v. 기쁘게 하다 n. 기쁨, 즐거움   • delightful a. 유쾌한

I was delighted to read the messages.

나는 메시지를 읽는 것이 즐거웠어.

---

gratifying
[grǽtəfàiiŋ]
a. 만족스러운

satisfying, feeling pleasure

• gratify v. 만족시키다

It was gratifying to entertain others.

다른 사람들을 즐겁게 하는 것이 만족스러웠어.

---

warn
[wɔ́ːrn]
v. 경고하다

to tell someone not to do something

Today I found a warning message.

오늘 나는 경고 메시지를 발견했어.

delete
[dilí:t]
v. 삭제하다

to remove something from one's computer or website
- deletion n. 삭제

Some music files had been deleted.
어떤 음악 파일은 삭제되어 있었어.

confused
[kənfjú:zd]
a. 혼란스러운

unaware of what is happening or what to do
- confuse v. 혼동하다, 혼란시키다   - confusion n. 혼란

I was very confused. 나는 매우 혼란스러웠어.

material
[mətíəriəl]
n. 자료

component, substance

There was a written message, "You're not allowed to use these materials."
메시지에는 "당신은 이 자료를 사용할 수 없습니다"라고 쓰여 있었어.

cybercop
[sàibərkáp]
n. 사이버 경찰

a person who monitors the Internet looking for anything illegal

Am I going to be arrested by cybercops?
제가 사이버 경찰에게 체포될까요?

defect
[dífekt]
n. 결함

a mistake or an error
- defective a. 결함이 있는

Are there any defects in my materials?
제 자료에 뭔가 결함이 있나요?

illegal
[ilí:gəl]
a. 불법의

against the law, unlawful
- illegally ad. 불법으로

Mom, why do they think my materials are illegal?
엄마, 왜 그 사람들은 제 자료가 불법이라고 생각할까요?

copyright
[kápiràit]
n. 저작권

the right to use or reproduce a piece of writing or music

It's related to copyright laws.
그건 저작권법에 관련된 거야.

utilize
[júːtəlàiz]

v. 사용하다

to make use of something
- utilization n. 이용, 활용

But I didn't utilize the materials for anything other than my personal interest.

하지만 저는 그 자료들을 제 개인적인 관심 이외의 다른 용도로는 사용하지 않았어요.

property
[prápərti]

n. 재산

possessions, assets

Other people's creations should be treated like personal property.

다른 사람들의 창작물은 개인적인 재산으로 취급되어야 해.

theft
[θéft]

n. 절도

the crime of stealing

If you used the materials without the owner's permission, it's like theft.

네가 자료를 주인의 허가 없이 사용했다면, 그건 절도와 같은 거야.

assert
[əsə́ːrt]

v. 강력히 주장하다

to say something forcefully, to insist
- assertion n. 주장, 확언

If someone asserts copyright properties of their materials, you have to give it back to them.

만약 누군가가 자신의 자료에 관해 저작권을 주장한다면, 너는 그걸 그들에게 돌려주어야 해.

sue
[súː]

v. 고소하다

to start a legal case against someone

The owner may try to sue you for money.

주인은 돈을 받으려고 너를 고소하려고 할지도 몰라.

infringe
[infríndʒ]

v. 침해하다, 위반하다

to do something that is against the law
- infringement n. 위반 • infringe on ~을 침해하다, 위반하다

I didn't know I was infringing on their copyright.

저는 제가 저작권을 침해한 줄 몰랐어요.

consent
[kənsént]

n. 동의
v. 동의하다

the agreement to do something
- consenter n. 동의자, 승낙자

From now on, I'll obtain their consent before I use someone else's materials.

지금부터는 다른 사람의 자료를 사용하기 전에 그들의 동의를 얻을 거예요.

Check Again!

A Translate each word into Korean.

1. component ....
2. phenomenal ....
3. positive ....
4. ingenious ....
5. gratifying ....
6. assert ....
7. sue ....
8. property ....
9. defect ....
10. illegal ....

B Translate each word into English.

1. 혼란스러운 ....
2. 자료 ....
3. 사이버 경찰 ....
4. 저작권 ....
5. 사용하다 ....
6. 절도 ....
7. 삭제하다 ....
8. 새롭게 하다 ....
9. 결합하다 ....
10. 표현 수단 ....

C Fill in the blank with the appropriate word. Refer to the Korean.

1. I was d   to receive your letter.
   귀하의 편지를 받게 되어 기쁩니다.

2. I would like to thank all that visit my blog and leave c
   messages.
   나는 내 블로그를 방문해서 칭찬 메시지를 남기는 모든 분들께 감사를 드리고 싶습니다.

3. Photocopying a literary work is a common way of i
   on copyright laws.
   문학작품 복사는 저작권 침해의 흔한 방식이다.

4. You should obtain their c   before organizing the event.
   그 행사를 준비하기 전에 그들의 동의를 얻어야 한다.

5. The university sent a w   message alerting students not to
   give their username and password to anyone.
   대학은 학생들에게 사용자 이름과 비밀번호를 누구에게도 알리지 않도록 주의시키는 경고문을 보냈다.

Check More!

(A), (B), (C) 각 밑줄 친 부분에 알맞은 어휘를 짝지은 것으로 가장 적절한 것을 고르시오.

You can see and feel exactly what this teenage girl is going through. I can remember feeling very frustrated and **(A)** confused / infused sometimes in my teens. I can also remember my emotions swinging from one extreme to another. So, for example, I would get **(B)** incredibly / incredulously mad about something, usually something silly. Then I would get mad at myself about being so angry, and then get mad again about what made me angry. I seemed to have absolutely no control over these feelings. That's why I often relied on music for an **(C)** outlaw / outlet for stress.

	(A)	(B)	(C)
①	confused	incredibly	outlet
②	infused	incredulously	outlet
③	confused	incredibly	outlaw
④	infused	incredibly	outlaw
⑤	confused	incredulously	outlet

Chapter 11
Technology

Unit 36. Forgery should be stopped.

implement cutting-edge technologies

watch news about **fake** cell phones

Episode

Dad: We need to renew our passports.
Bomi: You said they only need to be extended.
Dad: New passports would be safer. • It's because to prevent forgery cutting-edge technologies, like holograms, are being implemented.

Dad said this right after the news that forgeries had been found.
Korean cell phones are popular. • In some countries, they almost monopolize the market. • Today we watched news about fake cell phones. • Evidently, the logos and designs on these cell phones are identical to those of Korean cell phones. • Consumers can be tricked, believing that they are purchasing genuine Korean products. • How come this happened?
Sadly, some Koreans were also accused of doing this. • They have allegedly been deeply involved in this matter. • Allegedly, they conspired with foreign business people. • They might expect to receive a fortune in return for this. • But the financial losses of Korean companies are immeasurable. • If these traitors are found guilty, they should be forced to compensate for the companies' losses. • I'm worried that the integrity of Korean products is being harmed. • What if people's view of Korean products is tarnished?

Bomi: Can it lead to diplomatic disputes?
Dad: I think so. • It could even develop into hostility between the involved countries. • Forgery laws must be enforced.
Bomi: I think the laws should be reinforced. • I didn't know that fake products could bring about so many problems.

아빠: 여권을 갱신해야겠다.
보미: 기간을 연장한다고 하셨잖아요.
아빠: 새 여권이 더 안전할 거야. 위조를 방지하려고 홀로그램 같은 최첨단 기술이 사용되기 때문이야.

아빠는 위조품이 발견되었다는 뉴스가 나간 바로 후에 이렇게 말씀하셨다.
한국 휴대 전화는 인기가 있다. 어떤 나라에서는 그 제품들이 시장을 거의 독점하고 있다. 오늘 우리는 가짜 휴대 전화에 관한 뉴스를 보았다. 분명히 이 휴대 전화의 로고와 디자인은 한국 휴대 전화에 있는 것과 똑같다. 소비자들은 속아서 자신들이 진짜 제품을 구입한다고 믿을 수도 있다. 어떻게 이런 일이 일어난 것일까?
슬프게도 몇몇 한국인들이 이런 일로 또한 고소되었다. 그들은 이 문제에 깊이 연루되어 있다고 한다. 주장에 따르면, 그들은 외국의 사업가들과 공모했다. 그들은 이것에 대한 대가로 돈을 받기를 기대했을 것이다. 그러나 한국 회사의 재정적 손실은 헤아릴 수 없다. 만일 이 반역자들이 유죄로 밝혀지면, 그들은 그 회사의 손실에 대해 보상을 해야 할 것이다. 나는 한국 제품의 완전함에 흠이 갈까 걱정이다. 만일 한국 제품에 대한 사람들의 생각이 안좋아지면 어떻게 하지?

보미: 그것이 외교 논쟁으로 이어질 수 있나요?
아빠: 그렇지. 그것은 관련된 나라 간에 적개심을 불러일으킬 수도 있어. 위조법은 실행되어야 해.
보미: 그 법은 강화되어야겠어요. 저는 가짜 상품이 그렇게 많은 문제를 야기하는지 몰랐어요.

renew
[rinjúː]
v. 갱신하다

to get a new passport, a license, or other document
- renewable a. 갱신할 수 있는

We need to renew our passports.
여권을 갱신해야겠다.

extend
[iksténd]
v. 연장하다

to make something last longer than before
- extension n. 연장 - extensive a. 광범위한

You said they only need to be extended.
기간을 연장한다고 하셨잖아요.

passport
[pǽspɔ̀ːrt]
n. 여권

a document that lets one travel to other countries

New passports would be safer.
새 여권이 더 안전할 거야.

cutting-edge
[kʌ́tiŋ édʒ]
a. 최첨단의

of the very newest technology, state-of-the-art

It's because to prevent forgery cutting-edge technologies, like holograms, are being implemented.
위조를 방지하려고 홀로그램 같은 최첨단 기술이 사용되기 때문이야.

implement
[ímpləmənt]
v. 이행하다

to put into action

It's because to prevent forgery cutting-edge technologies, like holograms, are being implemented.
위조를 방지하려고 홀로그램 같은 최첨단 기술이 사용되기 때문이야.

forgery
[fɔ́ːrdʒəri]
n. 위조품, 위조

a fake; the crime of forging money or documents
- forge v. 위조하다 - forger n. 위조자

Dad said this right after the news that forgeries had been found.
아빠는 위조품이 발견되었다는 뉴스가 나간 바로 후에 이렇게 말씀하셨다.

monopolize
[mənάpəlàiz]
v. 독점하다

to have a very large share of something
- monopoly n. 독점

In some countries, they almost monopolize the market.
어떤 나라에서는 그 제품들이 시장을 거의 독점하고 있다.

fake
[féik]
a. 가짜의, 모조의
n. 가짜, 모조품

not real, opposite of genuine

Today we watched news about fake cell phones.
오늘 우리는 가짜 휴대 전화에 관한 뉴스를 보았다.

evidently
[évədəntli]
ad. 분명히, 명백히

apparently
• evidence n. 증거   • evident a. 명백한

Evidently, the logos and designs on these cell phones are identical to those of Korean cell phones.
분명히 이 휴대 전화의 로고와 디자인은 한국 휴대 전화에 있는 것과 똑같다.

trick
[trík]
v. 속이다
n. 속임수, 기교

to deceive someone
• trickery n. 속임수

Consumers can be tricked, believing that they are purchasing genuine Korean products.
소비자들은 속아서 자신들이 진짜 한국 제품을 구입한다고 믿을 수도 있다.

genuine
[dʒénjuin]
a. 진짜의

not fake, real, authentic
• genuinely ad. 진정으로

Consumers can be tricked, believing that they are purchasing genuine Korean products.
소비자들은 속아서 자신들이 진짜 한국 제품을 구입한다고 믿을 수도 있다.

accuse
[əkjúːz]
v. 고소하다

to charge someone with wrongdoing and put on trial
• accusation n. 고소   • accuse A of B A를 B로 고소하다

Sadly, some Koreans were also accused of doing this.
슬프게도 몇몇 한국인들이 이런 일로 또한 고소되었다.

allegedly
[əlédʒdli]
ad. 주장에 의하면

based on someone's assumption
• allege v. 주장하다   • allegation n. 주장   • alleged a. 주장된

They have allegedly been deeply involved in this matter.
그들은 이 문제에 깊이 연루되어 있다고 한다.

conspire

[kənspáiər]

v. 공모하다,
음모를 꾸미다

to make a secret agreement to do something bad

• conspiracy n. 음모 • conspirator n. 음모자

Allegedly, they conspired with foreign business
people.

주장에 따르면, 그들은 외국의 사업가들과 공모했다.

in return for

[in ritə́ːrn fɔːr]

~에 대한 대가로

as a compensation for

They might expect to receive a fortune in return for
this.

그들은 이것에 대한 대가로 큰 돈을 받기를 기대했을 것이다.

immeasurable

[iméʒərəbəl]

a. 헤아릴 수 없는

unable to measure or calculate

But the financial losses of Korean companies are
immeasurable.

하지만 한국 회사의 재정적 손실은 헤아릴 수 없다.

traitor

[tréitər]

n. 반역자

a person who betrays their country or friends

If these traitors are found guilty, they should be
forced to compensate for the companies' losses.

만일 이 반역자들이 유죄로 밝혀지면, 그들은 그 회사의 손실에 대해 보상을 해야 할 것이다.

compensate

[kámpənsèit]

v. 보상하다

to make up for a loss

• compensation n. 보상

If these traitors are found guilty, they should be
forced to compensate for the companies' losses.

만일 이 반역자들이 유죄로 밝혀지면, 그들은 그 회사의 손실에 대해 보상을 해야 할 것이다.

integrity

[intégrəti]

n. 완전함, 흠 없음

completeness, absoluteness

I'm worried that the integrity of Korean products is
being harmed.

나는 한국 제품의 완전함에 흠이 갈까 걱정이다.

tarnish
[tá:rniʃ]

v. 더럽히다

n. 퇴색, 흠

to damage a reputation
- tarnished a. 더럽혀진

What if people's view of Korean products is tarnished?
만일 한국 제품에 대한 사람들의 생각이 안좋아지면 어떻게 하지?

diplomatic
[dìpləmǽtik]

a. 외교의

relating to different countries
- diplomacy n. 외교 • diplomat n. 외교관

Can it lead to diplomatic disputes?
그것이 외교 논쟁으로 이어질 수 있나요?

dispute
[dispjú:t]

n. 논쟁 v. 논쟁하다

a disagreement between people or countries

Can it lead to diplomatic disputes?
그것이 외교 논쟁으로 이어질 수 있나요?

hostility
[hastíləti]

n. 적개심, 적대 행위

feeling of disaffection; aggressive behavior
- hostile a. 적의가 있는, 적개심에 불타는

It could even develop into hostility between the involved countries.
그것은 관련된 나라 간에 적개심을 불러일으킬 수도 있어.

enforce
[enfó:rs]

v. 시행하다

to make people obey a law
- enforcement n. 시행

Forgery laws must be enforced.
위조법은 실행되어야 해.

reinforce
[rì:infó:rs]

v. 강화하다

to make something stronger
- reinforcement n. 보강, 강화

I think the laws should be reinforced.
그 법은 강화되어야겠어요.

Check Again!

A Translate each word into Korean.

1. hostility ....
2. allegedly ....
3. reinforce ....
4. tarnish ....
5. conspire ....
6. forgery ....
7. immeasurable ....
8. cutting-edge ....
9. implement ....
10. genuine ....

B Translate each word into English.

1. 가짜의 ....
2. 독점하다 ....
3. 속이다 ....
4. 완전함 ....
5. 분명히 ....
6. 갱신하다 ....
7. 연장하다 ....
8. 반역자 ....
9. 보상하다 ....
10. 시행하다 ....

C Fill in the blank with the appropriate word. Refer to the Korean.

1. He was a _____ of spreading false rumors.

   그는 거짓된 소문을 유포시켰다고 고소되었다.

2. China used international law to resolve d_____ disputes.

   중국은 외교분쟁을 해결하기 위해 국제법을 사용하였다.

3. C_____ technologies were used to renovate the old building.

   그 옛 건물을 개보수하는 데 첨단 기술들이 사용되었다.

4. Only a small number of the victims have been c_____ for the loss.

   소수의 피해자만이 손실에 대한 보상을 받았다.

5. They asked for a lot of money in r_____ for saving the child.

   그들은 그 아이를 구한 대가로 많은 돈을 요구했다.

Check More!

다음 밑줄 친 부분에 알맞은 어휘를 고르시오. 아래의 영영 풀이를 참조하시오.

Ethics begins with our being conscious that we choose how we behave. For instance, we can either tell the truth or tell a lie. These two possibilities are presented to us as options. We are capable of doing either one because we can control our actions. A stone, however, does not face these kinds of options because it cannot **(A)** distinguish / demolish between different courses of action. A stone can behave only in the way an outside **(B)** force / enforce makes it behave. Unlike a stone, a person can start an action by himself or herself. The difference, then, is that a stone is not conscious of possibilities, whereas human beings are conscious that they face **(C)** genius / genuine alternatives.

(A) to tell the difference: ....

(B) might; power; energy: ....

(C) authentic; real; true: ....

+ 접두사 over- / dis- / co-/com-

over-는 '무언가를 지나치게 하다' 라는 뜻의 단어를 만드는 접두사이다. dis-는 'apart,' 'not' 이라는 뜻의 접두사로, '무언가를 제거하다' 라는 뜻의 단어 혹은 반의어를 만든다. co-/com-은 'together,' 'with' 라는 뜻의 접두사로, '무언가가 함께 있다' 라는 뜻의 단어를 만든다.

over-

eat 먹다
over + eat = overeat 과식하다
ex) I always end up overeating during the holidays.
나는 늘 연휴 동안 결국은 과식하게 된다.

• **work** 일하다	**overwork** 과도하게 일을 시키다
• **burden** 부담시키다	**overburden** 지나치게 부담시키다
• **sleep** 잠을 자다	**oversleep** 늦잠 자다
• **flow** 흐르다	**overflow** 넘쳐 흐르다
• **step** 한 걸음 내디디다	**overstep** 지나치게 가다, 한도를 넘다
• **estimate** 평가하다	**overestimate** 과대 평가하다
• **dose** 복용량	**overdose** 과대 복용

dis-

agree 일치하다
dis + agree = disagree 일치하지 않다
ex) The first witness' testimony disagreed with the second witness'.
첫 번째 증인의 증언은 두 번째 증인의 증언과 일치하지 않았다.

• **close** 닫다	**disclose** 드러내다, 폭로하다
• **arm** 무장시키다	**disarm** 무장을 해제하다
• **allow** 허락하다	**disallow** 금하다
• **approve** 찬성하다	**disapprove** 찬성하지 않다
• **lodge** 묵게 하다	**dislodge** 이동시키다, 제거하다
• **infect** 감염시키다	**disinfect** 소독하다
• **grace** 기품, 고상함	**disgrace** 불명예, 망신

co-/com-

worker 일하는 사람
co + worker = coworker 같이 일하는 사람, 동료
ex) Jake is very popular among his coworkers.
제이크는 동료들 사이에서 매우 인기가 있다.

- **education** 교육
- **write** 집필하다
- **exist** 존재하다
- **operate** 작동하다
- **bat** 타구, 때리다
- **-bi-** 둘
- **promise** 약속하다

coeducation 남녀 공학
cowrite 공동 집필하다
coexist 공존하다
cooperate 협동하다
combat 전투
combination 결합, 조합
compromise 타협하다, 화해하다

On a Passport 여권에서

+surname 성

+given name 이름

+nationality 국적

+date of birth 생년월일

+sex 성

+date of issue 발행일

+date of expiry 만기일

VOCA
EDGE
RED

joodbye, Sara. I learned about the earth. I went to a natural science museum. I had

ra attends a community party. Mom's got a new hobby. Are they my bosses? Hoony

ighter clinic. The Volcanoes are back. We have great brothers. What historical figures d

elepathy between us! Sara goes to Turkey. Home decorating is not easy. Hoony thinks gir

war should be stopped. Mom, are you going to cut my allowance? Hoony is back fror

uld have been more careful. Forgery should be stopped. Hoony wants to explore out

ricane hit the village. We're teens. I had my cell phone taken away. Goodbye, Browni

e museum. I had a campus tour. If I were a judge,... How can we survive in a jungle?

osses? Hoony is money-wise. Hoony goes to an herbal clinic. We became a rescue team

cal figures do you want to meet? Are mom and dad compatible? I can't understand th

Hoony thinks girls have illusions about boys. I can't understand politicians. Wearing a

Hoony is back from an economics camp. construction a thriving business? How amazin

to explore outer space. I attended the Arbor Day ceremony. We can make the earth

odbye, Brownie Life is full of contradictions. Goodbye, Sara. I learned about the earth.

n a jungle? I became a Santa Claus. Sara attends a community party. Mom's got a nev

Chapter 12. Nature and Space

a rescue team. Grandma goes to a laughter clinic. The Volcanoes are back. We ha

Unit 37. Hoony wants to explore outer space.

n't understand this painting. There was telepathy between us! Sara goes to Turkey. Ho

Unit 38. I attended the Arbor Day ceremony.

Wearing an electronic tag is horrible. The war should be stopped. Mom, are you going

Unit 39. We can make the earth a better place.

low amazing our life has become! I should have been more careful. Forgery should

Unit 40. A super hurricane hit the village.

e the earth a better place. A super hurricane hit the village. We're teens. I had my ce

the earth. I went to a natural science museum. I had a campus tour. If I were a judge,..

got a new hobby. Are they my bosses? Hoony is money-wise. Hoony goes to an herb

Chapter 12
Nature and Space

Unit 37. Hoony wants to explore outer space.

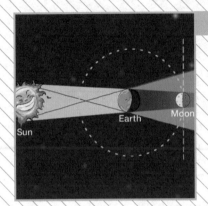

observe a lunar eclipse

think aliens will **abduct** kids

investigate the whole galaxy

Episode

Dear Diary,

Yesterday my family observed an amazing event. • It was a total **lunar eclipse**. • The earth, sun and moon were all **aligned**. • This kind of **celestial** event doesn't happen very often. • While observing, Hoony said that he wanted to **explore** other **planets** in outer space. • He thought it would be fun to communicate with **aliens**. • Seri asked Hoony, "Do you remember we thought aliens would **abduct** kids?" • Hoony and Seri made their own game titled **Extra-Terrestrials**. • They named their team **Expedition** from Mars. • They pretended to be **Martians**.

In the game, they were aliens exploring the **solar system**. • They used Hoony's rocket and called it an **artificial satellite**. • In their game, the artificial satellite was **orbiting** the solar system. • They called several balls **meteorites**. • They made the earth **collide** with the meteorites by throwing balls at one another. • They called this event **doomsday**. • If doomsday happened, all the people on earth would be **in jeopardy**. • It would be **catastrophic**.

Later we read a book about **astronomy**. • In the book, astronomically significant events were described in **chronological** order. • It told us about events that had happened over the last few **decades**. • Among them, the **explosion** of the spacecraft in 1986 was the most shocking. • It was funny to read about the animals that were **launched** into space. • We talked about what happened to the animals in space, where there is little **gravity**. • We looked at pictures of the animals whose heads sometimes became **swollen**. • According to the book, it was because their blood became concentrated in their heads in space. • We wondered if it was possible to explore the whole **galaxy**. • Hoony thought we could investigate the whole galaxy by sending **space probes**. • Hoony, you are **omitting** one important fact. • Our universe is vast.

다이어리에게,

어제 우리 가족은 놀라운 현상을 보았어. 전체 월식이었어. 지구, 태양과 달이 모두 일직선으로 정렬되었어. 하늘에서 일어나는 이런 종류의 현상은 자주 일어나지 않아. 그것을 관찰하는 동안, 후니는 외계에 있는 다른 행성을 탐험하고 싶다고 말했어. 그는 외계인들과 의사소통하는 것이 재미있을 거라고 생각했어. 세리는 후니에게 "우리가 외계인이 아이들을 유괴할 거라고 생각했던 것 기억하니?" 라고 물었어. 후니와 세리는 외계인이라는 이름을 붙인 그들만의 게임을 만들었어. 그들은 그들의 팀을 화성에서 온 탐험대라고 이름붙였어. 그들은 화성인인 양했어.

게임에서 그들은 태양계를 탐험하는 외계인이었어. 그들은 후니의 로케트를 사용했고 그것을 인공위성이라고 불렀어. 게임에서 인공위성은 태양계를 궤도를 그리며 돌고 있었어. 그들은 여러 개의 공을 운석이라고 불렀어. 그들은 서로에게 공을 던져서 지구가 운석과 충돌하게 했어. 그들은 그 사건을 최후의 심판일이라고 불렀어. 만일 최후의 심판일이 온다면, 지구에 사는 모든 사람들은 위험에 처하겠지. 그것은 매우 엄청난 재앙일 거야.

나중에 우리는 천문학에 관한 책을 읽었어. 그 책에는 천문학적으로 중요한 사건이 연대순으로 설명되어 있었어. 그 책은 지난 수십 년간 일어난 사건에 대해서 설명하고 있었어. 그것들 중에서 1986년에 우주선이 폭발한 것이 가장 충격적이었어. 우주로 쏘아 올려진 동물에 관해 읽는 것은 재미있었어. 우리는 중력이 거의 없는 우주에서 동물들에게 그 일이 있어났는지에 대해 얘기했어. 우리는 동물들의 그림을 보았는데 머리가 가끔 부풀어 올라 있었어. 책에 의하면, 그것은 우주에서 피가 머리로 몰리기 때문이야. 우리는 은하계 전체를 탐사하는 것이 가능한지 궁금했어. 후니는 우리가 우주 탐사선을 보내서 은하계 전체를 탐사할 수 있다고 생각했어. 후니, 너는 중요한 사실 하나를 빠뜨렸어. 이 우주는 광대해.

eclipse
[iklíps]

n. (해·달의) 식

an event where the earth comes between the sun and the moon so that you cannot see the moon

• a lunar eclipse 월식 • a solar eclipse 일식

It was a total lunar eclipse. 전체 월식이었다.

---

align
[əláin]

v. 정렬시키다

to position objects into one straight line

• alignment n. 정렬

The earth, sun and moon were all aligned.
지구, 태양과 달이 모두 직선으로 정렬되었다.

---

celestial
[siléstʃəl]

a. 하늘의, 천체의

relating to the sky and stars

This kind of celestial event doesn't happen very often.
하늘에서 일어나는 이런 종류의 현상은 자주 일어나지 않는다.

---

explore
[iksplɔ́ːr]

v. 탐험하다

to investigate an area to find something

• exploration n. 탐험 • explorer n. 탐험가

While observing, Hoony said that he wanted to explore other planets in outer space.
그것을 관찰하는 동안, 후니는 외계에 있는 다른 행성을 탐험하고 싶다고 말했다.

---

outer space
[áutər spéis]

외계

the area outside the earth's atmosphere

While observing, Hoony said that he wanted to explore other planets in outer space.
그것을 관찰하는 동안, 후니는 외계에 있는 다른 행성을 탐험하고 싶다고 말했다.

---

alien
[éiljən]

n. 외계인 a. 외국의

a creature from outer space

He thought it would be fun to communicate with aliens.
그는 외계인들과 의사소통하는 것이 재미있을 거라고 생각했다.

---

abduct
[æbdʌ́kt]

v. 유괴하다

to kidnap

• abduction n. 유괴

Seri asked Hoony, "Do you remember we thought aliens would abduct kids?"
세리는 후니에게 "우리가 외계인이 아이들을 유괴할 거라고 생각했던 것 기억하니?" 라고 물었다.

Extra-Terrestrial

[èkstrə təréstriəl]

n. 외계인

a. 지구 밖의

a creature that exists in another part of the universe

Hoony and Seri made their own game titled Extra-Terrestrials.

후니와 세리는 외계인이라는 이름을 붙인 그들만의 게임을 만들었다.

expedition

[èkspədíʃən]

n. 탐험대, 원정대

people on a journey

They named their team Expedition from Mars.

그들은 그들의 팀을 화성에서 온 탐험대라고 이름붙였다.

Martian

[má:rʃən]

n. 화성인

an alien who lives on the planet Mars

They pretended to be Martians.

그들은 화성인인 양했다.

solar system

[sóulər sístəm]

태양계

the earth and all the planets that move around the sun

In the game, they were aliens exploring the solar system.

게임에서 그들은 태양계를 탐험하는 외계인이었다.

artificial satellite

[à:rtəfíʃəl sætəlàit]

인공위성

an object sent into space to send information

They used Hoony's rocket and called it an artificial satellite.

그들은 후니의 로케트를 사용했고 그것을 인공위성이라고 불렀다.

orbit

[ɔ́:rbit]

v. 궤도를 그리며 돌다

n. 궤도

to move in a circle around another object

In their game, the artificial satellite was orbiting the solar system.

게임에서 인공위성은 태양계를 궤도를 그리며 돌고 있었다.

meteorite

[mí:tiəràit]

n. 운석

a large rock that floats in space

They called several balls meteorites.

그들은 여러 개의 공을 운석이라고 불렀다.

collide
[kəláid]

v. 충돌하다

to crash into something

• collision n. 충돌

They made the earth collide with the meteorites by throwing balls at one another.

그들은 서로에게 공을 던져서 지구가 운석과 충돌하게 했다.

doomsday
[dú:mzdèi]

n. 최후의 심판일

a day when a terrible and harmful event will happen

They called this event doomsday.

그들은 그 사건을 최후의 심판일이라고 불렀다.

jeopardy
[dʒépərdi]

n. 위험

danger, trouble

• jeopardize v. 위험에 빠뜨리다 • in jeopardy 위험에 처한, 위급한

If doomsday happened, all the people on earth would be in jeopardy.

만일 최후의 심판일이 온다면, 지구에 사는 모든 사람들은 위험에 처하겠지.

catastrophic
[kæ̀təstráfik]

a. 큰 재앙의

very dangerous, extremely harmful

• catastrophe n. 큰 재앙

It would be catastrophic. 그것은 매우 엄청난 재앙일 것이다.

astronomy
[əstránəmi]

n. 천문학

the scientific study of the stars and planets

• astronomical a. 천문학적인 • astronomically ad. 천문학적으로

Later we read a book about astronomy.

나중에 우리는 천문학에 관한 책을 읽었다.

chronological
[kràːnəládʒikəl]

a. 연대순의

arranged according to the sequence of events occurred

• chronology n. 연대기

In the book, astronomically significant events were described in chronological order.

그 책에는 천문학적으로 중요한 사건이 연대순으로 설명되어 있었다.

decade
[dékeid]

n. 10년

a period of ten years

It told us about events that had happened over the last few decades.

그 책은 지난 수십 년간 일어난 사건에 대해서 설명하고 있었다.

explosion
[iksplóuʒ∂n]

n. 폭발

an eruption, a blast

• explode v. 폭발하다 • explosive a. 폭발성이 있는

Among them, the explosion of the spacecraft in 1986 was the most shocking.

그것들 중에서 1986년에 우주선이 폭발한 것이 가장 충격적이었다.

launch
[lɔ́:ntʃ]

v. 쏘아 올리다, 발사하다

to send something into the air or into space

It was funny to read about the animals that were launched into space.

우주로 쏘아 올려진 동물에 관해 읽는 것은 재미있었다.

gravity
[grǽvəti]

n. 중력

the force that makes things fall to the ground

• gravitation n. 중력 • gravitational a. 중력의

We talked about what happened to the animals in space, where there is little gravity.

우리는 중력이 거의 없는 우주에서 동물들에게 어떤 일이 있어났는지에 대해 얘기했다.

swell
[swél]

v. 부풀다, 팽창하다

to become larger

• swelling n. 팽창

We looked at pictures of the animals whose heads sometimes became swollen.

우리는 동물들의 그림을 보았는데 머리가 가끔 부풀어 올라 있었다.

galaxy
[gǽləksi]

n. 은하계

a group of stars in the universe

• galactic a. 은하계의

We wondered if it was possible to explore the whole galaxy.

우리는 은하계 전체를 탐사하는 것이 가능한지 궁금했다.

space probe
[spéis pròub]

우주 탐사선

a small rocket sent into space to investigate

Hoony thought we could investigate the whole galaxy by sending space probes.

후니는 우리가 우주 탐사선을 보내서 은하계 전체를 탐사할 수 있다고 생각했다.

omit
[oumít]

v. 빠뜨리다, 생략하다

to leave something out

• omission n. 생략

Hoony, you are omitting one important fact.

후니, 너는 중요한 사실 하나를 빠뜨렸어.

Check Again!

A Translate each word into Korean.

1. omit ....
2. collide ....
3. doomsday ....
4. meteorite ....
5. catastrophic ....
6. orbit ....
7. celestial ....
8. decade ....
9. alien ....
10. abduct ....

B Translate each word into English.

1. 천문학 ....
2. 정렬시키다 ....
3. 탐험대 ....
4. 폭발 ....
5. 중력 ....
6. 부풀다 ....
7. 은하계 ....
8. 탐험하다 ....
9. 쏘아 올리다 ....
10. 태양계 ....

C Fill in the blank with the appropriate word. Refer to the Korean.

1. The next total lunar e   occurs on December 21, 2010.
   다음 전체 월식은 2010년 12월 21일에 일어난다.

2. Your phone messages are in c   order with most recent on top.
   여러분의 전화 메시지는 시간순으로 가장 최근 것이 제일 위에 온다.

3. A skier c   with another skier during the college ski championship.
   대학 스키 챔피언전 중에 한 스키선수가 다른 선수랑 충돌했다.

4. If there should be a spill, our coastlines and public health would be in j   .
   누출사고가 일어나면, 해안선과 공중 보건이 위험에 처하게 될 것이다.

5. The first a   satellite was Sputnik 1, launched by the Soviet Union on 4 October 1957.
   최초의 인공위성은 1957년 10월 4일에 소련이 발사한 스프트닉 1호였다.

Check More!

다음 밑줄 친 부분에 알맞은 어휘를 고르시오. 아래의 영영 풀이를 참조하시오.

We easily **(A)** omit / emit the important fact that animals use infrasound to communicate. Over the last few **(B)** decays / decades, biologists have found that whales, elephants, and some other animals also use infrasound. This **(C)** extremely / extensively low-pitched sound has been proved to be a means of communication. This infrasound has a special **(D)** merit / demerit: It can travel a greater distance than higher-pitched noise. Such long-distance communication is a must for animals such as giraffes or elephants that roam over wide areas.

(A) to forget; to exclude:

(B) ten years:

(C) tremendously; particularly:

(D) advantage; virtue:

Chapter 12
Nature and Space

Unit 38. I attended the Arbor Day ceremony.

hold a special **ceremony**

take care of environment

Episode

Dear Diary,

Sometimes we tend to **take** nature **for granted**, not realizing how valuable it is. • We often misuse nature, **calculating** only its economic value. • Our school held a special ceremony on **Arbor Day**. • All the students were wearing masks because of the **yellow dust**. • Our school principal **inaugurated** the event by planting a tree. • After the tree planting, he talked about the effects **pollutants** from yellow dust have on us. • He explained why yellow dust had increased in our **peninsula**. • He asked us what caused the **erosion** of soil. • He also asked us what caused **landslides** and **floods**. • We answered unanimously, "**deforestation**." • He emphasized again that we should be **vigilant** in taking care of our environment. • He also added, "If we don't preserve nature, it will **counterattack** humans." • After the ceremony, our class went to a **theme park**. • It was a popular **eco-friendly** park. • There were many **species** of plants and animals. • Animals, such as rabbits, were living in **colonies**. • Our teacher said that this area used to be a **landfill**. • Where did the garbage go? • It seemed **unaccountable**. • How on earth did plants grow in the **contaminated** soil? • The soil must surely have been **toxic**. • Actually, huge efforts had been made to successfully **neutralize** the toxins in the soil. • Thanks to the neutralization efforts, the **barren** land had become a park. • The **landscape** had completely changed. • Some **endangered species** are now able to live there. • That means their **habitats** have recovered. • In this place, they will not become **extinct**. • It made me very happy to see the theme park's **conservation** efforts.

다이어리에게,

가끔 우리는 자연이 존재하는 것을 당연하게 생각하고 그것이 얼마나 중요한지 깨닫지 못해. 우리는 종종 자연을 오용하며 자연을 경제적 가치로만 계산해. 우리 학교는 식목일에 특별 행사를 열었어. 모든 학생들은 황사 때문에 마스크를 쓰고 있었어. 우리 학교 교장 선생님은 나무를 심으면서 그 행사를 개최하셨어. 나무를 심고 나서, 교장 선생님은 황사의 오염물질이 우리에게 주는 영향에 대해 말씀하셨어. 그는 우리 한반도에서 황사가 왜 증가했는지 설명하셨어. 그는 우리에게 무엇이 토양의 침식을 일으키는지 물으셨어. 그는 또한 산사태와 홍수의 원인을 묻기도 하셨어. 우리는 만장일치로 "삼림 벌채"라고 대답했어. 그는 우리가 환경을 돌보는 데 주의해야 한다고 다시 강조했어. 또한 "우리가 자연을 보존하지 않으면, 그것이 인간을 역습할 것입니다"라고 덧붙이셨어. 행사를 마치고 나서, 우리 반은 테마파크로 갔어. 그곳은 인기 있는 친환경 공원이었어. 거기에는 많은 종류의 식물들과 동물들이 있었어. 토끼와 같은 동물들은 집단으로 서식하고 있었어. 우리 선생님은 이 지역이 쓰레기 매립지였다고 말씀하셨어. 쓰레기는 어디로 갔지? 그것은 설명이 안될 것 같았어. 식물들은 도대체 어떻게 오염된 토양에서 자랐을까? 토양은 틀림없이 독성이 있을 거야. 사실, 엄청난 노력 덕분에 토양의 독성이 성공적으로 중화되었어. 중화시키려는 노력 덕분에 척박한 땅이 공원이 되었어. 경관은 완전히 바뀌었어. 몇몇 멸종 위기의 동식물들은 지금은 그곳에서 살 수 있어. 그것은 그들의 서식지가 복구되었다는 것을 의미해. 그곳에서 그들은 멸종되지 않을 거야. 테마파크의 환경 보호 노력을 보는 것이 매우 즐거웠어.

take for granted
[téik fɔːr grǽntid]

당연한 일로 생각하다

to accept something as normal without thinking about it

Sometimes we tend to take nature for granted, not realizing how valuable it is.

가끔 우리는 자연이 존재하는 것을 당연하게 생각하고 그것이 얼마나 중요한지 깨닫지 못해.

calculate
[kǽlkjəlèit]

v. 계산하다, 평가하다

to decide how much money something is worth

• calculation n. 계산

We often misuse nature, calculating only its economic value.

우리는 종종 자연을 오용하며 자연을 경제적 가치로만 계산해.

Arbor Day
[áːrbər dèi]

식목일

a special day when many people publicly plant trees

Our school held a special ceremony on Arbor Day.

우리 학교는 식목일에 특별 행사를 열었어.

yellow dust
[jélou dʌ́st]

황사

yellow colored dirt that the wind blows to Korea from China

All the students were wearing masks because of the yellow dust.

모든 학생들은 황사 때문에 마스크를 쓰고 있었어.

inaugurate
[inɔ́ːgjərèit]

v. ~식을 행하다

to start an event with a special ceremony

• inauguration n. 개회 • inaugural a. 개회의

Our school principal inaugurated the event by planting a tree.

우리 학교 교장 선생님은 나무를 심으면서 그 행사를 개회하셨어.

pollutant
[pəlúːtənt]

n. 오염물질

poisonous or harmful chemical which can make one sick

• pollute v. 오염시키다 • pollution n. 오염

After the tree planting, he talked about the effects pollutants from yellow dust have on us.

나무를 심고 나서, 그는 황사의 오염물질이 우리에게 주는 영향에 대해 말씀하셨어.

peninsula
[pənínʃələ]

n. 반도

a long narrow piece of land joined to a main land, surrounded with water

He explained why yellow dust had increased in our peninsula.

그는 우리 한반도에서 황사가 왜 증가했는지 설명하셨어.

erosion
[iróuʒən]
n. 침식

wearing away of soil through wind and rain
- erode v. 침식하다

He asked us what caused the erosion of soil.
그는 우리에게 무엇이 토양의 침식을 일으키는지 물으셨어.

landslide
[lǽndslàid]
n. 산사태

a large amount of soil and rock that falls down the side of a mountain

He also asked us what caused landslides and floods.
그는 또한 산사태와 홍수의 원인을 묻기도 하셨어.

flood
[flʌd]
n. 홍수
v. 범람하다

a large amount of water that covers an area which is usually dry

He also asked us what caused landslides and floods.
그는 또한 산사태와 홍수의 원인을 묻기도 하셨어.

deforestation
[diːfɔ̀ːristéiʃən]
n. 삼림 벌채

removal of all the trees from a piece of land, logging
- deforest v. 삼림을 벌채하다

We answered unanimously, "deforestation."
우리는 만장일치로 "삼림 벌채"라고 대답했어.

vigilant
[vídʒələnt]
a. 주의하는,
   방심하지 않는

careful, watchful
- vigilance n. 조심

He emphasized again that we should be vigilant in taking care of our environment.
그는 우리가 환경을 돌보는 데 주의해야 한다고 다시 강조했어.

counterattack
[kàuntərətǽk]
v. 역습하다
n. 역습, 반격

to attack someone who has attacked you

He also added, "If we don't preserve nature, it will counterattack humans."
또한 "우리가 자연을 보존하지 않으면, 그것이 인간을 역습할 것입니다"라고 덧붙이셨어.

theme park
[θíːm pàːrk]
테마 파크

a large outdoor area where all the activities are usually based on a particular theme

After the ceremony, our class went to a theme park.
행사를 마치고 나서, 우리 반은 테마파크로 갔어.

eco-friendly
[èkoufréndli]

a. 친환경의

not damaging the environment

It was a popular eco-friendly park.

그곳은 인기 있는 친환경 공원이었어.

species
[spíːʃi(ː)z]

n. 종, 종류

a type of plant or animal of the same family or category

There were many species of plants and animals.

거기에는 많은 종류의 식물들과 동물들이 있었어.

colony
[káləni]

n. 집단, 군체

a group of people or animals that live together

Animals, such as rabbits, were living in colonies.

토끼와 같은 동물들은 집단으로 서식하고 있었어.

landfill
[lǽndfil]

n. 쓰레기 매립지

a place where garbage is dumped then disposed of

Our teacher said that this area used to be a landfill.

우리 선생님은 이 지역이 쓰레기 매립지였다고 말씀하셨어.

unaccountable
[ʌ̀nəkáuntəbəl]

a. 설명할 수 없는

difficult to believe or explain

• account v. 설명하다 n. 설명 • accountable a. 설명할 수 있는

Where did the garbage go? It seemed unaccountable.

쓰레기는 어디로 갔지? 그것은 설명이 안될 것 같았어.

contaminated
[kəntǽmənèit]

a. 오염된

polluted, poisonous

• contaminate v. 오염시키다 • contamination n. 오염

How on earth did plants grow in the contaminated soil?

식물들은 도대체 어떻게 오염된 토양에서 자랐을까?

toxic
[táksik]

a. 유독한, 독(성)의

very harmful, poisonous

• toxin n. 독소

The soil must surely have been toxic.

토양은 틀림없이 독성이 있을 거야.

neutralize

[njúːtrəlàiz]

v. 중화하다

to reduce acidic levels or effects of something

•neutralization n. 중화   •neutral a. 중성의

Actually, huge efforts had been made to successfully neutralize the toxins in the soil.

사실, 엄청난 노력 덕분에 토양의 독성이 성공적으로 중화되었어.

barren

[bǽrən]

a. 불모의

unprofitable, fruitless, opposite of fertile

Thanks to the neutralization efforts, the barren land had become a park.

중화시키려는 노력 덕분에 척박한 땅이 공원이 되었어.

landscape

[lǽndskèip]

n. 경관

all the features that are seen in an area of land

The landscape had completely changed.

경관은 완전히 바뀌었어.

endangered species

[endéindʒərd spíːʃi(ː)z]

멸종 위기에 있는 동식물

a type of plant or animal that has almost died out

•endanger v. 위험에 빠뜨리다   •endangered a. 멸종될 위기에 있는

Some endangered species are now able to live there.

몇몇 멸종 위기의 동식물들은 지금은 그곳에서 살 수 있어.

habitat

[hǽbitæt]

n. 서식지

the natural environment where a certain animal or plant lives

That means their habitats have recovered.

그것은 그들의 서식지가 복구되었다는 것을 의미해.

extinct

[ikstíŋkt]

a. 멸종된

dead and gone

•extinction n. 멸종

In this place, they will not become extinct.

그곳에서 그들은 멸종되지 않을 거야.

conservation

[kànsəːrvéiʃən]

n. 보호, 보존

saving and protecting the environment

•conserve v. 보호하다

It made me very happy to see the theme park's conservation efforts.

테마파크의 환경 보호 노력을 보는 것이 매우 즐거웠어.

Check Again!

A Translate each word into Korean.

1. barren ....
2. inaugurate ....
3. pollutant ....
4. unaccountable ....
5. contaminated ....
6. peninsula ....
7. erosion ....
8. toxic ....
9. conservation ....
10. deforestation ....

B Translate each word into English.

1. 친환경의 ....
2. 종 ....
3. 계산하다 ....
4. 경관 ....
5. 산사태 ....
6. 역습하다 ....
7. 집단 ....
8. 중화하다 ....
9. 쓰레기 매립지 ....
10. 서식지 ....

C Fill in the blank with the appropriate word. Refer to the Korean.

1. We often tend to take our parents for g_____ .
   우리는 종종 부모님을 당연하게 생각하는 경향이 있다.

2. Why did dinosaurs become e_____ ?
   공룡들은 왜 멸종되었죠?

3. Our citizens should be v_____ in protecting their security.
   우리 시민들은 자신의 안전을 지키는 데 주의해야 한다.

4. The Giant Panda is an e_____ species and highly threatened.
   자이언트 팬더는 멸종위기에 처한 종으로 매우 위협받고 있다.

5. The yellow d_____ that causes annual health concerns has returned early this year.
   매년 건강 우려를 일으키는 황사가 올해는 일찍 찾아왔다.

Check More!

(A), (B), (C) 각 밑줄 친 부분에 알맞은 어휘를 짝지은 것으로 가장 적절한 것을 고르시오.

There is healing power in flowers and in trees, fresh air, and sweet-smelling soil. Just walking through a garden or, for that matter, seeing one out your window, can lower blood pressure, reduce stress, and **(A)** ease / easy pain. Get out there and start digging, and the benefits multiply. While it may be basic and even old-fashioned, using gardening as a health care tool is blossoming. Some people even make an indoor **(B)** minimum / miniature garden in their apartment. New or remodeled hospitals and nursing homes increasingly come equipped with healing gardens where patients and staff can get away from **(C)** barren / barrel, indoor surroundings. Many also offer patients a chance to get their hands dirty and their minds engaged in caring for plants.

	(A)	(B)	(C)
①	easy	minimum	barrel
②	ease	miniature	barren
③	easy	minimum	barren
④	ease	minimum	barrel
⑤	ease	multiple	barren

Chapter 12
Nature and Space

Unit 39. We can make the earth a better place.

emerge as an **alternative**

watch a program **featuring** a goat

have a **green thumb**

Episode

Dear Diary,

Are economic development and nature **incompatible**? • News reports say that we have to **reduce** the amount of CO₂ emissions. • Many countries admit that nature **preservation** is preferable to economic development. • Large sedan cars **powered** by gasoline used to be popular. • Now small-sized **hybrid cars** are emerging as an alternative to them. • Companies will have to look for **bio-fuels** instead of **fossil fuels**. • They may feel **oppressed**. • But people are learning the lesson of **moderation**.

Recently, Seri and I talked about the food **crises** in some countries. • Seri used to be a supporter of **genetically modified food**, believing it could be an answer. • But frequent **exposure** to television environment channels changed her view. • One time she watched a program featuring goats at a cotton **plantation**. • The goats were fed genetically modified **cotton**. • After **prolonged** consumption of cotton, some goats were born with **deformed** legs. • After watching the program, she now **firmly** believes that genetically modified food is harmful. • Since she is **health-conscious**, she tries not to eat food from genetically modified products.

Seri has a **miniature** garden of cherry tomatoes. • She doesn't **have a green thumb**. • What is her **motive** for making her own garden? • She was just trying to find a way to use our family's **leftover** food. • She decided not to **discard** leftover food. • Instead, she decided to grow a garden and use it as **fertilizer**. • She learned that **decomposed** food makes the soil richer. • Her garden is a miniature **eco-system**. • As an environmentalist, she often says to me, "No more **disposables**." • Thanks to her, I try to **refrain** from using paper cups and plastic bags.

다이어리에게,

경제 발전과 자연은 양립할 수 없는 것일까? 뉴스 보도에 따르면 우리는 이산화탄소 배출량을 줄여야 해. 많은 나라들은 자연 보호가 경제 발전보다 바람직하다고 인정해. 휘발유를 연료로 하는 대형 세단은 인기가 있었어. 요즘은 소형 하이브리드 자동차가 세단의 대안으로 등장하고 있어. 회사들은 화석 연료 대신 바이오 연료를 찾아야 할 거야. 그들은 압박감을 느낄지도 몰라. 그러나 사람들은 절제라는 교훈을 배우고 있어.

최근에 세리와 나는 몇몇 나라의 식량 위기에 대해 이야기했어. 세리는 유전자 조작 식품을 지지했었고, 그것이 답이 될 수 있다고 믿었어. 그러나 TV 환경 채널에 자주 노출되자 그녀의 생각이 변했어. 그녀는 면 재배지에 있는 염소를 특집으로 한 프로그램을 본 적이 있어. 염소는 유전적으로 조작된 목화를 먹었어. 목화를 장기간 섭취한 후, 어떤 염소는 기형적인 다리를 가지고 태어났어. 그 프로그램을 본 후, 지금 그녀는 유전자 조작 식품이 유해하다고 굳게 믿고 있어. 그녀는 건강에 신경쓰기 때문에 유전자 조작 제품은 먹지 않으려고 해.

세리는 소형 체리 토마토 밭을 가지고 있어. 그녀는 식물을 잘 키우지 못해. 세리는 어떤 동기로 자신의 밭을 만들었을까? 그녀는 가족들이 먹다 남긴 음식을 사용하는 방법을 찾으려고 노력했어. 그녀는 남은 음식을 버리지 않기로 결심했어. 대신 그녀는 밭을 만들어서 그것을 비료로 사용하기로 했어. 세리는 분해된 음식이 토양을 더 비옥하게 만든다는 것을 배웠어. 그녀의 밭은 작은 생태계야. 환경주의자로서, 그녀는 종종 나에게 "일회용 물품은 더 이상 사용하지 마"라고 말해. 그녀 덕분에 나는 종이컵과 비닐백을 사용하지 않으려고 해.

incompatible

[ìnkəmpǽtəbl]

a. 양립할 수 없는,
   함께할 수 없는

disagreeing, very different

• incompatibility n. 양립할 수 없음, 상반

Are economic development and nature incompatible?
경제 발전과 자연은 양립할 수 없는 것일까?

reduce

[ridʒúːs]

v. 줄이다

to make something smaller in size or amount

• reduction n. 경감

News reports say that we have to reduce the amount
of CO_2 emissions.
뉴스 보도에 따르면 우리는 이산화탄소 배출량을 줄여야 해.

preservation

[prèzərvéiʃən]

n. 보호

protection of something from damage

• preserve v. 보호하다

Many countries admit that nature preservation is
preferable to economic development.
많은 나라들은 자연 보호가 경제 발전보다 바람직하다고 인정해.

power

[páuər]

v. 동력을 공급하다

to fuel or provide energy

Large sedan cars powered by gasoline used to be
popular.
휘발유를 연료로 하는 대형 세단은 인기가 있었어.

hybrid car

[hàibrid káːr]

하이브리드 자동차

a car that can use both gasoline and another type of fuel

Now small-sized hybrid cars are emerging as an
alternative to them.
요즘은 소형 하이브리드 자동차가 그 대안으로 등장하고 있어.

emerge

[imə́ːrdʒ]

v. 나타나다

to come out, to appear

• emergence n. 출현, 발생   • emergency n. 비상사태

Now small-sized hybrid cars are emerging as an
alternative to them.
요즘은 소형 하이브리드 자동차가 그 대안으로 등장하고 있어.

bio-fuel

[bàioufjùːəl]

n. 바이오 연료

the fuel made from newly harvested plants instead of gasoline

Companies will have to look for bio-fuels instead of
fossil fuels.
회사들은 화석 연료 대신 바이오 연료를 찾아야 할 거야.

fossil fuel
[fásl fjùːəl]

화석 연료

the fuel formed from the decayed remains of plants or animals such as oil and coal

Companies will have to look for bio-fuels instead of fossil fuels.

회사들은 화석 연료 대신 바이오 연료를 찾아야 할 거야.

oppress
[əprés]

v. 압박하다

to limit people from doing certain things

• oppression n. 압박   • oppressive a. 압박하는

They may feel oppressed.

그들은 압박감을 느낄지도 몰라.

moderation
[màdəréiʃən]

n. 절제, 완화

control of one's behavior to prevent excessiveness

• moderate a. 알맞은   • moderately ad. 온건하게

But people are learning the lesson of moderation.

그러나 사람들은 절제라는 교훈을 배우고 있어.

crisis
[kráisis]

n. 위기

a situation that will cause a lot of harm to people

• crises plural. crisis의 복수형

Recently, Seri and I talked about the food crises in some countries.

최근에 세리와 나는 몇몇 나라의 식량 위기에 대해 이야기했어.

genetically modified food
[dʒənétikəli mádəfaid fúːd]

유전자 조작 식품

food made by injecting foreign genes into their genetic codes

Seri used to be a supporter of genetically modified food, believing it could be an answer.

세리는 유전자 조작 식품을 지지했었고, 그것이 답이 될 수 있다고 믿었어.

exposure
[ikspóuʒər]

n. 노출, 드러냄

being affected by something, putting in view

• expose v. 노출시키다, 노출하다

But frequent exposure to television environment channels changed her view.

그러나 TV 환경 채널에 자주 노출되자 그녀의 생각이 변했어.

plantation
[plæntéiʃən]

n. 재배지

a large piece of farm used to grow plants

One time she watched a program featuring goats at a cotton plantation.

그녀는 면 재배지에 있는 염소를 특집으로 한 프로그램을 본 적이 있어.

cotton [kátn] n. 목화	a plant which produces fibers used to make cotton cloth **The goats were fed genetically modified cotton.** 염소는 유전적으로 조작된 목화를 먹었어.
prolonged [prəlɔ́:ŋd] a. 장기의, 연장된	continuing for a long time • **prolong** v. 연장하다 **After prolonged consumption of cotton, some goats were born with deformed legs.** 목화를 장기간 섭취한 후, 어떤 염소는 기형적인 다리를 가지고 태어났어.
deformed [difɔ́:rmd] a. 기형의	having an unusual shape • **deform** v. 불구로 만들다, 변형시키다 **After prolonged consumption of cotton, some goats were born with deformed legs.** 목화를 지속적으로 섭취한 후, 어떤 염소는 기형적인 다리를 가지고 태어났어.
firmly [fɔ́:rmli] ad. 굳게, 확고하게	strongly, inflexibly • **firm** a. 굳은, 확고한 **After watching the program, she now firmly believes that genetically modified food is harmful.** 그 프로그램을 본 후, 지금 그녀는 유전자 조작 식품이 유해하다고 굳게 믿고 있어.
health-conscious [hélθkànʃəs] a. 건강에 신경쓰는	taking good care of one's health **Since she is health-conscious, she tries not to eat food from genetically modified products.** 그녀는 건강에 신경쓰기 때문에 유전자 조작 제품은 먹지 않으려고 해.
miniature [míniətʃər] a. 소형의 n. 축소모형	small; a small version of a larger thing • **miniaturize** v. 소형화하다 **Seri has a miniature garden of cherry tomatoes.** 세리는 소형 체리 토마토 밭을 가지고 있어.
have a green thumb [hǽv ə grí:n θʌ́m] 원예를 잘하다	be good at gardening **She doesn't have a green thumb.** 그녀는 식물을 잘 키우지 못해.
motive [móutiv] n. 동기	a purpose for doing something • **motivate** v. 동기를 부여하다 • **motivation** n. 동기 부여 **What is her motive for making her own garden?** 그녀는 어떤 동기로 자신의 밭을 만들었을까?

leftover
[léftòuvər]
n. 나머지

some food that remains after people have finished using it

She was just trying to find a way to use our family's leftover food.

그녀는 가족들이 먹다 남긴 음식을 사용하는 방법을 찾으려고 노력했었어.

discard
[diská:rd]
v. 버리다

to get rid of something

She decided not to discard leftover food.

그녀는 남은 음식을 버리지 않기로 결심했어.

fertilizer
[fə́:rtəlàizər]
n. 비료

the substance that one puts on soil to make new plants grow better
• fertilize v. 비옥하게 하다, 비료를 주다

Instead, she decided to grow a garden and use it as fertilizer.

대신 그녀는 밭을 만들어서 그것을 비료로 사용하기로 했어.

decomposed
[dì:kəmpóuzd]
a. 분해된

chemically changed and rotten
• decompose v. 분해하다 • decomposition n. 분해

She learned that decomposed food makes the soil richer.

그녀는 분해된 음식이 토양을 더 비옥하게 만든다는 것을 배웠어.

eco-system
[ékousìstəm]
n. 생태계

ecological community

Her garden is a miniature eco-system.

그녀의 밭은 작은 생태계야.

disposable
[dispóuzəbəl]
n. 일회용 물품
a. 일회용의

the thing that is designed to be thrown away after use
• dispose v. 처분하다 • disposal n. 처분

As an environmentalist, she often says to me, "No more disposables."

환경주의자로서, 그녀는 종종 나에게 "일회용 물품은 더 이상 사용하지 마"라고 말해.

refrain
[rifréin]
v. 절제하다, 삼가다

to keep from doing
• refrain from ~을 절제하다

Thanks to her, I try to refrain from using paper cups and plastic bags.

그녀 덕분에 나는 종이컵과 비닐백을 사용하지 않으려고 해.

Check Again!

A Translate each word into Korean.

1. incompatible ....
2. reduce ....
3. emerge ....
4. discard ....
5. plantation ....
6. health-conscious ....
7. decomposed ....
8. fertilizer ....
9. prolonged ....
10. moderation ....

B Translate each word into English.

1. 노출 ....
2. 화석 연료 ....
3. 소형의 ....
4. 절제하다 ....
5. 위기 ....
6. 동기 ....
7. 기형의 ....
8. 생태계 ....
9. 일회용 물품 ....
10. 나머지 ....

C Fill in the blank with the appropriate word. Refer to the Korean.

1. You must have a green t   . I can't grow anything.
   당신은 원예에 솜씨가 있나 보군요. 저는 아무것도 키울 줄 몰라요.

2. Frankly, I began to feel o   by the criticism that I received.
   솔직히 나는 내가 받은 비판에 압박을 느끼기 시작했다.

3. I think the minister is wrong to support g   modified food.
   나는 그 장관이 유전자 조작 식품을 지지하는 것은 잘못이라고 생각한다.

4. He tried to r   from violence to achieve what he wants.
   그는 그가 원하는 것을 이루기 위해 폭력을 사용하지 않으려고 노력했다.

5. We have to deal with urban problems and nature p
   simultaneously.
   우리는 도시 문제와 자연 보존을 동시에 다루어야 한다.

Check More!

다음 밑줄 친 부분에 알맞은 어휘를 고르시오. 아래의 영영 풀이를 참조하시오.

You can certainly make bad quality wine from good quality grapes, but I **(A)** firmly / hardly believe that you cannot make good quality wine from bad quality grapes. What happens in the vineyard is crucial. To start with, you need well drained, not necessarily over **(B)** fertile / futile soil in order to make the vine's roots dig deep into it. The vineyard needs plenty of **(C)** exposure / exposition to the sun in cool climate areas. There needs to be enough rain, or in some cases, irrigation. With too little water, the grape skins become too tough and they fail to **(D)** ripen / liven.

(A) immovably, strongly:

(B) productive; fruitful:

(C) unveiling; display:

(D) to grow ripe; to become mature:

Chapter 12
Nature and Space

Unit 40. A super hurricane hit the village.

devastate homes and villages

try to **prevent** the outbreak of a plague

Episode

Sara emailed me.

Dear Bomi,

An El Niño event caused a super hurricane to hit villages along the Southern coast. • Residents were told to **evacuate** the area. • **Nevertheless**, a few people insisted on staying home, **risking** their lives. • **Immense** sea waves and huge **torrents** swept the whole village. • Most of the villagers were left **homeless**. • Their homes and village were **devastated**. • The destructive force was **formidable**. • It could be compared to the power of a **nuclear bomb**. • Victims are facing the problem of **scarcity** of food, clothing and **shelter**. • The media showed us pictures of their **agonized** faces. • The **extent of the** damage continues to expand. • The government **proclaimed** it a disaster area. • After several days, the hurricane's force **dwindled**. • Returning villagers sighed **wearily**. • There was little **trace** of their houses and properties. • **Nationwide** donations were collected. • Food and medicine were distributed by **humanitarian** organizations. • Wide scale **sterilization** efforts were made throughout the whole area. • The authorities are trying to prevent the outbreak of a **plague**. • Residents were recommended to drink only **boiled** water. • Now the government will provide social **welfare** to the villagers. • They will help the villagers to **rebuild** their homes as quickly as possible in order to prevent social **unrest**.

....

사라가 나에게 이메일을 보냈다.

보미에게,
엘니뇨는 거대한 허리케인을 일으켜서 남부 해안을 따라 위치한 마을들을 강타했어. 주민들은 그 지역에서 떠나라는 이야기를 들었어. 그럼에도 불구하고, 몇몇 사람들은 생명을 걸고 집에 남아 있기를 주장했어. 거대한 파도와 엄청난 급류가 마을 전체를 쓸어버렸어. 대부분의 마을 사람들은 집을 잃었어. 그들의 집과 마을은 완전히 파괴되었어. 파괴의 힘은 무시무시했어. 그것은 핵 폭탄의 위력과 비교될 수 있었어. 희생자들은 음식, 옷, 대피소가 부족한 문제에 당면하게 되었어. 방송에서는 우리들에게 그들의 괴로워하는 얼굴을 보여주었어. 피해의 범위는 계속 넓어지고 있어. 정부는 그곳을 재해 지역으로 선포했어. 며칠 후에 허리케인의 힘은 약화되었어. 돌아온 주민들은 지쳐서 한숨을 내쉬었어. 집과 재산의 흔적은 거의 찾아볼 수 없었어. 전국적인 기부 물품들이 모아졌어. 음식과 약품이 인도주의 단체에 의해 배포되었어. 광범위한 소독이 전 지역에 걸쳐 행해졌어. 행정 당국에서는 전염병이 발생하지 않도록 노력하고 있어. 주민들은 끓인 물만 마시도록 권고받았어. 이제 정부는 마을 사람들에게 사회복지 혜택을 줄 거야. 그들은 사회적 불안을 예방하기 위해서 주민들이 집을 가능한 한 빨리 다시 지을 수 있도록 도울 거야.

evacuate

[ivǽkjuèit]

v. 비우다, 대피시키다

to move out of a place to a safer place

• evacuation n. 비우기, 피난 • evacuee n. 피난자

Residents were told to evacuate the area.

주민들은 그 지역에서 떠나라는 이야기를 들었다.

nevertheless

[nèvərðəlés]

ad. 그럼에도 불구하고

regardless, still

Nevertheless, a few people insisted on staying home, risking their lives.

그럼에도 불구하고, 몇몇 사람들은 생명을 걸고 집에 남아 있기를 주장했어.

risk

[rísk]

v. 위태롭게 하다

n. 위험

to do something that might be dangerous

• risky a. 위험한, 아슬아슬한

Nevertheless, a few people insisted on staying home, risking their lives.

그럼에도 불구하고, 몇몇 사람들은 생명을 걸고 집에 남아 있기를 주장했어.

immense

[iméns]

a. 거대한

extremely large

• immensity n. 거대 • immensely ad. 거대하게

Immense sea waves and huge torrents swept the whole village.

거대한 파도와 엄청난 급류가 마을 전체를 쓸어버렸어.

torrent

[tɔ́:rənt]

n. 급류

a large amount of water flowing violently

• torrential a. 급류의

Immense sea waves and huge torrents swept the whole village.

거대한 파도와 엄청난 급류가 마을 전체를 쓸어버렸어.

homeless

[hóumlis]

a. 집이 없는

not having a place to live

Most of the villagers were left homeless.

대부분의 마을 사람들은 집을 잃었어.

devastate
[dévəstèit]
v. 철저하게 파괴하다, 황폐화시키다

to destroy an area totally
- devastation n. 초토화, 황폐화 • devastating a. 파괴적인

Their homes and village were devastated.
그들의 집과 마을은 완전히 파괴되었어.

formidable
[fɔ́:rmidəbəl]
a. 무시무시한

powerful, strong
- formidably ad. 무시무시하게

The destructive force was formidable.
파괴의 힘은 무시무시했어.

nuclear bomb
[njú:kliər bám]
핵폭탄

a type of weapon that will explode and destroy things

It could be compared to the power of a nuclear bomb.
그것은 핵폭탄의 위력과 비교될 수 있었어.

scarcity
[skέərsiti]
n. 부족함

shortness of supply
- scarce a. 드문 • scarcely ad. 드물게

Victims are facing the problem of scarcity of food, clothing and shelter.
희생자들은 음식, 옷, 대피소가 부족한 문제에 당면하게 되었어.

shelter
[ʃéltər]
n. 대피소, 피난처

a place for homeless people; a place that is made to protect people from bad weather or danger

Victims are facing the problem of scarcity of food, clothing and shelter.
희생자들은 음식, 옷, 대피소가 부족한 문제에 당면하게 되었어.

agonized
[ǽgənàizd]
a. 괴로워하는

extremely upset or hurt
- agonize v. 몹시 괴롭히다 • agony n. 고통

The media showed us pictures of their agonized faces.
방송에서는 우리들에게 그들의 괴로워하는 얼굴을 보여주었어.

extent
[ikstént]
n. 범위

the size or scale of something
- extensive a. 넓은

The extent of the damage continues to expand.
피해의 범위는 계속 넓어지고 있어.

proclaim
[proukléim]

v. 선언하다

to make something known to public formally
- proclamation n. 선언

The government proclaimed it a disaster area.
정부는 그곳을 재해 지역으로 선포했어.

dwindle
[dwíndl]

v. 감소하다

to become less, to reduce to low levels
- dwindling a. 감소하는

After several days, the hurricane's force dwindled.
며칠 후에 허리케인의 힘은 약화되었어.

wearily
[wíərəli]

ad. 피곤하게

in a weary manner
- weary v. 지치게 하다 a. 피곤한 - weariness n. 피곤함

Returning villagers sighed wearily.
돌아온 주민들은 지쳐서 한숨을 내쉬었어.

trace
[tréis]

n. 흔적

a sign that shows something existed there

There was little trace of their houses and properties.
집과 재산의 흔적은 거의 찾아볼 수 없었어.

nationwide
[néiʃənwàid]

a. 전국적인

involving the whole nation

Nationwide donations were collected.
전국적인 기부 물품들이 모아졌어.

humanitarian
[hju:mænətέəriən]

a. 인도주의적인
n. 인도주의자

helping and taking care of other people
- humanitarianism n. 인도주의

Food and medicine were distributed by humanitarian organizations.
음식과 약품이 인도주의 단체에 의해 배포되었어.

sterilize
[stérəlàiz]

v. 소독하다

to clean something so that there is no dirt and germs
- sterilization n. 소독   • sterile a. 살균한

Wide scale sterilization efforts were made throughout the whole area.

광범위한 소독이 전 지역에 걸쳐 행해졌어.

plague
[pléig]

n. 전염병

a disease that can quickly spread and kill many people

The authorities are trying to prevent the outbreak of a plague.

행정 당국에서는 전염병이 발생하지 않도록 노력하고 있어.

boiled
[bɔ́ild]

a. 끓인

heated to the point where liquid turns to gas
- boil v. 끓이다

Residents were recommended to drink only boiled water.

주민들은 끓인 물만 마시도록 권고받았어.

welfare
[wélfɛ̀ər]

n. 복지

well-being, the health and prosperity

Now the government will provide social welfare to the villagers.

이제 정부는 마을 사람들에게 사회복지 혜택을 줄 거야.

rebuild
[ri:bíld]

v. 재건하다, 다시 짓다

to build something again

They will help the villagers to rebuild their homes as quickly as possible in order to prevent social unrest.

그들은 사회적 불안을 예방하기 위해서 주민들이 집을 가능한 한 빨리 다시 지을 수 있도록 도울 거야.

unrest
[ʌ̀nrést]

n. 불안, 근심

the uneasy state, disturbance

They will help the villagers to rebuild their homes as quickly as possible in order to prevent social unrest.

그들은 사회적 불안을 예방하기 위해서 주민들이 집을 가능한 한 빨리 다시 지을 수 있도록 도울 거야.

Check Again!

A Translate each word into Korean.

1. evacuate ....   2. nevertheless ....

3. sterilize ....   4. dwindle ....

5. wearily ....   6. agonized ....

7. formidable ....   8. devastate ....

9. rebuild ....   10. torrent ....

B Translate each word into English.

1. 끓인 ....   2. 선언하다 ....

3. 부족 ....   4. 거대한 ....

5. 범위 ....   6. 복지 ....

7. 위태롭게 하다 ....   8. 흔적 ....

9. 전국적인 ....   10. 인도주의적인 ....

C Fill in the blank with the appropriate word. Refer to the Korean.

1. The country may be capable of making a n   bomb within 16 days.

   그 나라는 16일 이내에 핵폭탄을 만들 수 있을지도 모른다.

2. Let me introduce the women who r   their lives to defend human rights.

   인권을 수호하기 위해 목숨을 건 여성들을 소개해 드립니다.

3. The outbreak of p   affected the whole country.

   전염병의 발생이 전국에 영향을 주었다.

4. Fifty-five people were left h   after fire destroyed 12 houses in L.A. today.

   오늘 LA에서 12가옥이 화재로 전소된 후 55명이 집을 잃었다.

5. Social u   and protectionism are the two major risks of the world economic crisis.

   사회 불안과 보호주의가 세계 경제 위기의 가장 주된 위험 요소들이다.

Check More!

수능 기출 응용

(A), (B), (C) 각 밑줄 친 부분에 알맞은 어휘를 짝지은 것으로 가장 적절한 것을 고르시오.

What makes people behave in a **(A)** humiliating / humanitarian way? The ability to sympathize with others reflects the multiple nature of the human being. This may be one of the things that enable us to seek through literature an **(B)** enlightenment / enlargement of our experience. Although we may see some characters as outside ourselves – that is, we may not identify with them completely – we are **(C)** nevertheless / endlessly able to enter into their behavior and their emotions. Thus, the youth may identify with the aged, one gender with the other, and a reader of a particular limited social background with members of a different class or a different period.

	(A)	(B)	(C)
①	humanitarian	enlargement	nevertheless
②	humiliating	enlargement	endlessly
③	humanitarian	enlightenment	nevertheless
④	humanitarian	enlargement	endlessly
⑤	humiliating	enlightenment	endlessly

+ 접두사 astro- / counter-와 어근 -scrib / script-

astro-는 별이나 우주와 관련된 뜻의 단어를 만드는 접두사이다. counter-는
'against' 라는 뜻의 단어로, '무언가에 반대되다' 라는 뜻의 단어를 만든다.
-scrib/script-는 'to write' 라는 뜻의 어근으로, 글과 관련된 단어를 만든다.

astro-

logia ~에 관한
astro + logy = astrology 점성학, 점성술
ex) She has deep faith in astrology.
그녀는 점성술을 굳게 믿는다.

- navigate 항해   astronavigation 우주 비행
- -nomy 학문   astronomy 천문학
- physics 물리학   astrophysics 천체 물리학
- archaeology 고고학   astroarchaeology 천체 고고학
- compass 나침반   astrocompass 천측 나침반
- space 공간   astrospace 우주 공간
- photography 사진술   astrophotography 천체 사진술

counter-

clockwise 시계방향
counter + clockwise = counterclockwise 반 시계방향
ex) The special clock in the clock tower ran
counterclockwise.
시계탑에 있는 특이한 시계는 반 시계방향으로 움직였다.

- attack 공격하다   counterattack 반격하다
- act 행동하다   counteract 거스르다, 방해하다
- part 부분   counterpart 한 짝의 한쪽, 상대방
- balance 균형을 잡다   counterbalance 대등하게 하다
- productive 생산적인   counterproductive 비생산적인, 역효과의
- sign 서명하다   countersign 이어서 서명하다
- change 바꾸다   counterchange 교체하다

-scrib/script-

scribere 쓰다

script 필적, 대본

ex) That playwright changed parts of the novel in his movie script.

그 극작가는 그의 영화 대본에서 소설의 일부를 바꿨다.

- **scribe** 필기자, 서기
- **prescribe** 처방하다
- **inscribe** 비석 등에 새기다
- **scripture** 경전, 성전
- **postscript** 추신
- **transcript** 사본, 의사록
- **manuscript** 원고, 손으로 쓴 것

In Space 우주에서

+ space exploration 우주 탐사
+ space probe 우주 탐사기
+ space flight 우주 비행
+ space lab 우주 실험실
+ space shuttle 우주 왕복선
+ space station 우주 정거장
+ lunar module 달 착륙선

VOCA EDGE_RED

INDEX

VOCA EDGE_RED
Answer Key

Chapter 1_ Unit 1

Check Again!

A

1. 청소년, 청소년의
2. 순종적인
3. 반항적인
4. 일반적인
5. 얼다, 얼리다
6. 방해하다
7. 익명의
8. 무자비한, 심한
9. 사생활
10. 정의를 내리다

B

1. typical
2. energetic
3. prefer
4. chat
5. effective
6. reluctant
7. feast
8. squeeze
9. imitate
10. decorate

C

1. eager
2. stressed
3. vogue
4. concentrate
5. reluctant

Check More!

정답

(A) maturity
(B) adolescent
(C) understand
(D) institutions

해석: 나이로 우리 사회를 설명하고자 한다면, 네 가지 나이 집단을 생각해낼 수가 있을 것이다. 즉 유년기, 청소년기, 성인기, 노년기이다. 우리는 서로 다른 나이 집단의 사람들이 다르게 행동하는 것을 당연시 여긴다. 예를 들어, 30대 남자는 자기 나이에 맞는 행동을 해야지 청소년이나 노인처럼 행동해서는 안 된다고 생각한다. 마찬가지로, 인생을 살아나가면서 같은 나이의 사람들은 어떤 면에서 다른 나이대의 사람들보다 서로를 잘 이해할 것이라고 기대한다. 이것은 우리가 사회생활 가운데에서 기대되고 있는 행동 방식이지만, 엄격한 원칙에 의해 통제되는 공식적 기관들에도 적용할 수 있는 것은 아니다.

Chapter 1_ Unit 2

Check Again!

A

1. 좌절감을 느낀, 실망한
2. 연속하는
3. 억수같이 퍼붓다
4. 세게 닫다
5. 강요하다
6. 못되게 굴다
7. 후회하다
8. 진동하다
9. 강요하다
10. 알리다

B

1. transportation
2. temporarily
3. cancel
4. contact
5. indispensable
6. apologize
7. advice
8. refuse
9. furious
10. isolated

C

1. supposed
2. argument
3. attached
4. report
5. persisted

Check More!

정답: ⑤

해석: 다른 사람에게 상처를 준 적이 있는가? 그렇다면 당신이 잘못한 그 사람에게 연락을 해서 진심으로 용서를 구하라. 당신은 그 상처에 대해 사과해야 한다. 스스로에게 지금 당장 그것을 시행하겠다고 약속하라. 여러 해가 지난 후에도 사람을 찾는 것은 아직 가능하다. 그 사람이 죽었거나 정말로 찾을 수 없다면, 비슷한 행위로 고통을 받고 있는 다른 사람들을 어떤 식으로든 돕겠다고 약속할 수 있다. 당신의 결심이 확고하고, 분명하고 진지하다면, 당신은 그 감정과 기억을 제쳐두고 마음의 평화를 발견할 수 있을 것이다.

Chapter 1_ Unit 3

Check Again!

A

1. 친구
2. 상냥한
3. 염색하다
4. 운동 신경이 있는
5. 임신한
6. 귀여운
7. 똑같은, 동일한
8. 공감하다, 동정하다
9. 견딜 수 없는
10. 애도

B

1. heaven
2. cancer
3. mourn
4. immortal
5. funeral
6. elegy
7. balance
8. comfort
9. despair
10. grave

C

1. heartbreaking
2. blessing
3. pure-bred
4. unanimously
5. intensive

Check More!

정답

(A) depict

(B) identical

(C) unambiguously

(D) compensates

해석: 사물을 구별하는 것은 분리된 상태에서는 거의 힘들다. 얼굴 인식도 똑같은 방식으로 일어나는 것처럼 보인다. 그림 A에서 제시된 얼굴의 일부를 보여줄 때, 굴곡이나 선은 모두 얼굴의 생김새를 그려내기에 충분하다. 하지만 그림 B처럼 얼굴 생김새를 전체와 분리해 놓을 때는 결과가 다를 수 있다. 그림 B에서의 얼굴 생김새는 기본적으로 그림 A의 것과 동일하다. 그러나 전체와 분리되어 있어서 알아보기가 어렵다. 그림 C에서처럼, 분리된 상태로 제시될 경우 얼굴 생김새를 분명하게 알아보려면 그림 B보다는 더 자세한 묘사가 필요하다. 따라서 전체를 이해하는 것이 생김새를 알아보는 과정에서 상세함이 부족한 것을 보상해준다.

Chapter 2_ Unit 4

Check Again!

A

1. 모순적인
2. 성숙한
3. 생각하다
4. 완고한
5. 거꾸로 하다, 뒤집다
6. 포함하다
7. 관대한
8. 오해하다
9. 우위, 주도권
10. 사과하다

B

1. absorbed
2. atmosphere
3. situation
4. attitude
5. professional
6. desperately
7. divorce
8. impress
9. counselor
10. compromise

C

1. concerned
2. complimented
3. convinced
4. admit
5. absorbed

Check More!

정답: ⑤

해석: 아이러니하게도, 아주 많은 경험에서 나온 추측조차도 종종 비참할 정도로 빗나간다. 알버트 아인슈타인은 "핵에너지를 획득할 가능성은 전혀 없다"라고 말했다. 미래를 예측하는 일이 왜 이렇게 어려운 것일까? 다음에 무슨 일이 있을지 추측하려고 하지 않는 것이 현명한 것일까? 미래를 예측하지 않는 것은 자동차 앞유리 너머를 보지 않고 자동차를 운전하는 것과 같다. 우리는 미래를 예견해줄 수 있는 사람을 절실히 필요로 한다. 그들은 우리가 무수히 많은 가능성 있는 미래들을 하나 또는 적어도 몇 개로 압축시킬 수 있도록 도와준다. 우리는 현재를 바라보고 현재를 본다. 그들은 미래의 씨앗들을 본다. 그들은 다가올 세계를 돕기 위해 몰래 경계를 넘어가서 귀중한 정보를 가져오는 우리의 정찰대이다.

Chapter 2_ Unit 5

Check Again!

A

1. 간청하다
2. 예방접종을 하다
3. 예방 주사
4. 검사하다
5. 격리시키다, 검역하다
6. 떼어놓다, 분리하다
7. 시차로 인한 피로
8. 올라가다
9. 껴안다
10. 화물

B

1. complicated
2. reunite
3. restricted
4. domestic
5. baggage
6. procedure
7. fasten
8. shrink
9. extremely
10. vain

C

1. altitude
2. threatened
3. pleaded
4. quarantine
5. emigrated

Check More!

정답

(A) original

(B) complicated

(C) extremely

(D) coherent

해석: 그림 복구자들은 기술이 고도로 숙련되어 있다. 그러나 그들은 앞에 놓인 작품을 어떻게 해야 할지 정확히 알려면 원래의 화가가 되어야 할 것이다. 오물 제거와 같은 작업의 기술적인 측면은 복잡하지 않다. 중요한 것은 그림을 미술가의 원래 의도에 맞게 복원하는 것이다. 그렇게 하려면, 그들은 그림에 뭔가를 추가해야 할지 아니면 그대로 둘지를 결정해야 한다. 그들은 어떤 것을 수정해야 할지 말아야 할지를 결정하는 것이 매우 어려운 일임을 인정한다. "우리의 목표는 미술가의 의도를 존중하면서 그러나 동시에 시각적으로 일관된 작품이 되도록 하는 것입니다"라고 뉴욕 현대 미술관의 마이클 더피는 말한다.

Chapter 2_ Unit 6

Check Again!

A

1. 지구본
2. 동봉하다
3. 타원형의
4. 대륙
5. 반구
6. 빙하
7. 적도
8. 남극
9. 열대의
10. 후덥지근한, 습한

B

1. Arctic
2. geography
3. parallel
4. vast
5. inhabit
6. temperate
7. vertical
8. population
9. cultivate
10. horizontal

C

1. equivalent
2. mild
3. consists
4. related
5. longitude

Check More!

정답: ③

해석: 매우 무덥고 후덥지근한 날이었다. 어느 여름밤에 한 남자가 드넓은 숲과 들판이 내려다보이는 낮은 언덕에 서 있었다. 서쪽에 보름달이 낮게 드리워 있어서 남자는 때가 동틀 시간이라는 것을 알았다. 가벼운 안개가 땅에 내려앉아서 아래쪽 풍경을 부분적으로 감추었다. 그러나 그 위로 키 큰 나무들은 맑게 갠 하늘에 대비되어 선명한 덩어리로 보여졌다. 농가 두 세 곳이 안개를 뚫고 보였으나 당연히 그것들 어디에도 등불은 없었다. 사실 먼 곳에서 짖어대는 개 한 마리 외에는 생명의 흔적이나 암시는 어디에도 없었고, 그것은 고독한 광경을 더욱 강조하였다.

Chapter 3_ Unit 7

Check Again!

A

1. 거대한
2. 만성의
3. 사색하다
4. 우주
5. 철학자
6. 현상
7. 생기다, 유래하다
8. 분석하다
9. 재생 가능한
10. 구역, 구분

B

1. organism
2. fossil
3. observe
4. hypothesis
5. theory
6. evolve
7. anthropologist
8. mystery
9. explode
10. expand

C

1. originated
2. relief
3. exhibits
4. remains
5. phenomena

Check More!

정답
(A) aptitude
(B) hypothesis
(C) expanding
(D) range

해석: 나는 우리 아이들이 11살이나 12살에 치는 수학능력 시험의 결과에 기초해 진로를 결정하는 것이 좀 불공평하다고 생각한다. 아마도 당신은 아이들이 6학년 때 잘한다고 여겨진 분야가 고등학교 3학년 말이 되었을 때 그들이 우수한 분야와 같다는 가설을 믿지 않을지도 모른다. 중고등학교는 지평을 넓혀야 할 때이지 제한해야 할 때가 아니다. 학생들이 해야 할 단 한 가지는 다양한 분야의 과목을 중고등학교를 거치면서 공부하는 것이다. 고등학교를 마칠 무렵 그들은 대학교에서 무엇을 공부하고 싶은지 훨씬 더 잘 알 수 있을 것이다. 전문적인 공부를 해야 할 때는 대학교와 대학원에서이지, 그보다 더 일찍은 아니다.

Chapter 3_ Unit 8

Check Again!

A

1. 일류의, 명문의
2. 명성, 평판
3. 칭찬하다
4. 교대하다
5. 유능한
6. 수용하다
7. 교직원
8. 지침
9. 책임
10. ~할 만하다

B

1. supervisor
2. tolerate
3. assess
4. dormitory
5. luxurious
6. play
7. disturbance
8. co-ed
9. disappointed
10. term paper

C

1. term
2. prestigious
3. laundry
4. disturbances
5. assembled

Check More!

정답:
(A) prestigious
(B) handed in
(C) significant
(D) deserve

해석: 우리 간호학교는 우리나라에서 가장 명성 있는 학교 중의 하나이다. 어느 날 간호학 교수님이 우리에게 퀴즈를 내셨다. 나는 문제를 전부 쉽게 풀었다. 마지막 문제인 "학교를 청소하는 여자의 이름은 무엇인가?"를 읽기 전까지는. 나는 그녀가 키가 크고, 짧은 머리의 50대라는 것을 알았지만, 내가 어떻게 그녀의 이름을 안단 말인가? 나는 그 문제를 빈칸으로 남겨두고 시험지를 제출했다. 시험지를 거두면서 교수님은 마지막 문제가 중요하다고 말씀하셨다. 그리고 나서 그녀는 "여러분의 직업상 많은 사람들을 만나게 될 것입니다. 모두가 중요합니다. 미소와 인사를 건네는 것이 여러분이 하는 것 전부일지라도 그들은 여러분의 관심과 보호를 받을 자격이 있습니다"라고 덧붙이셨다. 나는 결코 그 가르침을 잊은 적이 없다. 또한 나는 그녀의 이름이 도로시라는 것을 알게 되었다.

Chapter 3_ Unit 9

Check Again!

A

1. 기사
2. 감정을 자극하다
3. 검열하다
4. 가두다, 제한하다
5. 망치다
6. 시대에 뒤떨어진
7. 기준, 표준
8. 성냄, 분노
9. 불합리한, 어리석은
10. 풍부하게 하다

B

1. deny
2. witness
3. betray
4. objective
5. violate
6. free speech
7. arouse
8. criminal
9. judge
10. objection

C

1. Undoubtedly
2. allowed
3. democracy
4. outdated
5. absurd

Check More!

정답: ②

해석: 만일 어떤 회사가 자신의 목표나 목적을 달성하지 못하고 있다는 것을 깨닫는다고 가정해보자. 이런 경우, 외부 경영자문가를 구하여 회사의 실적을 분석하고 좀 더 효율적으로 만들 수 있는 변혁을 권고하도록 하는 것이 유용할 수 있다. 이 경영자문가는 회사가 당면한 기회와 위기는 물론 회사의 강점과 약점을 좀 더 객관적으로 분석할 수 있다. 그러면 회사는 경영자문가의 조언에 근거하여 전략을 다시 짤 수 있다. 이런 방식으로, 회사는 의도한 결과물을 얻을 수 있을 것이다.

Chapter 4_ Unit 10

Check Again!

A

1. 정상
2. 미신적인
3. 정상
4. 당황한
5. 날카롭게 하다
6. 침략자, 약탈자
7. 나누다, 분배하다
8. 동기부여하다
9. 미개한
10. 미개인, 야만인

B

1. worship
2. orderly
3. tribe
4. limit
5. ultimate
6. precious
7. equality
8. keen
9. instinct
10. accustomed

C

1. survive
2. primitive
3. edible
4. spirits
5. boundary

Check More!

정답: ④

해석: 최근에 한국어에 관심을 가지는 외국인을 다룬 프로그램을 보았다. 지난 몇 년 동안 한국어에 관심을 가진 외국인의 숫자가 상당히 늘어났다. 그들은 한국어가 조직적이고 규칙적인 언어여서 배우기가 쉽다고 말한다. 한국어 프로그램에 참가하는 외국 학생들의 총 숫자는 지난해 말 약 4,700명에서 올해 서울에서만 3만 명 이상으로 늘어났다. 한국어를 하는 사람들은 오랫동안 대부분 한반도에 있는 사람들에게로 국한되어 왔다. 한국의 언어가 언젠가는 국제 사회에서 인기를 얻게 될 것이라는 것을 상상조차 하는 사람들이 드물었던 것도 당연하다.

Chapter 4_ Unit 11

Check Again!

A

1. 장애물
2. 준비하다
3. 과장하다
4. 기부하다
5. 지명하다, 선정하다
6. 독재자
7. 자원봉사하다
8. 고아원
9. 불만스러운
10. 기부자

B

1. loose
2. assist
3. process
4. recommend
5. superior
6. confirm
7. lend
8. confess
9. humorous
10. improvise

C

1. disguised
2. senior
3. superior
4. commands
5. nursing

Check More!

정답
(A) suggested
(B) contracts
(C) anxious
(D) arranged

해석: 피터 톰슨은 나와 긴밀한 업무 관계에 있는 사람인데 당신의 이름을 제게 언급해주면서 당신에게 연락해보라고 강력하게 제안했습니다. 피터가 제게 말한 바로는, 당신은 완구업계에서 아주 왕성한 활동을 하고 있으며 많은 영업관리자를 알고 있다고 합니다. 피터는 당신이 제가 계약하는 것을 도와줄 수 있을지도 모른다고 생각했습니다. 새로운 경쟁으로 인하여, 우리는 가능한 한 빨리 우리 제품을 시장에 내놓기를 간절히 원하고 있습니다. 다음 주 월요일에 제가 전화 걸어서 점심 식사를 하면서 이야기를 나눌 시간 약속을 잡아도 괜찮을까요?

Chapter 4_ Unit 12

Check Again!

A

1. 통역하다
2. 엄숙한
3. 전사
4. 1년에 두 번의
5. 후원하다, 후원
6. 다양성
7. 적수, 상대
8. 경쟁
9. 개회식, 시작
10. 적응하다

B

1. spectator
2. commercial
3. delegation
4. score
5. multinational
6. sophisticated
7. legendary
8. applaud
9. spectator
10. unmatchable

C

1. shaped
2. awe
3. ethnic
4. proceeded
5. oath

Check More!

정답: ③

해석: 미국은 언어 능력에 있어서 미개발 국가로 남아 있다. 이민자들은 자신들의 모국어를 엄청난 속도로 들여오고 있다. 하지만 대다수의 미국인들은 고집스럽게 1개의 언어만을 고수하고 있다. 다른 언어와 다양한 문화에 대한 무지는 미국이 전 세계 나머지 국가들과 거래를 하는 데 약점이 되고 있다. 오늘날 미국의 언어 정책은 주로 1개의 언어만 구사하는 미국인들에게 "외국"어를 가르치려는 노력으로 이 문제를 다룬다. 한편, 미국은 다양화에 대한 잘못된 두려움 때문이거나 이들을 강제로 동화시키려는 성급함 때문에, 소수 민족들에게는 기존의 이중언어 프로그램을 줄임으로써 이 동일한 능력을 없애려고 한다. 이민자들의 영어 무능력에 초점을 맞추기보다, 영어를 배우면서 동시에 그들의 모국어 능력을 유지하도록 권장하는 것이 어떨까?

Chapter 5_ Unit 13

Check Again!

A
1. 단조로운
2. 궤양
3. 명상
4. 정신의
5. 일과
6. 뻣뻣한
7. 동경하다, 감탄하다
8. 가르치다, 계몽시키다
9. 끈기
10. 고문

B
1. maintain
2. emphasize
3. value
4. strengthen
5. benefit
6. option
7. healing
8. emotion
9. recall
10. demonstrate

C
1. registered
2. lively
3. relieving
4. insight
5. purifying

Check More!

정답: ②

해석: 몇몇 한국 예술가들은 손으로 만든 한국의 종이인 한지를 제작하는 과정이 인간의 삶을 반영하고 있다고 말한다. 사실, 사람들의 하루하루의 삶이 이 종이 제작과정에서 보여진다고 말할 수도 있을 것이다. 그 과정은 나무에서 가지들이 잘리면서 시작된다. 그런 다음 가지들은 강하고 나긋나긋한 종이가 되기 위해 복잡한 과정을 거친다. 모든 불순물을 제거하기 위해 증기로 찌고, 삶고, 그리고 여러 번 헹궈진다. 또한 여러 시간 동안 두드려진다. 더 많이 두드려질수록, 실제로 더 강해진다. 이것은 사람들이 매일매일 부닥치는 어려움과 고난을 극복함으로써 더욱 지혜로워지고 강해지는 것과 비슷하다.

Chapter 5_ Unit 14

Check Again!

A
1. 완전히, 글자 그대로
2. 진공청소기로 청소하다
3. 거절하다
4. 계급제
5. 긴장감, 긴장
6. 훈련
7. 미친
8. 인정 없는
9. 사려 깊은
10. 장비

B
1. employer
2. executive
3. monitor
4. junior
5. leave
6. flexible
7. passive
8. justify
9. privilege
10. pessimistic

C
1. obligatory
2. permission
3. rehearsal
4. conflict
5. maternity

Check More!

정답
(A) equipment
(B) insane
(C) characterized
(D) perceive

해석: 빛이 무색이며 따라서 색이 우리 뇌 안에서 일어나야 한다는 것을 뉴튼이 말할 때 그는 어떤 장비를 사용했을까? "파동 그 자체는 색이 없다"라고 그는 썼다. 그 당시 사람들은 그가 제정신이 아니라고 생각했을지도 모르겠다. 그러나 그의 시대 이후, 우리는 빛의 파동이 각기 다른 진동 주파수에 의해 특징지워진다는 것을 알게 되었다. 그것들이 관찰자의 눈으로 들어오면 연쇄적인 신경화학 작용을 유발하고, 그것의 최종 결과물은 우리가 색깔이라고 부르는 내면의 심리적 이미지이다. 여기서 핵심 포인트는 우리가 색으로 인식하는 것이 색으로 이루어져 있지 않다는 것이다. 사과는 빨갛게 보일지 모르지만 그 원자 자체는 빨간색이 아니다.

Chapter 5_ Unit 15

Check Again!

A

1. 유효한
2. 회계, 계산
3. 지출
4. 만기가 되다
5. 협상가
6. 폐기
7. 언급하다
8. 사다, 구입
9. 누설하다, 폭로하다
10. 의기양양해서

B

1. purpose
2. surplus
3. acquire
4. barter
5. document
6. contract
7. brand-new
8. deal
9. convince
10. profitable

C

1. suspicious
2. obsessed
3. grinned
4. dispose
5. profitable

Check More!

정답

(A) obsessed

(B) valid

(C) confirm

해석: 많은 사람들은 우리에게 제공된 모든 정보가 신뢰할 만하다고 믿으면서 인터넷에 집착하는 것 같다. 휴대 전화, 인터넷, 텔레비전의 홍수 속에서, 우리는 우리 조상들이 뉴스가 마을 밖으로 멀리 전달되지 않는 순수한 세상에 살았다고 잘못된 상상을 한다. 매체가 우리 시대를 과거와 분명히 구분시켜 준다고 단정하는 것이 타당하지 않을 수 있다. 왜냐하면 우리는 과거에 정보가 어떻게 공유되어졌는지 비교적 거의 알고 있지 못하기 때문이다. 사실, 올림픽은 페르시아에 대한 아테네의 승리 소식을 전한 그리스 군인을 기린다. 우리 대부분은 많은 다른 예를 생각해 볼 수도 있을 것이다. 메시지 드럼, 봉화, 교회의 종, 배의 깃발 등. 그러나 그들의 원시성은 우리가 근본적으로 다른 세상, 즉 항시 즉각적으로 정보에 접근할 수 세상에 살고 있다는 느낌만을 확인해줄 것이다.

Chapter 6_ Unit 16

Check Again!

A

1. 소아과 의사
2. 자극하다
3. 진정시키다
4. 침술
5. 유전성의
6. 상상하다
7. 중독
8. 약초의, 식물의
9. 강제적인, 의무의
10. 인질

B

1. abuse
2. circulation
3. phobia
4. acknowledge
5. physician
6. inhumane
7. abruptly
8. hesitate
9. frantically
10. experience

C

1. pressure
2. sprained
3. glance
4. addicted
5. pulse

Check More!

정답: ①

해석: 동시대 작가가 쓴 신문과 책만 읽는 사람은 내게 근시안적인 사람으로 보인다. 그는 자신이 사는 시대의 편견에 전적으로 의존하고 있다. 다른 사람들의 사고와 경험에 의해 자극받지 않고 혼자서 생각하는 것은 기껏해야 하찮고 단조로울 뿐이다. 한 세기 내에서 분명한 사고와 훌륭한 취향을 가진 깨어 있는 사람들은 소수일 뿐이다. 그들의 작품 중에서 보존된 것은 인류의 가장 소중한 재산들 가운데 일부이다. 중세시대의 사람들이 서서히 무지로부터 해방될 수 있었던 것은 옛 시대의 몇몇 작가들 덕분이다.

Chapter 6_ Unit 17

Check Again!

A

1. 독이 있는, 독성의
2. 마비된
3. 제거하다
4. 해독제
5. 치명적인
6. 복부
7. 삼키다
8. 숨을 들이쉬다
9. 질식하다
10. 조심성 있는

B

1. casualty
2. biologist
3. prompt
4. unexpectedly
5. camouflage
6. rescue
7. respiratory
8. emergency
9. essential
10. instruct

C

1. nervous
2. distinguish
3. cope
4. critical
5. experimented

Check More!

정답
(A) simultaneously
(B) enjoyment
(C) extreme
(D) keep in mind

해석: 최근에 내 아내와 나는 친구집에 있었다. 우리는 친구가 전화통화를 하면서 동시에 문을 열어주고, 저녁식사를 확인하고, 아이의 기저귀를 갈아주는 것을 보았다. 우리들 다수도 누군가에게 말을 할 때 똑같은 행동을 하는데, 우리 마음은 다른 곳에 가 있다. 이런 일이 생기면, 우리는 우리가 하고 있는 것에 대한 즐거움을 잃을 뿐만 아니라 주의집중도 훨씬 덜하게 되고 효과도 떨어진다. 극단적으로 생각해서, 고속도로를 운전하면서 면도를 하거나, 커피를 마시거나, 신문을 읽는다고 상상해보자. 아마 사고를 부르는 것일지도 모른다. 어떤 일을 하든, 하고 있는 일에만 집중하라.

Chapter 6_ Unit 18

Check Again!

A

1. 분명히
2. 전염성의
3. 밀도
4. 방해하다
5. 우울증
6. 진단하다
7. 먹다, 소비하다
8. 쓰러지다
9. 주름
10. 악화시키다

B

1. motivate
2. anti-aging
3. laughter
4. decaffeinated
5. antibody
6. life expectancy
7. combine
8. apply
9. appetite
10. intellectual

C

1. impact
2. diagnosed
3. expectancy
4. interact
5. infectious

Check More!

정답: ①

해석: 음악에 어느 정도 반응하지 않는 사람은 거의 없다. 음악의 힘은 전염성이 강하다. 사람들은 서로 다른 방식으로 반응한다. 어떤 사람들에게 음악은 그것에 맞춰 춤을 추거나 몸을 움직이게 하는 주로 본능적이고 신나는 소리이다. 또 다른 사람들은 메시지에 귀를 기울이거나 형식이나 구성에 대한 지적인 접근을 하여 형식적인 패턴이나 독창성을 감상한다. 하지만 무엇보다, 어떤 종류의 음악에 감동하지 않는 사람은 거의 없다. 음악은 모든 범위의 감정을 다룬다. 우리를 기쁘게도 하고 슬프게도 하고, 무기력하게도, 힘이 솟구치게도 할 수 있으며 어떤 음악은 다른 것은 다 잊을 때까지 우리의 마음을 빼앗아갈 수도 있다. 그것은 무의식에도 작용하여 기분을 새롭게 하고 고양시키며 깊은 추억들을 열어젖힌다.

Chapter 7_ Unit 19

Check Again!

A

1. 현수막, 기치, 주장
2. 정체된, 막힌
3. 영감을 주다, 고무시키다
4. 동시대의, 현대의
5. 부정적인
6. 최면
7. 백혈병
8. 감탄한, 놀란
9. 유명한
10. 지탱하다, 기운내게 하다

B

1. grand
2. specialist
3. electric
4. block
5. magnet
6. fame
7. revive
8. genre
9. fanatic
10. meaningful

C

1. range
2. ride
3. passionate
4. receptive
5. insert

Check More!

정답: ②

해석: 현대 음악 작곡가가 여러분의 영웅으로 가장 먼저 선택이 될까요? 아니면 여러분이 동시대의 명화를 그린 화가를 생각해 낼까요? 여러분이 대부분의 사람들과 비슷하다면, 이 두 질문에 대한 대답은 "아니오"일 것입니다. 보다 가능성이 있는 것은, 스포츠 영웅이나 영화 스타가 여러분의 첫 번째 선택일 것입니다. 동시대의 미술과 음악의 세계는 사람들에게 영감을 주는 작품을 선사해주지 못한 것 같습니다. 더욱이 그들은 인간의 업적을 반영하지 못했습니다. 그래서 사람들은 현대 미술에 대한 흥미를 잃어버리고 자신들의 역할 모델을 찾기 위해 스포츠 스타와 다른 인기 있는 인물들에게로 눈을 돌렸습니다.

Chapter 7_ Unit 20

Check Again!

A

1. 유도하다, 권유하다
2. 손상되지 않은
3. 말재주 있는, 웅변의
4. 달성하다
5. 비범한, 우수한
6. 기간
7. 상대성
8. 능가하다
9. 아주, 전적으로
10. 전기

B

1. formula
2. statesman
3. physicist
4. patriotic
5. polish
6. fundamental
7. candidate
8. halt
9. embassy
10. non-violence

C

1. subscribe
2. elected
3. strenuous
4. pledges
5. Presidential

Check More!

정답

(A) induced
(B) destruction
(C) launched

해석: 소수의 사람들만이 한국의 야생 식물들의 가치를 인정해왔다. 그들은 이들 식물들의 아름다움에 매료된다. 식물들의 아름다움은 그 사람들로 하여금 이 식물들이 처한 비극적 현실을 발견한 후에 그들을 보호할 마음이 생기게 했다. 천연 서식지에 대한 무관심과 파괴로 인하여 몇몇 야생 식물들은 불확실한 미래에 직면한다. 이러한 상황을 고려해, 이 사람들은 한국에서 자라는 야생 식물들을 보호하려고 부단히 애써 왔다. 그들은 국민들에게 식물 종의 가치를 알도록 가르쳐 왔고 앞으로의 세대를 위해 야생 식물을 보존하기 위한 노력을 시작했다. 그들의 노력 덕분에, 더 많은 한국인들은 이제 그들의 소중한 야생 식물들의 온전한 가치를 이해한다.

Check Again!

A

1. 영향력 있는	2. 항해, 항해하다
3. 자질	4. 직관, 직감
5. 박애주의자	6. 추방하다
7. 폭군	8. 인물
9. 도피하다	10. 암살하다

B

1. foundation	2. primary
3. nurture	4. adventurer
5. prodigy	6. mercy
7. priceless	8. subordinate
9. eternal	10. toxic

C

1. regime
2. money-oriented
3. astronomical
4. commitment
5. ventures

Check More!

정답: ③

해석: 수학은 르네상스 미술에 분명 영향을 주었다. 르네상스 미술은 여러 가지 면에서 중세 미술과 달랐다. 르네상스 이전에, 회화 속의 사물은 실제 모습이라기보다는 평면적이고 상징적이었다. 르네상스 동안 미술가들은 회화를 개혁했다. 그들은 회화 속의 사물을 정확하게 그리길 원했다. 사물의 필수적인 형태를 인간의 눈에 보이는 것처럼 원근감 있게 그리는 데 수학이 사용되었다. 르네상스 미술가들은 기하학을 사용하여 원근법을 성취하였으며, 그것은 실제 세계에 대한 자연주의적이고 정확하고 3차원적 표현으로 귀결되었다. 수학을 미술에 응용하는 것이, 특히 회화에서, 르네상스 미술의 가장 중요한 특징 중의 하나였다.

Check Again!

A

1. 변덕스러운, 기질상의	2. 말의, 구두의
3. 가속하다	4. 진정시키다
5. 보완하다	6. 시간을 잘 지키는
7. 늦은, 지각하는	8. 꾸물거리다
9. 아는 사람	10. 신중한

B

1. complain	2. extend
3. similarity	4. confirmation
5. spouse	6. contrast
7. appointment	8. reckless
9. frighten	10. persuade

C

1. respects
2. bond
3. overdue
4. consequently
5. revenge

Check More!

정답
(A) comfort
(B) Consequently
(C) boredom
(D) complain

해석: 1800년대 선원들은 힘든 삶을 살았다. 그들은 그들이 배를 타고 불렀던 단순한 노랫가락에서 드문 위안을 찾았다. 결과적으로, 그 노래는 선원들에게 소중한 친구였고 그들이 팀을 이루어 일할 수 있도록 도와주었다. 이 노래들 중 다수가 수년간 지속되어 왔다. 어떤 뱃노래들은 오랜 여행의 지루함을 깨뜨려주었다. 또 다른 뱃노래들은 갈망과 외로움의 감정들을 표현하도록 도와주었다. 아직도 뱃노래들은 선원들이 자신들의 힘든 삶에 대해 불평하도록 해준다. 대체로 뱃노래는 선원들의 선상 생활을 덜 고달프게 해주었다.

Chapter 8_ Unit 23

Check Again!

A

1. 감상하다, 평가하다
2. 애매한, 중의적인
3. 표현하다, 그리다
4. 이해하다
5. 사색하는
6. 수분
7. 상처입기 쉬운, 연약한
8. 비율
9. 원기 왕성하게
10. 대칭의

B

1. masterpiece
2. crack
3. evaluate
4. sculpture
5. subconscious
6. invisible
7. vivid
8. comparatively
9. complete
10. preceding

C

1. concrete
2. vague
3. mutual
4. underlying
5. abstract

Check More!

정답: ③

해석: 시는 우리를 감동시켜 시인의 감정에 공감하도록 하거나 시인의 상상력이 창조해낸 사람들의 감정과 공감하도록 해준다. 우리는 그들의 투쟁, 연약함과 실패를 목격한다. 우리는 그들의 사랑과 상실, 기쁨과 슬픔, 희망과 두려움을 어느 정도 마치 그것들이 우리의 것인 양 느낀다. 우리는 이따금 그들의 불안과 슬픔으로 고통을 겪지만, 그 경험으로부터 기쁨을 얻는다. 시는 우리에게 우리 자신의 삶에서 빠져 있는 것을 제공한다. 즉 상상에 의한 즐거움을 경험하는 것이다. 이것이 우리가 일상생활에서 시를 감상하는 이유이다.

Chapter 8_ Unit 24

Check Again!

A

1. 목초지
2. 직관으로 알다
3. 마구를 채우다, 이용하다
4. 뽑다, 짜다
5. 친밀감
6. 농부
7. 이용하다, 착취하다
8. 가축
9. 풀을 뜯어먹다
10. 일관되게

B

1. essential
2. innocent
3. meek
4. rural
5. harvest
6. honor
7. plow
8. vicious
9. wretched
10. urge

C

1. Manual
2. destined
3. identifies
4. provide
5. herd

Check More!

정답
(A) innocent
(B) intuition
(C) interactions
(D) communicate

해석: 여러분 자신이 다른 사람의 말에 끼어들고 있다는 것을 눈치채기 시작할 때, 여러분은 이것이 단지 악의 없는 습관에 지나지 않는다는 것을 알게 될 것이다. 이것을 바로잡으려면, 여러분이 망각하는 순간에 말하려는 것을 멈추기 시작하기만 하면 된다. 자신에게 참고 기다리라고 주지시켜라. 여러분 차례가 오기 전에 다른 사람들이 말을 마치도록 내버려두어라. 여러분은 직감적으로 이 작은 행동의 직접적인 결과로 여러분 삶 속의 사람들과의 교류가 얼마나 좋아지게 될지 깨닫게 될 것이다. 여러분이 의사소통하는 사람들은 자신들의 말이 듣고 경청된다고 느낄 때 여러분 주변에 있는 것이 훨씬 더 편안하다는 것을 느끼게 될 것이다.

Check Again!

A

1. 찬란한
2. 과소평가하다
3. 피상적인
4. 번창하다, 융성하다
5. 통합된
6. 간과하다
7. 종교적인
8. 비위생적인
9. 웅장한
10. 기하학의, 기하학적인

B

1. sacred
2. pray
3. taboo
4. insufficient
5. fast
6. distort
7. establish
8. pioneer
9. architecture
10. attraction

C

1. legacies
2. depicts
3. aesthetically
4. prejudices
5. biased

Check More!

정답: ①

해석: 1990년대 중반 이후 외국인들에게 한국어를 가르치는 것이 조용하면서도 꾸준히 성장하였다. 이제 많은 대학들이 한국과 해외에서 한국어 프로그램을 제공하고 있으며, 한국어 학습자들을 위해 많은 교재가 제작되고 있다. 그러나 아주 소수의 외국인들만이 이러한 발전으로 인해 혜택을 받아왔다. 여전히 외국인들에게 한국어를 가르치는 일의 중요성은 과소평가되는 것 같다. 따라서 대부분의 외국인 노동자들은 가르친 경험이 거의 또는 전혀 없는 한국인 동료나 자원봉사자들에게서 배우고 있다. 그러므로 외국인 노동자들에게 한국어를 가르치기 위한 더 좋은 교육 프로그램을 구축하는 것이 필요하다.

Check Again!

A

1. 다재다능한, 다용도의
2. 공예품, 수공품
3. 재배치하다
4. 장식
5. 선풍적인
6. 위치를 바꾸다
7. 재배치하다, 재배열하다
8. 비실용적인
9. 두드러진
10. 직업, 경력

B

1. artistic
2. postpone
3. elaborately
4. perceive
5. decorative
6. modify
7. self-confident
8. concept
9. coincidence
10. selective

C

1. skeptical
2. scheme
3. substantial
4. interjected
5. self-confident

Check More!

정답:
(A) devoted
(B) career
(C) skeptical
(D) shelter

해석: 평생 문학에 대한 애정으로, 곤잘레스는 사람들이 문학에 더 접근할 수 있도록 하는 데 헌신해오고 있다. 그가 로스앤젤레스에서 이발사로서 성공적인 직업생활을 한 후에, 캔자스 메리스빌로 이사왔을 때 그는 지역사회에서 독서에 대한 갈증이 아주 널리 퍼져 있음을 발견했다. 그는 1990년에 이발소 안에 500여 권의 책을 소장한 도서실을 열어 고객들이 책을 읽도록 도왔다. "많은 사람들이 책을 읽고 싶어했지만, 도움을 받을 곳이 어디에도 없었죠"라고 곤잘레스는 말했다. 처음에는 많은 사람들이 그의 생각에 회의적이었지만, 그의 노력은 전국적으로 알려져서 2003년에 리빙스턴 상을 수상하였다. "곤잘레스 씨는 사람들이 영혼의 쉼터를 찾을 수 있도록 도왔다"라고 리빙스턴 위원회는 적었다.

Chapter 9_ Unit 27

Check Again!

A

1. 추론하다
2. 무시하다, 얕보다
3. 같은, 동등한
4. 분수
5. 숨기다, 은폐하다
6. ~의 탓으로 돌리다
7. 내주다, 포기하다
8. 흥분된, 동요한
9. ~의 경향이 있는, ~하고 싶어하는
10. 남자다운, 힘센

B

1. ideal
2. irresponsible
3. virtue
4. appealing
5. popular
6. secure
7. exhausting
8. victim
9. warm-hearted
10. feminine

C

1. attributed
2. illusions
3. prevalent
4. discrimination
5. martial

Check More!

정답:

(A) victims

(B) responsible

(C) issue

(D) risk

해석: 사냥 사고 건수가 올해 급격히 증가했다. 피해자는 사냥감으로 오인된 사냥꾼과 등산객들이 대부분이었다. 이 피할 수 있는 사고들의 책임이 누구에게 있는지에 관한 질문들이 피해자와 피해자 가족들에게서 제기되고 있다. 그들은 적절한 조치를 취하지 않은 경찰을 비난한다. 사실, 경찰은 자격 있는 사냥꾼들에게 허가증을 발급하고 사냥 시즌에는 환하고 색깔이 화려한 옷을 입을 것을 등산객들에게 권고하고 있다. 물론 경찰은 추가로 몇몇 경보를 발효하거나 기타 예방조치를 해야 한다. 하지만 자신들의 안전을 보장할 책임이 있는 사람은 피해자 자신들이다. 그들은 수수한 옷을 입고 혼자 있을 때는 깊은 숲속에서 목숨을 거는 모험을 하지 말아야 한다.

Chapter 9_ Unit 28

Check Again!

A

1. 인종차별주의
2. 풍자의, 비꼬는
3. 유행병, 유행
4. 요건
5. 자격
6. 엄격한
7. 정중한
8. 보수적인
9. 소수
10. 특성

B

1. nominee
2. corrupt
3. policy
4. investigate
5. politician
6. vanish
7. transparent
8. liberal
9. official
10. handicapped

C

1. Supreme
2. two-faced
3. imprisonment
4. illustrates
5. bribery

Check More!

정답: ⑤

해석: 여러분의 아들들과 딸들이 허트고등학교에서 지난 3년 동안의 학업으로 학업요건을 모두 완수하였음을 알려드리게 되어 매우 기쁩니다. 이들이 우리 학교에 들어온 지가 바로 어제 같은데 이제 자랑스럽게 졸업장을 받게 되었습니다. 우리의 오랜 역사에서 성공한 많은 졸업생들과 다르지 않게 여러분의 자녀도 세상으로 나아가 정치, 경제, 문화, 교육 분야에 성공적으로 참여할 것입니다. 졸업식은 허트고등학교 강당에서 다음 주 금요일에 열릴 것입니다. 학교를 대표하여, 여러분과 가족을 초대하고자 합니다. 거기에서 뵙기를 고대합니다.

Chapter 9_ Unit 29

Check Again!

A

1. 사설
2. 자존심, 자부심
3. 도발하다
4. 동화되다
5. 찬반양론
6. 직면하다
7. 논쟁의, 논란의 여지가 있는
8. 찬성론자
9. 반대론자
10. 유괴

B

1. murder
2. electronic
3. worth
4. resident
5. defend
6. priority
7. journalist
8. bully
9. harass
10. emission

C

1. panic
2. humiliated
3. crime
4. worth
5. offender

Check More!

정답

(A) provoke

(B) experiments

(C) panic

해석: 환경심리학자들은 예측할 수 없는 고음의 소음이 해롭다는 것을 오래 전부터 알고 있었다. 그것은 분노와 같은 부정적인 감정들을 불러 일으킬 수 있다. 실험에 따르면, 110데시벨의 소음에 노출된 사람들은 문제해결 능력이 감소하는 것을 경험했다. 그러나 실험자가 소음이 언제 발생하는지를 예측할 수 있거나 "공포단추"로 소음을 차단할 능력이 있을 때는 부정적인 효과가 사라졌다.
우리는 늘 소음공해가 없는 작업환경을 누릴 만큼 운이 좋지 않다. 하지만 소음이 있는 환경을 우리가 책임지고 있다고 느낄 때, 우리는 불안과 나쁜 실적으로 고생하지 않을 수 있다.

Chapter 9_ Unit 30

Check Again!

A

1. 양심
2. 강력한
3. 파견하다, 발송하다
4. 난민
5. 영토
6. 원자폭탄
7. 점령하다
8. 내쫓다, 내몰다
9. 상상의, 가상의
10. 조약

B

1. strategy
2. justice
3. blame
4. lack
5. demolish
6. infrastructure
7. explicit
8. declare
9. violent
10. feasible

C

1. Assault
2. resources
3. terms
4. cease-fire
5. broke

Check More!

정답: ③

해석: 독특한 상품만을 내놓는 것이 시장의 성공을 보장하지는 못한다. 또 다른 중요한 요인은 그 시장을 이루고 있는 지역공동체에 맞는 상품을 제공하여 시장에 대한 반응력을 높이는 것이다. 이것은 각 나라, 공동체, 개인이 독특한 특성과 필요를 가지고 있음을 이해하는 것이다. 이것은 지역과 개인적 차이에 대한 민감성을 요한다. 다른 말로 하면, 힘든 과제 중의 하나는 "세계적" 측면에만 너무 많은 강조를 하는, 한가지로 모든 것에 다 맞추려는 전략을 피하는 것이다. 심지어 국가를 "개발된" 또는 "부상하는" 등으로 분류하는 것도 위험하다. 면밀히 분석해보면, "부상하는" 국가도 서로 다 굉장히 다를 뿐만 아니라 수많은 독특한 개인과 공동체로 구성되어 있다.

Chapter 10_ Unit 31

Check Again!

A
1. 안정된
2. 기업가
3. 상품
4. 집회
5. 풍부한
6. 세계화
7. 역경
8. 적절한, 충분한
9. 절약하는, 검소한
10. 부과하다

B
1. soar
2. bankrupt
3. agricultural
4. protest
5. financial
6. recession
7. sentiment
8. imported
9. restrain
10. commute

C
1. amendment
2. measure
3. laid
4. comply
5. unemployment

Check More!

정답: ①

해석: 수년간 일기예보 센터를 지휘했던 앨런 피어슨이 경보체계에 불만이 있었던 한 부인에 대해 말한다. "그녀가 전화를 해서 회오리바람 경보 때문에 지하실에서 다섯 시간 동안 갇혀 있었는데 아무 일도 일어나지 않았다고 항의했어요"라고 앨런 피어슨이 말한다. "나는 그녀를 놀라게 하고 싶지 않았으며 다만 그녀가 알고 있기를 바랐다고 설명하려 했죠. 불행히도, 5개월 후에 같은 일이 또 일어났어요. 그때는 진짜로 화가 나 있었고, '무슨 조치가 이루어졌어야죠'라고 기상청에 불평을 했어요."

Chapter 10_ Unit 32

Check Again!

A
1. 저평가하다
2. 학자
3. 인용하다
4. 모으다, 축적하다
5. 대략
6. 심오한, 깊이 있는
7. 품질보증서
8. 예치하다
9. 수료증, 증명서
10. 소중히 여기다

B
1. infinite
2. interest
3. graph
4. prospect
5. insurance
6. investment
7. real estate
8. finite
9. millionaire
10. analyst

C
1. honors
2. stock
3. prosperous
4. insured
5. Presumably

Check More!

정답
(A) Presumably
(B) electronic
(C) profound
(D) extinct

해석: 텔레비전의 출현 이래로, 소설은 이미 죽은 것이 아니라면 죽어가고 있다는 소문이 있어 왔다. 전자 매체와 컴퓨터 게임들이 더욱 영향력을 떨치게 되면서 아마도 인쇄 지향적인 소설가들은 사라질 운명인 것처럼 보이는 듯하다. 요즘, 많은 젊은이들이 책을 읽는 것보다 인터넷을 검색하는 것을 선호하는 것 같다. 그리고 종종 그들이 찾는 것은 심오한 지식이 아니라 빠른 정보이다. 사람들은 문학적 허구가 멸종된 종들처럼 박물관에 보존되어야 할 구식 장르가 될 운명이 아닌지 궁금해할지도 모른다.

Chapter 10_ Unit 33

Check Again!

A

1. 수도의, 대도시의
2. 구별하다
3. 복제하다
4. 달라지다, 바꾸다
5. 유기농의
6. 이식하다
7. 익은
8. 소출, 수확
9. 비어 있는
10. 질, 품질

B

1. botanist
2. overcrowded
3. transform
4. retirement
5. multiply
6. thriving
7. booming
8. modernized
9. blueprint
10. construction

C

1. dwells
2. restricted
3. adapt
4. migrated
5. transformed

Check More!

정답: ②

해석: 다른 모든 산업들처럼, 장미산업도 시장의 변화하는 상황에 적응해야 한다. 과거에는 꽃가게가 지역의 독립 자영업자일 가능성이 높았다. 이들은 농부에게서 장미를 구입한 도매상들에게서 장미를 샀다. 발렌타인데이 같은 특별한 날에는 수요가 많아져, 장미 12송이 가격이 품질에 관계없이 거의 두 배 정도 올랐다.

오늘날에는 대형 슈퍼마켓 체인, 여러 지역에서 직접 판매하는 도매상, 직접 전화 판매업자들이 장미 공급자에 포함된다. 장미의 낭만은 경제적 실체로 대체되었다.

Chapter 11_ Unit 34

Check Again!

A

1. 장애
2. 첨단 기술의
3. 상상할 수 없는
4. 채택하다, 양자로 삼다
5. 혁신적인
6. 이상한
7. 피사체, 대상
8. 변하게 하다, 전환하다
9. 제대로 작동하지 않다
10. 독특한

B

1. client
2. conference
3. utility
4. portrait
5. referee
6. devise
7. three-dimensional
8. specimen
9. interactive
10. conceive

C

1. revolutionary
2. transfer
3. transmit
4. conventional
5. drastic

Check More!

정답

(A) unique
(B) sewn
(C) devised
(D) instruction

해석: 인간이 발명한 최초의 진정한 스포츠 기구는 공이었다. 고대 이집트에서, 돌 던지기는 아이들이 가장 좋아하는 놀이였다. 그러나 잘못 던진 돌이 아이를 다치게 할 수도 있었다. 그러므로 이집트인들은 던져도 덜 위험한 것을 찾게 되었다. 그래서 그들은 독특한 놀이기구인, 아마도 최초의 공이란 것을 개발한 것 같다. 그것들은 처음에 풀이나 나뭇잎을 실로 함께 엮어서 만들어졌고 나중에 동물의 가죽을 꿰매서 깃털이나 건초를 채워서 만들어졌다. 비록 이집트인들은 호전적이었지만, 그들은 평화로운 놀이를 할 시간을 내었다. 머지않아 그들은 수많은 공놀이를 생각해 내었다. 아마도 그들은 재미보다는 교육을 위해 공놀이를 한 것 같다. 공을 가지고 노는 것은 젊은이들에게 전쟁에 필요한 스피드와 기술을 가르치기 위한 하나의 방법으로 주로 간주되어졌다.

Chapter 11_ Unit 35

Check Again!

A

1. 구성요소
2. 놀랄 만한
3. 긍정적인
4. 독창적인
5. 만족스러운
6. 강력히 주장하다
7. 고소하다
8. 재산
9. 결함
10. 불법의

B

1. confused
2. material
3. cybercop
4. copyright
5. utilize
6. theft
7. delete
8. update
9. combine
10. outlet

C

1. delighted
2. complimentary
3. infringing
4. consent
5. warning

Check More!

정답: ①

해석: 여러분은 이 10대 소녀가 겪고 있는 것을 정확히 보고 느낄 수 있다. 나는 10대 시절에 가끔 아주 좌절하고 혼란스러웠던 것을 기억한다. 또한 내 감정이 한 극단에서 다른 극단으로 널뛰었던 것을 기억한다. 그러니까 예를 들면, 무엇인가에 대해 믿기지 않을 정도로 화를 내곤 했다. 대개는 한심한 것들이었다. 그리고 나면 그렇게 화를 낸 나 자신에게 화를 내고, 다시 나를 화나게 만든 것에 대해 화를 내곤 했다. 나는 이러한 감정을 전혀 조절하지 못했던 것 같다. 그래서 나는 자주 스트레스를 배출하는 수단으로 음악에 의존했다.

Chapter 11_ Unit 36

Check Again!

A

1. 적개심, 적대 행위
2. 주장에 의하면
3. 강화하다
4. 더럽히다
5. 공모하다
6. 위조품, 위조
7. 헤아릴 수 없는
8. 최첨단의
9. 이행하다
10. 진짜의

B

1. fake
2. monopolize
3. trick
4. integrity
5. evidently
6. renew
7. extend
8. traitor
9. compensate
10. enforce

C

1. accused
2. diplomatic
3. Cutting-edge
4. compensated
5. return

Check More!

정답
(A) distinguish
(B) force
(C) genuine

해석: 윤리는 우리가 어떻게 행동할 것인지를 선택하는 것을 의식하는 데에서 시작한다. 예를 들면, 우리는 진실을 말할 수도 있고 거짓을 말할 수도 있다. 이들 두 가지 가능성은 우리에게 선택안으로 제시된다. 우리는 우리의 행동을 통제할 수 있기 때문에 두 가지 중의 하나를 할 수 있다. 그러나 돌멩이는 이런 선택안과 마주하지 않는다. 왜냐하면 그것은 서로 다른 행동의 차이를 구분하지 못하기 때문이다. 돌멩이는 외부의 힘이 행동하도록 만드는 대로만 행동할 수 있다. 돌과 달리, 인간은 스스로 행동을 시작할 수 있다. 그렇다면 차이점은 돌멩이는 가능성에 대해서 의식하지 않지만 반면에 인간들은 자신들이 진정한 선택안들과 마주한다는 것을 의식한다는 것이다.

Chapter 12_ Unit 37

Check Again!

A
1. 빠뜨리다, 생략하다
2. 충돌하다
3. 최후의 심판일
4. 운석
5. 큰 재앙의
6. 궤도를 그리며 돌다
7. 하늘의, 천체의
8. 10년
9. 외계인
10. 유괴하다

B
1. astronomy
2. align
3. expedition
4. explosion
5. gravity
6. swell
7. galaxy
8. explore
9. launch
10. solar system

C
1. eclipse
2. chronological
3. collided
4. jeopardy
5. artificial

Check More!

정답
(A) omit
(B) decade
(C) extremely
(D) merit

해석: 우리는 동물이 의사소통의 수단으로 초음파를 사용한다는 중요한 사실을 쉽게 잊는다. 지난 수십 년에 걸쳐, 생물학자들은 고래, 코끼리, 그리고 기타 몇몇 동물들이 초음파를 사용한다는 것을 알아냈다. 이 지극히 낮은 음이 의사소통의 수단이라는 것이 입증된 것이다. 이 초음파는 특별한 장점을 가지고 있다. 이것은 높은 소음보다 훨씬 더 먼 거리를 갈 수 있다. 이런 원거리 의사소통은 넓은 지역을 돌아다니는 기린이나 코끼리 같은 동물들에게는 필수다.

Chapter 12_ Unit 38

Check Again!

A
1. 불모의
2. 식을 행하다
3. 오염물질
4. 설명할 수 없는
5. 오염된
6. 반도
7. 침식
8. 유독한, 독(성)의
9. 보호, 보존
10. 삼림 벌채

B
1. eco-friendly
2. species
3. calculate
4. landscape
5. landslide
6. counterattack
7. colony
8. neutralize
9. landfill
10. habitat

C
1. granted
2. extinct
3. vigilant
4. endangered
5. dust

Check More!

정답: ②

해석: 꽃, 그리고 나무, 신선한 공기, 그리고 달콤한 토양에는 치유하는 힘이 있다. 그 문제에 관해서라면, 그냥 정원을 걷는 것 또는 창 밖으로 보는 것만으로도 혈압을 낮추고, 스트레스를 줄이고 고통을 완화시킬 수가 있다. 나가서 땅을 파기 시작해보라. 그러면 혜택이 배가될 것이다. 기초적이고 심지어 구식인 것 같지만, 건강 도구로써 원예를 하는 것이 한창이다. 어떤 사람들은 심지어 그들의 아파트에 실내 미니 정원을 만든다. 신축 또는 리모델링 병원들과 양로원들은 환자들과 직원들이 황량한 실내 환경에서 벗어날 수 있는 치유 정원들을 설치해 놓고 있다. 또한 다수가 환자들에게 직접 손을 더럽히고 식물을 가꾸는 데 마음을 쏟을 수 있는 기회를 제공한다.

Chapter 12_ Unit 39

Check Again!

A
1. 양립할 수 없는
2. 줄이다
3. 나타나다
4. 버리다
5. 재배지
6. 건강에 신경쓰는
7. 분해된
8. 비료
9. 장기의, 연장된
10. 절제, 완화

B
1. exposure
2. fossil fuel
3. miniature
4. refrain
5. crisis
6. motive
7. deformed
8. eco-system
9. disposable
10. leftover

C
1. thumb
2. oppressed
3. genetically
4. refrain
5. preservation

Check More!

정답
(A) firmly
(B) fertile
(C) exposure
(D) ripen

해석: 확실히 질 좋은 포도에서 질 낮은 포도주를 만들 수는 있지만 질 낮은 포도에서 질 좋은 포도주를 만들 수 없다는 사실을 나는 굳게 믿고 있다. 포도밭에서 어떤 일이 일어나는지가 중요하다. 우선, 배수가 잘되어야 하는데 포도의 뿌리가 땅속 깊이 뿌리내리기 위해 반드시 지나치게 기름진 토양일 필요는 없다. 포도밭은 기후가 시원한 지역에서 태양에 많이 노출되어야 한다. 충분한 비가 필요하고 또는 어떤 경우에는 관개시설이 필요하다. 물이 너무 적으면 포도껍질이 너무 뻣뻣해져 익지 않는다.

Chapter 12_ Unit 40

Check Again!

A
1. 비우다, 대피시키다
2. 그럼에도 불구하고
3. 소독하다
4. 감소하다
5. 피곤하게
6. 괴로워하는
7. 무시무시한
8. 철저하게 파괴하다
9. 재건하다, 다시 짓다
10. 급류

B
1. boiled
2. proclaim
3. scarcity
4. immense
5. extent
6. welfare
7. risk
8. trace
9. nationwide
10. humanitarian

C
1. nuclear
2. risk
3. plague
4. homeless
5. unrest

Check More!

정답: ①

해석: 무엇이 사람들로 하여금 인도주의적으로 행동하게 할까? 다른 사람들과 공감할 수 있는 능력은 인간의 다양한 본성을 반영한다. 이것은 우리가 문학을 통하여 경험의 확대를 추구할 수 있도록 해주는 것들 중의 하나일 수 있다. 우리는 어떤 인물들은 우리 자신들과 관계 없는 자로 간주할 수 있지만, 즉 우리가 그들과 완벽하게 동일시할 수 없을지는 모르지만, 그럼에도 불구하고 우리는 그들의 행동과 감정으로 들어갈 수 있다. 따라서 젊은 사람이 노인과 동일시하고, 한 성이 다른 성에게(남성이 여성에게 또는 여성이 남성에게), 그리고 특별히 제한된 사회적 배경에 속한 독자가 다른 계층이나 다른 시대의 일원들과 동일시할 수도 있다.

Note